WARW
THE KINGMAKER

ENGLAND at the time of
Warwick the Kingmaker

North Sea

Spurn Head
(Ravenspur)

Cromer
Caister Castle
Norwich

The Wash

Tattershall
Castle Rising
King's Lynn

In

ark
Grantham   Croyland   Bury St. Edmunds   Harwich
Stamford
n Mowbray   Fotheringhay   Cambridge
ster

L A N D   Margate

Northampton   Olney   Sandwich
ntry   Stony   Hatfield   Canterbury Dover   Calais
Warwick   Stratford St. Albans Barnet Thames Gravesend   Boulogne
Banbury   London   Maidstone
ipping
Norton   Woodstock Oxford   Bodiam Castle
Burford
esbury   Windsor
Cheltenham   Reading   Guildford
oucester
Newbury

Winchester   Dieppe

stow   Bath   Salisbury   Southampton Portsmouth
istol
Wells   Isle of
Poole   Wight   English Channel
Cerne Abbas   Harfleur Seine
Corfe Castle   (Havre) Honfleur
Bridport Weymouth

Exeter   Barfleur
                         St Vaast-la-Hogue
            Cherbourg   Valognes

F R A N C E

Strait of Dover

0   10   20   30   40   50   60
Scale of Miles

Pitcher

Paul Murray Kendall was Professor of English Literature at the University of Kansas in Lawrence. Earlier he held the same Chair at Ohio University in Athens, Ohio, where he became a Regents Professor Emeritus. In 1970 he was awarded an Honorary L.H.D. (Doctor of Humane Letters) by Ohio University. He spent several years in Europe while carrying out the research for his books. He was the recipient of numerous awards and fellowships, including the Guggenheim. Paul Murray Kendall died in 1973.

Also by Paul Murray Kendall

Richard III
Louis XI (Phoenix Press)
The Yorkist Age
The Art of Biography
The Story of Land Warfare
My Brother Chilperic (novel)

As Editor

Richard III: The Great Debate

Dispatches with Related Documents of Milanese Ambassadors in France and Burgundy, 1450–1483, vol. 1: 1450–1460, edited with translations by Paul Murray Kendall and Vincent Ilardi

Dispatches with Related Documents of Milanese Ambassadors in France and Burgundy, 1450–1483, vol. 11: 1460–1461

WARWICK
THE KINGMAKER

Paul Murray Kendall

PHOENIX
PRESS

5 UPPER SAINT MARTIN'S LANE
LONDON
WC2H 9EA

A PHOENIX PRESS PAPERBACK

First published in Great Britain
by George Allen & Unwin in 1957
This paperback edition published in 2002
by Phoenix Press,
a division of The Orion Publishing Group Ltd,
Orion House, 5 Upper St Martin's Lane,
London WC2H 9EA

Phoenix Press
Sterling Publishing Co Inc
387 Park Avenue South
New York
NY 10016-8810
USA

A CIP catalogue record for this book is available
from the British Library.

Printed and bound in Great Britain by
Clays Ltd, St Ives plc

ISBN 1 84212 575 3

Contents

Part Five *"Setter-up and Plucker-down of Kings"* (*1469–1470*)

Part Six *The Lancastrian* (*1470–1471*)

Illustrations

Edward IV
Elizabeth Woodville, wife of Edward IV
Henry VI
René, Duke of Anjou
John, Duke of Calabria
Louis XI
Philippe de Commynes
Louis XI by Fouquet
Philip the Good and Charles the Rash
Margaret of York
Antoine, Bastard of Burgundy
Warwick's Navy
Middleham Castle
Battle of Barnet

MAPS

GENEALOGICAL TREE

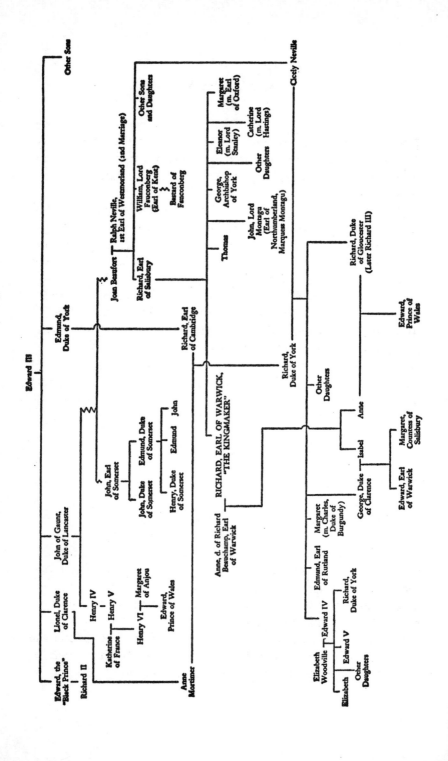

Preface

RICHARD Neville, Earl of Warwick—called The King-maker—has been relegated to a famous oblivion: is there any other man in English history so well known and so little known about?

The chroniclers of his age recorded his deeds and registered his impact, but passing time has been cruel to whatever revelations of himself were left in his restless wake—letters, portraits, impressions jotted down by contemporaries. Tudor writers were set upon erecting the Wars of the Roses into a pattern of God's justice, in which the quarrel of Lancaster and York was triumphantly resolved by the victory of Henry Tudor over Richard III at Bosworth Field and the establishment of Henry's dynasty. In this divine pattern Warwick had no real place. He was merely part of the hurly-burly of a civil strife from which the Tudors had rescued England. Thus Shakespeare displays him in the three parts of *Henry VI*, a bellicose baron of a turbulent time, whose voice is lost in the din of events.

After the Elizabethan age, no one found it worth while to attempt a biography of Warwick until, in 1891, Professor Charles W. Oman produced his *Life*—really a history of Warwick's times and deeds—which has since remained the standard work. Present-day interest in economic, constitutional, and administrative studies leaves Warwick outside the focus of scholarly attention, for his career throws little light on any of these subjects. Furthermore, he represents a direction that history did not take. He was molded by an age of endings and beginnings, the collapsing reign of Henry VI; and though he helped to create a new monarchy which would rule England until 1688, he soon revolted against his own handiwork.

But in the canons of biography it is an article of belief that the past is worth recapturing for its own sake. If the epoch of Lancaster and York is viewed for what it was rather than for the seeds of the future it engendered, Warwick bestrides the two middle decades of the fifteenth century. The pilgrimage of mankind is, at bottom, a story of human energy, how it has been used and the ends it has sought to encompass; and the life of the Earl of Warwick unfolds the tale of how one of the great vitalities of the fifteenth century chose, and was driven, to exercise its force. Warwick's prime meaning is the reach of human nature he exemplifies and—type of all human struggle—the combat he waged with the shape of things in his time.

Warwick has been called the last of the barons, but his identification of himself with the figure he persuaded the world to believe in gives some cause for him to be considered one of the first of the moderns. His career was a gigantic failure, not so much because he reached higher than he was able to grasp but because he poisoned his character in the course of reaching—sold what he was for what he thought he ought to be. Yet there was magnanimity in him, and if he is not quite a tragic protagonist, he is a memorable human being. He refused to admit that there were disadvantages he could not overcome and defeats from which he could not recover, and he had the courage, and vanity, to press his game to the end. In other words, he is a Western European man, and in him lies concentrated the reason why that small corner of the earth, in the four centuries after his death, came to dominate all the rest.

To pluck Warwick's life out of the past, those parts of his time to which he was most intimately attached must come too, or the specimen will wither. The waning Middle Ages, flushed with the germinating forces of the Renaissance, produced a blaze of princes. Warwick stands at the center of a great political duel—the first fire of nationalism—waged by Edward IV of England and Charles, Duke of Burgundy, and Louis XI of France. Whatever may be the case today, in the fifteenth century the personalities of dominant men counted for a great deal. If, considering the labyrinth of modern economic and ideological pressures, Warwick's politics seem simple, they were exercised in a world of characters who were far from simple and whose intricacies were the labyrinth in which Warwick drove on his career. Therefore, I have had to allow King Edward and King

Louis and Philip and Charles of Burgundy to intrude their flamboyant selves into this biography.

In order to come at Warwick's character, I have made inferences from the facts, and I have lightly fleshed out scenes, here and there, with touches of detail which, if not documented for the particular moment, are vouched for by the general customs of the age. Such surmises and reconstructions I have tried to make clear, either in the text or in the notes, so that the reader will not be at a loss to distinguish between documented fact and conjecture. All passages dealing with Warwick's motivations, thoughts, feelings, are, of necessity, conjectural. To avoid such conjectures would be to confess that it is impossible to write a biography of Warwick; I believe that there is sufficient information about the man to discern the essential pattern of his character. I have not invented any scenes, incidents, or conversations. To create a portrait, I have occasionally extended points of fact into lines, but I have intruded no points of my own.

In "Notes on Sources" I have identified, chapter by chapter, important quotations and passages of special interest; I have also indicated conjectures and discussed knotty or disputed points of evidence. Dialogue not in quotation marks has been reconstructed from source materials in which the dialogue form was implicit. The biography is based entirely on the historical sources provided by Warwick's own time, sources which are scantier than the Tudor chroniclers but, I believe, much more reliable.

I am much indebted to the staffs of the British Museum Reading and Manuscript rooms, and the Institute of Historical Research of the University of London, and to Miss Catherine Nelson of the Ohio University Library. For both aid and encouragement, I am especially grateful to Alec R. Myers, Senior Lecturer in Medieval History, the University of Liverpool; to Dr. George P. Cuttino, Professor of History, Emory University; and to Dr. Edward Hodnett, Professor of English, Ohio University. I am deeply grateful to the John Simon Guggenheim Memorial Foundation for the aid and stimulation afforded me by the award of a Fellowship. That the biography got itself written at all is due mainly to my two Carols, who endured with equanimity and helped with zest.

Now you see the deaths of so many great men in such a brief space of time, men who have worked so hard to grow great and to win glory and have suffered so much from passions and cares and shortened their lives; and perchance their souls will pay for it.

To speak plainly, as a man who has no literary skill but only a little first-hand experience, might it not have been better for these to have chosen the middle way in things?—that is, not to have worked so hard, to have undertaken fewer enterprises, felt a livelier fear of offending God and persecuting people and to have contented themselves with taking their ease and honest pleasure?

Their lives would be the longer, illnesses would come later, their passing would be the more widely regretted, and they would have less reason to dread death.

Philippe de Commynes

Part One

The Yorkist

(1428-1456)

I

The Eve of Fame[*]

NO LIKENESS exists of Richard Neville, Earl of Warwick. He may have found himself too busy to sit for one of the Flemish masters, or perhaps the chances of time have robbed us of his face. Symbolically, his portrait should be part of a triptych—Warwick in the center panel flanked on either side by portraits of Louis XI of France and Edward IV of England. These kings were his friends and his debtors. One of them turned out to be his deadliest enemy—except for himself. The other he enchanted and was enchanted by, and neither came well out of the bargain they struck. He played at winning and losing kingdoms with these monarchs, though he himself could never wear a crown. He believed he could rule without it, and for a time he convinced the world of his belief. Thus, he is known as the maker of kings. But the pith of his story lies in how he was undone by kings.

The pedestal Warwick wrought so that he could climb as high as monarchs was half rainbow, half stone: an amalgam of legend and deeds forged by the vitality of his character. As he passed through towns and villages, he diffused an aura of fame and splendor as perceptible as sun or rain. He was not only the mightiest of English earls, or even the champion of the House of York. He was Warwick, a power unto himself. He was not tied to his native soil, and he acknowledged no bar of rank or custom to his hopes. Warwick's generation took him for granted, like many another manifestation of God's unfathomable Providence. The chroniclers note his fiery passage across their scene with much the same acceptance they accord to the appearances of *stella comata*. He is simply *there*.

* The star indicates a note in which evidence is discussed or additional information is supplied. An unstarred number indicates a note simply naming sources. Notes begin on p. 376. Brackets show text pp. referred to.

For one whose fame blazed so high, Richard Neville arrived upon the stage of mighty affairs comparatively late, and his arrival was sudden. The first decisive moment in men's careers is not easily discerned, the occasion on which the dream within whispers *now* and the man sallies forth upon the errand of his will. But in Richard Neville's life the moment can be pin-pointed.

On a May morning in 1455 he found the clue to greatness in the town of St. Albans, when he was twenty-six.

On that day Louis XI was still the Dauphin of France, a man of whom Warwick had no more than heard, a man of whom Louis' father, Charles VII, had heard only too much and was about to descend upon with an army. In the fields outside St. Albans the future Edward IV was with Warwick, but he was only Edward, Earl of March, then, a precocious boy of thirteen, already wearing armor. Within the town lay Henry VI, King of England, surrounded by the lords who ruled in his name. Henry, too, should be somewhere brushed into Warwick's triptych, glimmering in the background like a ghost—a long-jawed defenseless face with its high nose only emphasizing the lonely, bewildered innocence of the dark eyes.

At eleven o'clock that morning the Earl of Warwick stood armed beneath his war banner at the head of hundreds of men wearing his badge of the Ragged Staff. In the meadows on either side of him, his father Richard, Earl of Salisbury, and his uncle-by-marriage Richard, Duke of York, were likewise arrayed for battle. Within the hour Warwick's moment will have struck. But now, as he stands waiting upon the commands of his father and uncle, he is no more—for all that anyone can see—than what he has become as a consequence of the family into which he was born, the marriage his father made for him, and the time of violence in which he was bred.

In the nerveless fingers of that sad-eyed king within St. Albans, the bonds of order had been unraveling for a generation. Henry was then thirty-four, and he had been King since he was nine months old. Ruler he had never been. His father, Harry the Fifth, and his mother, Katherine of France, had left Henry, and England, a fateful legacy—French conquests which mired the nation morally and physically in a long losing war and a taint of insanity in the infant Henry's blood passed on by Queen Katherine from her father, the mad Charles VI.

Richard Neville was born a few months before Joan of Arc raised the siege of Orléans; he reached his majority as the English were being finally beaten out of France; and in the interval he experienced in the turbulent North the worsening climate of disorder as the nobles took the law into their own hands while factions at court fought to pillage helpless King Henry's purse and wield his prerogative.

Richard had come into the world on November 28, 1428, the first son of Richard Neville, shortly to become Earl of Salisbury, and his wife Alice, the heiress of that earldom. On his father's side he was sprung from a hardy northern tribe who had been rooted in their lands for centuries. His grandfather Ralph, sixth Lord of Raby and first Earl of Westmorland, was the master of estates in the Bishopric of Durham and of the castles of Sheriff Hutton and Middleham in Yorkshire, which made him the rival of the Percys for pre-eminence in the North.

Ralph had reared a huge family by two prolific marriages. His first wife gave him nine children. His second, Joan Beaufort, daughter of John of Gaunt, bore him nine sons and five daughters, all but three of whom survived infancy. Although the Raby lands and the earldom went to the offspring of the first marriage, Joan's children were destined to eclipse them in worldly fortunes. Inheriting the great Yorkshire castles upon her husband's death, Joan passed them on to her eldest son Richard, the Earl of Salisbury. Most of her other sons were matched with heiresses of baronies. Four of her daughters soared much higher. Catherine wedded the Duke of Norfolk; Anne, the Duke of Buckingham; Eleanor, the Earl of Northumberland; and the youngest, Cicely, called the "Rose of Raby," married Richard, Duke of York.

By the time Richard Neville was ten years old, his father had extended this web of alliances by arranging Richard's marriage to Anne Beauchamp, daughter of the Earl of Warwick. It was an advantageous match, though not—to all appearances—a brilliant one, for Anne had a brother, Henry, who would inherit the earldom.

Richard grew into manhood in the restless backwash of a great enterprise failing and a realm falling into anarchy. Feudal ties were dead. The King's government lacked both moral authority and force. Lords maintained armed bands of retainers, recruited from yeomen and gentry who had come back from the French wars habituated to violence. Richard's father used this system—called livery and maintenance—to provide him with soldiers for the borders and with followers to support his position in the North.

Within the loosened fabric of society savage customs lingered. Down in Winchester a condemned thief who had prolonged his life by accusing many men falsely was at last "appealed" by an honest tailor. The men were clad in white sheepskins from head to foot, given each an ash club with an iron point, and set to fighting in "the moste sory and wrecchyd grene that myght by founde a-bowte the towne," neither having had food or drink and "yf they nede any drynke, they moste take hyr [their] owne pysse." At the first blow their weapons broke. They fell to fighting with nails and teeth. Suddenly flinging the tailor to the ground, the thief leaped on him and bit his privy parts. In an agonized convulsion, the tailor got to his knees, seized the thief's nose in his jaws, and gouged an eye with his thumb. The thief then confessed his lies and was hanged; the innocent tailor was given a pardon, became a hermit, and died shortly thereafter.[1]

Of Richard's early years little is known. His father was a plain, prudent man, rather colorless in personality but vigorous in the conduct of affairs. One thinks of him being called "Good old Salisbury"—a hard-bitten, not very imaginative Yorkshireman. After serving in the French wars, he became a member of the royal council and, like Nevilles before him, he held the wardenship of the West Marches toward Scotland. Though the lands of his earldom were in the South and he exerted a growing influence in the capital, his heart lay in the North with his wardenship and his Yorkshire castles.

Young Richard and his brothers Thomas and John were prob-ably trained in arms and knightly accomplishments at Sheriff Hutton and Middleham (George, the youngest son, heading for Oxford and a career in the Church). The North was in Richard's blood, and it nourished his first experiences with the turbulent society of his day. This region of wild spaces and fierce loyalties and baronial "menies" of fighting men, with craggy castles and great abbeys scattered over the lonely moors, was a breeding ground of violence and civil strife. When Richard was still only a lad, the children of Ralph's first marriage set out to recover the Yorkshire estates which Joan Beaufort had bequeathed to the Earl of Salisbury. Both sides armed their tenants, indentured for all the retainers they could afford, and were soon locked in a miniature war. In this hard school of raids and skirmishes young Richard Neville probably rode at his father's side and learned to manage arms and command men. The Earl of Salisbury repelled the in-vaders and kept possession of the estates.

Before he was eighteen, Richard was actively helping his father on the West Marches. Though England and Scotland were in a period of nominal truce and the Scots were busily fighting among themselves for control of their boy-king, James II, the borders were always unruly. Richard and his father commanded the gar-risons of Carlisle and smaller outposts, led raids to punish sheep-stealing and village-burning, and negotiated breaches of the truce with Scots envoys. In 1446 King Henry acknowledged young Richard's good service by appointing him joint Warden with his father after Salisbury's term expired. By this time he had won the spurs of knighthood.

The year before—in 1445 when Richard was sixteen—there was introduced into the growing anarchy of England a beautiful French Princess, a year younger than Richard, whose life was to be strangely and terribly intertwined with his. Within a decade he would be calling her an evil bitch and levying mortal war against her party, and not much more than a decade after that he would humbly acknowledge her as his sovereign lady and marry his daughter to her son.

This girl, Margaret of Anjou, niece of Charles VII of France, was brought to England as a bride for the meek and monklike King Henry. The dominant faction at court, led by the Earl (then Marquess, then Duke) of Suffolk and the Duke of Somerset, had arranged the marriage as a means of putting an end to the ruinous French war. Young though she appeared to be, Margaret was already a learned and high-spirited and imperious woman. Duchesses were required to go on their knees before her when they spoke, and the Mayor of Coventry discovered that when he headed a procession escorting her from his city, he must bear in his hands his mace of office, as he was accustomed to doing only for the King himself.[2]

Margaret of Anjou was a tincture dropped into the troubled brew of English politics which precipitated animosities and grievances into two bitterly opposed forces. With King Henry docilely following her lead, she openly embraced the party of Suffolk and Somerset, which had made her marriage and wanted peace with France. She set her face against the first subject of the kingdom, Richard, Duke of York.*

He was a man of moderate temper and moderate abilities, hardworking, forthright. He was also the undoubted—but unacknowledged—heir to the throne, and behind that claim lay hidden an even more dangerous one: since he was descended from Lionel, Duke of Clarence, Edward III's second son, as well as from Edward's fifth son, Edmund of Langley, he might be considered to have a better title to the crown than Henry VI himself, who derived from Edward's fourth son, John of Gaunt.† York also possessed the largest estate in the realm, a record of duty conscientiously performed, and a connection by marriage with the most powerful family group in England, the Nevilles.

Margaret of Anjou brought no peace at home and no peace with France. Conscious of their strength, the French insisted on the surrender of Maine—bulwark of Normandy—and when Suffolk and Somerset foolishly broke the truce to sack the city of

---

* He became so after the death of Henry V's brother, Humphrey, Duke of Gloucester, in 1447.
† See genealogical table, p. 10.

Fougères, Charles VII's armies stormed into Normandy in the summer of 1449 and quickly drove out the English. Within two years, all the English holdings in France were lost, save Calais.*

These disastrous years were the making of Richard Neville's fortune. His wife's brother Henry, now Duke of Warwick, suddenly died in 1447, leaving a daughter of four as his heiress. As the French armies were beginning to break into Normandy, this child succumbed. In July of 1449 Richard Neville was created, in his wife's right, Earl of Warwick and was likewise given Henry's honor of ranking as premier earl of the realm.

It was a magnificent accession of wealth and power—lands, lordships, manors, castles, privileges. Not only was the new Earl master of the Beauchamp estates but through his wife's mother, the heiress of the Despenser and Monthermer families, he swayed an even larger domain. He was baron of Elmley and Hanslape, lord of Glamorgan and Morgannoc. The heart of his holdings reached in a great arc from South Wales through Herefordshire, Gloucestershire, and Worcestershire, including well-nigh a hundred manors and a score of castles. More than half a hundred estates were scattered in the counties of Warwick, Oxford, Hertford, Northampton, Nottingham, Stafford, Rutland, Cambridge, Norfolk, Suffolk, Essex, Kent, Sussex, Hampshire, Berkshire, Wiltshire, Devon, and Cornwall, and in the far North he owned the stronghold of Barnard Castle, perched high above the Tees.

While the new Earl of Warwick remained quietly in the background, the realm, stirred by the losses in France and by misgovernment at home, rocked in violent upheavals. In the spring of 1450 the Commons demanded Suffolk's head, and though Queen Margaret persuaded Henry merely to banish him for five years, his ship was intercepted by a vessel in the Strait of Dover, he was beheaded in a small boat, and head and trunk were flung upon the Dover sands. Two bishops of the court party were murdered. In June, Jack Cade roused thousands of Kentishmen to his banners and lorded it in London for four days, but after he and his fol-

* In 1453 old Talbot, Earl of Shrewsbury, attempting the reconquest of Guienne, was defeated and killed at the battle of Chatillon.

lowers accepted a royal pardon, he was quickly hunted down and killed. In these events Warwick played no discernible part.*

Then in the autumn of 1450, the Duke of York, whom the Queen's party had thought to get out of the way by appointing him Lieutenant of Ireland, returned to England to demand a reform of the government and the ousting of the Queen's favorite, the Duke of Somerset. The Earl of Salisbury and the Duke of Norfolk, York's brothers-in-law, gave him their support, and the Earl of Warwick, following his father's lead, came to London "with a mighty people arrayed for war" to swell York's military power.

But Somerset and the Queen could count on strong baronial support, and by the summer of 1451 they had been able, despite York's popularity, to get rid of Parliament and frustrate the Duke's attempt to bring Somerset to trial. When, early in the following year, York took up arms to enforce his demands, Salisbury and Warwick succeeded in negotiating an agreement whereby York disbanded his army on the promise that Somerset would be removed from court. Instead, the Queen kept Somerset in power, York was delivered into their hands, and Warwick and Salisbury helplessly stood by while their kinsman was forced to swear his obedience in a public ceremony at St. Paul's.

But the Nevilles had learned their lesson. Warwick and Salisbury returned to their estates, determined to back York to the hilt when the right time came.

It came in the following year. In midsummer Henry VI went mad at Clarendon, lapsing into an animal-like stupor from which nothing could rouse him. Three months after, Queen Margaret gave birth to a son.

No longer able to act in the King's name, Somerset lost control of the government to the Duke of York in the autumn (1453) and was committed to prison. Warwick became a member of the

---

* On May 5, 1450, Warwick came to Leicester with more than 400 men (*Paston Letters*, I, p. 127). A month later, as trouble began to break out in Kent, he was gathering another force (*Notes and Queries*, May, 1919, V, 12th Series). Apparently, however, he took no part in the King's feeble operations and probably remained throughout the summer in armed watchfulness on his estates.

royal council early in December. After the Christmas holidays, London grew tense with fears and rumors. The court lords came back to town bringing powerful menies. The Yorkists had also gathered large forces. The Earl of Warwick—for the first time showing the immense resources of his earldom—sent ahead a thousand men to ensure a safe entry into London, and with a second bristling fellowship, he escorted his uncle, the Duke of York, to the capital. King Henry's incapacity and London's support of York prevented an outbreak.[3]

After it was shown that the King was hopelessly mad—Warwick was one of the examining committee [4]—the Lords of Parliament, in April (1454), made the Duke of York the Protector of the Realm, and the Earl of Salisbury became Chancellor. Warwick's youngest brother George shared the family fortunes by being promised the first available bishopric, even though he was not yet old enough to be ordained bishop.

York's power scarcely outlasted the year. By Christmas the Queen had succeeded in nursing Henry back to sanity. At the beginning of February (1455) she was able to command Somerset's release. York was relieved of his protectorship and Somerset triumphantly resumed his control of the government.[5]

Though the Earl of Warwick had jumped into a position of power in York's regime, he had seemingly done little more than second his father, perhaps being content to let the age sicken and his hopes mature. Now twenty-six years old, he had had sufficient experience of government and war to be aware that he could win men's hearts by the force of his personality, that he commanded energies beyond those of his peers. He must have sensed a depth of will yet untapped, a capacity to order events yet untried. His future lay coiled within him like a spring.

Within a few weeks of York's overthrow, he took the first of the steps which were to lead him to the meadows outside the town of St. Albans.

II

St. Albans

IN THE early spring (1455) the Earl of Warwick got word of a secret conference at Westminster, to which only Somerset's adherents were invited. There followed the news that a council of peers was to meet at Leicester in late May, in order to provide for the King's safety. Warwick, Salisbury, and York had not received invitations, and there was no doubt who, in Somerset's opinion, were the parties threatening the King.

From Warwick Castle horsemen rode in many directions bearing Warwick's summons to the men of his estates, his friends, and his retainers. Other messengers took the long road to Sandal Castle in Yorkshire, where the Duke of York had begun gathering his forces, and to the Earl of Salisbury's stronghold at Middleham. In the first days of May the roads leading to Warwick were bright with red jackets displaying the Earl's emblem of the Ragged Staff. The castle was becoming an armed camp. Headed by the officers of Warwick's estates, companies of yeomen archers arrived ahorse or on foot, wearing steel caps and padded leather "jacks" (tunics) with bows on their shoulders, a sword or leaden maul in their belts, and a quiver of cloth-yard shafts slung behind. Knights and squires rode in beneath their banners, encased in brigandines or steel corselets or—if they were rich enough—in full plate armor, the heaviest that had yet been devised.

About the middle of May, the Earl of Warwick led a band of a thousand men or more eastward across the Midlands. Somewhere along Ermine Street he joined the army of Salisbury and the Duke of York. York's eldest son, Edward, Earl of March, was at his father's side. Even for that century the boy was precocious in the bearing of arms, for he was only thirteen. He was big and strong for his age, bright of face, intelligent, happy-tempered, and fearless. This likely and likable lad was to become Warwick's greatest friend and his deadliest enemy.

26

By the time the Yorkists halted at Royston, they had received word from their agents in London that Somerset and the King, surrounded by lords pledged to the court party, were about to start northward from the city. Warwick, York, and Salisbury drew up an appeal to their sovereign, declaring that for their own safety and the King's they were coming to him, armed, in order to dispel the lies of their enemies. Next day they moved southward to Ware. News came that Henry and his lords were marching up Watling Street. It appeared that the advance of the Yorkists had been discovered and that Somerset was trying to slip around them in order to reach the rendezvous at Leicester. On the evening of May 21 they sent a second appeal to the King, enclosing a copy of the Royston manifesto. They may as well have saved ink and parchment, for Somerset pocketed both communications.[1]

During the evening of the twenty-first the lords at Ware learned that the King's force had halted for the night at Watford. They divined, or were informed, that Somerset would make for St. Albans. In the darkness of early morning began the race for the little town dominated by the great abbey. When the Yorkists reached the eastern outskirts some time after seven o'clock, they found their entrance barred and the banners of their enemies planted within. Pulling their army into the meadows to the southeast of the town, Warwick, York, and Salisbury decided on yet another appeal to the King. This time it was couched in blunt terms: "Please it, your Majesty royal, to deliver up such as we will accuse. This done, you to be worshipped as a most rightful King. We will not now slack until we have them, or else we, therefore, to die."

The royal heralds soon returned with a document bearing the King's seal but obviously drafted by Somerset: "I shall know what traitors dare be so bold to array my people in my own land. I shall destroy them, every mother's son. . . . Rather than they shall have any lord that here is with me, I shall this day myself live and die."

Warwick, York, and Salisbury showed the message to their captains. It was clear that they had no choice but to fight or

suffer a traitor's death. The Yorkist force of about five thousand
men was almost double the King's, but save for the three leaders,
it contained no men of note except Lord Clinton and Sir Robert
Ogle. Somerset, on the other hand, commanded well-nigh a
quarter of the peerage of England, but these lords were not accompanied by large retinues.

As the morning lengthened with the passing back and forth
of messengers, the Yorkist leaders were arranging their forces in
three divisions aimed at the southeastern side of the town. St.
Albans was defended by a crude ditch-and-embankment with
barriers that could be swung across the principal entries into the
market place. Commanding the wings of the army, York and
Salisbury drew up the bulk of the Yorkist troops so that they
fronted the barriers across two lanes that led up to Holywell–St.
Peter's Street.

In the meadows between, Warwick's center division faced
the ditch along the gardens of the houses on Holywell Street.
His Midland archers were backed by a band of six hundred men
brought from the northern Marches by Sir Robert Ogle. York
and Salisbury, the experienced commanders, would lead the main
assault. Warwick would threaten the defenses along the ditch,
but his detachment was mainly intended to give support to the
two wings.

At eleven o'clock in the morning, York and Salisbury suddenly gave the signal to attack. Their men rushed against the
barriers, taking their enemies by surprise. But the two lanes
were narrow, the Yorkists crowded together. Only a few of
them at a time could come to grips with the enemy. Somerset's
outposts, hastily seizing weapons, were able to hold back the
first assault. Church bells sounded the alarm. Reinforcements
came streaming down the lanes to bolster the defense. Despite
desperate assaults, the barricades could not be forced. The minutes
wore on. York's cause began to look grim.

Meanwhile, the Earl of Warwick was studying the strength
of the ditch-and-palisade. When he saw that the assaults of his
father and uncle had been halted, he discarded his subordinate
role. The enemy position appeared to be thinly defended; Sir

Robert Ogle was eager for action. At Warwick's order the six hundred northern footmen were massed in a wedge with the archers on the flank and in the rear. Warwick looked up and down the meadows. York and Salisbury were still unable to break through. He seized his moment.

Standing beneath his banner with his men-at-arms gathered round him, the Earl signaled his trumpeters. As the shrill call rang out, Sir Robert and the men of the Marches raced for the palisade, the archers covering their charge with a hail of arrows. When Ogle reached the ditch, the archers swarmed across the meadow, Warwick and his mailed knights in their midst. Ogle's men flung themselves up the embankment upon the defenders. One fierce clash of steel and they were across, the red-jacketed bowmen at their heels.

The Earl clambered up the palisade. Ahead, Ogle's men were pouring through the gardens. Waving on the archers, Warwick led his men-at-arms forward on the run. Men dashed through the houses and along garden sides. The archers burst into St. Peter's Street, yelling "à Warwick! à Warwick!" Ogle's Northerners had swung into the lanes and were slashing at the backs of the troops defending the barricades. Now Warwick's banner was planted in the street. Warwick and his knights were fighting with enemy men-at-arms trying to cut down the archers. The Earl shouted and pointed to a ragged line of footmen rushing to support the men-at-arms. Warwick's Midland archers let loose a volley that broke the charge.

Shouts of triumph sounded in the lanes. York and Salisbury had smashed across the barriers and were driving Somerset's men before them. St. Peter's Street was a hell of swords and glaives and whining arrows. Warwick was clearing a path so that his archers could fire toward the market place. There stood a ring of mailed nobles surrounding the King's banner and the slight figure of Henry himself. "Spare the commons!" Warwick was shouting. "Aim for the lords!"

An arrow-storm struck the defenders of the King. They began to melt away. Footmen were fleeing across gardens and through fields. Men in the polished armor of lords lumbered toward the abbey. Somerset's host had been broken to pieces. Warwick, York, and Salisbury approached the peaked King, standing alone and bewildered in the doorway of a house, his neck bleeding from an arrow-graze. Down on their knees they went, beseeching Henry the Sixth for his grace and swearing they never meant to harm him. Helplessly he nodded his head. The battle was over.

Men in broken armor were strewn about the street. The mighty Edmund, Duke of Somerset, lay slain beneath a tavern sign. The Earl of Northumberland had been killed and the fierce Lord Clifford, and the Duke of Buckingham's son soon died of his wounds. Somerset's heir, the Earl of Dorset, was so sorely hurt that he was carried away, helpless, in a cart. The Duke of Buckingham, hurt, managed to reach the abbey. So did Lord Dudley, with an arrow in his face. The handsome Earl of Wiltshire had shamefully fled, "for he was afraid of losing of beauty," says a chronicler. While Warwick, York, and Salisbury were escorting the King to the abbey, their men happily pillaged the baggage and appropriated the horses of the Lancastrian lords.[2]*

Next day the King was brought back to his capital. In solemn procession Henry rode between York and Salisbury with Warwick in advance bearing the sword of state. The most violent enemies of the Yorkists were dead or in hiding. The Queen was powerless. York was again master of the realm.

But the Earl of Warwick's position had altered. To the fifteenth century, war was still the birthplace of glory. Though Sir Robert Ogle led the decisive assault at St. Albans, he was a captain in Warwick's command, and the emblems of the Ragged Staff had shone bright in St. Peter's Street. Warwick's dashing attack had won him a military reputation and a sudden fame.

In reconstituting the government, York took the office of Constable. Since York's kinsman, Thomas Bourchier, Archbishop of Canterbury, was already Chancellor, Salisbury could not resume the chancellorship, and he was apparently content to let his son claim the high place due the Nevilles. The Archbishop's brother, Viscount Bourchier, was made Treasurer. What was to be the portion of Warwick? His new stature had kindled his ambition. He felt within himself the urgent demand of talents and capacities which he had hitherto exercised only in his dreams. Confidently he asked for the office which the dead Somerset had held, and York before him: a powerful but dangerous eminence and—in this time of internal strife and war with France—one of misty opportunity. The Earl of Warwick was made Captain of Calais.[3]

He still remains, however, a figure in outline, inseparable from the general picture of York's troubled government. The *Paston Letters* and official documents offer only brief glimpses of him, bits of action which suggest that he was feeling his way toward the style of greatness and beginning to tune himself to the effect he made upon the world.

He took into his charge the badly wounded Earl of Dorset, now Duke of Somerset and heir of the Beaufort line. If he hoped to make a friend of young Henry, he utterly failed, for the new Duke of Somerset was to spend the rest of his short life seeking vengeance. He had better fortune with Sir John Wenlock, formerly the Queen's Chamberlain, who had also fought against the Yorkists at St. Albans. The battle having shaken him loose from his allegiance to the court party, Warwick received his overtures with such a warmth of courtesy that in a few weeks he was converted into a devoted adherent. When Parliament met in July, the Commons, perhaps as a compliment to Warwick, elected Wenlock their Speaker.

On one occasion at least, Warwick's new sense of power pushed him into a display of imperious temper. When Lord Cromwell, an adherent of the Queen's, ventured to excuse himself before King Henry of any responsibility for the battle of St. Albans, Warwick stormed into the royal chamber and to the King's face swore hotly that Cromwell was the man who had begun all the trouble. So fierce was Warwick's wrath that at Cromwell's nervous request the Earl of Shrewsbury lodged himself and a body of his retainers close to Cromwell's dwelling.

Though the Yorkist Parliament passed a bill consigning to oblivion the unfortunate conflict at St. Albans, the blood which had been spilt inflamed the passions of the court party and turned the struggle between York and the Queen into a mortal combat.

The sons and friends of the dead lords chafed to retaliate. The climate of anarchy deepened. The strain of these times soon proved too much for King Henry's wits and in October he once more fell into a stupor of madness. York again became Protector. In a few weeks he had to hurry into the West Country to extinguish a bitter feud between the Earl of Devonshire and Lord Bonvile. Warwick assumed charge of the Yorkist government in London, but he could do little except keep up the outward show of authority. Queen Margaret was desperately nursing her husband that she might use his name against her enemies, and by February of 1456 he had again recovered the frail measure of his sanity. The Duke of York loyally relinquished the protectorship, but the Yorkists maintained their slender hold upon the government.[4]

During these months the new Captain of Calais had not been able to fulfill his office. Under the command of the dead Somerset's deputies, the garrison had refused to acknowledge the authority of the Earl of Warwick. Most of the trouble was unpaid wages, as usual. At the end of the year Warwick finally demanded in Parliament to be discharged of all responsibility for what might happen to Calais, since his efforts to take command had been thwarted. With the French ever threatening this last English foothold on the Continent, Parliament quickly made arrangements to give security to the Staplers of Calais, who then paid the garrison's vast arrears of wages, amounting to almost £50,000. Late in April (1456) the government of the town was surrendered to Warwick's representatives.[5]

He himself remained in England, however, for the fruits of the victory at St. Albans were withering away. Queen Margaret, as a correspondent of the Pastons wryly noted, was "a great and strong laboured woman." [6] Having now assumed direct command of the court party, she was setting about to undermine York's position with all the fierceness of her passionate nature. She had penetrated York's chief weakness: his power depended upon his controlling the King but he could not keep public sympathy if he held the royal family in obvious duress. When spring came (1456), she boldly took her little Prince and, shaking off the oppressive atmosphere of Yorkist London, went off to her great manor of Tutbury. Before the end of the summer, she had managed King Henry's removal to Coventry.

The Yorkist lords retired watchfully to their estates, York to Sandal and Warwick to Warwick Castle. The Queen had moved into royalist Cheshire, striving to rally hearts to her baby Prince. Tension grew like thunderheads in the summer weather. A rumor swept London that there had been another battle, with Viscount Beaumont killed on the Queen's side, Warwick "sore hurt," and a thousand men slain. As the summer of 1456 passed, the Queen gathered her loyal lords about the court, each bringing a stout band of warriors. At the end of September she made use of the King's name to summon a great council at Coventry.

The Earl of Warwick and the Duke of York either miscalculated the Queen's strength or rashly decided to confront their enemies at whatever odds. They arrived in Coventry to find themselves in a trap. The Queen summarily dismissed their kinsmen, the Bourchiers, from the chancellorship and treasurership. They themselves could neither protest nor retire: they were excluded from the council board, their movements were closely watched, and their retinues were jostled in the streets by the belligerent fellowships of the court lords. Neither Warwick's popularity with the commons nor York's genuine attempt to provide good government mattered now.

Warwick and York were commanded to appear before the King. In the audience chamber they were ringed round by the somber faces of their enemies and compelled to listen to a humiliating lecture delivered by the Duke of Buckingham. They were upstarts, Buckingham declared. They had outrageously troubled the realm to satisfy their selfish ambitions. Though they fancied their greatness, they were, in fact, no more than what their sovereign chose to make them, and they had only his goodness to lean on. Then Buckingham and the court lords fell on their knees, beseeching King Henry to show no more mercy to York and Warwick if they dared to "inquiet" the realm.

Henry nodded his head. But the ordeal was not yet over. Uncle and nephew were required to swear this submission on the Holy Evangels and confirm it with parchment sealed. Only then were they permitted, officially, to make their departure from the court.

They were in great peril. The young lords who had lost their fathers at St. Albans panted for blood. Secretly they prepared to fall upon York and Warwick as they left Coventry. But the Duke of Buckingham desired peace and he was York's brother-in-law. He managed to warn York of the ambush. Warwick and his uncle succeeded in slipping away unharmed.[7]

Though the Duke had been shorn of all power in the government, Warwick had not lost his captainship. Either he had already gained such popular approval that the Queen dared not remove him or else she hoped to be well rid of him when he crossed the Channel. York returned quietly to his estates at Wigmore. The Earl of Warwick, taking his wife and two small daughters with him, at last went over the sea to his town of Calais. Undaunted by the Queen's seizure of power and alert to what fortune might offer in these confused and dangerous times, he sailed across the Channel to continue the quest of greatness.

In this same season there was descried in the waters near Weymouth a portent which might have been taken as a presage of Warwick's future. A cock was seen "coming out of the sea, having a great crest upon his head and a great red beard and legs of half a yard long, and stood in the water and crew three times. And every time that he crew, he turned him round about and beckoned with his head towards the north, the south, and the west, and he was of the colour of a pheasant, and when he had crowed three times, he vanished away."[8]

Part Two

The Captain of Calais

(1456-1461)

I

"As Famous a Knight"*

CALAIS had fallen to the English more than a hundred years before, as a result of Edward III's victory at Crécy. People liked to talk of it as the springboard of a renewed assault upon France, but the men of business knew that its real significance was commercial. Here was located the Wool Staple, whose merchants held a monopoly of the export of most of the wool grown in England; here the traders of the great Flemish cities must come to buy bales of the indispensable stuff for their busy looms.

The heavily fortified town was protected by the Tower of Rysbank, dominating the harbor, and by the castles of Guisnes and Hammes, which guarded the entries into the twenty square miles of marsh and flat making up the English territory. The combined garrisons numbered perhaps two thousand men-at-arms and archers, the only professional army the realm owned.

When the Earl of Warwick assumed personal command in the fall of 1456, Calais stood in a precarious state. The garrisons were not up to strength; the soldiers were mutinous for lack of wages; the walls had begun to crumble. On several recent occasions the French had threatened to besiege the town, and even at the most peaceful times there were constant raids and skirmishes. The situation at sea was equally dangerous. The English fleet at this period consisted of a few large vessels and such merchantmen converted to warships as there was money to hire and fit out. For years the court had been too feeble to send forth a fleet, and Calais faced a Channel swarming with pirates and the aggressive flotillas of the French.

Only the ill feeling between Philip the Good, Duke of Burgundy—"The Grand Duke of the West"—and his more-or-less sovereign lord, Charles VII, had thus far saved Calais. The domains of Philip stretched in an arc from the North Sea to the dukedom and county of Burgundy in the east. Over Holland

and the rich Flemish cities he was master in his own right; as the lord of Burgundy he was a peer of France and a vassal of King Charles.* In fact, he had grown accustomed to acting as an independent ruler, though cherishing a sentimental regard for France, and he enjoyed the wealthiest and the most splendid court in Europe.

By the 1450s, Philip's pride and Charles VII's hope of reuniting France were showing themselves to be incompatible. It was Philip's refusal to allow French armies on his lands that had prevented Charles VII from beleaguering Calais. Only a few weeks before Warwick arrived there, Charles' ambitious and insubordinate son, the Dauphin Louis, fled from his appanage of Dauphiné and took refuge at the court of Burgundy. He was warmly welcomed by Philip, despite Charles' angry protests, and installed in the castle of Genappe with a handsome pension.

Philip never forgot that his father, John the Fearless, had been assassinated (1419) by the courtiers of Charles, then the forlorn Dauphin. As the price of accepting terms of peace (in 1435), he compelled Charles to make public acknowledgment of the wrong by agreeing to build chapels and chantries devoted to masses for John's soul. He also compelled Charles to surrender the great towns along the Somme River, which now formed the impregnable frontier of Flanders. He liked to remark that he might have been a King if he chose; his hearers had no difficulty understanding that there were many who wore crowns but only one Duke of Burgundy.

Yet Philip was extravagantly proud of being the first Peer of France. Although he had avenged his father's murder by allying himself with Henry V, the bitterest regret of his life was that he had not been present at the great battle of Agincourt, on the French side. When Charles VII's recalcitrant son, Louis, arrived on Flemish soil—as Warwick was preparing to cross to Calais—he dispatched word that he was hurrying to throw him-

---

* Most of his territories in the Low Countries and the county of Burgundy—the Franche-Comté—were nominal fiefs of the Empire. His Burgundian holdings were actually separated from his Flemish domain by Alsace and Lorraine, but he was able to command free passage through those lands.

self at Philip's feet, like a child seeking the protection of his father. Horrified, the Duke sent messengers spurring to Louis with agitated remonstrances. On no account must the heir of France abdicate his dignity by coming to meet the Duke of Burgundy! If he persisted, Philip would run as hard as he could in the other direction, for a whole year if necessary!

When the Duke approached the castle where Louis was impatiently awaiting him, the fugitive rushed down the stairs to greet his dearly beloved benefactor. The Duchess of Burgundy flew after him, lest he demean her husband and herself by an act of shocking impropriety. When they reached the courtyard, she clung to his arm to prevent him from running to greet the Duke. Philip had arrived at the castle clad in the furs and jewels and followed by the cavalcade of courtiers that betokened the amplitude of his power. At the outer gate, however, he ordered his princely train to remain behind, dismounted from his horse, and walked alone into the courtyard. When he caught sight of Louis, he bared his head and bowed his knee humbly to the ground. Then he advanced gravely toward his guest and, ignoring the outstretched arms and cries of gratitude, once more knelt before the Dauphin. Shaking himself loose from the Duchess, Louis pulled Philip to his feet and fell into his arms. Both men burst into tears.

Such was Philip's rigid respect for the French monarchy. But when Charles demanded the return of his son, that was another matter. Philip held himself answerable to no man and ruled as he pleased. "He has given shelter to a fox that will one day devour his chickens," Charles remarked wryly. He understood his son very well indeed.

Louis never tired of expressing his undying thanks to the Duke of Burgundy, and he flatteringly courted the friendship of Philip's heir, Charles, Count of Charolais. At Genappe, Louis treated the Count to what poor delights he could afford (on Philip's bounty): hunting, story-telling, and abusing Charles VII of France. Not many miles distant, at Calais, the Earl of Warwick, whose destiny was to be mortally intermingled with theirs, was exerting himself in more ambitious enterprises—but then he had much farther to climb than they. The heir of France was already thirty-three; the heir of Burgundy, ten years younger. Richard Neville, the heir of whatever his will and his talents could win him, was entering his twenty-ninth year.

He was welcomed at Calais by the Mayor and the wealthy merchants of the Staple. He listened to the reports of the Marshal, the Treasurer, the Victualler, and the lieutenants in charge of Guisnes and Hammes. He reviewed the garrisons and inspected his ships of war in the harbor. Riding through the Pale, he stared across the lands of Philip of Burgundy, whose friendship with England meant prosperous trade, and might mean more, and he gazed to the south at the territory of the Adversary, King Charles of France.[1]

The experience was an elixir. He was loyal to the Duke of York, but he recognized that he was no longer inseparable, as a personality, from the cause of York. He was in absolute command of military power and free to act as he chose in an explosive but inviting situation. His imagination was stirred by the situation of Calais—a little empery, a challenging promontory which overlooked England and France and Burgundy. He saw something even more compelling, which gave shape to all his hopes—a first hazy vision of himself as a unique and decisive personality printing a remarkable impact upon his age.

Unleashing his vitality, he thrust out in all directions. He paid his soldiers, increased their numbers, inspired them with his aggressiveness, and soon won their loyalty. The merchants, impressed by his zeal to ensure the safety of their trade, were not long in opening their purses to him, nor did he hesitate to deplete his own funds to eke out the slender supply provided by the government. Quickly perceiving the importance of the Kentish ports to his position, he set about making friends in Dover and Sandwich and Lydd and Romney. He enlisted shipmasters to teach him the arts of navigation and marine warfare. In those days, naval tactics were simple and direct: a fierce game of ram, board, and overpower. He was soon as much at home on ships as at the head of an armed cavalcade. He had quickly grasped that the offensive strength of Calais lay in its command of the sea, and he saw himself leaning in aggressive mastery upon the Channel.

When word arrived in the spring of 1457 that a mighty power of the French was coming against Calais, he sprang into action. Readying his garrison and his little navy, he appealed to the men of Kent for victuals and supplies. Zealously, they gathered provisions, loaded them aboard whatever ships lay in the harbors, and conveyed them to the storage vaults of Calais. To follow up his success, the Earl paid a visit—almost like a progress—to his kinsman Thomas Bourchier, the Archbishop of Canterbury, in his great cathedral town. There he summoned before him the men of Sandwich and Canterbury, feasted them and charmed them, "and thanked them of their good hearts and victualing of Calais and prays them to continue." [2]

The French decided to exert their power on the sea. The gallant Piers de Brézé, Seneschal of Normandy, was given charge of the fleet. He was not only the favorite minister of Charles VII but also a devoted friend to Margaret of Anjou; and it seems probable that she had begged him to do what he could to injure the Earl of Warwick. Warwick had not yet scraped together enough ships to take the offensive in the Channel. The task of meeting the naval challenge of the French belonged to Henry Holland, Duke of Exeter, who for ten years had been Admiral of England. But the partisan Exeter, so ready to smite the Yorkists whenever he could, took no measures to prepare a fleet, and the Queen's government were, as usual, busy with their own interests and short of money.

Putting to sea, Brézé soon discovered that Warwick's Calais was too tough a nut to crack, and after cruising the Channel without opposition he decided to hit Warwick's source of supply, and England's pride. Landing a strong force of men one summer dawn, he suddenly assaulted the port of Sandwich by land and sea, smashed into the harbor, plundered and ravaged the town through the daylight hours, and retired well-nigh untouched. For months afterward folk along the coasts trembled at the vaguest rumor of a French attack, while the rest of England seethed in humiliation and outrage.

Even the arrogant court faction could not face this storm.
What popular clamor was demanding they were forced with
bitter hearts to grant. Warwick was the man! cried the kingdom.
Only the vigorous Captain of Calais could restore England's naval
fortunes and her prestige. Early in October the Earl of Warwick
was given the special office of Keeper of the Sea for three years.
He was in a position to see that the award did not remain a mere
title. He secured the grant of the entire subsidy of tunnage and
poundage, except in the ports of Sandwich and Southampton. He
was likewise promised £1,000 in ready money from the revenues
of the Duchy of Lancaster, and when it was slow in forthcoming,
the King's council managed to provide him with £500 from the
Chancery fees.[3]

As the spring of 1458 approached, the Earl was using his new
resources to fit out as many ships as he could come by. Con-
centrating them at Calais, he dispatched scouting vessels to watch
the Channel. On Trinity Sunday morning, May 28, one of these
ships came flying into the harbor with tidings that twenty-eight
sail of Spaniards, sixteen of them being "great ships of forecastle,"
were approaching from the southwest. The Earl of Warwick
at once issued battle orders to his little fleet. While sailors rigged
his five ships of forecastle, three carvels, and four pinnaces,
archers and men-at-arms were marching down to the quays and
boarding the vessels. That same night the fleet cleared port. At
dawn the Earl of Warwick came upon the great navy of the
Spaniards, allies of Charles VII, their sails filling the dim sky
of morning and their hulls towering above the English flotilla.
The Earl had never fought at sea. He was woefully overmatched.
He immediately gave the order to attack.

At a signal from the flagship, his little squadron, marshaled in
tight formation, changed course. Headed by the five men-of-war,
it sailed directly for the heart of the enemy line. The Earl stood
beneath his banner on the forecastle, men-at-arms and master
mariners gathered about him. Gunners waited by the scattering
of cannon mounted on the decks. Archers and pikemen braced
themselves against the shock of ramming. Arrows whined above
their heads; missiles from the enemy artillery crashed into oaken

timbers. Warwick waved a gauntleted hand. Trumpets sounded his signal to open fire. With a roar the guns belched their stone cannon balls. Archers loosed volleys of arrows at the fast-approaching decks, thick with soldiers. The English vessels crashed into the hulls of their enemies.

Grappling hooks bit into wood. With a rush and a great shout of "à Warwick! à Warwick!" the English swarmed up the sides, slashing through the Spaniards massed at the rails. Warwick hoisted himself onto the Spanish ship, his household knights clearing a path for him with their swords. Then it was hack and thrust at close quarters, with the Earl and his men hewing their way along the deck. English archers clambered up masts to pour their fire on the rear ranks of the foe. Onward drove the banner of the Ragged Staff, leaving a trail of dead and wounded. Then the remaining Spaniards were crowded aft into a helpless mass and forced to surrender. They were quickly stowed below; soldiers and sailors were told off to man the vessel; Warwick led the rest of his men back to his flagship and the two men-of-war swung clear.

Drifting over the sea, English and Spanish ships were everywhere locked together in combat, except for a group of enemy merchantmen fleeing with all the sail they could make. Spotting two ships of forecastle crowded upon one of his pinnaces, Warwick gave orders to ram. In a few minutes he and his men were again fighting their way onto enemy decks.

Six hours the engagement lasted. The Spaniards recaptured some of their vessels and the English crews, but Warwick and his men continued to grind down the Spanish fleet, and the train of prizes grew steadily larger. At last, when his sailors were spread dangerously thin and his soldiers exhausted, the Earl permitted the Spaniards to draw off, after forcing them to agree to an exchange of prisoners. Though he had lost no ships, eighty of the attackers lay dead on bloody decks and some ten score were sorely hurt. His men had fought for him magnificently. More than two hundred Spaniards had been killed and five hundred wounded; one or two ships had been sent to the bottom; and six vessels, almost a quarter of the Spanish fleet, had been wrested from the enemy. Warwick sent hastily for more ships, intending to attack again, but the Spaniards were able to limp on to the ports of Flanders.

One of the Earl's soldiers, John Jernigan, spoke for all England when he wrote to a friend, "As men say, there has not been so great a battle upon the sea these forty winters." [4*]

The unhappy realm, hungry for redress of its martial pride, rang with Warwick's great exploit, and the men of Kent gave him a worshipful adherence that he was never to lose. England was a power in the world again; the Earl of Warwick was the author of her resurrection. Beyond the seas, through the courts of Europe, ran the fame of the English Earl. The legend of himself, already vivid in his own mind, he had now begun to impose upon the world.

While Warwick was smiting the enemies of England on the seas during these years, he was also attuned to events and attitudes in England, and he was alert for opportunities to show himself the friend and protector of English merchants.

It was a time of bitter frustration for the trading classes. The Queen's government was too weak and too irresponsible to support the interests of English commerce abroad. Court lords often instigated acts of piracy against alien shipping, heedlessly enriching their own purses while the merchants suffered from the retaliation invoked by foreign governments against English goods. There was no redress. When, in January of 1453, the Mayor of London and a delegation of burgesses complained to the Chancellor against Lord Bonvile for his plundering of Burgundian shipping, they received the usual shuffling answer. "With one voice" they irefully burst out, "Justice! Justice! Justice!"; but there was nothing the Chancellor could do except to retire in fear.[5] Despite the angry protests of the Merchants of the Staple, the Queen's favorites also issued licenses to their adherents and their Italian business agents which allowed them to evade the Staplers' monopoly on the sale of wool. Hence, with the increasing hostility to the government, there developed an acrid prejudice against foreign merchants, especially the Italians and the Germans of the Hanse towns. In the year Warwick came to Calais, London was rocked by an anti-Italian riot which turned into so dangerous a demonstration against the Queen's regime that the court lords sent to restore order precipitately quitted the city.

Not many months after Warwick reached Calais, he seized a chance to show his sympathy for the Staplers and the other London traders. Learning from his friends in the capital that a group of Italians, armed with licenses to avoid the Wool Staple, were loading three ships with wool and cloth, the Earl encouraged some of the Calais garrison to man a few vessels and called on his sailor friends at Sandwich to join the game. The little fleet sailed up the Thames, fell upon the three vessels loading at Tilbury, and carried them off to Calais. Though the government sent fierce letters to the London magistrates, demanding restitution of the goods and punishment of the malefactors, the Londoners did nothing at all—except cheer the Earl of Warwick.[6]

In the summer of 1458, only a few days after Warwick had defeated the Spaniards, he was again prowling the Channel when he intercepted a Hanseatic fleet freighting salt from the Bay of Bourgneuf. Warwick demanded that the Easterlings dip their flags for the Captain of Calais. Upon their refusing, he forthwith ordered an attack, won a quick and easy victory, and coasted back to port with a great train of prizes. This stroke once again sent his name soaring in England; the key of national greatness in which he pitched his plundering of the Easterling fleet jibed with the temper of the merchant class and the hearty xenophobia of the mass of Englishmen. This feat was to get him into a difficulty, however, which almost cost him his life.

Meanwhile, he never let up his aggressive tactics. When the Channel was quiet, he sent soldiers on raids into France and did not scruple to jab at Burgundian territory now and again, advertising by burned villages, ransoms, and booty that Calais was a beachhead of power, not a beleaguered town.

In July of 1459 Warwick was again in Kent. Feted like a hero and followed like a king, he had no trouble recruiting a great fellowship and hiring vessels for them to man. Cruising the seas a little later, he came upon two carracks of Genoa, hull deep in precious goods, and their escort of "three great Spanish ships which were stuffed with men of war." In a two days' running battle he captured one of the carracks and the three warships. Then did silk and spices go cheap in English ports as the Earl's name grew even dearer to the English nation. While the Queen's faction was sinking deeper into unpopularity and impotence, and the Duke of York bided his time, the Earl of Warwick was establishing himself in the hearts of his countrymen as the Champion of England.[7]

He had all along taken a wider view of his position, however. He meant to be the statesman as well as the Captain of Calais. The Yorkist party stood for a renewed attack upon France, and even before he left England Warwick was enthusiastically seconding his uncle's attempts to stir up profitable trouble in that kingdom.

For some years York had been negotiating with the Duc d'Alençon, a discontented prince who would aid an English invasion if he were properly rewarded. In the summer of 1455 an English herald arrived in the town of La Flèche (near Le Mans). At dawn next day he was led by devious ways to Alençon's lodgings, smuggled in the back door, and introduced into the ducal bedroom. Alençon was stretched out naked on the bed attended by two Barbary goats. Making the herald take an oath of secrecy—by promising to cut his throat and throw him in the river if he did not swear—the Duke delivered a message for the Duke of York: next year the time would be ripe for invasion, which Alençon would aid by delivering key Norman towns in return for lands, money, and the marriage of his daughter to York's eldest son, Edward. The English herald and a herald of Alençon's then took this offer to London, where they were joined two months later by another agent of the Duke's.

When York arrived in the capital in late November, he and the Earl of Warwick gave audience to Alençon's representatives. Warwick showed his ardor for the cause by sweeping Alençon's seal to his lips and passionately assuring the Duke's envoys that "he would live and die to accomplish the will of the noble prince d'Alençon if he had to sell and mortgage all his lands." Such a flamboyant gesture Warwick's blunt father, the Earl of Salisbury, could never have made. Warwick had inherited his tireless constitution from the hard-bitten lords of Raby, but his exuberance and histrionic *brio* must have come from other strains. As for the Duc d'Alençon, in December he sent a drunken laborer to Calais with a message; meeting a friend in Lisieux, the laborer spilled the whole plot; the friend promptly reported it to the Archbishop of Narbonne, who reported it to the King. On the last day of May, 1456, Joan-of-Arc's famous companion-in-arms, Dunois, clapped Alençon under arrest in Paris, and that was the end of the invasion.[8]

The Earl of Warwick had not been long at Calais before he drew himself forcibly to the attention of Philip of Burgundy by the depredations his men were committing on land and sea. Negotiations were opened. Early in July, 1457, Warwick rode out to an open field near Oye with an array of archers and men-of-arms, including two of his most famous swashbuckling captains. There he met an embassy escorted by the Count d'Estampes and Antoine, the Grand Bastard of Burgundy. Warwick and d'Estampes, both remaining on horseback, conferred amicably, the Earl sparing no pains to impress Duke Philip's representative by his princely bearing.

D'Estampes refused Warwick's invitation to dismount and partake of a feast, which the English had thoughtfully arranged nearby—the Burgundian fearing that if the French happened to descend on them, the attack might be ascribed to his treachery —but the Bastard of Burgundy and other nobles were happy to accept Warwick's cheer while d'Estampes kept guard. Then the Earl led Philip's envoys back to Calais, while d'Estampes returned to Philip to make a "fine, lengthy, high" relation to his master on the subject of Warwick as a "gentil chevalier."

The negotiations at Calais got nowhere, however, for the disputes at issue were a tangle of private grievances and claims and Warwick's men were, most of them, a tough, intransigent collection of freebooters. The English rudely refused to moderate their demands or offer compromises. Warwick, as befitted his dignity, left the haggling to his officers, but he was eager to cultivate the Duke of Burgundy's good graces and, on the surface at least, he tried to persuade his men to find a friendly solution. On the other hand, he may have been quite content to underline the martial vigor of Yorkist Calais. The Burgundians, realizing that they were "beating cold iron," withdrew to report their failure to the Duke at Hesdin.

Faced by the growing hostility of Charles VII, Philip was eager to gain the friendship of the Captain of Calais and of the Yorkist party, who were the enemies of his enemies, the King of France and the Queen of England. Therefore he and his councilors decided to swallow their pride and accept the English conditions for a settlement. At Calais, an agreement was quickly concluded and arrangements were made for another parley in October.

By the following spring, Warwick was hinting to the Duke of Burgundy that he was willing to entertain more ambitious proposals than truces and merchandising pacts, and he had so established himself in Philip's esteem that at the beginning of May (1458) the Duke was writing him private letters "touching some secret affairs." On May 27 Philip sent an array of notables to negotiate with the Earl, headed by the Count d'Estampes, the Bishop of Toul, and the Marshal of Burgundy. Their company of five hundred cavaliers arrived at Calais a few days after the English fleet had returned to port following the great struggle with the Spaniards, a victory which gave Philip further cause to appreciate Warwick's talents.

Under the cover of negotiating a renewal of the truce between England and Burgundy, the Earl and the Burgundians came to a secret understanding, virtually a Burgundian-Yorkist alliance, which afterward, as Chastellain notes, led to "hautes merveilleuses fins." Charles VII, suspicious of the undue cordiality between the Captain of Calais and the Duke of Burgundy, sent spies into Flanders to ferret out what was going on. No less a person than Charles' King of Arms, Normandy, was caught disguised as a merchant, and when his belongings yielded letters that betrayed his mission, he cooled his heels for a while in the prison of Lille Castle.[9]

In the latter part of the year (1458), Warwick was in the thick of negotiations so full of devious chicane that they were a veritable school of international intrigue. His follower, Lord Wenlock, secured a commission from the Queen's government to broach a triple marriage alliance to Charles VII—three English princes to wed three French princesses—as the means of bringing about peace between England and France. Wenlock also received permission to travel by way of the Low Countries in order to convey a greeting to the Duke and Duchess of Burgundy. To Warwick and his friends, the latter enterprise was the real purpose of the mission. Wenlock, received by the Duke and Duchess at Mons at the end of October, proceeded secretly— in the name of Henry VI and the Duke of York—to offer the marriage alliance to Duke Philip, only with a Burgundian cast of brides. Henry VI's son, the Duke of York's eldest son, and young Henry, Duke of Somerset, were proposed as husbands for the heiress of the Count of Charolais and the princesses of Bourbon and Guelders.

The Duchess of Burgundy was favorably impressed by the idea; and since Wenlock had shortly to take his leave in order to meet French negotiators at Rouen, she promised to send him a written assurance of Burgundy's interest in the proposal. Wenlock then made his offer of marriages and truce to the French, the brides this time being daughters of Charles VII, the Duke of Orléans, and the Count du Maine. As the Yorkists had expected, King Charles returned a politely evasive answer, which ended the matter. On reaching Boulogne, Warwick's agent immediately reported to the Duke and Duchess of Burgundy the whole course of his talks with the French, even dispatching copies of the chief documents which had been exchanged. He added two comments, designed to keep Philip and Charles at odds: (1) Philip should, above all things, cherish the fugitive Dauphin; (2) the French were eager to make a truce in order to prevent the English from aiding the Duke of Burgundy if Charles VII attacked him.

By this time, however, Philip's Duchess had become suspicious of Wenlock's lack of credentials for the marriage proposal and wrote to him that she could not send the assurance she had promised until she had official word from King Henry and the

Duke of York that they really wanted the alliance. At the same time, this disappointing answer and the entire story of Wenlock's double dealing were betrayed to Charles VII by a French spy at the court of Burgundy.[10]

By the early spring of 1459, Margaret of Anjou was publicly striving to oust Warwick from Calais, and the Earl decided it was high time that he himself visited Duke Philip. He probably had little doubt of his ability to deepen Philip's regard for him by a personal meeting; and Yorkist-Burgundian friendship had grown rich in possibilities, now that Warwick's party in England were being pushed toward open conflict with the Queen's government and Charles VII appeared on the verge of making war on Burgundy. Philip, in his turn, appreciated the value of Yorkist allies; he had also been touched by the reputation of the Earl of Warwick. He loved to view life as a chivalric game, and even the English town chroniclers, far more prosaic than the court of Burgundy, were writing of the Earl as a paladin of old:

"No lord of court took the jeopardy nor laboured for the honour of the land but only he, for the which manhood and his great policy and his . . . fortifying of Calais . . . all the commonalty of this land had him in great laud and charity . . . and all other lands in likewise: and so [he was] reputed and taken for as famous a knight as was living." [11]

Chivalry was no longer a positive force in the world. Its religious idealism, which had softened the fierceness of a ruder age, was now exhausted. But it lingered in men's minds as an habitual form of thought, a convenient pattern of meaning, and its outward rites and symbols were still observed. Even Chastellain, who wrote the history of the court of Burgundy from direct observation, could not help seeing Philip and his son Charles as high embodiments of chivalry, though he knew their terrible rages, the harsh punishments they visited on rebellious cities, and the arrogant manifestations of their worldly pride.

The court of Burgundy was now the stronghold of chivalric display in Western Europe, the last blaze of medieval aspirations and illusions in a world that was moving on to a more complex view of life, a rawer approach to reality, a more naked and more knowing pursuit of experience and power. The shrewd, wily, ambitious fugitive at Genappe, Louis the Dauphin, represented the coming age. Feudalism still dominated France; and the whole apparatus of feudalism, with its petty magnates defying the royal power, Louis was resolved one day to destroy. For him, chivalry was merely the vain cloak of feudalism; he would play upon its romanticism for his own ends but its empty ostentation and its pretentious claims he despised.

When Warwick paid his visit to the Duke of Burgundy in the spring of 1459, he discovered a new world of experience.[12]*

The Burgundian court was as rigid and minute in its etiquette as it was lavish in its ostentation of riches. When, for example, a relative of the Duke of Brittany visited the Count of Charolais' wife, it required a council of state to decide that the visitor must make two obeisances, upon which the Countess might advance three steps.* For his first meeting with the bold Master of Calais, Philip would have no wish to stint either his accustomed pomp or his natural amiableness.

Warwick was received in an audience chamber swathed in gorgeous tapestries. Surrounded by his chief courtiers, the Grand Duke of the West kept his estate upon a canopied dais—probably standing, for he had little use for sitting down and despite his age he stood as straight as a tree. He wore his favorite dress, black velvet, that winked and flashed with an array of gems; around his shoulders he displayed a collar of gold and precious stones from which depended a golden fleece, the insignia of the famous chivalric order he had founded. Now in his early sixties, Philip had a long, bony, dark-complexioned face with fierce eyebrows and vivid dark eyes and prominent veins that swelled and corded when he was seized by one of his tempers. He was still a vigorous tennis player and ardently followed the chase, both in the field and in my lady's chamber. As for his character: his word was his seal (except in the game of love, as he himself admitted); he was as trusty as fine gold and whole as an egg—so we are assured by his devoted chronicler, Chastellain.

* The ceremonial of the court of Burgundy passed to the sixteenth-century court of Spain and thence to the Versailles of Louis XIV.

After Warwick and the Duke had exchanged formal greetings, the serving of exotic spices and preserves brought the audience to an end. The actual negotiations of state were to be managed by the ducal council. To please the Earl's eye and palate, there would be banquets, receptions, perhaps a joust, these interspersed with informal talks between the genial Duke and his guest. In all likelihood, Philip showed the English Earl his treasures of plate, his band of musicians, his paintings, his library filled with precious manuscripts bound in jeweled leather. If Warwick visited the Duke's kitchens, he would find even the chief cook ensconced in a raised chair, with a wooden ladle in his hand to taste soup and beat the scullions.

The court of Burgundy attempted to realize in high colors and rich stuffs and elaborate manners the medieval view of aristocratic life as romantic and heroic. A few years after Warwick's visit, a young Englishman reported that there was never such a fairyland of wealth and ceremony outside of Camelot. By comparison, the castles Warwick lived in, the palaces of Henry VI, were but rude and barren habitations. The Earl could not fail to be impressed by this opulent grandeur. He, too, had conned chivalric romances and liked to think of himself in chivalric terms. Yet in his ambitions and his vigorous grasp of political possibilities, he was much closer to Louis the exiled Dauphin than to Philip. The medieval view of life was static; the institutions and orders of society were as unchanging as the immutable hieratic chain of being which stretched from God down to the meanest creature. In the castle of Genappe, Louis, however, was dreaming of the day when he should mold France into a nation such as Europe had never seen; and the Earl of Warwick had already sensed that from the tensions and disorders of the times he might create for himself a position beyond the settled bounds of rank, the fixed ideas of power. While Warwick aimed at glory, his hard upbringing in the troubled North and his experience in the bitter party strife of England had quickened him to seek it in realer, harsher, more tangible terms than the blazon of knightly jousts or the pageantry of courtly ceremony.

Probably what struck Warwick more forcibly than the riches

of Philip's court was the impact of its symbolism. This liturgy of highly decorated surfaces and elaborate forms created an arresting image of greatness, and, like most men of his time, Warwick was accustomed to weighing entities, ideas, values, by the images which represented them. The magnificence Philip displayed in the rhetoric of jewels and etiquette, Warwick was stimulated to express within the periphery of his own personality. Lacking the tradition of, the training in, chivalric pomp, he perhaps found Philip's symbolism somewhat fantastic. But he must have been impelled by his own heightened self-consciousness and flair for drama to appreciate more fully, from his experience at Philip's court, the importance of tone and style in persuading the world of his greatness.

As for the Duke of Burgundy, he had been moved by Warwick's knightly exploits, and the Earl's proud bearing did not disappoint his expectation. Warwick succeeded in sealing a firm bond of friendship with Philip and in strengthening the informal alliance which united the House of Burgundy and the Yorkists against Charles VII and Margaret of Anjou.

These were the Earl's great days: the shape of the legend and the shape of the facts very nearly correspond. Even the earnest old Abbot Whethamstede, in the unworldly confines of St. Albans, was roused to a fervent chronicling of Warwick's deeds. By daring, hard work, and force of personality he had transformed the beleaguered outpost of Calais into a seat of independent power and made himself the most renowned of Englishmen. Never again would he enjoy such an untrammeled authority or be able to spend his energies and ebullience so happily and so freely. His career at Calais represents in its most attractive form the translation of his character into action. Better far for him if, slipping into some parallel universe where the flux of things were averted, he could have gone on to the end as the Captain of Calais.

Twice during these three years he crossed to London. The first occasion came about through an attempt by the lovers of peace in the King's council to reconcile the Yorkists with the court party. The leaders of both sides appeared in the capital early in 1458 with large retinues of armed men, Warwick arriving on February 24 at the head of six hundred troops smartly appareled in their red jackets flaunting the emblem of the Ragged Staff. This display was viewed with heartburning by the Duke of Exeter, whom Warwick had displaced as lord of the sea, and the young Lancastrian lords came with bristling fellowships of steel that revealed their bellicose temper. But the peacemakers had their day, at least so far as appearances went. York, Warwick, and Salisbury agreed to found a perpetual chantry, at a cost of £45 yearly, in behalf of the lords and all others slain at St. Albans; and, in a sort of money-composition smacking of the barbaric *wergild*, York paid over 5,000 marks (about £3,300) to the Dowager Duchess and the Duke of Somerset, while Warwick made a similar provision of 1,000 marks to the Cliffords. Since both payments, however, were in the dubious coin of assignments on the treasury that York and Warwick held for long-overdue salaries and expenses, it is doubtful that they lost or the recipients gained more than a token sum. On March 25 this unlikely "love-day" was completed by a ceremony as pathetic in its irony as naive in its symbolism. The King and Queen and the newly reconciled lords walked in procession to St. Paul's. Henry was preceded first by the Earl of Salisbury and the young Duke of Somerset pacing hand in hand; then by the Earl of Warwick with his special opposite, the Duke of Exeter; while behind the King followed the Duke of York escorting the Queen. Of these actors only Margaret of Anjou would die a natural death, and she, broken-hearted and crownless.[13]

Warwick's second visit to London occurred in the autumn of the same year (1458) and revealed the hollowness of the reconciliation. His overenthusiastic attack upon the salt fleet of the Easterlings in this summer gave the Queen an opportunity she was quick to seize. On July 31 Sir Richard Woodville and others were commissioned to examine "persons having knowledge of a conflict on the sea between Richard, Earl of Warwick, and his retinue and certain of Lübeck under the King's friendship." He was summoned to Westminster in October to report on the situation at Calais and explain his attack on the salt fleet. On

November 9 he entered Westminster Hall, accompanied by a retinue of attendants. Numbers of men of the royal household, lounging about the hall, glowered upon the party. After Warwick had gone on alone into the council chamber, the King's menials began to jeer at the men who bore the badge of the Ragged Staff. The language grew hot on both sides. Somebody drew a dagger. In an instant men were slashing at each other with whatever weapon they had at hand. Up from the pantries and the kitchens streamed servants of the King brandishing knives and cleavers . . .

In the council chamber the Earl heard desperate cries of "Warwick! Warwick!" He rushed into the great hall, was immediately beset by men of the royal household intent on making an end of him. Surrounded by his outnumbered retinue he fought for his life. His friends on the council forced their way to his side. Slowly they cut a path down the hall. Once they were in the open air, Warwick and his men made a break for their barges. Just in time they pushed out into the Thames beyond the reach of their pursuers. Whether the riot was an accident or an ambush, no one knows.

Convinced that the court party had tried to murder him, Warwick warned his father and uncle of what had happened and returned to his impregnable little realm across the Channel. The Queen, declaring that he had provoked the outbreak, demanded that he resign his captainship to the young Duke of Somerset. Warwick retorted that Parliament had confirmed his appointment and only Parliament could withdraw it. Margaret summoned a Great Council of nobles—more manageable than a Parliament— in order to secure confirmation of the ouster. Warwick then publicly proclaimed that at the cost of abandoning all his lands and whatever he owned in England, he would not give up Calais. Before the Council could act, it was discredited by a lawless deed that shocked the realm. One of the Queen's most ardent adherents, the fierce unruly Duke of Exeter, fell into a dispute with the Justices. In the very palace of Westminster he dared to lay violent hands on a Justice, hustled the man into his barge, conveyed him to the Tower of London, and incarcerated him. Because of the public outcry that followed, the sessions of the Council were hastily broken off.[14]

But by the summer of 1459 the Earl was receiving ominous tidings from York and Salisbury. The Queen and her lords had decided that they were strong enough to crush the Yorkists. Margaret of Anjou and her little son kept open house in Cheshire, while King Henry set up his standard at Coventry. It was clear that the court party were assembling a powerful host.

Warwick realized that his kinsmen must fight for their lives. Confidently he promised to bring a band of six hundred trained men of the Calais garrison to the rendezvous at Ludlow, where the Duke of York was gathering his forces. By the middle of September, Warwick was ready to cross the Channel, leaving Calais in the charge of his father's brother, Lord Fauconberg. At the last moment there was a slight hitch. Warwick's captains appeared before him. Their men were uneasy, fearing that this expedition might jeopardize their allegiance to King Henry. They, too, wanted no part of a traitor's name. Warwick assured them that he and his kin were acting to defend themselves against the court party. But the captains would not agree to sail until the Earl swore an oath that he would not lead them against their sovereign. The King's name was still potent, despite the misgovernment of the Queen's favorites.

II

Disaster at Ludlow

THE EARL of Warwick came in the style to which he was accustomed—like a potentate, boldly swinging up from Sandwich toward London and issuing a proclamation to the realm. After pointing to the wrongs of the kingdom and the lawlessness of the court party, he declared that the Yorkists were loyally assembling in arms only to preserve their safety while they besought King Henry to redress these evils. On September 20 he entered London at the head of two hundred men-at-arms and four hundred archers, led by two of the most famous captains of the French wars, Andrew Trollope and John Blount.[1]

The Mayor and Aldermen offered the Earl a cordial greeting. Citizens thronged the streets to wave their caps and give a *Huzzah!* for the famous Captain of Calais as he rode, smiling and nodding, at the head of his smartly turned out band clad in the familiar red jackets. Spending only a night and morning in the capital, he took the road for Warwick Castle. On his march across half England he encountered no opposition. As he passed through towns and villages, the people swarmed to see him, mothers holding up their babes to behold the most renowned knight alive. But beneath the cheers there was a significant silence, the silence of those who look on rather than take part. Neither in London nor the shires did men flock to join the wearers of the Ragged Staff. Nobody had made them feel it was their quarrel, this strife of lords, even though many of them heartily detested the Frenchwoman and her pack of favorites.

Though Warwick had shot up in the world during the past five years, he was moving toward Ludlow, as he had marched on St. Albans, a partisan of the Duke of York, leading his personal retinue to join the seignorial fellowships of his kinsmen in opposing the lords of the court. His manifesto was a defense of his action and an assertion of his dignity rather than an attempt to rouse the people to his banner. Warwick had transformed himself into a national hero, but the Yorkist cause had not moved on from the days of '55. Either the Earl had not yet realized the new possibilities of his position and had not perceived the futility of re-enacting the same narrow pattern of armed protest by a baronial faction, or he thought it safest for the moment to follow without demur the lead of his chief, the Duke of York.

When he arrived at Warwick, he discovered that his estates had been plundered and his tenants harried by the Lancastrians. The Midlands were alive with Lancastrian war parties. While the Earl of Salisbury was on the march from Middleham to Ludlow, he was intercepted at Blore Heath on September 23 by an army under Lords Audeley and Dudley. His outnumbered band fought so fiercely, however, that the Queen's army fell back, leaving many of their fellows stretched on the earth, Lord Audeley slain, and Lord Dudley taken prisoner. Two of Warwick's brothers, Sir John and Sir Thomas Neville, were captured in pursuing the enemy too boldly. When dark fell, Salisbury circled the Lancastrian position and went on safely to Ludlow. It appears that a whimsical Augustinian friar covered his withdrawal by firing cannon all night. He explained to the Queen's men the next morning that he had shot off the guns only in order to keep up his courage.

A day or two later, Warwick almost had the same experience as his father. As he passed through Coleshill, his troops brushed against a party of the Duke of Somerset's men, but Warwick's band were well mounted and they got safely away before the Duke could bring up his forces.

At Ludlow, Warwick found his father and his uncle in the company of their most faithful adherents, including York's two sons, Edward, Earl of March, now seventeen, and Edmund, Earl of Rutland, a year his junior. York had conceived no better way of securing control of the King than the same appeal to arms he had used at St. Albans, but the Yorkist position at Ludlow was far more precarious than it had then been. Now the Queen's party had taken the initiative and mustered beneath their banners a much larger force than York's. Warwick, for all his aggressive confidence, could see immediately that there was no hope but to stand on the defensive. The Yorkists forwarded to the King the same sort of manifestoes they had sent five years before. Warwick displayed his prestige by dispatching a statement of grievances and accusations in his own name.

The Queen's party countered with an offer of pardon to all who would lay down their arms, and the royal army continued to move on Ludlow. In the meadows of the river Teme just south of the town, the Yorkists constructed an embankment blocking the road from Leominster up which the Lancastrians were advancing, planted their few guns in carts, and hoped that the flooding waters and their barricade would make their position impregnable.

In the early evening of October 13 the King's army drew up about a mile south of the entrenchments. When night had fallen, Andrew Trollope and most of the Calais garrison slipped across the embankment and fled to the security of the King's pardon. Trollope knew the precise strength of the Yorkists and all their plans; the men he led were the most experienced troops in York's host. After a desperate consultation Warwick, York, and Salisbury decided that they could do nothing but flee, even though York must leave to the Queen's mercy his Duchess and his two youngest sons, Richard and George. The troops were ordered to disperse in the darkness as best they could. With only a small escort the three leaders and York's two older boys galloped westward through the night.

In Wales the little cavalcade divided. York and Edmund of Rutland made for Ireland, while the Nevilles and Edward, Earl of March, headed for the Devon coast and Calais. Accompanied by Sir John Wenlock and guided by John Dynham, a bold Devon squire, Warwick and his companions made their way safely to Dynham's manor. His stalwart mother hid the fugitives while John spent every penny the family possessed to buy a small vessel and hire seamen. Down the Severn estuary they sailed, around the tip of England, and with a lucky wind soon reached Guernsey, which Warwick held as a fief of the crown. On receiving news from Calais that the stronghold was still his, the

Earl set sail once more, to find a triumphant welcome on November 2 from Lord Fauconberg, the townspeople, and the soldiers of the garrison. Some weeks after, came the happy tidings that the Duke of York and his son Edmund had been warmly greeted at Dublin.

It was reported that when Warwick and his companions put off from the north Devon coast and directed the sailors to set a course to the west, the seamen replied in terror that they knew not the way, and at this perilous moment the Earl of Warwick himself took the tiller, bade the sails be shaken out, and steered the ship to Guernsey.[2]

III

The Calais Earls

WARWICK'S adventure had lasted only six weeks, but it appeared to have undone him. The Yorkists were driven from England, their followers taken or helpless, their claim to represent the will of the realm blasted by an overwhelming defeat. Warwick's great estates were gone. He could guess that in a few weeks a Lancastrian Parliament would strip him of his earldom and attaint him of treason. He was a landless outlaw. The garrison and burghers of Calais welcomed their fugitive captain warmly but with anxious hearts. Many must have been dubious and downcast, feeling themselves a forlorn crew, threatened now by the might of England as well as beleaguered by the French, and fatally tainted with the stigma of their lord's treason.

But the Earl was still the master of Calais. He was riding the momentum of a highly romantic escape. And he was something that no loss of lands could diminish nor any Parliament demean: he was Warwick, "as famous a knight as was living." To his soldiers and townsfolk he showed himself undaunted by misfortune. The Yorkists had suffered a temporary reverse, that was all. Why should his people despond when Calais was still theirs, bestriding the Narrow Seas, and still theirs were the hearts that had made her the most renowned bastion in Europe? As to the means of defending themselves against a world of enemies—they were the hope of England and the masters of the sea. Let the Queen and her unpopular minions betake themselves to defense! He promised his men their wages and led them on raids into France to exercise their courage and give them booty. He ordered his mariners to set their keels once more proudly furrowing the Channel.

The magic of his assurance blotted out disaster. The drooping town burst into a bloom of aggressive spirits. The Merchants of the Staple, even though they were now shut off from their supplies of wool, reportedly lent the Earl £18,000 for his soldiers' pay.[1] The Queen's party had hurriedly requested Continental rulers to give Warwick no aid and to forbid their ships' putting into Calais, but the Earl went on issuing the customary safe-conducts to foreign traders, whose vessels continued to bring goods into his harbor; and the Duke of Burgundy sent his Marshal and the Seigneur de Lannoy to signify his unabated friendship.

The moment Warwick recoiled into his stronghold, he had begun his return. This time, he meant to exploit his resources to the full. He would carry on York's struggle, but not by York's methods nor in the shadow of York's leadership. This time, his coming would express himself and his hold upon English hearts. York's faction had suffered a humiliating defeat, but not York's cause of governmental reform. And Warwick henceforth meant to identify himself with the cause rather than the faction.

While the Earl of Warwick was speedily reanimating his forces, the Duke of Somerset lay at Sandwich, holding a royal appoint-ment to the captainship of Calais and a band of soldiers to make it good. Toward the middle of November, Somerset put to sea, apparently still uncertain of Warwick's whereabouts. His force included Andrew Trollope and most of the men who had fol-lowed Trollope into the King's camp. When the Duke approached the harbor of Calais, he was greeted by a heavy cannonade which proclaimed Warwick's presence. Angrily refusing to put back to Sandwich, he sailed a little way down the coast to Scales' Cliff, disembarked the men in his squadron, and marched to Guisnes Castle. After Trollope had offered the garrison a payment of wages, they opened their gates and let the Duke take possession of the stronghold. He was not joined, however, by the remainder of his forces still at sea.

The Kentishmen manning the ships were friends of Warwick, and taking advantage of a strong wind, they allowed their vessels to be blown into Calais harbor. Down to the wharves strode the Earl of Warwick, in polished armor and rich furs, ac-companied by his knightly retinue and a guard of archers. He gave the sailors his best welcome, shaking the hands of their captains, calling many of the men by name, thanking them for their trusty service, and sending them off with coins jingling in their pockets to fill their stomachs with meat and to drink his health. Then his bearing changed as he came to the captives, whom his archers had herded into line. Slowly he passed down the ranks of Somerset's frightened troops. Those whom he recognized as belonging to Trollope's band he dispatched to the dungeons. His expression softening, he addressed the remaining soldiers like the "lodestar of knighthood" that the balladeers called him. He had no quarrel with them nor with any honest Englishman. What was their will? He would accept them into his service, if they so chose, or return them to their homes. They might speak out without fear.

Most of them summoned enough courage to say that they desired to serve the King. Warwick listened to them courteously, praised their loyalty, and arranged for them to be transported back to England. The prisoners, however, received short shrift. They had betrayed the Yorkist army; worse yet, perhaps, they had turned their backs on the Captain of Calais. They were promptly executed. Warwick then unloaded Somerset's stores and sent an exuberant message to his rival at Guisnes: he thanked God, not him, for the goods he had provided!

The Duke of Somerset waged daily warfare with the Calais garrison, sending raiding parties along the causeway and harrying the farmers bringing provisions to the town. This drain on his men and armaments he could not long have endured, for few supplies got through to him from England, except that the French came to his aid with horses, armor, and money.

Richard Neville was not averse to wearing Somerset down, and he had powerful friends of his own. The Duke of Burgundy concluded a three months' truce with him, arranged to supply provisions, and winked at the raids Warwick's men conducted across Burgundian territory against the French. To Charles VII's protests Philip returned an empty answer, and he showed himself equally unfriendly to Queen Margaret's party. When his commercial treaty with King Henry expired, he did not seek to renew it.

Warwick had no intention of basking in Burgundy's flattering support and idly skirmishing with the Duke of Somerset. Lord Rivers lay at Sandwich fitting out ships and readying men to go to Somerset's aid. Warwick was kept intimately informed of his plans by the Kentishmen who daily slipped across the Channel to join him or bring him news. On January 15 (1460), as Rivers was about to set forth, Sir John Wenlock and John Dynham sailed into the harbor at dawn, surprised Rivers' troops before they could offer effective resistance, captured all the ships in the port, took Lord Rivers in his bed and his son Sir Anthony Woodville as he came riding from London. The townspeople looked on with joy. In the late afternoon the raiders returned to Calais with their prisoners and their booty, leaving behind them the tidings of their exploit to strike consternation in the hearts of the court party and to trumpet to the realm that the Earl of Warwick would soon make good his return.

There ensued at Calais a night scene which Rembrandt would have enjoyed painting. It was said that Rivers and his son were kept aboard ship till dark because the people of the town so hated them, but the sequel suggests that Warwick's sense of the dramatic was at work. When darkness fell the Woodvilles were led into the market square to confront the lords of Calais. One hundred sixty torches lit up the faces of the crowd, the cloaks and armor of the Earls.

"Knave's son!" old Salisbury began on Rivers, and the crowd roared. There followed a harsh diatribe against Rivers for daring to call the Yorkists traitors when in fact it was Rivers and his men who were the traitors and the Calais Earls the King's true men. The Earl of Warwick took a haughtier tone, reminding Rivers that he was but a squire's son who had made himself by marriage (to the Dowager Duchess of Bedford) and was therefore unworthy to speak in any terms of the lords of the King's blood. Then the young Earl of March had his say, and all three of them rated Sir Anthony Woodville in the same vein.[2] Satisfied with his scene, Warwick committed the Woodvilles to no worse a fate than a sojourn in prison. Impossible now for the master of Calais to remember that but for his father's marriage to an Earl's daughter and his own to Anne Beauchamp, he would have been only Sir Richard Neville, a North Country knight.

Before spring came (1460), Warwick was bending all his energies on military preparations. His agents in Kent were stirring the people to ready themselves for his arrival. Night and day men with armor on their backs sailed into the harbor of Calais to join his cause. The sailors of the port towns, scorning the King's officers sent among them, slipped across the Channel to bring to their friend food, arms, news. The tidings were increasingly favorable. In defeat the Yorkists had won a widespread, popular sympathy; and the Queen's party were exacerbating the realm by their arrogant misrule.

The Lancastrians had summoned a Parliament in November to pass a bill of attainder against their principal enemies; the confiscated estates of the rebels were distributed piecemeal to bolster the loyalty of their adherents. After the raid on Sandwich the government flooded the country with commissions of array, fierce orders to seek out traitors, demands for money. A thrill of anger ran through the kingdom when it was learned that the Duke of Exeter and the Earls of Wiltshire and Shrewsbury had wantonly sacked the Duke of York's town of Newbury, hanging a number of its citizens. On receiving a royal command to raise troops, the city of London dared reply that its ancient liberties were being infringed. The hearts of the citizens were further hardened by the execution of a lawyer and a group of his friends who were caught in the act of smuggling munitions to Calais. The master of the King's ordnance was murdered between Dunstable and St. Albans as he was bringing a train of armaments to London. Ballads satirized the government; placards nailed on church doors called for the return of the Yorkists; ribald songs attacked the Queen.

This beautiful and indomitable princess, this pitifully distracted woman, suffering herself and bringing suffering to the realm, had been reared to think of dynasty rather than the public weal, had been forced by her husband's feebleness into the savage arena of contending factions, and, blind to any obligation but that of protecting the inheritance of her son, had now reduced herself to depending on a group of recklessly selfish nobles, heedless of where their greedy partisanship was leading them. After the sack of Newbury, the Earl of Wiltshire deserted Queen Margaret in fear, stuffed five carracks with the plunder he had amassed, and, giving out that he meant to go against the Calais Earls, sailed apprehensively about the Narrow Seas until he at last took temporary refuge in Holland. The Queen's government staggered on. When spring came, a new flood of commissions to raise men and resist traitors was loosed upon the realm, the peremptoriness of their language betraying the desperate impotence of the royal authority.[3]

More than parchment was needed to avert the rising power of the Earl of Warwick. In March he boldly set out for Ireland to concert plans with the Duke of York. He found him established as absolute master in Dublin, for the Irish had gratefully remembered the excellence of his rule in 1449–50. Two months the Duke and the Earl spent in canvassing their hopes and discussing their strategy. The Duke of Exeter, in the meanwhile, fitted out a fleet and was now cruising westward, hot for his rival's head.

In late May Warwick sailed from Ireland, bringing with him his mother, who had managed to escape from England. Off the south Devon coast the Earl found Exeter's fleet blocking his way. Though it was larger than his own, he gave the signal for battle, only to see the Duke's vessels turn in disorder and straggle back into Dartmouth harbor. Exeter's captains had brought him word that his crews would mutiny rather than attack the Earl of Warwick.

As soon as Warwick arrived at Calais, the great stronghold burst into activity. By day the docks swarmed with ship-fitters and porters loading arms. By night boats big and small sailed into the harbor bringing men and supplies. Osbert Mountfort, one of Trollope's officers, was now at Sandwich preparing to reinforce the Duke of Somerset. In the third week of June, Warwick struck his opening blow. Led by Lord Fauconberg, a force from Calais fell again upon Sandwich and after a sharp fight won the town and captured Mountfort. Fauconberg's men seized munitions and stores; messengers flaunting the badge of the Ragged

Staff spurred through Kentish villages shouting their tidings;
enterprising Kentishmen altered proclamations of Jack Cade to fit
the present circumstances and scattered them through the shire;
streams of men poured into Sandwich to join the Yorkist banners.
It was not a raid but a beachhead.

At the last moment Warwick received a notable accession to
his cause. This was an Apostolic Legate, Francesco Coppini. He
was a naive, mercurial little Italian, an iridescent bubble of a
man, whose liveliness and eloquence so impressed Abbot Whethamstede that he thought Coppini's words seemed to drop from his
lips like dew. Made a bishop in 1458 under the patronage of
Francesco Sforza, Duke of Milan, Coppini had come to England
in 1459, officially as a representative of the new Pope, Pius II,
and unofficially as an agent of Sforza. The Pope, eager to unite
the Kings of Europe for a crusade against the Turk, had sent Coppini to secure England's adherence to the cause and had instructed
him to help allay, if he could, the dissensions in the kingdom. On
the Duke of Milan's behalf, however, Coppini was eager to promote an English descent upon France to distract Charles VII from
supporting Angevin pretensions in Naples against Sforza's ally,
King Ferrand. Intoxicated by his elevation among the powerful
of the world, he apparently never perceived that the two missions
were incompatible. Though he was received with great respect,
when he arrived in England early in 1459, he could get no more
than a perfunctory hearing from the Lancastrian court. In December Pius II hopefully gave him full legatine powers, but the
Queen's party were too much occupied with their dangers even
to recognize his new authority, and when they turned haughty
at his venturing to suggest peaceful overtures to the Yorkists,
he angrily left the country in the late spring of 1460 and went to
Bruges. As a representative of the Duke of Milan, he was warmly
welcomed by Philip of Burgundy and the Dauphin Louis, who
were as eager as Sforza to do Charles VII a bad turn.

When the Earl of Warwick, upon his return from Ireland,
learned that the Legate was at Bruges, he set about wooing his
good will. Nobody knew better than Richard Neville how to
win the ebullient little bishop. Soon perceiving from hints in

Coppini's letters that the Legate longed to promote an English invasion of France, Warwick was quick to make clear that his party cherished this very aim, as it cherished its loyalty to King Henry and the good of the realm. Coppini eagerly dispatched an appeal to Henry to give ear to Yorkist demands, enclosing copies of letters in which the Earl pledged his love of peace and the King's welfare.

Warwick then persuaded him to venture to Calais. There at the Citadel Coppini found the famous Captain waiting to bend his proud knee to the Legate's greatness. A trio of doughty lords—Salisbury, March, and Fauconberg—came forward to share the Legate's blessing.

Coppini began to talk of further appeals to Henry and the virtues of patience, but Warwick led him onto the battlements, showed him the harbor crowded with vessels being rigged for the sea, the docks swarming with soldiers about to embark.

The Yorkists, Warwick declared, could afford no more delay. They must take the flood tide of their cause, secure in their consciences that they sought only the lands and offices rightfully theirs, the reformation of the government, the good of the King—and the opportunity of reasserting the English claim to France. The most holy apostolic Legate they looked upon as a father. His cause was theirs. In the harbor lay a stately ship, waiting for him. Now was the moment for him to fulfill his glorious mission by coming to King Henry in their very company. In a solemn document of state the lords of Calais would subscribe to all that Warwick had promised. The Earl summoned March, Salisbury, and Fauconberg. Parchment was duly inscribed and the four lords attached to it both their sign manuals and seals . . .

Little Coppini, swept away by an eloquence equal to his own and a force of character far superior, cried enthusiastically that he would go with them.[4] It was Wednesday, June 25. On the sands below the Tower of Rysbank sailors had just hacked off the head of Osbert Mountfort because he had dared challenge the Warwick legend by going over to his King.

The next morning the Earl of Warwick's armada sailed for

Sandwich, transporting a force of some two thousand men and an Apostolic Legate. They were coming to an England sodden with the worst summer weather in a hundred years, but primed to hearken to the trumpets of the Captain of Calais.

IV

"Marvellous Things"

WARWICK had seized the forelock of time, and in the following six months, time responded, with a dazzling acceleration of events.

Pausing in Sandwich only long enough to muster the waiting bands of Kentishmen to their banners, the Lords of Calais set out for Canterbury. Their march was heralded by messengers and manifestoes. They were coming, they proclaimed, to put an end to misrule and rescue their abused sovereign from the clutches of the court party. By nightfall Warwick and his chieftains were kneeling at the tomb of Thomas à Becket. Three famous captains joined them at Canterbury. As they rolled toward London, thousands of men were drawn to their banners by the name of Warwick and the hope of better days.[1]

The capital was held for the court party by a little group of noblemen headed by Lord Scales, who strove to stiffen the backs of the city magistrates. These made a gesture of manning walls and refusing admittance to the Calais Earls, but when a herald arrived with Warwick's plain question, "Will you join our just cause?" the Mayor immediately gave way to the enthusiasm of the common citizens, and Lord Scales and his fellows took refuge in the Tower. A Convocation of the clergy—among them, Warwick's youngest brother George, now Bishop of Exeter—gave no sign of deploring the imminent arrival of the Yorkists.

On the evening of July 1 Warwick's motley host encamped on Blackheath. Next morning Londoners streamed across the bridge to welcome them into the city, led by the Mayor and a number of the bishops, including George Neville. Like a conqueror Warwick rode to St. Paul's to make an offering, and then retired to his headquarters at the Grey Friars while his followers camped in the meadows around Smithfield. At nine on the morning of July 3, the Yorkists proceeded to St. Paul's. Within were

70

assembled most of the great ecclesiastics of the realm, surrounded by a throng which packed every inch of the cathedral and overflowed into the streets outside. Warwick himself harangued the multitude, dramatically laying his cause before the ecclesiastics of the realm and the commons of the capital for judgment. Then he called for the Cross of Canterbury, which his host had borne at their head. March, Salisbury, and Fauconberg gathered round him. The four lords placed their hands on the Cross and swore by God, His Mother, and all the saints of Heaven, that they were liege men to King Henry. The crowd cheered as lustily as Warwick could have hoped.

The moment he returned to his headquarters, he plunged into decisions. He knew that he must move quickly, while the momentum of popular support was still gathering force and before the court party could bring their full strength to bear. He had learned that the King's hastily assembled army was now encamped at Northampton. It was decided that Salisbury, aided by Lord Cobham and Sir John Wenlock, should remain in London to besiege the Tower. That very afternoon the first contingents of footmen, commanded by Lord Fauconberg, began moving northward out of the city. On Friday, July 4, the main body of the Yorkist host departed, and the rear guard followed the next morning. Warwick was accompanied by a notable spiritual power: York's kinsman, Thomas Bourchier, Archbishop of Canterbury; George Neville, Bishop of Exeter; the bishops of Ely, Salisbury, and Rochester; and the Apostolic Legate himself, trembling at the thought of a battle but dizzy with visions of his sway over men and things.[2]

Coppini had made a brief extempore speech to Convocation, which respectfully acknowledged his legatine authority. A long letter he wrote to King Henry was read aloud at Paul's Cross on July 4. Taking a high tone, he dwelt on his own toils and dangers, declared the honorable motives of the Yorkists, told Henry that he had only to follow the instructions of Coppini, threatened him with defeat if he remained blind to his country's good, and in a fine passage of self-inflation reminded him of "that tremendous day of judgment, when we will all stand before the tribunal

of Christ [and] I will require a reason for each thing you have
done, especially for so much shedding of English blood . . . I
have spoken!" This same day, caught up in the excitement of the
army's departure, he penned a vivid account of events to the Pope,
which would be brief, he wrote, because "we are all in a whirl to
go to meet his royal majesty," but he could give Pius a few minutes while the horses were being got ready. Warwick is "in-
credibly beloved by all." The people are marvelously grateful to
Coppini himself because they recognize that the Yorkists have
been brought back "as it were on my shoulders"—or rather, he
hastily amends—"on those of the church and your holiness."
There are good hopes for peace, and for such glory to the Church
and Pope as perchance were not even known in earlier days—if,
that is, "continued pontifical favour and authority are granted
me." [3]

The Yorkists marched slowly northward through heavy rains.
Two days they spent at Dunstable, laying final plans and waiting
for the arrival of their footmen, slogging through muddy lanes.
Warwick sent to the King's camp a delegation of bishops, headed
by the Bishop of Salisbury. Since they came proudly with an
armed escort and since Salisbury less than a year before had
acted as Henry's emissary to the Yorkists at Ludlow, the embassy
served only to arouse the anger of the Duke of Buckingham, commanding the King's army. He refused to let them see Henry,
scarcely listened to their message that the Calais lords sought only
to state their case to the King, and informed them bluntly, "The
Earl of Warwick shall not come to the King's presence, and if he
comes he shall die."

Warwick sent two more messages, both scornfully rejected.
Little Coppini, hovering in the rear of the army, was letting it be
understood that all who fought for Warwick would have the
Church's absolution and all who opposed him faced excommunica-
tion. The Earl had pushed his host forward to the top of rising
ground which overlooked the meadows by the river Nene and,
beyond, the town of Northampton. Across a lazy bend in the
Nene the Lancastrians had constructed a great arc of ditch-and-
embankment, letting in the waters of the river to turn the ditch

into a moat. Formidable though the field was, this badger's defense confessed the weakness of the court party. The embankment bristled with guns, but from the hilltop Warwick could see that they lay mired in rain water and useless.

On the morning of July 10, the Earl sent a formal defiance borne by a herald-of-arms: "At two o'clock I will speak with the King or I will die." At the announced hour the Yorkist host advanced down the slope to the assault. Lord Fauconberg commanded the right wing; young Edward, Earl of March, bearing his father's banner, had been given charge of the left; Warwick led the center. Bravely their men waded the ditch, scrambled for footing on the embankment, were hurled back sodden and blinded with mud. But in a few minutes the Earl of March received a signal from Lord Grey de Ruthyn, who commanded the Lancastrian right wing opposite him. Ruthyn's troops began shouting and waving their enemies to come on. March plunged forward with his soldiers. Hands were stretched down to haul them over the barricade. Then the young Earl and his men hurled themselves on the flank of Buckingham's center. In no time the whole Yorkist army had swarmed across the muddy palisade.

The Lancastrian ranks broke under the shock. Fugitives plunged wildly into the river or fought to reach the single narrow bridge that led to Northampton. Drowned bodies cumbered the Nene. There was a last frantic clash of steel before the King's headquarters. The Duke of Buckingham, the Earl of Shrewsbury, Viscount Beaumont, Lord Egremont lay dead near the royal tent, surrounded by a scattering of knights and squires. Some three hundred of the Lancastrian troops were killed or drowned. Warwick had given orders before the battle to spare the King and the commons and seek out the leaders.

The Earl and his lords knelt before King Henry, swore themselves his loyal vassals and true lovers of the realm, escorted him with due reverence to the convent of St. Mary de Pratis on the hilltop, and then in stately procession led him to Northampton. While Warwick was fighting for the stakes of power, the old game of love and death had had its moment. "That good knight, Sir William Lucy . . . heard the gun shot, and came into the field to have helped the King, but the field was done before he came; and one John Stafford, a Yorkist, was aware of his coming, and loved that knight's wife and hated him, and anon caused his death." [4]

A few days later the Yorkists entered London with Henry and conveyed him ceremoniously to the Bishop of London's palace, Warwick with bared head bearing the sword of state before the King. Not many hours afterward, the Tower surrendered.

It looked like the days of '55 all over again, but only on the surface. Then, the Yorkists had won a contest between seignorial retinues, as they lost a similar contest in '59. Warwick had rebounded from Calais with such success because he rallied the people of southern England and London to his banners, and, winning over the Papal Legate, secured the support of many of the higher clergy. The leadership of the Yorkist party likewise showed a change from the days of '55. Salisbury had retired into the background in favor of his sons. The man around whose name and claim the party had sprung into being—the Duke of York—was far off in Ireland. If the dashing young Earl of March had brought himself to public notice by carrying off the victor's palm at Northampton, he was considered to be Warwick's friend and protégé rather than the Duke's representative.

The Earl of Warwick immediately proceeded to form a government, a Neville government. He appointed his brother George, Bishop of Exeter, still only in his middle twenties, to the Chancellorship; Viscount Bourchier once again became Treasurer; Edward, Earl of March, and Sir John Wenlock took seats in the King's Council, which was dominated by old Salisbury. Parliament was summoned to meet on October 7.

"Thus one may say," a foreign observer reported, "that today everything is in Warwick's power and the war at an end, and that he has done marvellous things." [5]

V

The Crown

BUT WHERE was the Duke of York?

When he and Warwick laid plans together in Ireland, the Earl had perhaps assured him that the Calais Lords commanded sufficient power to defeat the Queen's party without York's immediate assistance. York may have wanted to hold back for fear of offending English prejudices if he brought in an army of the much-disliked Irish; he also had motives for wishing to appear in England as a harbinger of peace, after the brawling was over. Warwick certainly knew that his uncle would not arrive in June. By the time he had formed his government, he may have learned, or guessed, the real reason why York chose to postpone his coming until Parliament met.

Meanwhile, the enemies of the Yorkists were beginning to raise their heads again. The moment the tidings of Northampton had reached Queen Margaret at Coventry, she and her young Prince fled westward for Wales, escorted by only a handful of attendants. She was waylaid on her journey and robbed, but she managed to come safely to Harlech Castle. Since much of Wales remained loyal to the Lancastrian Jasper Tudor, Earl of Pembroke, she was soon able to recruit a following. In the Southwest and the North, Lancastrian magnates were gathering their adherents.

Interesting political rumors were now running through London. It was whispered that Warwick would elevate his protégé, the Earl of March, to the throne. Tales purporting to prove the bastardy of Margaret's son were being widely asserted. Other stories hinted that the Earl of Warwick would shortly lead a descent upon France, supported by the Duke of Burgundy. York's name appeared only casually in the gossip. It is impossible to tell whether these tales were trial balloons put about by Warwick's agents or whether they merely reflected the feverish speculation in the streets.

Warwick was well aware that his position was less solid than it looked in London. His government did not command the obedience of the whole realm—woe to an emissary of the Ragged Staff who should be captured in the Southwest or Wales or the North! He had secured a powerful hold on the Yorkist party and the people of southern England, but the absence of the Duke of York left an uneasy hiatus in affairs. Rather than chance a rupture with the Duke by emphasizing his own power in a campaign to consolidate his regime, he chose to mark time until the titular head of his cause appeared.

But he took the occasion during these months of late summer and early fall to remind the realm that the Yorkists were wedded to the Holy Church; he cultivated his personal popularity by showing himself in Kent, East Anglia, and the Midlands; and he sought industriously to counter the menace of foreign enemies and propagate his good understanding with the Duke of Burgundy.

In early August the Yorkist chieftains made a pilgrimage to Canterbury to give thanks for the triumph. Coppini came too, and Warwick, desirous of maintaining his close relations with the Duke of Burgundy, encouraged the Legate to think that an invasion of France might soon be possible. Zestfully writing in sympathetic ink between the lines of his ostensible letter, Coppini informed the Duke of Milan that with a little pushing the Yorkist lords would attack Charles VII, expressed his hopes for a marriage alliance between Philip of Burgundy and the Yorkists —"who through my hands have won back the state"—and pressed for Sforza's aid in getting him a Cardinal's Hat, which he pictured King Henry and Warwick as longing to see him wear. With the Hat and a license from the Pope to operate secretly in England, he was ready to perform even greater wonders. The fact was, Warwick wanted to use the Legate's name for all it was worth, and after he learned that Pope Pius might be willing to grant the Hat if King Henry nominated Coppini as an English

Cardinal, the Earl arranged for the Legate to be given a royal license to accept a bishopric in England.[1]

After holding several councils of state at Canterbury, Warwick crossed to Calais, armed with the royal authority to take possession of Guisnes. The Duke of Somerset could not endure to wither longer on the vine. He met the Earl at Newnham bridge, kissed him, swore never to take arms against him or his, gave up Guisnes and fled into France. Richard Neville quickly returned to England with his wife and two daughters and his mother to begin a triumphal progress. After presenting his ladies to the King at Greenwich, where he was much feted by the Yorkist court, he came to London for another splendid welcome, battalions of children with banners piping his praises and the citizens huzzahing "as if he had been a God." The Earl and Countess went on to visit their estates, which had been plundered by the Lancastrians, and then rode as pilgrims to Our Lady of Walsingham in Norfolk. When some adherents of the Queen got word of his movements, they seem to have made an attempt to ambush him, but he returned in safety to the Midlands, where his progress became a tour to stamp out Lancastrian opposition and win the allegiance of townsmen and gentry.

During these summer journeyings he diligently applied himself to foreign affairs. Philip of Burgundy had hastened to express his gratification at the victory of Northampton and to hint that he would openly ally himself with the Yorkists if they invaded France in the coming spring. Warwick encouraged the Duke to believe that he would fulfill this program, going so far as to angle for a marriage alliance of some sort, as Coppini had optimistically mentioned. Yorkist prospects were still too uncertain for Philip to take up this proposal immediately, but he promised to send an imposing embassy to negotiate a treaty. By this time Warwick had learned that Margaret of Anjou was dickering with the Scots, who had been raiding the borders, and that Charles VII was stirring Mary of Guelders, mother of the boy-King James III, to aid the Lancastrians. The Earl called upon Philip, who was uncle to the Dowager Queen of Scots, to counter this French and

Lancastrian diplomacy; and the Duke of Burgundy promptly dispatched a great lord of his court to Scotland in the Yorkists' behalf. Warwick was also in touch with the wily fugitive at Genappe, Louis the Dauphin, who, like Philip, was hoping for a Yorkist invasion to harry his father.

The political situation at the Burgundian court was curious, for whereas Philip and Louis were hand in glove with the Yorkists, Philip's heir, Charles, Count of Charolais, was an equally ardent Lancastrian. He was at odds with his father at the time, hating Philip's favorites, and he laid great store by his descent, through his mother, from John of Gaunt, Duke of Lancaster. He had struck up a friendship with Henry, Duke of Somerset, and helped that young man to while away his unhappy hours at Guisnes by treating him to dinners at Ardres and taking him hunting. They had even cooked up a scheme whereby Henry would surrender Guisnes to Charles, but Charles' father would not hear of it. Now, as Philip and Louis worked with Warwick against France, the Count of Charolais, getting word that Charles VII was preparing to aid Margaret of Anjou, offered to take command of an invasion of England, which assistance the French King coldly declined.

In September one of the Dauphin Louis' officers, the Seigneur de la Barde, arrived in England to cement the Dauphin's friendship with the Earl of Warwick. Warwick gave him a courtly welcome, providing him with a safe-conduct to travel at will for the next three months between Burgundy and England. La Barde became so warmly attached to the Earl that he embraced Warwick's fortunes like a personal adherent.

At the end of September the Earl of Warwick rode to London for the meeting of Parliament. The opening session, which George Neville, the Chancellor, addressed on Tuesday, October 7, contained no Lancastrian magnates, and the representatives of the shires and towns looked hopefully to Warwick to restore the realm. Yet he was not free to exercise this leadership. He and the Parliament were still awaiting the arrival of Richard, Duke of York. He gave no sign of being at odds with his uncle, but when the Duke at last appeared at Westminster, on Friday, October 10, the Earl of Warwick remained at his city headquarters in the Grey Friars. Landing in Cheshire in early September, York had lingered on the way to London, having been commissioned to investigate disturbances in a number of towns in the West. Perhaps the commission had been issued to delay his arrival until Warwick had established his hold on the Parliament, but, more probably, the Duke had solicited the authority in order to collect adherents and postpone his appearance at Westminster until Parliament was sitting to receive him.

When York entered London on October 10, he came with trumpets and clarions blowing before him and above him the full arms of England waving on his banners. To the chamber of the Lords he made his way, strode without a word to the empty throne, put his hand on it— The peers, stunned, gave no welcoming shout. York frowned at them. At last his kinsman, the Archbishop of Canterbury, asked timidly if he wished to go to see the King. "I know no man in England," he replied haughtily, "who ought not rather come to see me than I go to him." [2] With that declaration, he made his way through Westminster palace to the royal chambers, commanded the doors to be broken down, and took possession of the apartments, while Henry scuttled fearfully into his wife's suite. York had returned to make himself King.

Managed however adroitly, it would have been a doubtful and dangerous maneuver. The Duke handled it badly. His accumulating bitterness against the Queen, his weary years of seeking to oust the Queen's party, the stimulation of his regal reception in Ireland—these forces had combined to thrust upon him a role he could not manage. Being essentially a plain and honest man, he was uneasy, and his uneasiness made him brusque and blustering.

There was no more business done at Westminster that day. Lords and Commons alike were bewildered, apprehensive, resentful. The people of England were sentimentally attached to their sad-witted monarch. The Yorkists had sworn to reform the government by rescuing, not removing, King Henry. Lords took counsel with their friends and dependents. Members of the Commons returned to their city lodgings in dismay. The alehouses and public places of London were buzzing with the news.

To the Earl of Warwick at Grey Friars old Salisbury came hurrying to report the scene at Westminster and the indignation it was arousing. Warwick's temper flared. Immediately seeking out Thomas Bourchier, Archbishop of Canterbury, he pointed to the ill the Duke was doing the Yorkist cause, and urged him to bring York to his senses. But the Primate replied weakly that he was afraid of arousing the Duke's displeasure.

Warwick then took barge himself for Westminster. He found the entrances to the palace bristling with York's soldiery, the corridors crowded with York's household men and retainers. Entering the apartments of state which York had appropriated, Warwick came upon his uncle leaning on a sideboard. With him were his sons Edmund, Earl of Rutland, who had accompanied him into Ireland, and Warwick's friend Edward, Earl of March. Warwick and York greeted each other with outward cordiality, but once the formalities were observed, the Earl launched into a protest against York's proceeding. York haughtily refused to hear of any retreat from his just claim. The two men came to high words.

Young Rutland made matters worse by a brash interruption: "Fair cousin," he remarked condescendingly to Warwick, "be not angry, for you know that it is our right to have the crown. It belongs to my father here, and he will have it, whatever anyone may say."

The Earl of March, hitherto silent, at once interposed: "My brother, annoy no man, and all will be well."

Warwick, seeing that more words would only precipitate a a quarrel, curtly took his leave of the Duke. But he beckoned aside the Earl of March, sensing that his intelligent and popular young companion in arms might serve as a mediator. Affectionately he pressed him to attend a conference of lords which he intended to assemble at Blackfriars on the morrow. York's son replied that he would not fail to be there. Clearly, he recognized as well as Warwick that his father was making a mistake, and, clearly, too, Warwick had succeeded during the past year in winning his staunch friendship.[3]*

By the time the informal council met at Blackfriars next day,

Warwick's temper had cooled and he was all politician. The Yorkist hold on the country was insecure enough without inviting calamity by a rupture within the party. Warwick worked with all the adroitness he could muster to knit up his relations with the Duke and yet block his purpose. He was careful to take no step without the approval of Edward of March and to emphasize his loyalty to the Duke of York. With Edward's good will, he drew up a patient statement of reasons why he, his colleagues, and the citizens of London were opposed to the Duke's design. In the first place, the proceeding would bring only more trouble to a realm still plagued by discord; second, Edward himself, the Duke's heir, as well as Warwick and the other lords, had given their word to protect King Henry and by that solemn undertaking had won the adherence of most of the realm; and, third, the people of London were so fond of Henry that they would never stand for his deposition. Warwick persuaded two bishops, Lord Audeley, and a worthy citizen to bear this message to Westminster. They found York sitting in council like a King. And like a King he returned the answer, after consulting with his advisers, that he meant to be crowned, and that in short order.

With Edward at his side, Warwick quietly persisted, however, in seeking to soften the Duke's stubbornness. He hinted to York that a compromise which would preserve the Duke's rights could certainly be found. He tactfully sounded the opinions of the lords and bishops. With engaging familiarity he consulted the chief citizens of the capital, warming their hearts and winning their trust.

While he worked delicately behind the scenes, he stage-managed a parliamentary process designed to check his uncle's precipitancy until a solution could be reached.

The Lords called upon the Justices to deliver an opinion on York's title to the throne. The Justices decided, however, that so high a subject was manifestly beyond their competence. The sergeants of the law were next appealed to, but they declared that if the matter was too high for the Justices, it was certainly above *their* learning. When the Lords then asked the King for his view, he hopefully requested them to draw up all the objections to

York's claim which they could muster. They were able to adduce five, mainly centered on the oath they had all taken to Henry and the length of years during which the House of Lancaster had ruled. These objections were submitted to the Duke of York. His advisers promptly returned an answer to each objection and reaffirmed the Duke's undeniable claim by right of blood.

This comedy consumed the better part of October, by which time Warwick brought the Duke of York to realize the dangerous unpopularity he was incurring. The Earl also worked out a compromise which he found Lords and Commons willing to accept and which he was now able, with the aid of the Earl of March, to press upon the Duke as the best bargain he was likely to get.

By parliamentary enactment the Duke of York was recognized as heir to the throne, Prince of Wales, and Protector of England. Henry was to continue as King as long as he lived, York and his sons swearing to do nothing to shorten his life.

It was a patchwork business that took the bloom off the Yorkist cause and weakened the Duke of York's hold upon the country. But Warwick emerged from the squabble with increased prestige. Margaret Paston wrote to her husband on October 21, "There is great talking in this country of the desire of my lord of York. The people report full worshipfully of my lord of Warwick." To John Paston, in London as a member of the Commons, his friend Friar Brackley had also written giving him earnest advice and adding, "If ought come to my lord of Warwick but good, fare well ye, fare well I, and all our friends! for by the way of my soul, this land were utterly undone, as God forbid." [4]

On October 31, the Duke of York and his two sons swore before Parliament their adherence to the settlement. That evening torches flared on files of armed men as York and his followers removed King Henry—against his will—from Westminster to the palace of the Bishop of London. The Duke bore himself as proud as a King, he and Rutland venting their disappointment by saying openly that the crown on Henry's head was theirs by every right. But the crowds in the streets of the capital were yelling, "Long live King Henry and the Earl of Warwick!" Next day Henry wore the diadem in procession to St. Paul's, Warwick bearing the sword of state, the Earl of March holding the King's train, and York riding moodily alone. At a banquet that night, however, Warwick did his best to show his regard for his uncle, and York made the friendly gesture of announcing the appointment of Warwick's brother John as the King's Chamberlain.

A few days later, Warwick's father was made Great Chamberlain of England; two of his closest adherents received important offices, John Dynham being appointed Chancellor of Ireland and Sir John Wenlock, Chief Butler; while Warwick himself closed his grip on the Narrow Seas by securing the offices of Constable of Dover Castle and Warden of the Cinq Ports.

He was also appointed Keeper of the Sea during the winter season, for the enemies of the Yorkists were now stirring ominously. Queen Margaret had sailed to Scotland to beg for aid. The French were reportedly readying an invasion. The Lancastrian magnates of the North—the Earl of Northumberland, Lords Clifford, Neville, Dacre—had thoroughly pillaged the estates of the Duke of York and the Earl of Salisbury and were moving to a great rendezvous at Hull. In early December the Duke of Somset, who had left France in September to assemble his followers in the Southwest, joined with the Earl of Devon and marched to Hull at the head of almost a thousand men.

It was the older generation of Yorkist leaders who elected to lead an army northward. York and Salisbury may have felt a special responsibility to the harassed tenants of their estates; York was probably also aware that his position, for all that he was heir to the throne, had been eclipsed by Warwick and hoped to refurbish it with a military triumph. The Duke and the Earl, with their sons Edmund of Rutland and Sir Thomas Neville, set forth on December 9 at the head of a small army. The Earl of March departed on the same day to raise men in the Marches of Wales. The Earl of Warwick, supported by his brother George, the Chancellor, and his brother John, the Lord Chamberlain, and his kinsman by marriage, the powerful Duke of Norfolk, remained in the capital at the head of the government.

In this uneasy moment he assembled the officers and chief citizens of the city to ask them if they were willing to help protect their King and their homes. They replied with a zealous affirmative. The municipal council set a special watch at night, ordered the gates shut and guarded, and required each householder to hang a lantern with a burning candle in front of his dwelling. It was well to remind the city where its loyalties belonged. In the name of her son the Queen had recently written to demand London's obedience. A letter followed in the same vein from the Earl of Pembroke and soon after one from the Earl of Northumberland. To these communications the London council made no reply. Warwick had also to look abroad, for it was said that the French were contemplating a descent upon the Isle of Wight. Striving to ready a fleet, the Earl appointed his follower Geoffrey Gate, Governor of the Isle, and sent him off to guard against invasion. The French made no move after all, but Gate captured Edmund Beaufort, the Duke of Somerset's brother, and sent him and his men prisoners to Calais.

The Earl of Warwick kept his Christmas in London. The situation was too uncertain to permit him to take his ease in the country. There was no news of importance from the North: York had established his forces at his castle of Sandal for the holiday season. London was quiet, but there was a feeling of doubt and apprehension in the city.

A few days after the New Year Warwick received tidings of a stunning disaster.

The Duke of York's army had been smashed at Wakefield by the Lancastrians. Rashly issuing forth from Sandal Castle to meet a far superior force of the enemy, York and his son Rutland and Sir Thomas Neville were slain along with hundreds of their men. The Earl of Salisbury, captured in the battle and sent to Pontefract Castle, was dragged from his prison cell the next morning by a mob and beheaded by the Bastard of Exeter. The heads of the Yorkist leaders were thrust atop one of the gates of the city of York, the Duke's being surmounted in derision by a paper crown. It was said that the Lancastrian host would begin rolling south at any moment.

VI

"Like Another Caesar"

YET, though the torrent of defeat at Wakefield had swept away the older stalwarts of the Yorkist party and the way south lay open to the Lancastrian horde, this violent reverse was by no means a complete misfortune for the Earl of Warwick's cause or for the Earl himself. The earlier generation of leaders was stained with the weary baronial bickerings of the '50s, and York had clouded his reputation by reaching for the Crown; whereas Warwick, having identified himself with the popular will, stood forth as the champion of the nation, and his protégé, the handsome young Earl of March, had nothing on his record but his bravery, his charm, and his loyalty to the Earl.

Undoubtedly the tidings of Wakefield plunged Warwick into grief for the horrible end of his father, the death of a brother, the loss of his uncle and his cousin Edmund; and undoubtedly he was shaken by the danger now looming in the North. But he must also have appreciated, with leaping imagination, that the battle had disposed of his awkward rivalry with Richard of York, swelled his resources with the earldom of Salisbury and the great estates of Middleham and Sheriff Hutton, and left him sole master of the King and of those parts of the kingdom which did not hold for Queen Margaret.

How long those parts would be Warwick's was now in the balance. Scarcely had the Earl heard the black tidings when messengers were galloping into the capital with alarmed inquiries, promises of aid, reports of shock and despair and anger. The disaster at Wakefield had sent a thrill of fear through the counties south of the river Trent.

Within a few hours of receiving the news, the Earl of Warwick set about rallying his forces. He appealed to the London council to lend him money for the defense of the realm. In good spirit they parted with 2,000 marks and graciously released a group of

his servants who had been arrested for attacking a citizen's house.
Commands sped to the Yorkist captains to arm every man they
could bring to their banners. The Duke of Norfolk was soon gathering adherents in East Anglia; the Earl of Arundel and Viscount
Bourchier, in the southern counties. Lord Bonvile and Sir Thomas
Kyriell and Sir John Neville were calling up their retainers.
George Neville, the Chancellor, sent forth a stream of writs for
the maintenance of order, the seizure of rebels and rioters, the
arrest of those who were shipping food to the Lancastrians. Armed
men, riding and on foot, began to pour into the capital without
waiting for a summons—gentry with clusters of servants and
retainers, commons in leather jackets and bows on their shoulders. News arrived daily of Yorkist leaders having to restrain
throngs of people from rushing mob-fashion to hurl themselves
against the Northerners. It appeared that Warwick, once again
riding the momentum of a popular cause, would soon be moving
northward at the head of a great army.

In a swirl of activity the Earl was seeking everywhere to shore
up his power. Conscious of the European stage, he wrote letters
to Coppini's friend, the Duke of Milan, the Pope, and Philip of
Burgundy, minimizing the defeat at Wakefield and expressing his
confidence in the future. To bolster the prestige of his government, he asked Philip to send immediately the Burgundian embassy which had been promised. Though the Duke was not quite
willing to give such overt support—fearing that if he did so a
Lancastrian victory might bring both Margaret of Anjou and
Charles VII down on him—he dispatched a contingent of hand-
gunners as an earnest of his good will. The Dauphin Louis, too,
wrote reassuringly to the Earl, and the Seigneur de la Barde remained faithfully at Warwick's side, apparently taking command
of the Burgundian troops.

With the Pope, Warwick assumed a haughty tone: If, as you
indicate in your former letters, "you value my allegiance and the
allegiance of all those who are conscientiously aiding the King
and the Legate," you must give prompt evidence of your backing. The fact was, Coppini had become the butt of malicious
tales put about by the Lancastrians, who scorned his pretensions

and said that the Pope had disowned what his Legate had done. Even in the Yorkist camp the little Italian's lordly airs got him into trouble, for Warwick admitted to Pius II that one of the reasons Coppini needed the Cardinal's Hat was to avert "envy and opposition on the part of our two Archbishops. . . ." [1] Still, when the Legate proposed that he try his accomplished hand at negotiating with Queen Margaret, Warwick let him go ahead. The venture might gain a little time; at the least, it would show that the Yorkists were working for the repose of the realm.

Coppini concocted a peace proposal that would have stirred to anger a much less spirited woman than Margaret of Anjou. Strewing his missive with lengthy references to his own nobility, self-sacrificing labors, and wisdom, he alternately lectured and threatened the Queen. He began propitiously by observing that in a previous communication to him she had "displayed too great passion." He pointed out that there was now an opportunity for peace if Margaret and her lords "will attend to the wise counsel of the Apostolic Legate." They "must not be arrogant because of the trifling victory they have won." The people of southern England are incensed because of their cruelty and if they do not listen, "they will see more than 200,000 desperate men rise against them. . . . With the tears of our heart we beg them to try to avoid this."

Coppini did not hesitate to give Warwick military advice, counseling the Earl to remain on the defensive until Easter while he pursued his "negotiations." He was still dunning the Duke of Milan to help him secure the Cardinal's Hat, and he took to invisible ink again to explain his diplomacy and let Sforza know that "I shall have effected wonders if the affair succeeds"— which was true enough.

Warwick had in mind a more substantial job for Coppini, however. He wanted the Legate to come into camp when the army was finally assembled, give his benediction to all soldiers fighting for the Yorkists, and publicly excommunicate, in the name of the Holy See, all who took arms for Lancaster. Coppini agreed, but as tidings of the Queen's mighty power multiplied and the time grew nearer, he decided that he could not risk the apostolic legation in such dangerous circumstances. The weather was bad, he told Warwick, and he was not feeling well, and . . . and perhaps he had better temporarily leave England. Warwick kept his thoughts to himself, gave the little bishop an escort as far as Gravesend, and Coppini boarded a ship at Tilbury. It went aground on a sandbank, was chased by a French privateer, and almost foundered in a storm, before the badly shaken Legate finally "got away from the uproar of the barbarians"—as a Milanese ambassador wrote his master—and landed at Brill. He was soon writing as exuberantly as ever, nagging the court of Milan about the Hat. If the Pope will "supply fire to the bombard I will make the report resound beyond England." The bombard, however, would shoot no more rockets. Though the envoys of the Duke of Milan wrote to their master that Coppini was a veritable Aristotle on English affairs, it was not long before the Pope received a full report of his indiscretions. A year later Coppini had been stripped of his bishopric and immured in an abbey for life. He made a better monk than a bishop, was Pius' dry verdict.[2]

Meanwhile, the Lancastrians were covering the North with their arms. After a secret interview with the Queen Mother of Scotland, Margaret of Anjou brought a force of Scots with her when she joined her host at York about January 20. Before the end of the month the Lancastrians were swarming southward, displaying the banners of the Dukes of Somerset and Exeter; the Earls of Northumberland, Devon, and Shrewsbury; Lords Clifford, Roos, Grey of Codnor, Wells, Willoughby, Dacre, Greystoke, and Fitzhugh; and numbers of knights, squires, and gentlemen. Somerset was in command; Andrew Trollope led the van and directed the march; the fiery Queen Margaret and her small son rode in the midst of the host, all the great lords wearing the Prince's livery of black and red with ostrich feathers.

Soon refugees were streaming southward in panic, and dreadful tidings were borne through the shires by a succession of messengers. Advancing on a thirty-mile front, the Lancastrian army was devastating the country as if it were a foreign land. A train of burning villages marked their course. Towns were pillaged, abbeys sacked, barns and manor houses gutted. The very churches were robbed of vestments, chalices, pyxes. Women were raped; men tortured to reveal where they had hidden their wealth, and killed at the least show of resistance. Grantham, Stamford, and Peterborough were given over to every form of violence, and it would soon be the turn of Huntingdon, Royston, and Melbourne. The Croyland chronicler records the terror of villagers and monks as they worked frantically on their fenny island to barricade themselves against these hordes. His sigh of relief can be heard clear across the centuries as he writes exultingly after the invaders had passed Croyland Abbey by—"Blessed be God who did not give us for a prey unto their teeth!" [8]

While these reports were telling Warwick that time had run out, there came a piece of good news from the West. After the Earl of March, at Shrewsbury, got word of the disaster to his father, he hastily assembled his forces. He was starting for London when he learned that the Earls of Wiltshire and Pembroke had landed in Wales and were gathering men. Instantly he turned back, came up with the Earls at Mortimer's Cross in Herefordshire. On February 3 he broke their army and scattered it in flight. Then, having heard of Margaret's advance, he set out eastward with all speed.

The Earl of Warwick was still in London. He had had to cope with enormous difficulties. The structure of the Yorkist government, shallowly rooted, had been shaken by York's overthrow. Royal officers appointed by York and Warwick were not settled in authority. The Queen's victory stunned men's minds. But Warwick had moved immediately to take control. Men rallied to his banners even before they were bidden. All southern England was fired by the depredations of the Lancastrians and the tidings that the Queen had promised to let her hordes pillage the counties south of the Trent.

Yet, from the first days of January, when Warwick was the embodiment of vitality and decision, there had come an enigmatic change. In many districts the gentry and towns raised armed forces but received no marching orders. Fellowships of soldiers rode about aimlessly. In the county of Norfolk, Lancastrian sympathizers confused these Yorkist bands with false tidings, slowed their march by breaking down bridges, attacked their stragglers, and seized castles under the color of guarding them for the King. A number of Warwick's lieutenants had clearly failed in their duty, but the Earl did not stir from London, even into the Home counties, to combat this confusion. He issued no commissions of array * until the end of January, and they were mainly directed to the counties of the South, the Thames valley, and East Anglia. Not until Edward of York's success at Mortimer's Cross, apparently, did he send Sir John Wenlock to establish liaison with his victorious protégé; and though the Midlands were the critical no-man's-land of the moment, Warwick did not ride northward to rally the strong Yorkist following in this region nor even dispatch commissions of array to its chief counties.

He stayed in London, permitting the Queen's forces to gobble up the manpower and the resources of the heart of England.

The weeks of January and early February, 1461, are crucial in the study of Warwick's character, but only a faint sketch of his outward life remains. Something had gone amiss. The industry, the ebullience, which had exploited to the full the possibilities of Calais, faltered in the face of a larger and more complex situation. To all appearances, Warwick's exuberant imagination had outpaced his political shrewdness and his experience in making war, so that he grasped for shadows, fouling the impetus of popular enthusiasm and letting time—of which he had hitherto been the master—slip away from him. His proper style was boldness, the panache of aggressive action. Like Hamlet he had held that the readiness was all. Now, he did not even attempt to put the Midlands at his back before hurling himself on the Lancastrians.

"He is like another Caesar in these parts," one of his agents wrote to the Duke of Milan.[4] This glowing analogy more truly reveals the color of his dream than the actuality of his performance. Dazzled by the show of greatness, he had not quite closed his grip on its substance.

* Commissions of array were customarily issued to a number of prominent men in each county, empowering them to summon the people of the county to arms in the King's defense.

Before the end of January, Warwick had caused his brother, Sir John Neville, to be created Lord Montagu. He took pains to assume his dead father's office of Great Chamberlain of England, a largely honorific post which contributed little to his needs in this hour. Then, on Sunday, February 8, while the southern and eastern counties of the realm rocked in fear and confusion, and bewildered troops chafed to be led against the enemy, the Earl of Warwick arranged in the Bishop of London's palace a chapter meeting of the Order of the Garter. With traditional pomp, he and Sir John Wenlock and Lord Bonvile and Sir Thomas Kyriell were solemnly elected to the Order.[5] The host of Queen Margaret, terrorizing the Midlands, had already rolled to within a week's march of the capital.

VII

Warwick's Protégé

NOT UNTIL February 12 did Warwick ride out of London at the head of his army, accompanied by the Duke of Norfolk, the Earl of Arundel, Lord Bonvile, Lord Montagu, Sir Thomas Kyriell, a gentleman named Lovelace who had been appointed leader of the commons of Kent, and lesser captains. King Henry they brought with them, not trusting a London stripped of Yorkist arms. By this time Queen Margaret's army had overrun most of the Midlands.

On reaching St. Albans, Warwick decided to go no farther. Abandoning his star, he meant to stand on the defensive.

He had learned that Margaret's unwieldy host was slowly advancing on a front which stretched from Bedford to Royston. On her left straggled the wild bands of Scots and border toughs, more interested in plunder than battle, while on the right were concentrated the archers and men-at-arms brought by her lords, the effective fighting strength of her army. Warwick strung out his forces along a line extending some four miles eastward from the outskirts of St. Albans to a heath called No Man's Land beyond the village of Sandridge. This position blocked both roads coming down from Luton. Warwick assumed that when the Queen discovered his whereabouts she would follow one of these routes.*

His front spread over a countryside of thickets and hedgerows, a position which was hard to assail but which also made for slow communications between his widely spaced wings. He spent the next four days constructing elaborate defense works, the like of which had apparently never been seen in England before. The

* As a consequence of the military heritage from the Dark Ages and of the tradition of chivalry, medieval strategy was elementary compared with that of classical times. It was taken for granted, when an army drew up in battle formation, that the opposing force would duly assault it head-on. Flank attacks were almost unknown.

bowmen were given large mobile shields with swinging "doors" which the archers opened to deliver their arrows and then clapped to. These "pavisses" were studded with threepenny nails so that when the enemy rushed forward, the archers could throw down the shields as mantraps. Accessible points of attack were sewn with thick-corded nets, bristling with nails, and to protect the flanks of the army from cavalry, great wooden lattices, also full of nails, were placed at likely openings. Over all the approaches were scattered caltrops, iron hedgehogs whose points were a peril both to man and horse. Warwick had brought artillery with him, too, and the latest development in infantry fire-power, the handguns of the Burgundian contingent, which shot lead pellets or iron-tipped arrows or wildfire. It was, for those days, a massive and marvelous field position, but it did not continue the theme of aggressive valiancy by which the Earl had attained his fame at Calais.[1]

A stout band of archers were stationed in St. Albans to guard the western flank. The left wing of the host, commanded by Lord Montagu and including the Kentishmen under Lovelace, stretched eastward through crofts and enclosed fields; Warwick commanded the center and reserve; the Duke of Norfolk was in charge of the right wing far out on No Man's Land. Behind the center position, under a great oak tree, King Henry's tent had been pitched.

In his concentration upon defensive measures Warwick had apparently neglected to send out sufficient scouts, or they had served him badly, or they had been swallowed up by the Lancastrians. On the afternoon of February 16 the Queen's army was much closer to him and far more dangerous than he realized. Upon reaching Luton, it suddenly swung westward and overwhelmed a Yorkist outpost at Dunstable. Long before dawn the Lancastrians were marching down Watling Street to strike St. Albans from the northwest. Their advance guard thrust into the town in the early morning. Warwick's archers were alert, however, and the enemy could make no headway against the storm of arrows they loosed. But by this time Lancastrians were pouring through the fields north of St. Albans and soon broke into the eastern end of St. Peter's Street. After a bloody skirmish, the archers were smashed. By noon the Queen's host stood poised on the Yorkist left flank. It was considerably larger than Warwick's army (perhaps 12,000 men against 9,000); it had swept unopposed through the heart of England; its unexpected attack had thrown the Yorkists into confusion.

The moment Warwick learned that the Lancastrians were in St. Albans, he made a desperate effort to swing his army round to meet the coming attack. The left wing under Montagu, now the Yorkist front, was forced to abandon its prepared positions and form a line facing westward, while Warwick worked to bring up forces from the center and the right wings to its support. Numbers of men, shaken by the tidings that the enemy host was upon them, groping through hedges and thickets, were confused by their officers' urgent commands and straggled aimlessly. Support troops from the rear worked their way slowly along narrow trails. In the midst of the confusion and uncertainty, the Lancastrian army assaulted Montagu's forces. Gone now was the protection of pavisses, nets, caltrops. Men snatched swords and axes and leaden mauls and battled to hold back the massive wave of the enemy.

Warwick was urging on the reinforcements from the rear wings. Montagu worked to shore up his line. For a moment it looked as though the Yorkists might consolidate their position. But once again treachery delivered a decisive stroke. The Kentish-man Lovelace, who had been bribed or frightened into turning Queen's man, suddenly led his band of warriors over to the Lancastrians.* The Queen's troops surged into the gap. Montagu's wing began to crumble. At one moment Warwick led a mounted counterattack which drove a temporary wedge into the enemy advance but could not halt it. The Yorkist ranks dissolved into a hopeless confusion of struggling men. Most of the handguns failed to work or backfired.

The patchwork countryside, fatal to Warwick's communica-

* He had apparently been captured at Wakefield and released by the Lancastrians upon promising to betray the Yorkist cause (see Waurin, II, p. 264).

tions, now slowed the Lancastrian attack, split up the fighting into groups of men slashing at each other in crofts and clearings. By late afternoon, however, the Queen's troops were everywhere breaking through. Montagu, shielding the remainder of the army, held his position until he was captured. His stand and the difficult terrain gave Warwick the chance to rally the shreds of his center and right wings and get them away from the field under the cover of darkness. King Henry was found under the oak tree, reportedly laughing and singing. His attendants, Lord Bonvile and Sir Thomas Kyriell, had remained at his side on his promise to protect them. They were beheaded in a day or two. Lord Montagu would probably have shared the same fate, except that the Duke of Somerset's brother was a prisoner at Calais and Somerset feared reprisals.

Across a sodden February countryside, rain beating on the men's heads as they slogged through miry lanes, Warwick led the wreck of his badly beaten host. He had no thought of attempting to fall back on London. The citizens would never defend their walls for a defeated army against the triumphant Lancastrian advance. The capital was doomed, must fall by the next afternoon. By back-country ways Warwick was making for the one hope of his cause, young Edward of York and his victorious fellowship now driving eastward by forced marches. The situation looked desperate. King Henry was retaken by the Queen, Warwick's reputation for victory broken, his brother at the mercy of the enemy, and his badly mauled force in low spirits. Yet the Earl spoke cheerily to his men and his eye flashed with confidence. Magically, he had regained his old resiliency. Action had worked like a tonic on his imagination, disciplining it to grapple efficiently with the dire shape of things. As he had rebounded from the disaster at Ludlow in '59, so now, riding at the head of a bedraggled fellowship, with the stink of defeat in his nostrils and the realm apparently lost, he was already planning his return to power.

Again as he had done after Ludlow, he instantly perceived that, to retrieve defeat, a new approach was needed. The old issue— how to keep control of King Henry—had been exploded by the

Queen's victory. Henry, after all, was only a puppet stamped
with the royal arms. Futile to try to rouse men to recapture
a puppet. Needless to seek again the shelter of that discredited
authority. Half of England could still be roused to fight, out of
hatred of the Queen and her plundering horde—if men could be
given a new banner to rally to. That new banner Warwick was
now fashioning in his mind. There was no longer any need of
Henry. Warwick could produce another King, a better King.

Warwick and Edward met in the Cotswolds, at Burford or
Chipping Norton. Summoning their chief captains, they quickly
retired to confer. The Earl sketched his tale of disaster.

Where was the King? Edward wanted to know.

You are the King, Warwick told him.

Edward was flushed with victory, young and valiant and intelligent . . . and a Plantagenet. He immediately embraced War-
wicks' proposal.[2]*

At this instant came well-nigh incredible tidings: London had
not fallen! The citizens were showing amazing courage; the
Queen, amazing hesitancy. The combination had produced something of a miracle, and Warwick and Edward were in precisely
the mood to make the most of miracles. They struck for the
capital, sending ahead the news of their coming.

A wave of terror had swept over the city when it learned that
the Yorkists were overwhelmed at St. Albans. Shops were closed,
streets deserted, as men huddled in their homes, burying valuables, or took arms to patrol the walls with the Mayor. York's
widow hurried aboard a ship bound for the Low Countries her
two youngest sons, George (later Duke of Clarence) and Richard
(later Duke of Gloucester and afterward Richard III). The London magistrates had no thought but to surrender; their one hope
was to secure a promise that the city would not be pillaged. They
hastily sent a delegation to the Queen and welcomed a group
of Lancastrian knights. But as Wednesday and Thursday passed
during these negotiations, the commons of London discovered,
first, that the Northern horde was not at their gates and, second,
that the Queen, in order to conciliate the city, had sent the bulk
of her army back to Dunstable. The mass of citizens so took heart

that on Friday, when the Mayor and Aldermen were about to send forth a train of carts laden with food and money that Margaret had demanded for her army, they rose in arms, plundered the carts, seized the keys to the gates of the city and refused to let anyone pass out. The food disappeared into their bellies; as for the money—"I wot not how it departed," noted a chronicler who was present. "I trow the purse stole the money." [3] Over the weekend the harried magistrates proposed that the Queen send an embassy to treat openly before the citizens, but by the time she had agreed, some Lancastrian bands, pillaging in the outskirts, had been set upon and beaten into flight; and by the beginning of the following week there were no more negotiations. Margaret of Anjou hesitated. Perhaps she had at last become alarmed by the terrible reputation her marauders had fastened on her banners and feared that London might be ravaged if her army attacked it. Meantime, her Northern ruffians were deserting or wandering about the country in search of plunder. On Monday and Tuesday she remained, irresolute, at St. Albans.

The first rumors after the battle had left Warwick's whereabouts a mystery. Then it was bruited in the streets that he had been taken by the Queen and was held a secret prisoner. Later there were tales that he had fled to Calais or was hiding in the vicinity of London. But by Monday, February 23, reports were coursing through the city that he had joined with Edward of York and was marching to relieve the capital. By Wednesday the Lancastrian scouts had confirmed this news to their generals. In angry frustration the Queen and Somerset and Sir Andrew Trollope—knighted after the battle, during which he admitted modestly to killing fifteen men while his foot was caught in a caltrop—gave the signal for their unruly host to retire. Deprived of the sack of London, Lancastrian bands swept bare the country in their retreat, leaving a train of suffering and devastation as great as that which they had previously wrought. On Thursday, February 26, the Yorkist advance guard rode through the gates of the city.

The following day, the Earl of Warwick and Edward of York were given a tumultuous welcome. With an army not half the size of the Queen's they had saved the capital, and the Londoners took them to their hearts. As Warwick would one day discover, London was henceforth to look upon the cause of York as its own. In a day or two the citizens put their feelings into a jaunty saying: "Let us walk in a new wine yard, and let us make us a gay garden in the month of March with this fair white rose and herb, the Earl of March."

Warwick, meanwhile, having got the reins of time in his fingers again, drove forward his design at top speed. Two days after he entered the capital, he arranged an assemblage of soldiers and citizens in St. John's Fields. In order that Edward might not appear to be merely the choice of the Nevilles, he had hastily summoned to the city what friendly nobles and bishops were within call, and, on this Sunday, March 1, he stayed in the background while the highest officer in the kingdom—who happened to be his glib-tongued young brother George, the Chancellor—ascended a platform to harangue the multitude.

Did they think King Henry, feeble of mind and captive to Queen Margaret, was worthy to rule over them?

Nay! Nay! they roared.

In that case, would they take the heir of York, Edward of March, to be their King?

Yea! they shouted. Yea! Yea!

A delegation of captains bore to Edward, at Baynard's Castle, the news that, being the true inheritor of the crown in blood, he had been chosen King by "plain election" of nobles and commons.

Two days later Warwick issued a proclamation summoning the people of London to Paul's Cross at nine o'clock the following morning. There, on Wednesday, March 4, Edward was again ceremoniously acclaimed King. Then he rode to Westminster Hall to take his seat in the marble chair as Edward the Fourth.

George Neville was confirmed as Chancellor, Wenlock as Chief Butler, and Bourchier as Treasurer. Lord Fauconberg became a member of the royal council. Warwick kept all the offices he had already amassed. In staging Edward's elevation to the throne, he had once again demonstrated his capacity to distill from the lees of defeat a bold, new wine of hope.

But the great Lancastrian host remained to be dealt with. It had now withdrawn into southern Yorkshire, Henry and Margaret making their headquarters at York. Somerset and his captains succeeded in drawing fresh forces to their colors, so that the army was even more formidable than when it had rolled to the gates of London.

The Earl of Warwick counseled immediate pursuit, and the new King was as eager as he to take the flood tide of their enterprise. Men were flocking into London to join their banners. The Duke of Norfolk hurried off to East Anglia to raise more troops. Warwick, commanding the York host, was readying the van of the army within a few hours of Edward's elevation. On March 6 a proclamation was issued to the realm asserting Edward's right to the throne, denouncing the crimes of the Lancastrians, and summoning all men between sixteen and sixty to join the King in their best array. Warwick welcomed another contingent of men sent by Philip of Burgundy, dispatching grateful letters to Philip and the Dauphin Louis. He took pains to emphasize that he was still the leader of the Yorkist host, and he showed his confidence in victory by mentioning that he had fitted out a fleet in order to prevent Margaret from escaping to the Continent. The Seigneur de la Barde was preparing to march with his friends at the head of the Burgundian troops, bearing the lily banner of the Dauphin.

An emissary of the Milanese ambassador to the court of Burgundy listed the reasons why, at this moment, the Yorkists were hopeful of victory, despite the mighty army of the Queen: (1) Edward had inherited from his father a "great lordship" in Ireland and England and engaged popular sympathy because of the cruel wrongs the Queen had done him; (2) the Earl of Warwick stood at the young King's shoulder; (3) London, "the wealthiest city in Christendom," was "entirely inclined" to Edward and Warwick; (4) the temper and moderation of the two Yorkist chiefs had won good opinions everywhere.

On Saturday, March 7, Warwick left London "with a great puissance of people," marching northward by the western Midlands in order to recruit additional forces. Four days later Lord Fauconberg followed with the foot soldiers; and on March 13 King Edward set out. At Coventry, Warwick had the good fortune to capture the Bastard of Exeter, his father's executioner, whom he promptly sent to the block. The townsmen were able to raise forty armed men immediately and sent three score more to join him a few days later. Burgesses of other towns, yeomen tenants of Warwick's estates, and the Yorkist gentry of the district swelled the bands of the Ragged Staff. Somewhere north of Trent, the Earl united his forces with those of Fauconberg and the King. The Duke of Norfolk's stout fellowship of men from East Anglia had not yet come up, but Warwick, leading the van of the army, pressed forward. Scouts brought word that the Lancastrians had taken a battle stand north of the river Aire, between the villages of Saxton and Towton.

On Friday, March 27, Warwick's advance guard occupied the crossing of the Aire at Ferrybridge, and the Earl set his men hastily to repair the bridge, broken down by their enemies. That evening he and Lord Fitzwalter established their camp on the north bank of the river. In the first light of dawn a Lancastrian force led by Lord Clifford took the Yorkists by surprise. Fitzwalter fell vainly trying to rally his confused troops. After a desperate struggle, the Earl of Warwick, wounded in the leg by an arrow, managed to make good his retreat across the bridge with the bulk of his force. On the Continent it was reported that the Earl, supposing that the whole of the Queen's host was upon him, lashed his steed back to Edward's headquarters, leaped from the saddle, cut the horse's throat, and, drawing his sword, swore that he would die before he budged another foot.

By the time the rest of the Yorkist army came up, Clifford had once again damaged the bridge and was holding the opposite bank in force. Perhaps it was the memory of Queen Margaret's flank attack at St. Albans that prompted Warwick to send Lord Fauconberg up the Aire to Castleford. Crossing there unopposed, he discovered that Clifford was retiring, having got wind of his maneuver. By a speedy advance Fauconberg caught Clifford's force on the march. Clifford, the slayer of Edmund of Rutland at Wakefield, died with an arrow in his throat, and his men were driven pell-mell back upon the Queen's host, which had made no attempt to support his victorious sally. By Saturday evening, the whole Yorkist army, except for Norfolk's wing, had crossed the Aire and were encamped a little to the south of Saxton village, scarcely a mile from their enemies.

Palm Sunday, March 29, came in with a gray and bitter dawn. A harsh wind drove snow in the faces of the Yorkists as they formed up in battle order. Lord Fauconberg, a grizzled little man with the heart of a lion, commanded the left wing; Warwick, the center; the King, the reserve. Though Norfolk with the right wing was still on the road and the Yorkists knew themselves to be outnumbered, their lines of armed men trudged doggedly forward in the snow. Fauconberg, Warwick, and the King, with their household knights and captains clustered about them, marched at their head. Now the wind was shifting uneasily, blowing in gusts from every quarter. Mounting a slope, the Yorkists heard a roar of hate and beheld the Queen's great host waiting for them on the other side of a small depression.

They stood ranged in massive steel ranks—most of the chivalry of England, such as it had become—a forest of banners flaunting beneath the leaden sky the colors of their long lineage. The Lancastrian lords had come to the field with their tenantry and retainers, determined to crush the parcel of upstart nobles who had dared rouse the ordinary people of England to overthrow the old comfortable way of things. Behind, in the city of York, lay a lovely dark-haired, dark-eyed Queen—the blood of Charlemagne in her cheek and the pride of feudal France in her look— whose high spirit had showed them the path of glory. These mailed chieftains, in their turn, represented to their yeomen tenants the objects of accustomed loyalty and the assurance of accustomed duty. Some twenty-five thousand strong the Lancastrian host stood, the full muster of the Queen's cause, the greatest armament ever assembled for battle on the soil of England. They were packed onto a narrow plateau bounded on the right and to the rear by Cock Brook, now in flood, and on the left by the highroad to Tadcaster.

Few lordly banners waved above the Yorkist army. They could boast only one Earl, Warwick himself, and but a handful of barons—little Fauconberg, Stanley, Scrope of Bolton, Clinton, and Grey de Ruthyn. The mass of the army were but farmers and tradesmen and country gentry. At full strength their force was scarcely more than two-thirds the size of the Lancastrian array, and a quarter of their host was still on the march. But these men had just passed through the towns ruined by the Lancastrians, and they were fired to fight for the safety of their homes. They had confidence in the leadership of their famous knight, the Earl of Warwick. They were following the flag of a genial, valiant young King they themselves had helped to choose.

The wind, beginning to blow from the south, was now driving the snow full in the faces of the Lancastrians. Taking advantage of this omen, Fauconberg sent his archers forward to deliver a volley into the enemy mass. The Queen's archers replied, but they were half-blinded by the snow and their arrows fell short. Again Fauconberg's bowmen fired into the close-packed ranks across the shallow ravine. Stung beyond endurance by these volleys, the Lancastrian host plunged into the dip and flung themselves upon the Yorkists.

The line gave way a little under the weight of numbers. Up and down the plateau men hacked and thrust at each other with sword, bill, battle-axe. Warwick, holding the center and right, was bearing the brunt of the attack. Surrounded by his household men, he stood in the forefront of the battle, slashing at the masses of the enemy until he saw that his line had steadied. Then, his household closing in front of him, he retired to take horse. Up and down the line he moved, watching for weak places, shouting orders and encouragement, dismounting to thrust into the melee with fresh troops.

Slowly, as the deadly minutes passed, the numbers of the enemy began to tell. Foot by foot, the Yorkists yielded ground. Messengers sped to King Edward, crying for reinforcements. Forward he went with a detachment of the reserve, plowed into the battle line, laid about him furiously, a six-foot-four-inch giant in mail of proof. When the line stiffened, he withdrew to lead a detachment to another weak spot. Yet, despite his prodigies of valor and Warwick's unflagging efforts to shore up the ranks, the Yorkists were pressed back and back.

But Norfolk was coming hard now—an ailing man already marked for death, urging his troops up the road to Saxton. On the plateau men now had to clamber over mounds of the dead and wounded to get at the enemy; there were pauses in the struggle while bodies were dragged away. Tirelessly Edward of York—the most awesome warrior on the field—hurled himself into gaps in the line to beat down the enemy advance and cheer the hearts of his men. Warwick, too, and Fauconberg bolstered their ranks with continual sallies.

But the Yorkists' reserve was well-nigh gone and their line had been forced back almost to the southern edge of the plateau, when out of the snow the Duke of Norfolk and his men appeared. Quickly they swung to the east side of the field. With a shout they fell upon the left flank of the Lancastrians. Yet, so closely packed were the enemy, that Norfolk's assault made little impression at first. The deadly fight wore on into the afternoon, perhaps the longest struggle ever fought by Englishmen of the Middle Ages. At last, the Northerners grudgingly began to give ground. The Yorkists drove forward, heartened by impact of Norfolk's fresh troops and the growing weariness of their enemies. In another hour the Lancastrian lines were faltering. Then the Queen's host broke up into swarms of fleeing soldiers. The bridge over Cock Brook was jammed. Men in heavy armor frantically plunged into the stream, to find death in its icy waters.

The war steeds of the Yorkists were hurried forward from the horse-park. Trumpeters shrilled the signal to pursue. "Seek out the lords! Spare the commons!" Warwick and Edward were shouting. The Yorkist cavalry charged forward. As twilight thickened, they were driving across the plain toward the city of York, cutting down the fugitive Lancastrians. The plateau between Towton and Saxton was heaped with the slain. Bodies cumbered Cock Brook.

Night fell upon the bloody ruins of the House of Lancaster. As soon as they had got word of the disaster, Queen Margaret, the Prince, and Henry fled northward from York, accompanied by the Dukes of Somerset and Exeter. The Earl of Northumberland, more than half a dozen barons, many knights and squires, including Sir Andrew Trollope, lay dead upon the field or were slain in the pursuit. The Earl of Devonshire was taken at York and executed; the Earl of Wiltshire suffered the same fate a few days later. The strength of Lancaster was broken in one day, and the breaking cost the lives of perhaps 10,000 men.[4]

When Warwick and Edward entered York, next day, they found their captive kinsmen, Lord Montagu and Bourchier's son Lord Berners, awaiting them. After a sojourn in the city to reestablish order, the King and the Earl moved northward to exert their sway over Yorkshire. Warwick entertained Edward at Middleham and accompanied him as far as Durham. By this time Henry and Margaret had bought their welcome into Scotland by surrendering the frontier fortress of Berwick.

King Edward now turned southward to establish his government in the capital and prepare for his triumphant coronation. The Earl of Warwick chose to remain in the North, keeping his brother Montagu with him. There were pressing reasons enough to account for his decision. Forces must be gathered to hold the Marches, for Queen Margaret would be urging on the Scots to invade England; the North was in a state of confusion and disorder; areas of Yorkshire and most of Northumberland were in Lancastrian hands.

Yet, there were probably other motives as well. Young Edward had won at Mortimer's Cross, while Warwick was badly beaten at St. Albans, and the King had achieved the greater renown at Towton. Handsome, genial, gallant, he had touched the imagination of the realm. At Westminster the Earl of Warwick would inevitably be obscured by the new-crowned King, and comparisons would offer themselves which Warwick had no wish to be drawn. By remaining in the North with Montagu, however, while brother George, the Chancellor, headed the government in London, Warwick maintained a pre-eminence of place which challenged no comparison. That the young King might enjoy at ease the acclamations of the capital and the pomp of the coronation, the Earl of Warwick, bulwark of the kingdom, would stand guard against the peril in the North.[5*]

He was now in his thirty-third year. He had fathered only two frail daughters, Isabel, aged nine, and Anne, four years younger; and it was apparent that his wife, Anne, would bear him no more children. During the years since he had sailed for Calais in the autumn of '56, he had ceaselessly driven onward, through perils and reverses, to the mastery of England. He had lived in his armor; he fed on action; and he had found no defeat too crushing to be retrieved and no ambition too high to be encompassed by his vitality and his hold on men's hearts.

Part Three

Master of
the Realm

(1461-1464)

I

The Earl and the King

FOR THE next three and a half years the Earl of Warwick
labored to stamp out Lancastrian resistance in the North.
During these years the causes of York and the House of Neville
were apparently identical. Richard Neville felt no distinction between the word of Warwick and the King's prerogative, and
Edward showed himself content with this assumption. Their relationship, like their division of authority, was amiable and un-
defined. Edward spent most of his days in the southern and
Midland parts. Warwick governed in the saddle from the periphery of the realm.

Two-thirds of this period he spent in Yorkshire and Northumberland on the hard service of raids, skirmishes, sieges. The
remaining months he was on the road from Middleham to London or riding into Kent to outfit a fleet, or attending Parliament
at Westminster, or negotiating with foreign envoys. There were
no intervals of rest, few occasions for hunting, for taking his ease
with his wife and two daughters in the great hall of one of his
castles. Of his private life in these years nothing is known. The
chroniclers faithfully attest his impact upon the kingdom as the
Patent Rolls attest the plenitude of his powers; but not a glimpse
survives of Richard Neville in undress—writing to his wife, sport-
ing with his friends, tending his private affairs. He is Warwick,
Hammer of the Scots and Lancastrians, Lord of the North, Mentor and Partner of his grateful sovereign. "Conductor of the
kingdom under King Edward," his enemy, James Kennedy, Bishop
of St. Andrews, called him.[1] He could now leave to others to put
into words the vision of himself which he had projected upon
the world.

The long campaign in the North was a rough, perilous enterprise, harassed by raids from across the border and sea-borne in-
vasions, slowed by treachery and relapsed allegiance. Lancastrian

chieftains, now attainted and landless, had only their oath to King Henry to cling to, and the bitter hope of revenge. In the northern parts of the kingdom, slow to change allegiance, they were always able to gather bands of men to their banners. Under color of aiding the House of Lancaster, the Scots were eager to do what damage they could, and soon the French were contributing ships and men.

It was harsh work, without glory, but Warwick pressed on. He had constantly to recruit men, to find money to pay them, to supply them with food and arms and shelter. His operations were carried out in one of the wildest parts of England: sweeps of moor and waste and swamp and forest. During a siege or in the smallest skirmish he might be cut off by a chance arrow, or be caught in ambush and delivered to the revenge of Queen Margaret. Lord Montagu carried much of the burden of the fighting, and at the most critical times many Yorkist chieftains came north to aid in the struggle, but Warwick bore the responsibility of command as well as the daily dangers of this guerrilla warfare.

After the blazing years of '59 and '60, his nerves demanded action, excitement, a perpetual doing. Life was a moving platform that must go ever faster, farther, and higher; he himself would provide the acceleration. Perhaps his quenchless vitality had led him to feel that existence itself was an adventure of the Earl of Warwick. Long before Shakespeare wrote the words, Warwick's genius had whispered in his ear, "Time hath, my lord, a wallet at his back,/Wherein he puts alms for oblivion." He identified himself with his fame, and he needed the pressure of labors and cares to maintain the shape of his identity.

He was probably moved by his pride as well as by his temperament. The chief man of the realm must deal with the chief task of the new regime. At Westminster, he would be, in appearance, but the servant of a King, the luster of his greatness dimmed by the forms of subservience he must respect. The cutting edge of his will would be sheathed in the scabbard of the King's authority. However happy Edward was to do his bidding, his exercise of power would be cloistered in the royal chambers, hidden from the sight of the realm. In the North, he was the direct master of men and events, and he transmitted his wishes to his sovereign by messages and brief meetings which maintained his power without shadowing his pride.

While he planned operations at Middleham Castle or led his tough fellowship of soldiers across the moors in search of Lancastrian war bands, the force of his authority was diffused through the kingdom by his kinsmen and agents. His stalwart brother John, Lord Montagu, was his second-in-command in the North. His work as Keeper of the Sea was performed for him by his uncle, Lord Fauconberg, now Earl of Kent. His brother George headed the machinery of government at Westminster. Faithful agents like John Wenlock (now Lord Wenlock) and Louis Galet and Thomas Kent spoke with his voice in the royal council and headed the chief diplomatic missions which were sent abroad. Streams of riders wearing the badge of the Ragged Staff clattered over the drawbridge of Middleham Castle, bringing messages of state from Westminster, bearing the Earl's mandates concerning domestic affairs, foreign policy, military campaigns. Heralds and messengers from abroad mingled with the stream. Rulers on the Continent coupled the names of "my lord of Warwick" and "King Edward" when they spoke of England. Official letters were sent to the Earl as well as to the King, and the Earl's response was more eagerly awaited than his sovereign's.

Yet, in the style of greatness, Richard Neville was still what he had been for a dozen years, the premier Earl of England, but no more than an Earl. After the coronation, on June 28, King Edward scattered titles liberally. He created his brother George, aged twelve, Duke of Clarence, and shortly after gave his brother Richard, aged nine, the dukedom of Gloucester. His kinsman by marriage, Viscount Bourchier, was made Earl of Essex and one of Bourchier's sons became Lord Cromwell. With a lavish hand Edward bestowed baronies on the young men who had been his most intimate companions in arms: William Hastings, William Herbert, and Humphrey Stafford of Southwick. The House of Neville did not fare as well—but then, Warwick's brother John had become Lord Montagu and his brother George was confirmed as Chancellor, before Towton was fought. Warwick's uncle,

Lord Fauconberg, was advanced to the earldom of Kent; his
followers, Sir John Wenlock and Sir Robert Ogle, became barons.
In a peerage that now scarcely numbered forty members, Edward's particular friends held about a third of the places, Richard
Neville's about half; almost all the remainder were loyal Yorkists.

The Earl himself had received no new honors.

Was he too proud to ask—and Edward too obtuse to give
without being asked? Were his feelings like those of the House
of Rohan: "Roi ne veux, Prince ne daigne, Rohan suis"? While
Warwick was entertaining his sovereign at Middleham after the
battle of Towton, they had undoubtedly discussed the coronation honors list. In all likelihood, Edward had hastened to tell his
friend and mentor to take any dignity he wished. But what reward
could enhance the fame and power which Richard Neville had
achieved as Earl of Warwick? He had won for that title a meaning that no dukedom could enlarge. In remaining Warwick, he
emphasized that he stood apart from the hierarchy of the English
peerage and that his honors were of his own getting. He also
emphasized the reach of his pride. Was it not he who had bestowed the ultimate title upon Edward?

If Warwick had experienced any uneasy moments after Towton as he assessed King Edward's high spirit and noted his popularity, the Earl's misgivings were quickly dispelled. Edward was
nineteen years old, the handsomest man in the kingdom, radiant of
health, wonderfully winning with his sunny, frank, amiable
manner; fond of a good story, a brave man (if he was convivial),
and a pretty girl. He was resolved to rule justly and restore the
realm to order and prosperity. He publicly demonstrated the
seriousness of his purpose by having the hand of one of his servants hacked off at the Standard in Cheapside because the man
had dared strike another in the presence of the judges in Westminster Hall. When John Paston, involved in a land dispute,
sought to gain the King's ear, Edward let Paston know that he
would hold with him in his right, but as for favor, he would show
no more to one man than to another, not to anyone in England.
He managed to keep a keen eye on affairs and was all business
when he was listening to his council. But Edward's blood ran hot

with the love of life; he was exuberantly sensual and ready for pleasure. Though he had already established himself as one of the greatest warrior kings of England, he genuinely disliked war and would take his ease when he could. In these first months of his reign, he showed himself happy to taste the delights of his crown and leave its burdens to the Earl of Warwick.

The wintry gloom of Henry VI was banished from the royal palaces, to be replaced by youthful laughter, love songs, the aroma of summer flowers. At Westminster, Edward revelled with Hastings and Herbert and vied with them in pursuing the girls attracted to his gay court. Chambers flashed with satin and velvet and cloth of gold and jewels and the new honorific decoration Edward had devised, a collar of suns and roses.* Music sounded on the terraces and in the great halls, inflaming hearts already high with wine, sounding an obbligato to kisses and sighs and broken promises. When Edward and his court followed the good weather to Windsor for hunting, trestles heavy with roasted swans and sugared dainties were stretched in the shade of the great oaks, and silken tents grew like gargantuan flowers on the lawns. On other days Edward and his courtiers glided down the Thames in gilded barges to Greenwich or up to Shene, jousted at Eltham, feasted at Westminster, made love by moonlight and torchlight, rose at dawn to hear Mass, broke their fast with a mess of meat and ale, and quickly took horse to be beforehand of the sun in their pursuit of what the day might bring. The Duke of Milan's envoy, Count Dallugo, whirled from banquet to hunting party, was soon laid up with gout. Impressed and a little bewildered, he reported that the new King was chiefly inclined to pleasure. He soon inclined to it also and concentrated his diplomacy on securing some of the famous English dogs and horses for his master.[2]

In the middle of August Edward accompanied the Count to Sandwich, receiving such a welcome as he passed through towns

---

* Suns: in memory of the three suns which, reportedly, were shining in the sky just before Edward won his victory at Mortimer's Cross. Roses: the white rose of York. There was no red rose of Lancaster; when Henry VII came to the throne, he displayed a red Tudor rose. The term, Wars of the Roses, was a sixteenth-century invention.

and villages that it seemed to Dallugo he was adored like a god. His train had been swelled by two surprising additions, Lord Rivers and Rivers' son Anthony, Lord Scales. After Warwick had released them the previous summer from their Calais prison, they had promptly gone over to the Lancastrians and both fought for King Henry at Towton. Warwick had captured them a few weeks before and sent them to the Tower, but here they were at Edward's elbow, not only pardoned but taken into favor. When Dallugo questioned them—not very tactfully—about the cause of Lancaster, they told him that it was irretrievably lost.[3]

But it was the stirring of Lancaster that had brought King Edward, reluctantly, from London. Much of Wales was still loyal to King Henry, several strong castles being in the grip of the Earl of Pembroke. Edward had sent off Lords Herbert and Ferrers of Chartley to raise an army in the Welsh Marches, and he now intended to take command of operations himself. But he moved westward at a leisurely pace. It was early September before he reached Ludlow Castle, and soon deciding that Herbert and Ferrers were fully capable of handling the campaign, he ambled unhurriedly back to London. On the way he paused at Stony Stratford, near which town happened to lie the principal seat of Lord Rivers. There, at Grafton Regis, Edward probably spent a little time with a beautiful young widow, Rivers' eldest daughter Elizabeth.[4] Of this lady the Earl of Warwick, who knew almost all that was going on in the realm, knew nothing at all. By the beginning of autumn King Edward had returned to the pleasures of Westminster Palace.

Months before, Warwick had begun his long struggle in the North. This campaign etches the outline of his life for the next three and a half years; yet during this time he was becoming increasingly occupied with the direction of England's foreign policy —the issue that was to shape the rest of his career. In the mesh of Warwick's days, action and policy are intertwined; but the tale of action—the tale the chroniclers tell—offers itself as a prelude to the tale of policy.

II

Labors in the North

TWO MONTHS after the battle of Towton, the Scots were pouring over the western border, led by Queen Margaret herself and a party of Lancastrian chieftains, in order to lay siege to Carlisle. Not many days later, however, Lord Montagu routed the invaders, slew six thousand of them according to report, and drove them back across the border. Warwick, in the meanwhile, was dealing in similar style with a Lancastrian raiding party that penetrated to the bishopric of Durham. In order to command all the military resources in the North, he secured from Edward the office of Warden General of the East and West Marches. Then he and Montagu began systematically working their way northward, mopping up pockets of resistance, reducing castles. By the beginning of October, they had captured the strongholds of Alnwick and Dunstanburgh in Northumberland. Warwick was able to ride south for the opening of Parliament on November 4.

The Earl had no program to offer Parliament beyond what the exigencies of the moment dictated: he and Edward prudently refrained from asking for any money; they arranged for the customary attainder of their enemies and the confiscation of estates. The Commons showed themselves sensitive to Warwick's position in the realm. They elected a connection of his, James Strangways, as their Speaker, and they prompted Strangways to deliver a congratulatory address to their sovereign which pointedly revealed where their confidence lay. After praising King Edward's prowess in battle and neatly touching on his "beauty of personage," his humble subjects besought him to take into his trust such persons as had merited his favor by assisting him to establish his right to the throne. Thus, the evils rife in Henry's reign would be repressed and justice and right maintained.

While Warwick and Edward were turning over in their minds the old design of invading France, the country was suddenly shaken by alarms. Early in February (1462), the Earl of Oxford and his eldest son were detected in a Lancastrian conspiracy and immediately executed. Rumors swept London that Queen Margaret's party, backed by French and Scots, was about to invade England from Wales, the Channel Islands, and the North simultaneously. The day after Oxford was arrested (February 13), Warwick took the emergency office of Keeper of the Sea for a period of three years. He rode down to the Cinq Ports to speed the outfitting of his ships, made a quick trip to Calais to inspect its defenses, drove seamen and dock workers at such pace that an English fleet sailed into the channel before the end of February.

The French mounted no invasion, but in Scotland the political faction headed by the Bishop of St. Andrews was again readying men to support Lancastrian incursions. Two weeks after Warwick returned to London from Sandwich (March 5), he was riding northward. Warwick's old friend, the Dauphin Louis—who had become King Louis XI of France the preceding July (1461)— had just sent him a more intimate friend, the Seigneur de la Barde, whose mission was to feel out Yorkist intentions. Warwick was so eager to haggle or harry the Scots into making terms that he brought la Barde along with him and conducted his diplomacy on the road.

After pausing at York, he went on to Carlisle and sent word to the Scots Queen Dowager, Mary of Guelders, that he had attractive proposals to make to her. At this very time, Margaret of Anjou, borrowing £290 from the Scottish Queen, set sail for France in order to make a direct appeal to King Louis; and Mary, who genuinely wanted peace with England, found herself free to meet Warwick and his staff of envoys at Dumfries.

The Earl's attractive proposals took the form of a matrimonial barrage: the boy-King James III and his sister to marry a sister and brother of King Edward, and Edward himself to espouse Mary of Guelders. There were other reasons besides the Dowager's years and uncertain importance why this last match was an odd offer. Mary was widely reputed to be the mistress of one of the Scots lords, and it was even now being reported that only a few weeks before, when Henry, Duke of Somerset, returned to Scotland after begging help from King Louis, she had persuaded her love to try to poison the Duke because he had boasted to Louis of his "carnal copulation" with her.[1] Even in an age when marriage was regarded as a business proposition by all but the lowest orders of society, this proposal showed Warwick to be far from squeamish in his matrimonial plans for his sovereign. It is doubtful if Edward had any wish to take an aging, notorious Scottish bawd to wife. Perhaps Warwick had not had time to consult him; perhaps the Earl was merely flattering Mary into a compliant mood by pretending to offer her the handsomest Prince in the world. In any case the Bishop of St. Andrews refused to countenance the negotiations, a condition on which Warwick insisted, and the conference at Dumfries came to nothing.

But Warwick led his border fighters on such destructive raids into Scotland that by June the Scots were happy to come to Carlisle in order to sign a summer truce. Then the Earl set Lord Montagu and Lord Hastings and other captains to besieging some of the Northumberland castles which during the winter had again fallen into Lancastrian hands.

Meanwhile, Margaret of Anjou had signed a treaty with Louis XI. In return for a promised alliance and a mortgage on Calais (after it was hers), she received a slender supply of men, ships, and money, and King Louis released from prison her gallant friend Piers de Brézé to lead her invasion. The expedition sailed in October, picked up King Henry and a few troops on the coast of Scotland, and landed at Bamburgh Castle, Northumberland, on October 25 (1462).

The event found Warwick in Yorkshire. Hastily he set about gathering men, sending urgent messages to the King to come northward with all the strength he could make. In a few days he received a commission to raise his standard in the North as royal Lieutenant and shortly after he learned that Edward was on the way.

Based at Bamburgh and Dunstanburgh, the Lancastrians and their French allies soon captured Alnwick and began an advance to the south, expecting to rally the countryside; but when Margaret and Brézé heard of the forces being arrayed against them and surveyed the paucity of men who had joined their colors, they hurriedly broke their field. King Henry was packed overland back to Scotland; Alnwick, Bamburgh, and Dunstanburgh were garrisoned with French and Scots under the command of the Duke of Somerset; and the Queen and Brézé hastily took to their ships, promising to return with an army of Scots. As usual, Margaret suffered a romantic disaster. A tempest overwhelmed the fleet and she barely escaped with her life, thanks to a fishing boat which deposited her and Brézé at Berwick. Some six hundred French who had taken refuge on Holy Island were killed or captured.

By early December the banners of the Earl of Warwick were planted before the three castles. His tactical ingenuity and administrative talent, misapplied at St. Albans, now found an appropriate situation in which to be exercised. The elaborate leaguer which he established might even be compared with the "classical" sieges of the seventeenth and eighteenth centuries. Bamburgh on its great thrust of rock overlooking the sea was well-nigh impregnable against assault and Alnwick and Dunstanburgh were almost as strong. Though not victualed for a long siege, they were stuffed with powerful garrisons who had been promised the succor of a Scots host.

While King Edward lay bedridden at Durham with an attack of measles, Warwick pressed the sieges with an army of some seven thousand men, including all the chief Yorkist captains. Montagu was given command of the siege of Bamburgh, assisted by Lords Ogle, Strange, Say, Grey of Wilton, and Lumley. The Earl of Kent (little Fauconberg) and Lord Scales lay before Alnwick; and the rigorous, learned John Tiptoft, Earl of Worcester—who enjoyed cutting off heads and would one day have his own cut off by Warwick—was investing Dunstanburgh with Lords Scrope, Greystoke, and Powis, and Sir Ralph Grey. Warwick himself commanded a strong force in reserve. The whole operation was based on Newcastle, where the Duke of Norfolk was in charge of receiving supplies by land and sea and conveying them northward to the Earl's headquarters at Warkworth Castle, a few miles from Alnwick and only a short distance from the other two castles. Daily Warwick took horse to inspect the progress of the sieges, sending up victuals, munitions, reinforcements wherever they were needed. The reserves stood ready to repel sorties or to mask the three besieging forces from attack by the relieving army that the Scots were loudly threatening to send down.

In the face of this implacable machine, the fiery Duke of Somerset and his captains lost heart, despite the promises of their allies to the north. Offered not ungenerous terms, Bamburgh surrendered the day after Christmas and the next morning Dunstanburgh followed suit. The soldiers were permitted to march away, leaving their arms behind. The captains were given pardon with life only, but the Duke of Somerset was immediately taken into Edward's favor and showed his good intentions for the future by joining Warwick's host, which now lay concentrated in a position to besiege Alnwick and make a front against the anticipated attack by the Scots.

On January 5 the Scots army duly appeared, led by the Earl of Angus and Piers de Brézé, "the best warrior of all that time." Though the Yorkists had received ample notice of their coming, Warwick was afflicted by a flurry of nerves like that which had seized him during Clifford's surprise attack at Ferrybridge and somewhat like the bewilderment that had apparently scattered his faculties for a moment as Queen Margaret fell upon his flank at the second battle of St. Albans. The volatility of temperament which cheered men's hearts when all was going well and gave such radiance to his graciousness, sometimes bestead him ill in moments of crisis. Warwick appeared to be as startled by the Scots as if they had descended out of the blue. Hurriedly he pulled his men back from their siege emplacements and led his whole army in a helter-skelter retreat to a position between the castle and a marsh which would be difficult for his enemies to assail. True, Warwick's men had lain many days in the field, chilled and sodden with rain; it may well be that Brézé and Angus had managed to scramble together a host of Scots that outnumbered the English army. But Warwick's soldiers had just tasted victory, they were well armed, they were led by experienced captains; and they might have been expected to give the Scots a sound beating.*

Fortunately for Warwick, the enemy were bewildered by the retirement of the English and halted suspiciously before the castle. The garrison of Alnwick took the opportunity of joining their allies, leaving the fortress undefended. The Scots then retired. Next morning Warwick occupied the last of the great Lancastrian strongholds.

This success provided him with an interval in which to pay a funereal tribute to his father and his brother Thomas and his recently deceased mother. Disinterred at Pontefract, the bodies of the Earl of Salisbury and Sir Thomas Neville were placed in a chariot drawn by six horses and conveyed southward by Warwick and Montagu and a retinue of their followers. At Bisham Abbey, founded by one of their ancestors, the cortege was greeted by a family gathering—George Neville, Bishop of Exeter and Chancellor; Lord Fitzhugh and Lord Hastings, Warwick's brothers-in-law; young George, Duke of Clarence, and Elizabeth, Duchess of Suffolk, representing their brother King Edward; Warwick's sisters, Lady Stanley and Lady Margaret of Salisbury, and his sister-in-law, Lady Montagu. On February 15, 1463, the triple interment was performed with great ceremony. Two weeks earlier at Fotheringhay, King Edward had arranged a similar observance for his father and his brother Edmund.[2]

By April (1463), Warwick had come to London to attend Parliament and negotiate with an embassy representing both Philip of Burgundy and Louis XI. But in a few weeks his tale of action was renewed. On the last day of May tidings arrived that the North was once more aflame. When an army of French, Scots, and Lancastrians under Piers de Brézé appeared in Northumberland, the commanders of the three great castles promptly turned traitor and delivered them into the hands of the enemy. The weary labor of '61 and '62 was all to do again. But Warwick

* Some of the English chroniclers take the opposite view—that it was the Scots who lost a great chance for victory by not attacking; but this sounds like a patriotic covering up of Warwick's failure to give battle. See Warkworth, p. 2; Worcester, p. 780 (Works listed in Bibl., p. 375).

and Montagu galloped northward with undiminished vigor. By July they were able to lead a large army against Queen Margaret and Brézé, who had concentrated their forces to besiege Norham Castle. The two Nevilles smashed the enemy host and penetrated miles into the Lowlands, returning only when their supplies were exhausted.

It was a decisive victory. Discouraged at last and no longer welcome in Scotland, Margaret of Anjou sailed for the Continent with her son and her faithful friend, Brézé; King Henry was forced to take precarious shelter at Bamburgh Castle. By late autumn the Scots were eager to come to terms, and Warwick made it clear that the English genuinely desired their friendship. On December 3 he and Montagu welcomed King Edward to York. A Scots embassy appeared a day or two later, and on December 9 a truce was signed to last until October, 1464. Though the great fortresses in Northumberland still held out, this truce ruined Lancastrian hopes in the North.

In January and February (1464) Warwick helped King Edward to put down a ripple of disturbances in the Midlands. Toward the end of March he came once more to London to negotiate with Louis XI's ambassador, Jean de Lannoy. Though there was still work to be done in the North, Warwick's mind was now intensely occupied by his dealings with the King of France.

Before he could finish his talks with Lannoy, however, the usual bad tidings arrived from Northumberland: Somerset, who had turned traitor at the end of the year, was raiding the countrysides from his base at Bamburgh, supported by Hungerford, Roos, and all the other Lancastrian chieftains still in arms. King Edward set out northward before the end of April, and Warwick soon followed, after bidding Lannoy a hasty farewell. Galloping for Yorkshire by a different route, the Earl was not aware that on May 1 Edward rode over from Stony Stratford to Grafton Regis, Lord Rivers' seat, for a visit of several hours, about which he told his household nothing when he returned. "Now take heed," writes the chronicler Gregory, "what love may do, for love will not nor may not cast [foresee] fault nor peril in no thing."

It turned out that Warwick's stalwart brother John mastered

the Lancastrians by his own efforts. On the way to Norham Castle, to escort a Scots embassy to York, he skillfully eluded an ambush, then pounced on the enemy at Hedgeley Moor and scattered them in flight, killing Sir Ralph Percy, one of the principal rebels.

After he had brought the Scots safely to York and returned to Newcastle, Lord Montagu discovered that the Lancastrians had reunited their forces and reared their banners along the Tyne, daring him to give battle. He at once accepted the challenge, came up with the rebels outside Hexham, and won a crushing victory over them. The Lancastrian captains who escaped death on the field were captured and dispatched to execution in the chief towns of the North. So ended Henry Beaufort, Duke of Somerset—nine furious years after his father's death at St. Albans—and Hungerford and Roos and some twenty-five others.

Two weeks after Hexham Field, John Neville received his reward. In the palace at York, with Richard and George Neville looking on, King Edward bestowed upon him the princely earldom of Northumberland, forfeit by the Percys since the battle of Towton. The three mighty Nevilles then negotiated a truce with the Scots to endure for fifteen years.

Warwick was now eager to be off to France to meet King Louis, but he agreed to Edward's suggestion that no one but himself deserved to bring his long work in the North to completion. With his brother John, the new Earl of Northumberland, he led a strong force to oust the Lancastrians once for all from the three great castles on the Northumberland coast, all of them ill-victualed and filled with dispirited fugitives from Hedgeley Moor and Hexham Field.[3] Alnwick and Dunstanburgh quickly surrendered. Bamburgh was impelled to hold out by the desperate exertions of Sir Ralph Grey, who was exempted from the King's pardon. Warwick sent the defenders a fierce summons by his herald: We will besiege this castle seven years if necessary. For every gunshot that hurts a wall of this royal stronghold, this jewel, a Lancastrian head will fall.

On Grey's refusal to surrender, Warwick opened fire with the train of heavy ordinance he had brought with him—the great guns "Newcastle" and "London" and "Dijon" and "Edward" and "Richard Bombartel" and others—while his archers rained arrows against the ramparts and his cavalry stood ready to frustrate any attempt at escape.[4]

This siege exemplifies Warwick's attitude toward the making of war. Just as he had defied traditional ideas of rank and power, so too did he disregard the chivalric idea of warfare (though not its trappings), which still lingered hazily in most men's thinking. Though the spirit of chivalry was absent from the battlefield, its outward form, the method of fighting which its tenets had inspired, still paralyzed strategy and tactics. The knight on horseback continued to hold the dominant position. He was expected to lead his forces directly against the enemy and to fight in the forefront of the battle. Gunpowder was still looked upon somewhat askance, the more so since handguns were often found to backfire and James II of Scotland had been killed in 1461 by the bursting of a cannon.

Among the English, the greedy struggle to hold King Harry's French provinces and the bitterness of civil strife had reduced chivalry to the display of occasional jousts and the habit of knightly tactics. The French monarchy under Charles VII had built up a formidable artillery, but the numerous counts and seigneurs still saw themselves as "preux chevaliers." Philip of Burgundy and his son Charles, who had done little fighting for a quarter of a century, were always presiding over tournaments in the public squares of the Flemish cities, where knights thundered against each other in the lists, flaunting their ladies' tokens on their sleeves or wearing golden chains on their legs that all might behold their bondage to love.

More clearly than anyone else in the England of this age, the Earl of Warwick, it seems, perceived the revolution that gunpowder was making in the art of war, and he sought to adopt his tactics to the actualities, rather than the conventions, of combat. At the second battle of St. Albans he had shown his interest in the new possibilities of fire-power. He took pains, during his northern campaigns, to develop a train of artillery, for use in sieges or battle. Cannon, he saw, saved time, saved lives; therefore he used cannon whenever he could.

Unlike his fellow captains, he did not rush into the front of the fray. To fight on foot diminished a captain's control over the general conduct of the battle, and meant, besides, that if the enemy proved victorious, flight was almost impossible and defeat equaled death. Warwick usually led his soldiers on foot into the thick of the conflict, then took horse and commanded the engagement from behind the front line until opportunity beckoned and he crashed into the battle at the head of his reserve. He preferred the opportunity of fighting again, to knightly derring-do. Bred in the violence of Henry VI's reign and touched by the spirit of the coming age, he fought simply in order to win, and what means would achieve success he was eager to adopt. This attitude probably explains the curious insistence of the Burgundian chroniclers that Warwick showed himself a coward in battle, a charge that appears to have no justification and that is not repeated by the English writers. These Continental historians apparently were trying to say that Warwick's method of making war offended against the canons of chivalry.[5*]

"The most famous living knight" more nearly resembled in his outlook, if not his fame, the *condottieri* of the future than the paladins of the past. This was but one of several paradoxes developing in the regime which Warwick and Edward had established after Towton. The Yorkists were not only the party of governmental reform; they had taken their stand on legitimacy (York's precedence in blood over Lancaster), orthodoxy, and romantic traditionalism—a return to a glorious past. They had, for example, pressed charges of heresy against Bishop Peacock, the ecclesiastic with Lancastrian friends who, in attempting to confute the followers of Wyclif, had embarrassingly suggested that much Catholic practice could not be supported by reason; and they had attacked the court party for plundering the church revenues and denying the Papal Legate.

Yet Warwick had taken a haughty tone to the Pope; neither he nor Edward showed marked signs of piety or of reverence for the rights of the Holy Church; they squeezed heavy contributions out of the clergy, and Edward saw to it that an assessment raised to support the Pope's crusade against the Turks was deposited in his own pocket; and the ecclesiastics they chose for councilors and emissaries were generally men of affairs rather than dedicated churchmen. As for the glorious past (a vague concept popular in all ages of medieval thinking), Warwick and Edward were steadily moving, in practice if not altogether by design, toward the development of a strong central authority untrammeled by the baronial opposition which had so often contested the prerogative of kings; and though the Yorkists had promised to retrieve the French conquests of Henry V, the Earl of Warwick's thoughts were even now concentrated on making a final peace with his friend Louis XI, while he watched his cannon battering Bamburgh Castle.

"London" smashed at the walls so powerfully that great chunks of masonry went flying into the sea; and "Dijon," a shining piece of brass, sent a cannon ball crashing into Sir Ralph Grey's chamber, knocking him unconscious beneath the debris of the stone ceiling. The garrison seized this opportunity to capitulate, and when Sir Ralph Grey came to, he was taken off to Doncaster, tried by the Constable of England, and hanged.

This surrender marked the end of Lancastrian resistance in England. A single castle, Harlech in Wales, held out a few more years, but the realm was now at peace and Warwick's and Edward's government unchallenged. What appeared to be the last flicker of Lancastrian hope was snuffed out a year later when King Henry, wandering helpless about the North with a handful of attendants, was captured in Lancashire and sent to the Tower. Far off in the Duchy of Bar, Queen Margaret and her son and a few faithful followers lived meagerly on a pension from her father and dreamed of better days.

Meanwhile, as the summer of 1464 passed, King Edward, still concealing his May-day visit to Grafton Regis, hearkened with his usual geniality to his friend Richard; and Richard, in his turn, was eagerly preparing for his long anticipated meeting with Louis XI.

III

Warwick's Friend the Dauphin

THE COMPLEXION of international affairs had altered since the days of '59 and '60, when Warwick was weaving schemes with Philip of Burgundy and his guest, the Dauphin Louis, to attack Charles VII of France.

While Edward was reveling at Westminster in the summer of 1461 and Warwick was beginning to subdue the North, there came news about the end of July that the King of France was dead (July 22). The Yorkists rejoiced, for the man whose banner had waved with theirs in the snows of Towton now occupied the French throne. Yet Warwick knew that the Dauphin Louis' eagerness to see an English invasion of France—their common bond—would certainly not be cherished by King Louis. The Yorkist hold on England was green; there were still plenty of Lancastrians in the world; and the Scots, allied now to Margaret of Anjou, would probably as of old take their cue from the French.

Busy though he was in the field, Warwick meant to keep foreign affairs at his finger tips, both because relations with France and Burgundy were of first importance to the Yorkist regime and because the Captain of Calais had acquired an appetite for the subtleties of diplomacy and the high game of dealing with Continental potentates. In the summer of 1461, Warwick edged cautiously onto the untried ground of Louis' attitude, as monarch, toward the House of York. Having flaunted their adherence to the Good Old Cause of Henry V, Edward and Warwick briefly flourished the Agincourt flags in the breeze of public rumor, but all the while the Earl was putting out friendly feelers across the Channel. Without waiting for any word from Louis, he arranged for an embassy, headed by his agent, Lord Wenlock, to cross to Calais, where Wenlock dispatched a request to the French King for safe-conducts to come into his presence. Nobody had better reason than the Captain of Calais to know how much England's future course depended on the surcharged personalities of Philip of Burgundy, his son Charles, Count of Charolais, and King Louis XI.

Philip was in his middle sixties now, still something of a spoiled, charming child living in a world of high fantasy. Never had a harsh reality broken in upon the perpetual spectacles of court and tourney by which he dramatized the fullness of his might and exercised his devotion to chivalry. Yet, if he was spoiled, his own skillful handling of affairs had permitted him to be so. Having first allied himself with England and then concluded peace with France at the right moment (1435), he was the only ruler and his were the only dominions to profit from the Hundred Years War, and in his prime he had governed his hodge-podge of lordships firmly but kindly, suffering only a few collisions with the proud burghers of his towns and beginning to mold his assorted sovereignties into a single regime.

Though his emblem, *le fusil* (flint-and-steel), aptly symbolized his famous temper, he was beloved by his people; for his terrible bouts of anger occurred only when he was crossed, and he was seldom crossed, and after a fit of rage he quickly resumed the benevolent disposition which earned him the name of "Bon duc." He knew how to touch hearts and imaginations. In order to demonstrate to his Hollanders, for example, how easily his power could subdue the bishopric of Utrecht, he exhibited publicly an array of plate worth 30,000 silver marks and, having poured 200,-000 gold lions into two chests, he invited one and all to try to lift them! Except for the limited liberties his great towns possessed in their charters, Philip's will was absolute, but his people forgave him even such annoying little tyrannies as his pleasure in gratifying favorite archers and less genteel servants by marrying them to widows and daughters of rich burghers—though it was noticeable that bourgeois maidens within his territories were affianced very young by their parents, and at least one widow took the precaution of rewedding within two days of her husband's death.

Philip was affable to all, of high or low degree, looking directly into the faces of those with whom he spoke, answering with charming courtesy, sealing his promises with his word alone, and bearing himself with a carriage that unmistakably proclaimed, *Je suis Prince*. He was affable, above all, to women, "quickly surrendering his heart to the wishes of his eyes." On his espousal, in 1430, to his third wife, Isabella of Portugal (mother of Charles), he assumed the motto, *Autre n'array* (I will have no other), but everyone took it for granted that he meant no other *wife*. By 1461 he had enjoyed some thirty known mistresses, who had borne him seventeen acknowledged bastards, the girls honorably endowed or installed in convents, the boys taken into courtly favor and surrounding Philip like the entourage of a Jewish patriarch.

Of late years, corruption and inefficiency had crept into his rule, as the aging Duke gave himself increasingly to the gear of the Round Table and left government to his favorites, the brothers Croy, Antoine and Jean, "new men" of burgher origin. The news of the death of his inimical overlord, Charles VII, he greeted with open pleasure and hasty preparations. Was he not the virtual guardian of the new King, his nephew Louis? And had not the fugitive a thousand times assured him of undying gratitude? As he made ready to accompany Louis to his coronation, only two problems disturbed Philip's mind: his yet unfulfilled vow to go on crusade and his unhappy relationship with his son Charles, Count of Charolais—both of which preoccupations were to play a part in the affairs of Richard Neville, Earl of Warwick.

No one in Europe was moved to higher resolves by the news of the fall of Constantinople in 1453 than the chivalric Philip. At Lille, on February 17, 1454, he had advertised his intentions to the world at the most renowned banquet of the century—the Feast of the Pheasant—in a style so barbarically gigantesque, ingenious, and rich that the Sultan might well hear and tremble. Masked spectators drawn from the farthest ducal dominions and even foreign lands were accommodated in raised tiers about a huge hall, blazoned with tapestries depicting the Labors of Hercules, the revered ancestor of the House of Burgundy. A buffet, guarded by a live lion, displayed riches of plate and *objets d'art*. Three tables supported marvelous "set pieces": a full-rigged galley with mariners loading cargo and setting sails; a landscape of lake and villages; a fortress besieged by an army; a grove of birds; a mammoth pasty holding twenty-eight musicians, whose strains alternated with the music of an organ and small choir enclosed in the replica of a church. At the head of the first table the "Grand Duke of the West," in a dress of black velvet flashing with 2,000,000 crowns' worth of diamonds, rubies, and pearls, played host to Burgundian chivalry, whose arms had been exercised that day in a great tournament.

The courses, each composed of many dishes, arrived in chariots of gold and azure worked by concealed machinery. Between courses the guests were treated to elaborate *entremets*, tableaux vivants or "acts" displaying edifying stories, a variety of mechanical monsters, and two trumpeters in fantastic garb sounding fanfares while seated back to back on a horse that had been trained to pace backward through the hall.

Finally appeared a Saracen giant leading an elephant. In a swaying tower on the beast's back was seated a disconsolate female figure representing the Holy Church (played by the chronicler and court servant, Olivier de la Marche). After a long plaint of the evils done her by the infidels, she appealed to the Knights of the Golden Fleece and all champions of right to draw swords in her defense. Then a live pheasant—a bird mysteriously symbolical—was ceremoniously carried into the hall, a golden collar starred with jewels gleaming about its neck. Philip of Burgundy rose to have his vow announced. To God his creator, to the glorious Virgin Mary, and then to the ladies and the pheasant he swore to undertake a crusade and, if possible, engage the Grand Turk himself in single combat, provided he was not prevented by unavoidable exigencies. Next, Charles of Charolais swore a similar oath, followed by a procession of Burgundian nobles, whose vows and provisos were minutely registered. A number of the oaths were frivolous or bizarre or hedged with obvious escape clauses. But Philip was serious, within the limits, that is, of his imaginative irresponsibility. Even as he prepared to escort Louis to his crowning, he was thinking that if he could join his now royal guest and his English friends in a bond of friendship, he might then embrace the high adventure of Richard Coeur de

Lion, provided only that he could reduce his pigheaded, passionate son to the obedience owing to a father, especially a father who was the mightiest Prince in Europe.

For Charles, Count of Charolais, was as stubborn and violent and proud as Philip, but in an entirely different pattern of physique and mind. If Philip modeled himself on King Arthur, Charles had early chosen the antique Roman type, the austere Marcus Aurelius with a hearty dash of Julius Caesar and Trajan. He was as earnest and reserved as Philip was genial; he passed down to his great-great-grandson, Phillip II of Spain, his prognathous jaw, his grinding industry, and his cold pride. Pomp and ceremony he did not love, as his father did, but fostered as the fitting accompaniment of his high estate. He had a remarkably good education, was a fine musician, composing chansons and motets, played an expert game of chess. He was eloquent in speech, when passion did not shake his thoughts, and he could reason far more cogently than his father. When he walked, he hunched forward and bent his gaze on the ground, absorbed in the heavy struggle of his ideas and feelings.

Ascetic hardihood was his prime métier—was not Trajan tireless in the saddle and Marcus Aurelius abstemious? He ate sparingly; he drank water, or wine much diluted with water; he was so rigidly faithful to his marriage bed that he was reproached for a continence not beseeming so great a prince. Heavy-shouldered and ribbed with muscles, he exposed himself to all weathers, ardently practiced the sports of the day, thundered against his opponents in the tourney with the reckless impetuosity of a poor knight set on making his fortune by arms. When in Holland, he went sailing in calm or storm in order to master in detail the art of seamanship and perfect his endurance; and he so loved the harsh weight of armor that it seemed as if he had been born in it.

"I never knew any man tougher," says Commynes. "I never once heard him say that he was tired, and I never saw in him the appearance of fear." He was harsh but tried to be just in his judgments; implacable in his enmities; all fire and rigor. In short, a formidable, difficult, and obviously ambitious young man.

About the time that Warwick came to Calais and the Dauphin

Louis fled to Burgundy (1456), the Count of Charolais had dared at last to show his bitter hostility to the Croys, who were henceforth to be the subject of most of his quarrels with his father. Out of his pride and ambition he hated them as upstart usurpers of the ducal government, which he himself longed to sway. The most famous quarrel of Philip and his heir, occurring in 1457, serves to illustrate their characters, their stormy relationship, and the role which the Dauphin Louis played in his exile.

A vacancy occurring in the household of the Count of Charolais precipitated the outburst. Charles had secured his father's permission to give the post to his friend the Lord of Hemeries, but the brothers Croy, feeling that their rights had been overlooked, persuaded Philip to bestow the office upon Jean de Croy's son, the Lord of Sempy. One morning in the middle of January, after the Duke had heard Mass and performed his private devotions in the chapel of his palace at Brussels, he summoned his son to him and said pleasantly, "Charles, I wish you to put an end to the strife between the Lords of Sempy and Hemeries over the chamberlainship, and I want the Lord of Sempy to obtain the vacant place."

"My lord," said Charolais, "you have already given me your promise in the matter. No mention at all was made of the Lord of Sempy, and I beg you, my Lord, to keep your promise."

"Déa!" said the Duke. "Let us have no more talk of promises. It is my privilege to give and to take away. And it is my will that the Lord of Sempy be settled in the office."

"Hahan!" Charles exclaimed (for so he always swore). "My Lord, I beg you, pardon me, for I am unable to do that. I hold by what you have promised me. It is the Lord of Croy who has cooked up this plot, I see it well."

"What? You will disobey me? You refuse to do my will?"

"My Lord, I will happily obey you, but that I will not do."

"Ha! You will cross my will, boy? Get out of my sight!"

In his rage Philip turned deadly pale; then his face flamed with a horrible color and he turned on his son Charles so fell and terrible a look that Charles' mother, who had heard this exchange of retorts, was terrified that her husband might do violence to her son. Hastily seizing Charles' hand and pushing him in front of her, she forced him out of the oratory and followed without saying a word to her lord.

Mother and son rushed up the stairs to the Dauphin's chamber. Louis instantly dismissed his suite. When the Duchess had poured out her woeful tale of Philip's anger, Louis was all concern—for himself—fearing that the quarrel might be somehow turned against him since it was occurring so soon after his arrival in the ducal dominions. He hurried off to the oratory to try to soften Philip's heart; but though he kneeled before the Duke—to the latter's horror—and tearfully pictured the distress of the Duchess and the repentant Charles, Philip was not to be moved.

There followed a scenario for opera.

The Duchess and her son, after Louis reported his failure with streaming eyes, retired to their chambers to lament their miserable case. Louis, the most heavily afflicted, belabored God with the plaints of his woe. The Duke, wild with anger, secretly took horse and set off at a gallop across country for his manor of Hal. A thick, cold night of rain and fog was descending. The ways were icy. The Duke lost all sense of direction. Four times his horse fell. Bruised and lame, Philip finally pulled the animal after him as he wandered through the bitter darkness of a thick forest.

Meanwhile, within the palace at Brussels, all was grief and dread as the hours lengthened and the Duke did not reappear. The lowliest grooms indulged in roulades of mournful bewilderment, while the Duchess and her son sustained high duets of woe (rather like Mozart's Donna Anna and Don Ottavio). The Dauphin leaped to horse and with a few followers galloped into the growing dark on a frantic search for his uncle. Finding no trace, he flung himself into a church dedicated to the Virgin, and on his knees before Her he sobbed out so piteous a wail that, his companions afterward declared, it was unmatched among mankind for sheer dolor. When he returned without the Duke to the palace, the entire household went to pieces, while Louis, pacing his chamber, sounded the changes—in a magnificent baritone recitative preserved by Chastellain—on the theme that he was the most unfortunate King's son ever born.

Meanwhile the Duke was wandering his perilous way, determined to endure any misery rather than return to Brussels. At last he found a peasant's hut, persuaded the owner to open his door, and fell upon a humble repast of coarse meat pie, cheese, and cold water. Then Philip safely made his way to a nearby village, where he spent the night in the dwelling of a servitor of his, and so finally betook himself to the castle of Genappe.

Joy immeasurable at Brussels when word came that Philip was safe! But this rejoicing was soon succeeded, on the part of the Duchess, Charolais, and Louis, by the awful question: What to do now? Finally Messire Philippe Pot, a favorite of the Duke's and a brave, witty gentleman, was sent to Genappe.

Finding the Duke in his bedchamber having his bruised leg rubbed, Philippe Pot greeted him with a broad smile:

"Good day, my Lord, good day! What's this? Are you playing King Arthur now or Messire Lancelot?"—

Philippe hit the mark. The Duke laughed, settled into a vein of joking, was soon persuaded to return to Brussels. The Dauphin led the Countess of Charolais, great with child, into his presence. Charles' wife threw herself on her knees in an abandonment of weeping. Philip kneeled to the Dauphin. Louis pleaded piteously for the penitent Charles. At last the Duke agreed to relent, at the Dauphin's request. While the Countess covered Philip's feet with kisses, Louis hurried off to fetch Charles for the reconciliation.

The Duchess of Burgundy soon retired to a religious house, from which she seldom emerged. The Countess of Charolais gave birth to a baby girl, named Marie, who would one day become the greatest heiress in Europe. Louis held her at the font.

"Gods! What a godfather!" an unknown hand has noted in the margin of Chastellain's text. When Warwick's bloody corpse had lain more than a decade in the grave and the naked body of Marie's father had long since been found in the ice before the city of Nancy, and while King Edward IV hesitated in an agony of doubt, Louis XI would tear from his godchild and her husband, Maximilian of Austria, the provinces of Burgundy, Picardy, and the frontiers of Flanders.[1]

Now, at the end of July, 1461, Louis at Avesnes was awaiting the arrival of Philip and Charles to escort him to his coronation. It is said that he had dabbled in the black art to hasten his father's death; he certainly consulted astrologers; and on hearing the news, he had a few hasty Masses sung, then decked himself in red —which was quite proper *—and took his company on a gay hunt. For a while he refused to receive anyone who put on mourning for the late King.

Philip had sent forth a summons to all his vassals, and by the time the Duke and Charolais joined Louis, thousands had thronged to the rendezvous, eager to share in the golden shower of offices that was bound to fall upon the ducal dominions now that the grateful guest had become King. Alarmed at the prospect of feeding and managing this avid host, Louis persuaded Philip to limit their escort to some four thousand men, and the long caval-cade set off for Rheims, Louis borne along to his crowning by the extravagantly costumed chivalry of The Grand Duke of the West. On August 15 the solemn sacring in Rheims cathedral was brought to its climax when the *doyen* of French peers, Philip the Good, placed the crown of France upon Louis' head and shouted, "Vive le Roi! Montjoye Saint-Denis!" The banquet that followed was all of Philip's providing—hangings, napery, plate, food, servants, chefs. From the spoil of Burgundy's treasure, trundled across France in a long line of carts, plate and *objets d'art* worth 200,-000 crowns were presented to Louis as a token of Philip's esteem. During the feast Louis became annoyed by the weight of the crown, casually took it off and put it on the table beside him, and went on talking. It was the sword of power *he* cared about, not the pompous scabbard.

On August 31 the new monarch made his state entry into Paris, dressed in a simple gown of white damask and an ordinary little hat. The admiring eyes and cheers went to Philip, who wore the fortunes of the House of Burgundy in a galaxy of jewels (said to be worth three millions in gold) sprinkled over his plumes and his robes and the trappings of his steed. Philip took up residence at his palace, the Hotel d'Artois, stuffed with hangings and plate.

* The new King of France, and he only, customarily wore red as the sign of mourning for his predecessor.

Louis settled himself in a modest dwelling. For the next three weeks the Hotel d'Artois was the center of the new reign, as Philip displayed his opulence in a series of fetes and balls. Louis seldom appeared and when he appeared, left early. He worked at politics; he worked at soliciting the powers of Heaven; and, it is said, he went wandering at night through the lowest haunts of Paris, sampling the wares and the talk of the brothels, listening in taverns to the opinions of petty burghers and scamps—making contact with the people who, to him, spelled France.

In these three weeks Philip was shaken out of his dream of benevolently helping his former guest to guide the destinies of the realm. Louis scattered a few posts and favors among the Duke's followers; but the only Burgundians he endowed lavishly with offices and privilege were the two men who dominated Philip the Good and were hated by the Count of Charolais, the brothers Croy. Though Louis continued to protest his gratitude, Philip discovered, as day followed day, that the King did not intend to consult him about policy. His followers were assaulting his ears with a growing chorus of disillusion and outrage as the offices they hoped for were given to other men. His own request to have his French fiefs exempted from the jurisdiction of the Parlement of Paris was somehow mysteriously ignored. He himself—Louis' dear, dear uncle—was actually reproved for favoring the cause of York!

This unlooked-for rebuff came about when word arrived that Edward's and Warwick's ambassadors lay at Calais awaiting safe-conducts to appear before the King of France. While Louis was at Avesnes, he had been confronted with the news that two emissaries of Queen Margaret, the Duke of Somerset and Lord Hungerford, had arrived with safe-conducts signed by Charles VII. Louis, under Philip's eye, circumspectly ordered the Lancastrians to be taken into custody. Since then, the Count of Charolais had been begging Louis to show favor to his friend, Henry of Somerset. When Philip requested that the King of France countenance the triumph of York by receiving Lord Wenlock, Louis faced a conjunction of the two external problems that were to dominate his reign: his relations with England

and his attitude toward the House of Burgundy. He chose a devious course, symbolical of his rule to come. While he assured the Duke that he could never be indifferent to the slightest wish of his former host, he managed to convey his reproachful surprise that Philip should champion the avowed enemies of the realm, and he found pretexts to defer issuing the safe-conducts until Philip's pride forbade him to ask again.

Eager to be rid of the Duke of Burgundy and of Paris, a city he never loved, and to plunge into the delights of governing France, Louis did not wait for his uncle's departure (on the last day of September) but bade farewell to him on September 24 and went to Tours. He immediately welcomed Somerset and Hungerford to his court; he pressed the Count of Charolais to visit him, and when Charles approached the town early in October, Louis thoughtfully dispatched the Count's friend, Henry of Somerset, to greet him. The King bestowed on Charles the high office of Lieutenant-General of Normandy, with the understanding that the Count of Charolais would draw the fat pension attached to the post without being expected to govern the province. When it came the turn of Francis, Duke of Brittany, to enjoy his new overlord's smiles, Louis made sure that Charles of Charolais was well on his way home, for he had no wish for the two most independent feudalists in his realm to fall into friendship.

The Duke of Somerset he sent back to Scotland with kind messages and hints of aid for Margaret of Anjou. Still, though Lord Hungerford lingered at his court for further talks, Louis welcomed before the end of October an emissary of Warwick's, who remained with him till the following February. While he was shocking France by the furious vigor of his new rule—turning his father's officers out by the hundreds and sending streams of messengers galloping through his provinces with proclamations and commands—he set about the task nearest his heart, the management of foreign affairs, with much more subtlety and caution. He was suspicious of Edward and Warwick: they were young, martial; they had promised to invade France; they were riding the crest of a great victory. Their tentative advances might be no more than a screen for hostile designs. Besides, the House of Lancaster, dethroned but by no means impotent, might offer an opportunity to clip or blunt the claws of York. While Louis turned to fish happily in the troubled political waters of the Spanish peninsula and sought to keep Philip of Burgundy amused by ardent protestations of friendship, he tried to hold open two bridges across the Channel, one leading to Edward and Warwick and the other to Margaret of Anjou.

By this time (autumn, 1461), Warwick was as suspicious of the French King as the French King was of him, and Edward equaled, perhaps even exceeded, his mentor in his dubious view of Louis. With Wenlock and his colleagues stranded at Calais and news arriving that Lancastrian agents were being received at the French court, Warwick hastily arranged for Louis Galet, a diplomat well known in France ("this notable deceiver," the French called him [2]), to visit King Louis and keep a sharp eye on affairs. Meanwhile, he and Edward happily received overtures from Jean II, King of Aragon, and began dickering for an offensive alliance aimed at France; and Wenlock was instructed to negotiate a renewal of England's friendly relations with Philip the Good.

The Duke of Burgundy, somber and disillusioned after the lesson he had learned in Paris, was eager to feel the solid ground of English friendship under his feet. He gave Warwick's envoys a luxurious welcome at Valenciennes, treated them to banquets and audiences, and hired all the baths of the town for them to disport themselves in, complete with *filles de joie* to spice the languor of the warm waters. Warwick had gone so far as to propose the marriage of his sovereign lord with the sister of the Countess of Charolais. Philip was not quite ready to commit himself decisively to the still-green cause of York, especially with the new, disturbing image of Louis in his mind; but he heartily agreed to prolong the truce and intercourse of merchandise for a year; and, still nurturing the dream of reconciling England and France in order to embark upon his sworn crusade, he persuaded the English to let him sponsor an Anglo-Franco-Burgundian Diet to work out a durable peace.

Thus did Warwick counter the first devious moves of the French monarch, and so began the great political duel of the century between France and England, lasting until the deaths of Louis and Edward within a few months of each other (in 1483). There remains some doubt as to which of these was the winner. There is no doubt that Charles of Burgundy and Richard Neville, Earl of Warwick, were losers.

IV

Warwick's Friend
the King of France

EARLY in 1462, a messenger galloped into the town of Abbeville in the middle of the night, bringing to Charles, Count of Charolais, the tidings that his father had fallen dangerously ill. Soon after, the entire household of the Count were on their knees in supplication to Heaven for the Duke's recovery. Before he joined them, Charolais dispatched messages to the "bonnes villes" of the Burgundian dominions, requesting them to pray for his father, and sent word of the tidings to the magistrates of Abbeville. Leaping into their clothes, the aldermen ordered the bells of St. Vulfram's to be rung. The whole population of the town poured into the church, where they remained all night, kneeling or prostrate, weeping and beseeching God to spare their beloved ruler, while the bells never ceased their tolling.

Eventually Philip rallied. As he grew better, his physicians ordered his head shaved, and some five hundred of his nobles shaved their heads, too, out of loyalty to their lord. By July (1462) he had completed his convalescence, but the edge of his acumen and the pith of his vigor were gone. In the meanwhile, Charles of Charolais, the friend of Lancaster, ruled the ducal dominions—and got back some of his own against the Croys.

Philip's illness made unpleasant news for the Earl of Warwick and King Edward. The Earl had been contemplating a journey to the Burgundian court in order to strengthen Yorkist ties with Philip, but there was no point in talking to the Count of Charolais. The discovery of Oxford's conspiracy in early February (1462) * and rumors that Lancastrians were about to invade England from the Continent as well as from the North, deepened Warwick's sus-

* See p. 116.

picions of Louis. On the horizon glimmered the possibility of an alliance of Scotland, France, and Burgundy with the House of Lancaster.

While Warwick worked to put an English fleet to sea, King Louis made the next move. Worried by Warwick's courting of Jean II of Aragon, with whom he was not on good terms at the moment because he was eagerly meddling in the affairs of the Aragonese province of Catalonia, Louis determined to send an embassy across the Channel, in order to check England's flirtation with King Jean and to feel out Warwick's intentions toward himself. Since Philip the Good had already proposed an Anglo-Franco-Burgundian conference, Louis seized on this idea as the pretext for his diplomatic mission and persuaded Philip (just before Philip's illness) to make the embassy a joint one so as to sweeten it to English taste. He himself sweetened it still more by appointing as its chief the Seigneur de la Barde, who had fought beside Warwick and Edward at Towton.

When Louis' mission arrived in England at the end of February, King Edward had already started for the Midlands to raise men and money. Warwick greeted la Barde with genuine warmth for the man, if not with great confidence in the envoy. On hearing la Barde's message, Warwick showed England's willingness to treat with Louis by dispatching Thomas Vaughan across the Channel to make preliminary arrangements for the projected tripartite conference, and he and his brother George, the Chancellor (and the royal council they dominated), drew up instructions for an embassy to be headed by Lord Wenlock. The instructions suggest that in these first days of March, 1462, the Earl was quite aware of Louis' wiliness and Louis' troubles, for by this time Warwick had learned about the ambitious doings of the King of France and the discontent they were beginning to stir among the French nobility.

For his dealings with Burgundy (that is, with the Count of Charolais), Wenlock was instructed to negotiate for a three years' truce and intercourse of merchandise, provided that the ruler of Burgundy had been licensed by the French King—"of whom he calleth himself subject"—to treat with England. Warwick seems to have aimed at two ends in this proviso. Since the mention of such a license would gall Charles' pride, it might cause trouble between him and Louis which would redound to England's benefit; at least, it would prevent Louis—or Charolais, for that matter —from later slipping out of a treaty by declaring the Anglo-Burgundian clauses to be illegal. Wenlock was warned not to conclude the truce without the commercial agreement. He was also to try to soothe the Burgundians into consenting to an unfortunate petition of the English Parliament for the restraint of imports from the Low Countries. Failing in these negotiations, Wenlock and his colleagues were to accept a renewal of the old pact.

As for the French, the English envoys were to "keep themselves under generalities" in order that Louis' representatives might be the "first to break and open their intent." When negotiations got down to business, Wenlock was to remind the French that long before England claimed title to the realm of the lilies, her kings had ruled by lawful inheritance the provinces of Normandy, Guienne, Anjou, and Maine. Should the French be willing to restore these territories, England would agree to a three years' truce. If, in addition, Louis' envoys would consent to desert the Scots alliance, then the English would even look favorably upon establishing a final peace with France. Though Warwick was undoubtedly aware that Louis would rather cut out his tongue (an especial deprivation for him) than relinquish those great provinces to Yorkist rule, he was dangling before Louis' eyes what he knew must be a tempting lure—the tacit admission that the English might be willing to forego their claim to the crown of France, which had been the chief sticking point in Anglo-French negotiations for over a century and the avowed cause of the Hundred Years' War. If the French proved obdurate, Wenlock was to put up a stiff demand for Guienne at least, but that failing, to agree in the end to a truce.[1]

These arrangements were hastily made, for in the first week of March, Warwick was preparing to go north against the Scots.* He and la Barde were finding their reunion so pleasant, however,

* See p. 116.

that Louis' envoy decided to accompany the Earl in order that they might talk a little longer. As the two former companions-in-arms rode northward, they doubtless paused at Towton to renew their memories of the bloody field. When they reached York, the city fathers gave them a banquet.[2] In these intimate circumstances, recalling the old days when the Dauphin Louis was as ardent a Yorkist as any, la Barde tellingly made the point that his master desired nothing more than to gain the friendship of the Earl of Warwick, the maker of Edward and the ruler of England. Louis hoped that he and Warwick might together work out a durable peace. After all, they had common aims. Had not Warwick crushed the recalcitrant nobles of Lancaster? Louis, too, was struggling to bring his nobles under control. La Barde probably even hinted that the mighty Earl might find it to his advantage if he were willing to lend his aid to the King of France.*

Warmed in his pride and aware that Louis had good reason to seek the friendship of England, Warwick gave ear to la Barde's free disclosures. There began to take shape in his lively imagination a stroke of high diplomacy—might he not put an end to these wearisome Lancastrian incursions and bring the Scots to terms, by fashioning with the King of France a peace pact that would prosperously resolve a hostility as old as time and earn, perhaps, some magnificent expression of Louis' gratitude? He caught a tantalizing glimpse of himself as the arbiter of Western Europe, the Captain of Calais of the '50s a hundred times magnified.

But his duty on the borders was pressing. Before going against the Scots, he hastily requested King Edward to express to Louis England's desire for friendship, he wrote a very amicable letter in the same vein, and he demonstrated his interest in collaborating with the French King by arranging for Edward's communication and his own to be sped to France in the wallet of his personal officer-of-arms, Warwick Herald.

King Louis had more time for diplomacy than the Earl of

---

* Subsequent relations between Louis and Warwick suggest that la Barde threw out some such flattering hints. See below.

Warwick—time to let the implications and alternatives of his diplomatic ventures shoot along his nerves in *frissons* of eagerness and suspicion which thrilled his fertile imagination and spurred his will to make France a great state. As he pondered la Barde's report and the letters from Edward and Warwick, he perceived that he had touched the quick of Warwick's pride and ambition. He still had doubts of English good faith, however, for word had reached him that as soon as Warwick returned from the North, he would put to sea with a fleet in order to attack France, as he had promised King Jean of Aragon. Besides, the Scots and Lancastrians were still capable of making plenty of trouble for the Yorkists. Above all, there was the King of Aragon, with whom Louis was eager to ally himself, at whose court even now the Count of Foix was negotiating. In return for abandoning the Catalans to Jean, he might be able to close his grip on the border provinces of Rousillon and Cerdagne and thwart the menacing combination of England and Aragon.

The opportunity was too tempting. Louis dispatched Edward's and Warwick's friendly letters to the Count of Foix. "Seeing that they are so humble," these missives were to be shown to Jean II as proof that the English were only playing with him and really desired an alliance with France. The device worked. Early in April, Louis signed the treaty he sought for and confirmed it by an interview with King Jean in May.[3]

But what was he to do about the projected tripartite conference, with Warwick Herald waiting to carry back to England the safe-conducts for Wenlock's embassy? An alluringly complicated stratagem occurred to him. Zestfully he concocted—or was quick to employ—a useful indiscretion committed by Warwick Herald. Allegedly, while the herald was enjoying himself in Paris, he had rashly blurted out that the Yorkists feared the Count of Charolais as they feared the Devil and that if Philip died they would rush to make friends with France out of their distrust of Charles. With Charolais now ruling Burgundy in his father's illness, Louis was eager to stay in the good graces of his dear brother-in-law (Charles' first wife having been Louis' sister). Louis sent Warwick Herald home with pleasant assurances but not with the safe-conducts. He made these out, indeed, but he dispatched them to one of his officers, with orders to forward them to the Count of Charolais, along with the report of Warwick Herald's revealing utterance in Paris, and to inform the Count that Louis, out of his love, would leave entirely in Charolais' hands the decision to send or withhold the safe-conducts. The grim and sulphurous Charles did not, needless to say, dispatch them to England. Thus Louis thrust on the Burgundians the onus of breaking up the proposed peace conference and also cultivated his friendship with the Count of Charolais.

Having taken the plunge, the King of France pressed on his offensive against Yorkist England. He signed a treaty with Margaret of Anjou in June, and he released her friend, Piers de Brézé, from prison to lead her expedition . . . and to pay a great part of her bills. He exhorted the Scots to support the coming Lancastrian blow. Fired by the mortgage on Calais which Queen Margaret had yielded, he set about to besiege this last English stronghold in France, the ulcer in her fair flesh which he desperately longed to cure. With all his powers of persuasion he besought the aid of Philip of Burgundy, since Calais was encompassed by Burgundian territory. If Philip would allow free passage across his territories and contribute the ships of Holland and Zeeland to close the siege by sea, Charles of Charolais would be given command of this glorious enterprise.

Indignantly Philip refused to desert his alliance with York. Never would he permit Charles to accept such a command. He would not allow Louis to use his ships or cross his dominions. He even refused to have Louis' proclamations against England cried in his lands. Jean de Croy, now devoted to Louis' service, was required to carry to the King of France this fierce refusal.

Croy: The Duke will die before he allows it.

Louis: Why? Do I not have the power of moving supplies and men anywhere in my realm?

Croy: Sire, you certainly have the right, but all things do not happen according to reason. Neither my Lord nor his territories are like others. His people have not learned to be put upon and he could never bear it either.[4]

Angrily, fearfully, Louis drew back, jolted into awareness that he had tried to go too far, too fast. By the time Queen Margaret's expedition was preparing to sail, he had found additional reasons to stint his aid and give but perfunctory encouragement.

The Earl of Warwick provided the reasons. He had lost the game with Aragon—though it was not much of a game since England was in no shape to invade France even with Jean II's help—but as soon as Louis' attitude became clear, he gave the French King's intricate stratagems an answer in iron. He harried the Scots into making a brief truce. He pressed the war against the Lancastrians in Northumberland. And he aimed a direct blow at Louis by fitting out a great fleet, with which his uncle William, Earl of Kent (little Fauconberg), put to sea in the late summer. Down came the English upon the Breton coast, harrying the port towns, burning Le Conquet, near Brest, then sailing on unopposed to pillage the Île de Ré. Helpless and frightened, Louis was now in no mood to do very much for Margaret of Anjou.

On the diplomatic front, an English mission was dispatched to King Henry of Castile, who, though allied to France, had joined the Catalans against Louis and Jean of Aragon. In October, Wenlock headed an embassy to Burgundy, and before the end of the year England had once again renewed her all-important truce and intercourse of merchandise with Philip.

After the Earl of Warwick had chased Queen Margaret and Brézé back to Scotland and closed an unbreakable grip upon the three Northumberland fortresses, he sent word to the King of France (December, 1462), even before the castles surrendered, that England might be willing to let bygones be bygones and entertain peace offers. Warwick was more than ever eager to rid the North permanently of Scots and Lancastrians; having countered Louis' moves, he was clearly making overtures from strength, not weakness; and there still glimmered in his mind the prospect which his talks with la Barde had opened up.

Thrust had been answered by riposte. Honors were easy. The artist in Louis must have ruefully admired Warwick's skill, as the ruler, jettisoning all thoughts of pursuing the offensive against the Yorkists, now set himself to woo the friendship of the mighty Earl. In answer to Warwick's communication, he hastily ap-

pointed envoys to treat with the English at Calais; but no representatives of King Edward appeared. Warwick and his sovereign
did not want to jeopardize their negotiations with Castile. Jean
of Aragon, annoyed by Louis' gobbling up Rousillon and Cerdagne, was again turning to England. Warwick meant to wait
until Louis showed more positive signs of friendship than merely
appointing ambassadors.

Louis had still another motive for wooing England besides the
reasons Warwick had given him and those generated by mounting
difficulties within his realm. From the moment of his crowning
he had burned to buy back from Burgundy the Somme towns,
which pushed Philip's frontier all the way to Amiens, scarcely
sixty miles from Paris.* Philip's illness in 1462 had given Louis
a scare, for well he knew that the ambitious Count of Charolais
would never consent to sell back the towns; and the rebuff over
Calais which the Duke had administered the previous summer
served to increase his anxiety. If Louis came to terms with the
English, as Philip had been hoping, then the Duke might be
grateful enough to let the towns go.

King Louis made haste, therefore, (early in 1463) to respond
more positively to Warwick's overture. He sent word to Philip
from Bordeaux that he would gladly submit himself to the Duke's
desires and send representatives to a peace conference sponsored
by Burgundy. Philip, in consequence, notified England that he
was dispatching his councilor, Jean de Lannoy, a nephew of the
Croys, to make arrangements for a tripartite Diet. Lannoy sailed
in March, the official envoy of Philip but the actual servant of
King Louis and the bearer of Louis' amicable tenders to Warwick and Warwick's sovereign.

Edward and Warwick gave Lannoy a warm welcome. Money
was laid out for silks and gowns and quantities of food and drink
to express their hospitable feelings toward the Burgundian embassy. Lannoy soon made himself popular. He was a Knight of
the Golden Fleece and high in Philip's confidence. He was a

* The towns were ceded to Philip by Charles VII in the treaty of Arras
(1435), which vaguely provided for their repurchase at some future time
at a price of 400,000 gold crowns.

brave and convivial gentleman—chairman of the committee which had arranged the famous Feast of the Pheasant. Edward went so far, it is said, as to offer him a large bribe to work for English interests and liked Lannoy none the less for courteously refusing. The King and the Earl promised Lannoy to send envoys to a conference at St. Omer, at which Philip would use his good offices to make peace between England and France, and Warwick let Lannoy know that he and his brother George, the Chancellor, intended to head the English embassy.

But there were also informal interviews between Lannoy and Warwick, in which, it appears, Lannoy disclosed Louis' ardent desire to meet Warwick personally in order to arrange the destinies of the two realms they ruled. Louis even hoped that Warwick might consent to give him active aid—of a kind, of course, that would open up to the Earl prospects suitable to his talents and his greatness. Not long after, there arrived at Warwick's London inn a servant of the Seigneur de la Barde. He had been sent by King Louis to beg a greyhound of Warwick, as one sovereign might ask a favor of another, and he undoubtedly brought messages as well.

The Earl's imagination was entrammeled. After the Burgundian embassy departed, his agent Wenlock wrote to Lannoy that the English envoys would attend the Diet without fail and that the Earl of Warwick would be their chief.[5] But the news that de Brezé and the Scots had crossed the border sent Warwick galloping northward at the beginning of June (1463),* and no English embassy crossed the Channel. Even after the Scots were routed and Queen Margaret sailed for the Continent in despair, Warwick, in August, sent Philip of Burgundy the vague message that he would be unable to leave England for two months. By this time an English embassy had been commissioned, but it lingered day after day at Canterbury.

With Scotland not quite yet brought to terms and rumors running that the French were arraying a fleet and meant to besiege Calais, Warwick evidently decided that though he had shown Louis the hopelessness of the cause of Lancaster, the situa-

* See pp. 120–121.

tion was not yet ripe for his mission to the King of France, and he had probably discovered that Edward, too, was not eager for him to meet Louis at this time—though he had no suspicion that Edward's motives might be somewhat different from his own. Edward was ready, however, to fall in with Warwick's proposal that a partial *rapprochement* be offered the King of France. The English envoys, moving at last from Canterbury to Dover, were given the limited power of concluding a year's truce with France, on land only. As a hint to Louis that if all went well a mightier Neville would be willing to appear, Warwick saw to it that his brother George headed the embassy, which crossed the Channel shortly after the middle of August. Before the end of the month the Chancellor and Lord Wenlock had entered upon cordial talks with the French and Burgundian envoys at St. Omer. Philip remained at his wonderful palace in Hesdin, awaiting the arrival of King Louis, who was still in Paris.

But there occurred almost immediately a change of diplomatic climate. Like one of the goddesses who descended periodically from Olympus to disrupt the schemes of Greek and Trojan on the ringing plains of Troy, Margaret of Anjou, reaching Sluys from Scotland at the beginning of August, was determined to blast the St. Omer Diet, which boded ill for the House of Lancaster. For resources, she had only her unquenchable spirit and her protector, Brézé: "ne credence, ne argent, ne meubles, ne joyaux pour engaiger." Her small company of faithful followers, her son Edward, her seven woman attendants, depended even for their food on Brézé's purse.

Knowing his chivalric heart, she addressed herself, not to her avowed friend and cousin, King Louis, but to the enemy of her house, Philip of Burgundy. Even though the Yorkist envoys were due to arrive any day, Philip could not resist sending the gallant Philippe Pot to offer comfort, but also to prevent any attempt on her part to seek a meeting. But, though Pot warned her that the English at Calais knew of her arrival and were laying ambushes for her, the intrepid Margaret was not to be put off. Writing Philip that she was coming to see him, she set out for Hesdin without giving him time to object. At Bruges she left

her son and her followers. Disguised—or costumed—in the gar-
ments of a peasant woman, she drove off in a humble cart with
three of her attendants, guarded only by the ever-loyal Brézé.
Near Lille she was met by the Count of Charolais, who paid
her royal honors and lent her five hundred crowns. Not long
after, Philip, hearing that a band of English were lying in wait
for her near Bethune, sent her a guard of archers and promised
to grant her an interview, but only if she would come no nearer
Hesdin. On the second of September, even as the ambassadors at
St. Omer were beginning their talks, Philip rode over to St. Pol
to greet the beautiful and indomitable and fallen Juno.

She rushed into the street to meet him. He tried to pay his
gallant homage to her as a Queen. She tried to throw herself upon
him as a helpless Princess. It was an affecting scene, but she
could not move him to ruin the St. Omer Diet for the sake of
Lancaster. Entertaining her and Brézé at a banquet that evening,
he pointed out that King Louis was now determined to recognize
the House of York, and the next day he firmly took his departure
from St. Pol. Shortly after he was on the road, he dispatched
Margaret a rich diamond and a goodly sum of money for herself
and her little company. Then he sent his sister, the Duchess of
Bourbon, and the Duchess' daughters to comfort her. Charles of
Charolais and his knights honored her with a great tourney at
Bruges.

If Margaret could not ruin Yorkist-Burgundian diplomacy, she
at least stirred a high chivalric debate. Before dinner one day, she
invited the Count of Charolais to wash with her. "Knowing his
duty and following in the footsteps of his father [as a pattern of
courtesy]," he politely refused despite reiterated invitations. When
water was brought for her young Prince, the contest in etiquette
was repeated at length. The Count would have no part of washing
with the son of a King, though driven from his kingdom, while
Margaret and Prince Edward protested that such miserable and
unfortunate persons as they did not deserve the honor which
Charles insisted upon paying them. The argument waxed long
while the dinner cooled, but Charolais' inverted pride was in-
flexible. That evening the court at Bruges hummed with intense

discussion of the issue. Messengers sped to Philip at Hesdin with news of this weighty affair of protocol. In Philip's presence a great debate on the subject ensued between Philippe Pot and Philippe de Croy. Asked for his opinion by the Duke himself, Chastellain judiciously agreed with Philippe Pot that, far from being "overnice," as Croy maintained, the Count of Charolais had properly upheld the high chivalric etiquette of the court of Burgundy.

Having failed in her desperate mission, Margaret of Anjou soon retired to Nancy to meet her father, after which she settled with her ragged band of followers in his Duchy of Bar, to dream of revenge and await the turning of fortune.

But George Neville and John Wenlock—doubtless on instructions from Edward and Warwick—did not let Margaret's meeting with Philip pass without notice. They held themselves haughty, declaring that only at the Duke of Burgundy's request had England been willing, in the first place, to listen to overtures from France, and they insisted that the French at once agree to abandon the House of Lancaster. Louis' envoys did not have the power to make this promise. Obdurately the English refused to hear of any compromise or to proceed to other matters. They even squabbled with their good friend the Duke of Burgundy because he did not grace the negotiations with his presence. Philip was kept busy trying to soothe their feelings, but he did not stir from Hesdin.

The old Duke was tired and harried. He was again having trouble with his son Charles, who was furiously urging him to resist King Louis' blandishments. The Croys and Louis had somehow pushed him into a position he had actually wanted to avoid. Embarrassed by his interview with Margaret, he did not wish to face the questions of the nettled English envoys, nor did it suit his dignity to appear at St. Omer before Louis. Wearily he explained to the English that he must wait at Hesdin for the arrival of the King of France. Throughout most of September the diplomats haggled fruitlessly. It began to look as if Margaret had succeeded, after all.

But at last, on September 28, King Louis, having shaken himself free from an annoying Catalan embassy in Paris, rode eagerly into Hesdin. He was deeply disappointed that Warwick had not come to St. Omer, was still hoping that the great Earl would arrive a little later; but he zestfully looked forward to meeting the English envoys and also to closing his marvelous deal with Philip—a deal that must be consummated before Philip's dour, fierce son, whom Louis protested that he loved better than any man alive, succeeded his father as Duke of Burgundy.

Itching to exert his spells, Louis immediately went to work behind the scenes. On the last day of September the English rode to Hesdin to be received by the Duke of Burgundy. George Neville delivered an elegant address in praise of their host. In reply, Philip expressed his hope that now at last he could bring together the representatives of his friend, King Edward, and his sovereign, King Louis. The English balked, refusing to enter Louis' presence lest the act be taken as acknowledging that he was King of France (their own sovereign holding that title and this other being merely "le roi Louis"—of nowhere).

But Louis knew how to make use of Philip's hospitality. Two days later the stiff-necked envoys were treated to a delectable *fête champêtre* in the ducal park. Afterward, when they called on the Duke to thank him for his bounty, Philip remarked that there was only a door between them and the King of France and that he was sure King Edward would be displeased if they failed to pay their respects. There was nothing for the envoys to do but follow the Duke into Louis' chamber.

After Philip had made a graceful little speech of introduction, Louis welcomed the ambassadors, protesting that the Duke of Burgundy had been more than a father to him and that he owed to him his very crown. Then, before the English could freeze into diplomatic hauteur, Louis was among them, taking their hands, laughing and talking as easily as if they had long been familiars. George Neville managed to extemporize a smooth Latin greeting. Louis praised his eloquence, chatted in his best frank and easy style, asked many questions, declared emphatically that he wished King Edward well, who was, in truth, a "gentil Prince."

As for the main sticking point in the negotiations—his support of the House of Lancaster—well, there would be no more trouble about *that*, he implied with the best grace in the world. In the old days, before the Yorkist triumph, he and King Edward had been companions-in-arms, after all, and for his part, he was still eager for their friendship to continue. Letting his tongue get the better of him, he went so far as to disavow France's ancient allies, the Scots, declaring expansively that he would even help King Edward subdue them, if necessary (an imprudence which was promptly retailed to the next Scottish embassy that visited England).

In spite of themselves, the English were charmed and rode away to continue the negotiations in the best of spirits. Five days later, on October 8 (1463), a year's truce, for land only, was signed. It included both Burgundy and Brittany and pointedly ignored the Scots; and it was announced as the first step toward a peace conference to be held the following April.[6]

On the same day, King Louis consummated with Philip his marvelous deal. After the Duke of Burgundy recovered from his illness (July, 1462), he had restored the Croys to favor and quarreled with his son. Then was it that Louis anxiously undertook to persuade the Duke to sell back the Somme towns for 400,000 gold crowns. Philip wanted peace so that he could go crusading and "make his soul." He was depressed by his son's recalcitrance, yet determined to show that he was master. Louis' instruments, the brothers Croy, were ever at his ear urging him to accede to the wishes of the King of France. Perhaps he thought that Louis could never raise the money. By the late summer of 1463 he had given his reluctant consent. Instantly Louis delivered to him half of the vast sum. Philip had no choice but to seal his promise that he would surrender the cherished towns when the rest was paid. Meanwhile, the Count of Charolais was sending his father desperate pleas not to give up the towns and appealing to his friend Louis to cease, or defer, his efforts to conclude the bargain. But not even his fear of Charolais could restrain Louis now. Scraping together every bit of cash he could beg, borrow, cajole from his subjects, Louis had made up the full amount by the time he rode for Hesdin.

"Croy, Croy," Philip muttered helplessly after he signed away the towns, "it is hard to satisfy two masters."

Louis was now more eager than ever to meet the man who ruled England. He received word from Warwick at the beginning of November that the Earl hoped to cross the Channel before the end of the month, but by that time Warwick was preparing to negotiate with the Scots at York.

The King of France knew that he had made an implacable enemy of Burgundy's future ruler. He was already on bad terms with Francis, Duke of Brittany, with whom he had quarreled over feudal rights and ecclesiastical benefices. To keep these potential rebels apart, he had appointed Francis to the lieutenant-generalship of Normandy, after he had already given the office to Charles, in the hope that the two would quarrel. Instead, they became friends, and with Charolais glowering at his overlord, this friendship was doubly dangerous.

Having the Somme towns and the hope of Warwick to hearten him, Louis decided to challenge Charolais openly. He stopped the Count's pension for the lieutenant-generalship. He placed in charge of his new northern territories the Count of Nevers, whom Charles had forced to flee from Burgundy when Philip was ill. He worked at sowing further discord between Philip and his son.

But Charles and Francis were not his only enemies. The moment he was crowned, he had set about governing his realm with the zeal and impatience of a man too long kept out of his own. He hated the policy and officers of his father's regime. He wanted to know everything, control everything, reform everything, and at once. He burst over France like a volcanic eruption, jetting clouds of edicts, proclamations, commands. He removed taxes that pressed heavily on the middle class, meanwhile levying new ones here and there; he lopped off hundreds of offices that he thought inefficient. But with administrative business snarled for lack of clerks, he was forced to restore many of the offices; and with his treasury running dry, he was having to reimpose the taxes, visiting a cruel disillusionment on his people. He angered the Church by his too hearty interest in her government and by his insistence on taxing ecclesiastics like laymen. Most of all he angered his proud vassals, the nobility of the Lilies.

The lords who had served his father best, he promptly got rid of. Piers de Brézé and Antoine de Chabannes he stripped of their goods and locked up (later to win them back at great expense of money and energy and give them high office). He visited his scorn on any gorgeously dressed lord who appeared in his sight. He had the temerity to forbid all but himself to hunt within the realm of France, partly to show his authority, partly to encourage his seigneurs to convert their forests to agricultural land, partly to pocket the fees he charged for licensing exceptions. He dismissed noble hangers-on from his court. He gathered about him talented men of the middle class, his instruments rather than councilors, officers whom he made out of nothing, who were attached to him by the one bond he respected—self-interest—and whom he could easily dispense with if need be.

Jean de Lescun, his Marshal, was an old freebooter; Ambroise de Cambrai, his Master of Requests, had forged a Papal Bull to allow Jean d'Armagnac to marry his own sister. Two of these intimates have become legendary: Oliver de Daim (the Devil), his barber, who shaved him, doled out his pocket money, did secret police work, organized his endless journeys, sometimes served even as an envoy extraordinary; and the still more fearsome Tristan l'Hermite, whom Louis as Dauphin had dreaded like the fiend, yet who continued in his old office of Provost-Marshal, a sleepless, ruthless, astute Justicer, as pitiless and ineluctable as death—"a terrible man," Warwick's secretary called him.[7]

Louis had driven from his court the peerless paladin Dunois, companion-in-arms of Joan of Arc. He took the government of Guienne away from the Duke of Bourbon. He deprived Gaston, Count of Foix, of some of his appanages. He alienated the House of Orléans (nursing a dim claim on Milan) by allying himself with Francesco Sforza, whom he admired above all rulers. He alienated the House of Anjou (nursing a dim claim on Naples and linked by marriage with Lancaster) by allying himself with Jean of Aragon and making overtures to Yorkist England.

Now, in the winter of 1463–64, with Philip of Burgundy's health ebbing away and Francis of Brittany and Philip's heir exchanging too frequent and too friendly messages, with a coming and going of angry lords and an ominous buzz of discontent sounding throughout the duchies and counties of France, King Louis was nervously regretting his intemperate revenges, his too hasty reforms, the overexuberant display of his determination to subdue his feodality. With wonderful skill he was already beginning to recover himself, to secure the services of the men who could most help or most injure him; but the arch on which he must base his future was friendship with England and the keystone of that arch was Richard Neville, Earl of Warwick. His darting, subtle, fertile brain, addicted to ensnaring loyalties, pregnant with stratagems, and irrepressibly fond of testing its ingenuity, was now bent upon winning over the master of the Yorkist realm.

He had a taste for foreigners—being more Corsican than Napoleon in his distrust of the French, and far more adroit in drawing men of other lands to his services. He surrounded himself with Swiss, Scots, Germans, Flemings, Burgundians, Italians, Greeks, Portuguese, paid them liberally, treated them familiarly, never tired of dosing them if they were ill or of finding brides for them if they were marriageable. He used all his talents to make friends with the chief men in his neighbors' governments. He had won hearts at Sforza's court, and at the courts of Burgundy, Aragon, Castile, the Emperor of Germany. But the blue rose of his florilegium was to be the dashing, martial adventurer, the Earl of Warwick, ruler of the race he most feared and hated (he once expressed his love of the chase to an intimate by remarking that the only sport he preferred to hunting was killing Englishmen).

He must win Warwick to secure his desperately needed peace with England, but he did not stop there. He loved to juggle a thousand alternatives, however improbable. Might not more be done with the masterful Earl than merely persuade him to a treaty? Louis' mind flashed with visions. He loved to exhale an electric cloud of projects, possibilities, prophecies, which often confused his court as well as his enemies, but which served as a safety valve for a personality that delighted in, but was also wary of, its own ebullience. Might not the Earl perform services for Louis like those he had performed for Edward—or, at least, be played upon to desire such a role? Louis, utter misanthrope, knew that all men possess a nerve than can be touched. For Warwick, flattery was not enough. Money was beside the point. Ambition—that was it.

Spurred by his pride in his charms, by his urgent necessities, and by the Earl of Warwick's shrewd game of waiting till the moment was ripe, the King of France set on foot, early in 1464, his program of conquest.

Ready at hand were Warwick's officers and servants at Calais. He turned on them his consummate affability. Richard Whetehill, Warwick's Lieutenant, he addressed in seductive terms of familiarity. Sir Walter Blount, the Treasurer of Calais, he persistently besought to pay him a visit. He bestowed safe-conducts on other officers of the town, permitting them to travel in France at will. All the while, in these days of January and February, he was sending messages to Warwick, forwarded to the Earl by these officers at Calais. Whetehill, in enclosing a reply from his master, showed himself quite carried away by Louis' graciousness, promising to serve him "à mon petit pouvoir." The exchange of messages was directly concerned with the approaching visit to England of Jean de Lannoy, who had made himself so agreeable to the English the previous year. Louis had met Philip of Burgundy at Lille in February (1464), promised him ten thousand men for his cherished crusade, and then persuaded him to postpone his departure for the Holy Land till the truce between England and France was transformed into a permanent peace. In his letters to Warwick Louis embroidered his discussion of Lannoy's mission with hints that he longed to secure Warwick's personal assistance and that even the Earl's magnificence might somehow, perhaps, be enlarged . . .[8]

Lannoy sailed for England on March 18, 1464, followed by Louis' secretary, Le Begue.

V

The French Marriage

AS WARWICK slowly made his way southward from York in the early weeks of 1464, pausing in the Midlands to help Edward extinguish a smoulder of disorder, he was pondering the stream of missives from Louis.

This King of France, who wrote as if he and Warwick were companions and equals, seemed to understand what he himself had scarcely more than felt—that with his control of England's policy and resources, his rule of Calais and the Narrow Seas, his command of thousands of hardy followers, he was, in effect, a European power. Louis and he were much alike, the King of France seemed to say: adventurers really, breaking with the past, making good their new ideas of dominion. Warwick had crushed the old-fashioned barons of Lancaster, given England a new King and a powerful government. Louis, too, was set upon subduing *his* barons and creating a strong central authority. Might not Warwick now help to do for France what he had done for England? —but with a different sort of consequence for himself. Might he not win a virtual prerogative of his own, which would make him the buffer and arbiter between France and England?

These intimations, perhaps only vaguely articulated if articulated at all, spurred Warwick's developing conviction that peace must be made with the French. He had reason to think he was judging the issue on its merits: such a peace would spell the end of the Anglo-French war which had drained English energies and resources for generations; it would put a halt to Lancastrian and Scottish incursions; and it would stimulate a prosperous trade with the great markets of France. Yet the prospect for his own future probably fastened him more warmly to Louis' cause than he might otherwise have committed himself and caused him to brush aside the annoying fact that the people of England had no desire to link themselves with their old enemies.

By the time Warwick was waiting in London, in late March, to greet the Seigneur de Lannoy, he knew that Louis wanted not only a peace treaty but a marriage bond and an alliance aimed against Burgundy.[1*] The proposal that England join with France at Burgundy's expense would require a deal of careful persuading before Edward grasped its necessity. Warwick perceived that he must take his protégé gradually down the path; enough, for the present, to concentrate on the peace pact and the marriage. Thus, as Lannoy crossed the Channel, there fell, like a hint of twilight on the summer air, a faint obscurity between the Earl and his sovereign. For the first time, Warwick was not taking Edward into his full confidence; for the first time, he was pursuing a policy which acknowledged that there was a difference between the King's interest and his own.

About March 20, Warwick received the unpleasant tidings that Jean de Lannoy, landing at Dover, had been roughly handled by English officials. They were declaring, despite his credentials from Philip as well as from Louis, that Lannoy was no Burgundian but of Picardy and a hated Frenchman, and they were threatening to clap him behind bars. Warwick hastily dispatched servants to rescue Lannoy, arranged to have him ceremoniously escorted to London, and tried to make up for this inauspicious beginning by giving him a warm greeting and installing him in comfortable quarters at the House of the Preaching Friars near Ludgate. Meanwhile, Louis' secretary, Le Begue, remained trembling at Rochester until he too was enclosed in Warwick's protective mantle. There were Francophobes in plenty in England, but to threaten an envoy with arrest was going far. Was the attack inspired by someone at court?

Warwick saw to it that his followers and his brother George, the Chancellor, surrounded Lannoy and his colleagues with the façade of a hearty popular welcome, while at the council table at Westminster he worked out the terms under which he and his faithful officer, Lord Wenlock, were to treat. There were no real hitches, but the commissions were not issued until March 28.

Though Lannoy's main purpose was to pave the way for the Anglo-Franco-Burgundian Diet to be held in the late spring, Louis had conferred on him broad powers of negotiation. Edward's council, on the other hand, were disturbed by a well-authenticated report that an agent of Louis', Guillaume Cousinot, was at King Henry's side in Bamburgh Castle, and there were such persistent rumors of a French descent upon Calais that the garrison was reinforced. Warwick was not so ensnared in King Louis' web that he made light of Cousinot or forgot that the Northumberland castles were still in Lancastrian hands. Besides, the messages from Louis and the private talks he had already held with Lannoy indicated that no durable bonds could be forged until he and Louis conferred personally. Therefore he was content to approve a commission for Wenlock and himself that empowered them only to arrange a peace conference and treat for an interim truce by sea to complement the truce by land. Yet the King and the King's friends had not been so ready to agree with him as usual. Was Edward's pliant attitude beginning to stiffen and show signs of change?

Warwick made emphatically clear to Lannoy that Louis would have to do some explaining about Cousinot; * then official negotiations went smoothly. The truce by sea, to last like the land truce until October 1, was soon concluded and quickly ratified by Edward; and a tripartite conference to be held at St. Omer was arranged for early summer. On the basis of these harmonious proceedings, Warwick was then given powers to treat for a double alliance with France and Burgundy, even though that high subject was not to be settled until the St. Omer Diet brought Warwick and Louis together. Either Edward had himself proposed the commission or the Earl had arranged it as a screen for quite a different enterprise.

For in his private talks with Warwick, Lannoy was undoubtedly exploring the themes which had been broached in Louis' correspondence. Though the Anglo-French agreement was to be ne-

* Which Louis apparently did, for there is some evidence that Cousinot afterward claimed to have been captured by the Lancastrians. See Scofield, I, p. 324, note 1.

gotiated under the sponsorship of Philip the Good, Lannoy was proposing that it contain a hidden treaty which would link Edward and Louis in an offensive alliance against Burgundy. In order to make a gradual approach to this end, Warwick probably hoped to persuade Edward to a stipulation that, just as France must not countenance the enemies and rebels of the Yorkists, England would reciprocally oppose Louis' enemies and rebels; then he would tempt English merchants to break their long-established bonds with Philip by holding out to them prospects of even greater mercantile advantages in France.

When Warwick sounded his sovereign on these preliminary steps, he found Edward willing to listen as always and even to make an immediate move in the direction of better commercial relations with France. The King courteously granted Louis himself a license to ship to England a thousand tuns of wine; he issued letters of protection for four merchant ships of Bordeaux; and he intermitted until Michaelmas the prohibition against the importation of wine of Guienne. Affairs looked so promising that Warwick dispatched a herald to France to inform King Louis that the approaching Diet would undoubtedly satisfy most of his desires.

But the further reaches of the projected Anglo-French agreement Warwick did not open to Edward, nor did he mention a still more delicate and fascinating topic. Lannoy was now turning Louis' hints into more tangible proposals. Would the Earl be interested, Lannoy wondered, in a Continental appanage? Perhaps the very jewel of the Plantagenets, the dukedom of Normandy (provided, of course, that Warwick were willing to reside there in order to help Louis subdue his vassals)? Or would Warwick prefer to carve his reward out of the Flemish-Dutch dominions of the Duke of Burgundy, once that Duke was exterminated with Warwick's aid? The Earl cautiously indicated his approval, in principle, of these suggestions but pointed out that further clarification must wait upon his meeting with Louis. For the moment, these images of the future remained diffuse, a vapor struck by the sun of what-might-be into a rainbow to light Warwick's way to the bosom of the King of France.

The marriage alliance, however, which Lannoy was pushing enthusiastically and which called for much less elasticity of outlook on Edward's part, Warwick certainly discussed with his sovereign. King Louis had made the first known reference to this subject in the summer of '63. In the autumn, George Neville's embassy suggested—according to Louis—that Edward might be willing to wed Louis' daughter; but it is much more likely that the King of France himself broached the idea. In any case, Louis now thought his daughter too young for Edward—she might do for Edward's brother George—and offered him instead the hand of his wife's sister, Bona of Savoy. The proposal must have been discussed at the English court during the winter. With Lannoy to back him up, Warwick now urged Edward to close with this offer. Doubtless he pointed out, with a genial glance at Edward's licentious living, that it was time for the King of England to settle into matrimony and produce an heir; and he expatiated on the political advantages of cementing Anglo-French relations with a matrimonial alliance.

A faint barrier of darkness again divided the two men. Edward did not show himself averse to the proposal; but Warwick could not bring him to an outright agreement. He needed time to consider. The kingdom was not yet rid of Lancastrians. Was Louis' offer, after all, a firm one? The young monarch pleasantly, agilely, evaded Warwick's attempts to pin him down. Besides, Scotland was now eager to treat for a long truce, a matter of first importance, in which Warwick deserved to take the lead after all that he had done to bring the Scots to their senses.

The Earl, convinced that only a little more time and pressure were needed to secure Edward's agreement to the marriage, consented to conduct the negotiations with the Scots, assisted by his two brothers. In the end, however, Warwick needed a few more days to finish his talks with Lannoy.[2] George, the Chancellor, rode off to York without him. King Edward, too, started for the North, on April 28. Three days later, with Warwick's exhortations ringing in his ears, he paused for several hours at Grafton Regis, the home of Earl Rivers and of Rivers' eldest daughter, the widowed Elizabeth Woodville.

When the Earl of Warwick finally began his journey north-ward, he must have been thinking over the unmistakable shift in his relations with Edward. He knew that in his own mind there had fallen between himself and his sovereign the shadow of the King of France, the shadow of his new ambition. But as he assessed Edward's attitude, he was perhaps wondering if the shadow was even deeper than he had supposed. Had it been darkened by another shade, that of Edward's private reservations, Edward's ambitions? True, Edward had less cause than his mentor to be moved by the advantages of an alliance with the King of France. He had not had to deal at first hand with the tedious resurgences of the Lancastrians, and Louis had spent far less charm on him than on the Earl of Warwick. Still, he was ob-viously listening to, if not heeding, the Francophobes at court, and he was taking a lively interest in foreign policy, and in his own marriage.

Riding to join his brothers and the King in Yorkshire, Richard Neville had reason to give some thought to his position in the realm. If, as the Bishop of St. Andrews and others took for granted, he was the "conduiseur du royaume," he actually pos-sessed a multiplicity of authorities but no authority. Great offices gave him control of the North and of the Narrow Seas: he was Warden of the East and West Marches toward Scotland, and King's Lieutenant; as the master of Calais and the Cinq Ports, he controlled a powerful force of ships and seamen. Lesser offices extended his resources of patronage.

When the Parliament of 1461 passed an edict against livery and maintenance, the Warden of the Scots Marches was exempted from the provisions of the bill (in order to augment his army on the borders), and thus the Earl lawfully built up a great body of retainers, sworn to his personal service and wearing for all to see the badge of the Ragged Staff. The seafaring men of Kent, serving in his fleet and in his private vessels and remember-ing his naval victories, likewise gave him their staunch loyalty. The might of these authorities was supported by his vast estates in Wales, the Midlands, the South, and in Yorkshire. The latter were rich not in rents but in men, providing him with a host of warlike tenants and dependents; from the others he drew a princely revenue to swell his official salaries.

His brother George, Bishop of Exeter and Chancellor, and his brother John, Lord Montagu, his second-in-command in the North, his agents like Lord Wenlock and Thomas Kent, royal councilors and ambassadors, held an array of offices which multiplied his power; and the Earl exerted an even more pervasive spell upon the realm, diffused by the force of his general popularity, the tradition of his military prowess, the history of his services to the House of York. He was dowered too by health and vitality and now, at thirty-six, he was in the full ripeness of his prime.

Yet these resources—an almost inextricable intermingling of private strength and delegated authority—formed but the groundwork of his chief power, the influence he wielded over his former protégé, Edward of York. Like the Bishop of St. Andrews, the people of England took it for granted that what Warwick willed, the King was happy to command. When a friend of the Pastons got wind of Oxford's conspiracy early in 1462, he immediately advised Paston that "ye inform my lord of Warwick that he may speak to the King to make provision against this . . ."

Warwick took pains to emphasize and buttress his position. His ambitious brother George accumulated lands and customs concessions. To his brother John he relinquished the wardenship of the East Marches (in 1463) in order to reward and strengthen John's service in the North. He had already married one of his sisters to Thomas, Lord Stanley, a power in Lancashire and Cheshire; another sister became the bride of Edward's dearest friend, William, Lord Hastings (early in 1462). Encompassing the King's two brothers in his web of loyalties, he cultivated the friendship of the elder, George, Duke of Clarence (born 1449), and from late 1461 to 1464 he supervised the knightly education of Richard, Duke of Gloucester (born 1452), who lived in his household at Middleham Castle. On occasion, he could not resist measuring his opulence against the King's. The interment of his father, mother, and brother at Bisham Abbey, in February, 1463, markedly exceeded in splendor of ceremony and magnificence of company the obsequies Edward had performed for his father a month earlier.

Until the spring of 1464, the affable young King had appeared content to let Warwick do the hard work in the North and conduct domestic and foreign policy. He obviously admired and appreciated his cousin Richard. When it was necessary, he could labor diligently in the council chamber and rouse himself to ride watchfully up and down his still uneasy realm, but he was always ready to leave campaigning and negotiating to his mentor. Warwick enjoyed the toils of governing; Edward enjoyed the delicious perquisites of kingship. So it appeared. He did not seem to mind being surrounded by Nevilles and by the servants of their will. Had they not made him King? Did they not zealously shoulder the burdens of creating an orderly society?

In the spring of 1462 and again in the following year, Edward had given out that he was going against the Scots and started north, but each time he had got no farther than the Midlands. When it appeared that the Earl of Warwick would make a successful campaign without him, he lingered at Leicester or Fotheringhay, spent his leisure in coursing and feasting, and then ambled back to London. Nor did he mind letting the world know that he amused himself while Warwick toiled. In a letter to Jean de Lannoy (August 7, 1463), Lord Hastings boasted that "the noble and valiant lord, the Earl of Warwick," with only his Marchmen to help him, had so badly beaten a great army of Scots that King Edward at Fotheringhay was able to enjoy the chase and disport himself without a care in the world.[3]

Yet if Edward Plantagenet—who did not reach his twenty-first birthday until April 28, 1463—cheerfully acquiesced in Richard Neville's leadership, he did not live in Richard Neville's shadow. From the beginning of his reign he had set out to print himself upon his kingdom and to gain hearts for the Yorkist regime. His personality was no less winning than Warwick's, and though he was steeped in Nevilles, he had quietly garnered friends and followers of his own. Life at court was dominated by his three convivial young favorites, Lords Hastings, Herbert, and Humphrey Stafford of Southwick; and Edward was building up a staff of able officers devoted to his person.

Chief of these was one of the most brilliant personalities of the age, John Tiptoft, Earl of Worcester, whose learning and rigor were suggested in his bold features and cold, protruding eyes. He had returned to England from several years of study and pilgrimage abroad just in time to attend Edward's first Parliament in the fall of 1461. His talents were eagerly seized on. He was made a member of the King's Council on November 1; he became Justice of North Wales in the same month; and in December he was appointed Constable of the Tower. A few weeks later, Edward gave him the high office of Constable of England, with enlarged powers that made him the spearhead of the Yorkist drive to crush Lancastrian rebellion. In addition to being the arbiter of chivalry and president of courts-martial, the Constable was now given the authority to try rebels and traitors in arms, on simple inspection of fact. Two months after he assumed the constableship, he succeeded the Earl of Essex (Viscount Bourchier) as Treasurer of England. Yet he also took an active part in military operations, commanding the siege of Dunstanburgh in December of '62 and in the following year leading a fleet against the Scots and French. Resolute and capable, he worked in apparent harmony with the Nevilles, but he was not drawn within Warwick's orbit of allegiance. He was Edward's officer. So, too, was Sir Walter Blount—knighted on the field of Towton, then made Knight of the Bath at Edward's coronation. Though he began his rise as Warwick's treasurer at Calais, he gradually transferred his services and his affection to the King. Lord Grey de Ruthyn—who was shortly to be made Earl of Kent following the death of Warwick's uncle, little Fauconberg—and William FitzAlan, Earl of Arundel, attached themselves to Edward. Men of lesser name but greater capacities, like Sir John Howard, were working smoothly with the Nevilles but looking to the King for their cue.

Edward was also striving to win over former enemies. By temperament as by policy, he was quick to forget an injury and eager to make friends. This clement and statesmanlike object he pursued despite the grumbling of some of his subjects, who felt that the sun should shine only upon good Yorkists, and despite the probable lack of enthusiasm of the Earl of Warwick, who was a more ardent party man than the King himself, perhaps because he had to struggle in the North with the consequences of relapsed allegiance which Edward's mercy induced.*

The chief Lancastrian the King set himself to win was the fiery young Henry, Duke of Somerset. Henry's party feelings had been burned deep by the death of his father at the first battle of St. Albans (1455) and by the severe wounds he himself received in that skirmish. From the stronghold of Guisnes he had battled Warwick in 1459–60. He defeated the Duke of York at Wakefield and led the Lancastrian horde southward to St. Albans; he commanded Queen Margaret's army at Towton; he experienced King Louis' harshness, followed by King Louis' kindness, in the summer and fall of '61; he was a sworn friend of Charles, Count of Charolais; he headed the defense of the Northumberland castles in December, '62, and he had surrendered on the stringent terms of pardon with life only.

He was immediately conducted to the King, at Durham, and vowed to be Edward's liege man. To demonstrate his good faith, he requested a command in Warwick's army, and when the Scots suddenly appeared before Alnwick, he showed himself notably eager to do battle with his old friends. With a retinue of his followers, likewise pardoned, he then accompanied the King to London. Edward not only wooed his friendship out of policy; he felt sympathy and a deep affection for the unfortunate young Duke, and went to elaborate lengths to express his feeling.

Henry of Somerset was apparently of mercurial temperament, and, though he had cause enough at the moment to suffer attacks of depression and guilt, he seems to have been a victim of that darker melancholy which marked many men of this age, particularly on the Continent, where it may have been, in part, a fashionable pose. Olivier de la Marche, the well-known Burgundian chronicler, took for his motto, "Tant a souffert La Marche." When Philip of Burgundy's baby son succumbed, the

* See pp. 109–110.

grief-stricken Duke cried, "Had it pleased God to cut me off at that age, I would have been fortunate indeed!" Charles d'Orléans anticipated Hamlet in his plaint, "Je suis celluy au cueur vestu de noir." Even the much earthier Villon recorded, "Je m'esjouys et n'ay plaisir aucun." *

In England, the popular ballads of the period display this gloom and it pervades the life and the poetry of Edward's new friend, Anthony Woodville, Lord Scales, son of Lord Rivers. In Charles, Count of Charolais, the spirit of the age assumed the form of a hard, sullen, brooding reticence. Richard Neville, Earl of Warwick, and Louis XI were alike in being scarcely touched by it. Their sentience and their vitality had little time to sour. They expended themselves in the pursuit of power, the management of affairs, the exertion of their charm to win men. They worked off their sense of drama by displaying themselves (in different ways) rather than their *sensibilité*. As for Edward the Fourth, his native exuberance protected him from melancholy (until, in later years, he lost his ebullience and his sunny confidence). He was sensitive as well as sensual, however; his gay heart went out to the Duke of Somerset, and he dared put utter trust in young Henry Beaufort in an attempt to secure his happiness as well as his loyalty.

The King made full much of him; in so much that he lodged with the King in his own bed many nights, and sometimes rode a-hunting behind the King, the King having about him not passing six horses at the most, and yet three were of the Duke's men of Somerset. The King loved him well. . . . Edward made a great joust at Westminster, that he [Somerset] should see some manner sport of chivalry after his great labour and heaviness. And with great instance the King made him to take harness upon him, and he rode in the place, but he

---

* These expressions of gloom are perhaps heavier than the zestful declarations of "Renaissance" melancholy—as may be seen, for example, by comparison with a lyric of Lorenzo the Magnificent (who was well advanced in his teens before Charles d'Orléans died):

> Quant e bella giovinezza
> Che si fugge tuttavia!
> Chi vuol esser lieto, sia:
> Di doman non c'e certezza.

would never cope with no man and no man might not cope with him, till the King prayed him to be merry and sent him a token, and then he ran full justly and merrily, and his helm was a sorry hat of straw.

There is a Burgundian strain, a strain that perhaps helps to explain Somerset's friendship with the Count of Charolais; in any case, it provides an interesting intimation of the future, for Edward's court was soon to show itself receptive to Burgundian gestures and Burgundian influences.

The King saw to it that Parliament that spring ('63) restored the Duke to his forfeited titles and estates, made him several gifts of ready money, and bestowed annuities of £220 on his mother and on him. But when Edward moved northward in the summer and the men of Northampton beheld, with horror, their King guarded by Somerset and two hundred of Somerset's followers "well horsed and harnessed"—like "a lamb among wolves"—they rose in wrath and fear, stormed the royal lodgings and would have slain Somerset before Edward's eyes, "but the King with fair speech and great difficulty saved his life for that time, and that was pity . . ." Edward got Somerset safely away to Wales, and as a mark of his undiminished confidence, he dispatched Somerset's men to hold Newcastle, punctually paying their wages. But the King also appreciated the loyal hearts of the citizens, if not their violence, and he "full lovingly gave the commons of Northampton a tun of wine that they should drink and make merry. . . . Some fetched wine in basins, and some in cauldrons and some in bowls and some in pans and some in dishes."

But either the Duke had all along "thought treason under fair cheer and words," or the hatred of the Yorkist commons and covert slurs of Yorkist courtiers had proved unendurable. In early December of '63 he suddenly bolted from Wales for the North, having secretly written to his men in Newcastle to betray the town to him. He was almost caught in Durham, escaping "in his shirt and barefoot," and his followers in Newcastle were forced to flee for their lives. He managed to join King Henry at Bamburgh. Not many months later (May, '64), Warwick's brother John put an end to his violent story at Hexham Field.[4]

If Edward had wasted his kindness on Somerset—which is doubtful, since the King's generosity, contrasted with the Duke's betrayal, must have boosted Yorkist sentiment—there were many others, of lesser rank, whom he completely won over. Among these were the very serviceable members of the Woodville family —Lord Rivers and his eldest son, Anthony Woodville, Lord Scales ("men of very great valor," an Italian envoy noted [5]), and Anthony's four brothers and Anthony's six nubile sisters, including the eldest, the lovely widow, Elizabeth.

But the young King had not only achieved a court coterie, a devoted staff of officers, and a growing train of converted Lancastrians. While Warwick was establishing himself as Lord of the North and building a great fellowship of tenants, dependents, and retainers—the old baronial resource, but on a grander scale and in the King's service—Edward was actively cultivating the good will of the Midlands, East Anglia, and the southern parts of the kingdom, especially London and the Kentish inland towns. This was the most progressive, well-to-do, and enterprising region of England (with the addition of certain districts in the West), already touched by the secular and commercial spirit of the Renaissance; whereas the North was poor, disorderly, and old-fashioned. Edward seemed to have an affinity for townsmen and merchants. Having begun dealing in wool for his own profit, he was bending a sensitive ear to the interest—and prejudices— of English traders; and he treated the people of London with flattering but sincere bonhommie and familiarity. Besides, was he not *their* King? Had they not held their gates against Queen Margaret? Were they not the first to acclaim him? His gay and extravagant court was good for business. He ran up large bills with the victualers guilds, the vintners, the goldsmiths, the mercers and drapers, debts which gave an urgency to the loyalties of the citizens, as his masculine beauty and susceptible eye stimulated the loyalties of the citizens' wives.

Yet, if Richard Neville, Earl of Warwick, was pondering these manifestations of the King's spirit and independence, as he rode into the North in the spring of 1464, he found no reason to doubt his own mastery of the realm. He and Edward had worked wonderfully well together, on his terms. Not until Lannoy's visit, a month ago, had Edward shown any desire to cross Warwick's policy, foreign or domestic. Though he was exhibiting a strange stiffness toward Warwick's plan for amity with France—especially the marriage alliance, about which he was being annoyingly evasive, if genial—Warwick was still confident that he would soon be crossing the Channel to negotiate with Louis. His stalwart brother John's victories at Hedgeley Moor and Hexham * appeared to hasten the day, and the King had never shown himself more sensitive to Neville deserts than on that May morning ten days after the battle of Hexham (May 17), when he bestowed on John, Lord Montagu, in the presence of Warwick and brother George, the princely dignity of Earl of Northumberland.

While Edward and the three great Nevilles were completing their negotiations with the Scots at York (late May, 1464), Warwick confidently pressed his sovereign for full powers to conclude a peace with Louis and to sign the marriage treaty linking Edward and Bona of Savoy. Meanwhile, he sent a letter to the King of France, promising to meet him and the Burgundians at St. Omer by mid-August, and Edward obligingly dispatched the same assurance.[6]

Warwick Herald, just returned from his mission to the French King, had been dazzled by Louis' condescension, and how could Warwick fail to see in these attentions to his man the deep affection for himself cherished by the heir of St. Louis? Not only had the King of France talked to the herald in private—taken him companionably by the arm—but he had led him into the chamber of the Queen's two beauteous sisters, no chaperon being present, so that the herald might intimately behold the future bride of his sovereign, Bona of Savoy, whom he found as lovely as she was warranted; and he reported, too, that Louis was making special efforts to give Warwick a fitting welcome.[7]

Yet, though Edward had so willingly joined his promise to Warwick's and though he was still smiling, still attentive to his mentor's words, he would not commit himself to the treaty and

* See p. 122.

the marriage. He remarked that the three Northumberland castles remained to be taken, an operation that would crown Warwick's great labors in the North; and there was soon to be held a conference with the Scots over breaches of the truce. Finally, as the Earl reiterated his demands, the King pointed out that a matter so important as his marriage should be put before the chief men of the realm.

Warwick consented to accept a compromise which represented, after all, only a few weeks' delay. The Great Council of England—an assemblage of the lords spiritual and temporal—was to be convened toward the end of the summer to discuss reform of the coinage. Warwick agreed to submit his policy to the Council's consideration. Certain that he could secure the lords' approval, he insisted on only one condition. Since he had promised to appear at St. Omer by mid-August, envoys should immediately be sent across the sea to conclude a temporary treaty. These men were to be considered his own representatives as well as royal emissaries—commissioned by the King but furnished by the Earl with a fitting retinue (expenses to be paid by the royal treasury). So it was that in the middle of June, Lord Wenlock and Richard Whetehill left London with a train of almost a hundred men. They were officially empowered to extend the truce with France for a year; they were ordered by Warwick to explain that affairs in the North had unavoidably delayed his arrival but that he would without fail meet Louis in October to consummate their plans.[8]

But while Warwick and his brother John quickly reduced the Northumberland castles to submission and then negotiated breaches of the truce with the Scots (June–July, '64), the King was indulging—the Earl soon learned—in unseemly by-play.[9]* The Bastard of Brittany had slipped across the Channel incognito, ostensibly on pilgrimage to the shrine of St. Thomas à Becket; but he then found his way to King Edward, and he was clearly an emissary of Francis, Duke of Brittany, King Louis' very hostile vassal. Warwick next discovered that Edward was also being kind to a squire of the Count of Charolais—an even more inimical vassal of Louis'—whose appearance at court followed suspiciously on the Bastard's. Warwick, it seems—out of pride or confidence or an impulse of anger—sent posthaste to his friend, the King of France, an unconditional assurance that England would enter into no alliances and have no intelligence with any of his discontented nobles.*

The tale of disguised missions and covert plotting accelerated. Early in August there appeared two men passing themselves off as simple Breton friars. Warwick quickly learned that they were Francis of Brittany's Vice-Chancellor and confessor. While the Earl was chafing to secure his commission and be on his way to France, King Edward openly designated representatives to treat with the Bretons (August 12). Warwick was either not invited to take part or refused. Edward's learned, vigorous Constable, the Earl of Worcester, headed the negotiators. It was the first time since the triumph of the House of York that the Earl of Warwick had not conducted English diplomacy. Not many days later, there was signed a year's truce with Brittany, and William Hatclyf, a royal councilor, sped to the court of Francis for further conversations. This was not all. The treaty carried a stipulation which struck directly at King Louis and therefore at Warwick's policy: England was to supply three thousand archers to Francis of Brittany, if he was attacked by the French King, in return for which aid Francis offered free passage to an English army invading France. Edward now compounded this slight to the Earl of Warwick's wishes by blandly proposing—whether out of calculation or naïveté, Warwick could not be sure—that John Neville take command of these archers! The Earl sent his sovereign a curt, emphatic refusal: he would not allow his brother to leave England on a mission which he himself had had no part in arranging and which he did not consider in the interests of the realm.[10]

But as September arrived, Warwick prepared with undiminished confidence—albeit somewhat grimly and warily perhaps—

---

* Louis let it be known about this time that he possessed Edward's sealed word to this effect. He certainly did not have Edward's word and he may well have invented the whole matter. On the other hand, if he had received Warwick's assurance on the subject, it would be like him to transmute Warwick's word into "King Edward's seal." See Scofield, I, p. 351, note 1.

to attend the assembly of the Great Council at Reading. At this moment, King Edward took special pains to show his appreciation of the Nevilles, as if he acknowledged that the Breton pact was but a prank, a youthful gesture of independence. He conferred on John, the new Earl of Northumberland, an array of estates and authorities in the North, forfeited by the Percys; he gave the ambitious George a lovely chunk of heart's desire by nominating him for the archbishopric of York and authorizing him to take possession of its temporalities pending the Pope's confirmation. To Warwick himself, he presented a much more modest gift, but a thoughtful and pleasant one: a year's license for eight of the Earl's ships to export merchandise to Bordeaux and return with Gascon wine, which might be sold in any port of England.[11]

The Earl of Warwick rode toward Reading, meditating no doubt on Edward's increasing balkiness but quite certain that he was at last to meet the King of France and open up—what new conquest of experience?

VI

Waiting for Warwick

ABOUT the same time that the Earl of Warwick was preparing to attend the Great Council at Reading, there sailed into a small harbor near the port of Gorkum, in Holland, a swift, rakish bark which showed no pennons or markings to denote its owner. The captain went ashore, alone. Walking to Gorkum, he drifted into a tavern, soon fell into talk with the hostess and her customers. Casually he turned the conversation to Gorkum's chief resident, the Count of Charolais. When he learned that the Count was now at his castle, the stranger showed a persistent interest in Charolais' habits; he inquired at what times he went sailing, what other excursions he customarily made in the neighborhood, and how strongly he was escorted.

Accounting for his presence by explaining that he was a merchant-trader, he bade his tavern friends farewell and wandered, like a careless sight-seer, toward the outskirts of the town, where the Count of Charolais' castle was situated.

Here the Count had spent much of his time since Philip the Good, upon recovering from his illness in 1462, had quarreled with him over his treatment of the Croys and temporarily stripped him of privileges and revenues. On his arrival at Gorkum, Charolais had acted in the high style of one of the classic heroes he loved to read about. Summoning all his household around him, including stableboys and scullions, he disclosed to them that he was penniless. He meant no disrespect to his father, whom he revered above all men, in revealing the condition to which he had been reduced; he was only anxious about the welfare of his faithful servitors. He hoped that those who were in funds would remain with him, to await the turn of fortune. Those in want were given free leave to depart, the Count assuring them that if they came back when his prospects improved, they should have their old places and be rewarded for their patience. "Then were heard cries and sobs and with one accord they shouted, 'We all, we all, my Lord, will live and die with thee!' " As it turned out, Charles' courtiers hastened to contribute such sums that "everything went on as usual, and there was never a hen the less in the kitchen."

The stranger showed a surprising interest in the terrain about the castle, its proximity to the sea, its gates and towers. Finally climbing up the outer wall, he surveyed the grounds within and looked often in the direction of the beach. Suddenly he made the unpleasant discovery that he, too, was being surveyed, by a group of townsfolk who had been struck by his odd behavior. By the time he scrambled down the wall, more men had arrived. As the stranger tried to make off, the crowd pressed closer. Nobody laid a hand on him, but the faces were clearly suspicious and unfriendly. Then somebody recognized him and called his name. With that, the pseudo-merchant bolted for a church and sought sanctuary.

The Count of Charolais was immediately notified. He had the ship seized, but the crew had taken alarm and managed to melt away into the countryside. The "merchant" was removed from the church, put in custody, and closely questioned. He refused to admit any criminal purpose, giving muddled and contradictory replies.

But his identity was enough. He was the Bastard of Rubempré, a soldier of fortune ready to sell his sword in any enterprise. He had once belonged to the household of the Count of Charolais. He was known to be now in the service of the Count of Nevers, Charolais' deadly enemy. And the Count of Nevers was the officer and instrument of the King of France.

Inflammatory rumor flew through the Low Countries: Louis XI had tried to kidnap Charles, the heir of Burgundy! Itinerant friars spread the word, denouncing the perfidious King in fiery sermons. Nobles and townsmen alike boiled with excitement and anger. Then a more terrible fear swept the ducal dominions: Philip himself, far dearer than Charolais, was at Hesdin, on the very frontier of Picardy; Louis and Nevers were nearby, and Louis was expected at any moment to visit the Duke—or did he really intend, having captured the son, to swoop upon the father and with this double blow extinguish the independence of the House of Burgundy? Frantic messages were dispatched to Hesdin.

Guilty or innocent, Louis, when he heard the news, was appalled. It came at a wracking moment, when he was anxiously awaiting the long-delayed arrival of the only man, he conceived, who could extricate him from his difficulties, Richard Neville, Earl of Warwick.

King Louis had spent a nervous summer.

Clouds of seignorial wrath were gathering about him. The Count of Charolais was conspiring with Francis, Duke of Brittany, and Francis, Louis knew, was covertly appealing to England for soldiers and offering to aid an invasion. The King's weak and discontented brother Charles was listening to Louis' enemies. And there were others, many others. Even Charolais' father, Philip of Burgundy, was beginning to realize that Louis meant him no good.

In this deepening crisis Louis hung on Warwick's messages and fired off even more messages of his own. Exuding a feverish confidence, he assured everybody at his court that peace would be made . . . Bona would be married to King Edward . . . Warwick would soon be in France. Early in May he rushed up to the Duke of Milan's ambassador, crying that he had received great good news. Warwick was coming to Picardy in June to conclude a treaty—this disclosure interrupted by exclamations of joy and repeated thanks to God. Soon after, the ambassador penetrated the reason for Louis' optimism: peace will be made with England, he noted, because the King will give Normandy to the Earl of Warwick. Meanwhile, Louis' court were singing quite a different tune. King Edward, they thought, did not desire peace with France, and, even if he did, the English people would have none of it.

But Louis was well aware that his plans might come to nothing. This febrile excitement, obscurely related to his frantic religious observances, expressed the nervous excess of a personality tightly, skeptically, secretly concentrated on actualities. These superficial agitations gave release to a mind essentially *sec* and secular, a mind flexible and sinewy with infoliations whose heart no one ever plumbed. Louis' ebullience often drove him to imprudences of word and deed which he afterward took great pains to retrieve. He would say frankly to a man whose good will he had lost by some sally: "I have spoken as they tell me I shouldn't, but it gives me great pleasure, this vice, and I am willing to pay well for it"—this speech followed by handsome amends and rewards.

Through his permanent embassy at the French court—a striking innovation—Francesco Sforza, Duke of Milan, was trying in this season to weave a broader web than Louis' and Warwick's. His ambassador, Malleta, was working to promote papal mediation between France and England which would bring about a peace. Then Louis and Edward would join forces under the Pope's banner for a crusade against the Turk. Edward, it was thought, would be glad to get rid of the bellicose element among his subjects, and Louis had glibly promised the See of Rome ten thousand soldiers for four months, once an Anglo-French treaty was signed.

But the King of France openly despised the Pope for resisting his interference in church affairs and sending him surly envoys. When Alberic Malleta reported that the Holy Father was ill of gout and fever, Louis replied, "Have no fear, Messire Alberic. He won't die, because he's a bad Pope." Then he whipped off his hat and added hastily, "God pardon me!" Louis the Crusader!

Neither Warwick nor his friend the King of France had any interest in papal mediation or expeditions to fight the Turk. And Louis let slip to Malleta that, despite his public protestations of depending on his dear uncle of Burgundy to bring England and France together, he had set all his hopes on the Earl of Warwick. Yet the French wanted no treaty with England, for the lords of the Lilies were well aware that, freed from cross-Channel threats, Louis would sit on their necks harder than ever; and they were quite right in supposing that the English people had no stomach for embracing their ancient adversaries. The proponents of peace in the two realms appeared to be limited to the King of France

and the Earl of Warwick, both of whom reposed their confidence in the power of the Earl.

June came. Louis journeyed eagerly to Dompierre in Picardy,
bringing Bona of Savoy with him, to learn that he had but Wenlock and Whetehill to deal with and that they had powers only
to extend the truce another year. Hiding his disappointment, he
graciously accepted what they had to offer—Warwick's promise
to come in October and the year's truce—and led them to Dompierre to show off Bona, whom he had specially dressed for the
occasion. Promising Wenlock a reward if he helped to bring the
marriage off, he bade farewell to the English envoys with a present of plate. Then there arrived alarms from the coast, where it
was discovered that the Earl of Worcester was furrowing the
Channel with a fleet—certainly not at Warwick's bidding—and
Louis hurried off to look to the defenses of Normandy.

But perhaps Wenlock had brought some private word from
his master. Malleta believed that he could detect a change in
Louis' hopes after his talks with the English. Since Edward's subjects were so hostile to France, another solution was perhaps being explored. There might be concluded a series of truces hiding
a secret treaty of peace. Warwick, as early as his conferences with
Lannoy, may have been counting on this solution if he could
force no better one.

Up and down the roads of France Louis traveled this summer,
trying to ride off his anxieties, to be everywhere and see everything—as he was to travel throughout most of his reign—ignoring
the plaints of his saddle-galled entourage. Malleta, after only a
year with him, was pitifully begging to be recalled because, he
reported, he was so exhausted by endless journeys on horseback
broken by vile lodgings, that he'd had to have made a special
carriage to enable him to keep up with the King of France.

Louis took his whole household with him, so that he was always
at home and always equipped for the business of ruling. Along
the dusty roads he hurried on his *destriers,* accompanied by his
officers and servants and archer guard and followed by a long
line of pack horses and carts carrying his bedding, trunks, food,
furniture, wine cellar. On reaching a town, he avoided if he

could all ceremonies of welcome, lodged humbly, said little, asked much, ignored the festivities in his honor, and left suddenly— usually to the relief of his bourgeois hosts, for Louis' swarm of dogs turned his quarters into a kennel and the droppings of his pet birds ruined the furniture. When he came to a river, he loaded his company and baggage on boats, whatever the weather. If drought had lowered the water level, he had the channel dug out; if the stream was in flood, he commanded bridges to be broken down so that his vessels could pass. In the bitter cold, he had gangs of workmen breaking the ice before his flotilla. He maintained no fixed itinerary, changing direction abruptly to investigate a village or adore a relic. A poor clerk of Évreux, leaving the royal cavalcade to take a message to his Chapter and immediately setting forth with their reply, had to ride for sixty-six days before he caught up with his perequitating sovereign.

As the summer passed, menaces and disappointments thickened around Louis. The Count of Charolais tightened his relations with Francis of Brittany and let it be known that the moment his father was dead, he would levy war on his overlord. Francis, having somehow got wind of Louis' intention to offer Normandy to Warwick, disseminated to all the malcontent dukes and counts the news that their sovereign's real purpose in seeking to placate the English was to gain their aid in crushing his own vassals. Philip of Burgundy, Louis heard, was beginning to fear the marriage of Edward and Bona and was thinking of offering one of his nieces to the King of England.

A machination so ingenious and profitable that Louis could not resist it, further stirred the fears of his nobles and worsened his relations with the Duke of Burgundy. Philip of Bresse, the younger son of the Duke of Savoy, had got control of the dukedom and driven his feeble-witted father and older brother to seek the protection of the King of France. Sending Philip of Bresse a safe-conduct and fervid assurance of good will, Louis persuaded the young man to set foot in France, then promptly had him arrested and cast into the damp vaults of the chateau of Loches, while royal agents took over the government of Savoy. The young Prince being a godson of the Duke of Burgundy, Philip pleaded indignantly for his release, and when Louis refused his demand, he became the more aware of Louis' true feeling for his dear, dear uncle.

The more threatening his predicament became, the louder Louis cried up his certainty of Warwick's coming and the more fervently he sought to exploit the resources of Heaven—flinging himself on his knees, doffing his hat, and praying to the leaden images of saints fastened to its brim. He approached Providence under a curious duality of compulsions. His mind was so bound to earthly stratagems and values that he conceived the noumenal domain as very much like the phenomenal. God, indeed, was too distant, too mighty, and too vague for him to handle; but the army of God's saints did God's work on earth; and just as his own subordinates expected a return for services rendered, so was it clear that the saints, too—who obviously could not take care of everybody—would respond to him who showed the most tangible gratitude. Careful always to expend money only where it would work to his interest, he lavished donations on the heavenly host as a contribution to his own weal and to the prosperity of France.

Each week he had thirty-nine Masses celebrated in his behalf, to which were added fifty special Masses every month; he heard Mass every day; he confessed weekly; he daily isolated himself for a period of pious meditation (but thought nothing of imprisoning Cardinal Balue in an iron cage). Yet this regimen of religious observance was but a frame for his exploitation of heavenly resources. Saint Emerance cured him of a colic? He quickly built a chapel for Saint Emerance. He never cheated on the endless bargains he drove with saints. His letters are peppered with orders to create religious foundations, with references to vows and endowments and gifts and searches for new relics and new saints. He invested in gold chalices, gold pyx-covers, gold hearts, gold lamps, costly tapers. To St. Martin of Tours, one of God's most powerful executive officers, he offered a grill of wrought silver worth 3,000,000 francs.

Yet he meant to get value for his money. He investigated the saints as thoroughly as he watched his own subordinates. His letters abound with commands to inquire into the claims of shrines and miracle-working objects. He demanded that the rival pretensions of holy places, the exact powers of relics, the precise location of a saint's thigh, be minutely weighed and looked into. And he did not hesitate to pray the saints' help for his most scabrous undertakings.

If there was in him any genuine spark of love, of tenderness, if he felt any need of love and tenderness, this feeling—absent in his dealings with his family, his wife, his intimates, his children—showed itself in his perfervid adoration of the Virgin. Certainly She seemed more accessible than God and perhaps more human and realer even than the saints. Perhaps, too, since he loved to jeer coarsely at women,* he felt he must be the more attentive to the Virgin so that She would understand that he did not include Her in his ribald remarks. He particularly venerated Her image at Cléry (to whose intercession he attributed his capture of Dieppe in 1443), but he also honored Her at Tours, Chenusson, Saint-Lô, Embrun, and other places and he engraved Her sacred name upon his arms.

Yet there was a deeper, darker element in his response to the unseen and the eternal. He so zestfully enjoyed his physical powers, he saw the tangible in such decisive outline, that the intangible loomed the more terrible. He feared what was beyond the reach of his arm to manage, the reach of his personality to move, the reach of his intelligence to understand. In his nature there ran a morbid strain—perhaps derived from the madness of his grandfather, Charles VI—a strain related to his misanthropy and nervous excitation, which drove him to superstitious dreads and propitiations. To the men of his century, the unknown was awful, but it was more awful to him than to most. His ardent devotion to relics, pilgrimages, processions, is in part a gesture of fetishism. Beyond God he felt the presence of older and still more unfathomable forces. The dress he wore, the horse he was riding, at

---

* His shrewd, capable sister Yolande he called the least foolish woman in France.

the moment he heard evil news, he would never use again. Receiving in the Forest of Loches the tidings of the death of his new-
born son, he gave orders to lay waste the area.

He was at once too sublunary and too superstitious to experience true faith. His attempts to meet the Unknown fell on either
side of religion: practiced dealings with Providence and a primi-
tive propitiation of Fortune. The popular belief that the day of
Holy Innocents was unlucky,* he observed scrupulously, refusing to do business or receive anyone. Yet when Commynes dared
at a critical moment to ignore this fiat and interrupt his devotions, Louis "abruptly left his 'hours' and told me that it was not
at all necessary to observe the ceremony of the Innocents today."

By early September he was back at Abbeville, waiting with
mounting impatience for Warwick's arrival. An escaped English prisoner of war who had fallen into his hands he clothed in
the arms of England and of the Earl, put ten crowns in his pocket,
and dispatched him across the Channel as a gracious gesture. He
continued to send Warwick messages and he arrayed a special
company of guards to honor Warwick's coming. An usher of the
English court appeared, to say that Warwick would surely come
by the beginning of October. This comparatively humble messenger Louis treated like a lordly ambassador, having the man
eat at his own table and calling him "Monseigneur"—much to
the haughty disgust of Philip of Burgundy.

The days of September slipped away. At last Philip declared
that it did not sort with his honor thus to hang about waiting
for an English Earl. Through his agents Louis soon learned that
Philip had at last discovered the true feelings of the King of
France for the House of Burgundy.

One day when the Duke burst into a violent rage over Louis'
fawning on the English, the veins swelling in his old bony face as
he railed against the attentions Louis had paid to "King Edward's swineherd," his attendants sought to calm him by sug-
gesting that the reports he had heard might not be true. With

* The day of the week on which fell the anniversary of the Holy Innocents—December 28—was considered to be unlucky throughout the following year.

that, Philip furiously thrust a letter at them . . . and the real source of his passion was explained. It was a missive from Louis to Edward. Louis, by way of proving to the King of England that he wanted peace, indicated that it would leave him free to fall upon the Duke of Brittany and the Count of Charolais—"*My son!*" blazed the old Duke. Edward himself must have sent the letter to Philip; it was clear that whatever Warwick thought about France, the English King was happy to show his friendship for Burgundy by serving Louis an evil turn when he could.

At this black moment the King of France learned that the Bastard of Rubempré had been captured, that Charolais was accusing his sovereign of making an attempt to have him kidnapped, that excited rumors were coursing the Low Countries of his designs on Philip as well as Charles.

On Saturday, October 6, Louis sent word to the Duke, still at Hesdin, that he would visit him the following Monday. But Philip abruptly quitted Hesdin on Sunday, and went to Lille, where he embraced his son Charles and restored him to his favor.

Was Louis guilty of the kidnapping charge? There is no knowing. It was a wild, rash scheme, but Louis had been badly harried that summer and, much though he had learned since the first months of his reign, he was still capable of imprudences. He had certainly sought to inflame the ill-feeling between Philip and Charles; he had told Philip that he himself would be happy to take over the task of chastising the young man for his insubordination. Perhaps the success of his enterprise against Philip of Bresse had pushed him into a like machination against Burgundy, whereby, having Charles safely in his custody, he would bewilder and harry the aged, increasingly senile Duke into conceding frontier territories and acknowledgments of Louis' feudal sovereignty.

Perhaps he aimed at a quite different end—the end which he afterward admitted. At first he denied that he had ever heard of the Bastard of Rubempré, protested that he was as innocent as a babe of any plotting, and forbade his subjects so much as to discuss the topic in a tavern. Then he altered his story. He had learned, he said, that Francis of Brittany had perfidiously sent

representatives to treat with the King of England and that these
envoys were instructed to call upon the Count of Charolais on
their return journey. Therefore he had sent the Bastard of Rubempré to waylay them at Gorkum.

In any event, with Philip and Charles united in their suspicions of the King of France and with September having come to
an end without bringing his savior, the Earl of Warwick, Louis
was in low spirits. Still, he stayed on at Abbeville into October,
alone and palely loitering. The Italian ambassador thought that
if Warwick came, he would obtain anything he wanted from the
King of France.

By the tenth of October, however, trickles of news from across
the sea had swelled into a crushing disappointment which even
Louis could no longer gainsay.

Warwick was not coming.

VII

Quarrel

THERE was no such thought in the Earl's head as he arrived in Reading for the meeting of the Great Council.

The offer which the King of France dangled before Warwick had come at a moment when he was especially susceptible to intimations of the future. His great work in the North was accomplished. He was not inclined to sink into the ease of an Elder Statesman, benevolently proffering his advice to Edward at Westminster, or to retire to his estates and quietly enjoy the fame of his labors. He must have fresh tasks of high importance; life must soar on an ever up-turning curve.

Had it not been for King Louis' attentions, he might well have considered emulating the greatness of Harry the Fifth. The rumblings of discontent within the French monarchy and the friendship of Philip of Burgundy for the House of York sketched an opportunity for Warwick to lead an army into France. But the increasing independence of King Edward and the enticing implications of King Louis' proposals had turned his thoughts—if he had ever nursed such thoughts—away from winning another Agincourt. Warwick owned a mighty stretch of lands, but held no territory. Warwick governed a realm, but it was Edward's realm and there was always Edward's acquiescence to secure. No matter what great domains might be carved out of France, they would still be Edward's. King Louis' suggestions, on the other hand, spelled out a dominion for himself, a prerogative that would be all his own to sway. . .

He arrived in Reading, impatient to be off to France with an unlimited commission.

As a prelude to a formal meeting of the Great Council, King Edward convened a group of his intimate advisers, spiritual and temporal. To Warwick he was never more charming. Yet when the question of the treaty with France was raised, the Earl dis-

covered that the councilors closest to Edward were ready to
cast doubt on the sincerity of Louis' intentions. Louis, so they
said, was allegedly hostile to the Duke of Burgundy and the
Count of Charolais, who were good friends of England; it was
reported that Piers de Brézé, Queen Margaret's staunchest supporter, was now high in Louis' favor; and the arrest of Philip
of Bresse while he carried a safe-conduct did not look reassuring.
When Warwick attempted to dispose of these allegations, there
was produced at the council board a deposition by one Pierre
Puissant, who, captured by the garrison of Hammes, had declared
that King Louis was secretly plotting against England and Burgundy. Ridiculing this sort of evidence, Warwick insisted that
Puissant and his deposition be sent to Louis so that the French
King might have the opportunity of refuting the gossip. The
Council heeded Warwick's voice. King Edward said nothing.

He lounged at the head of the table, smiling upon them all. One
of Warwick's friends now brought up the question of matrimony.
All the King's subjects, he pointed out, were eagerly anticipating
their sovereign's marriage. They hoped that he would ally himself
as befitted his high blood and would most benefit his estate.

Yes, Edward heartily agreed, he truly wished to be married. He
went on: "Perchance our choice may not be to the liking of
everyone present." Genially he added, "Nevertheless we will do
as it likes us." He was still smiling.

Whom did he wish to marry? they asked him, thinking that
he was joking, having no doubt that he would approve Warwick's
choice.

Jauntily he told them that he would have to wife Elizabeth
Woodville, the eldest daughter of Lord Rivers.

Silence fell. Warwick did not deign to reply to this absurdity.
At last the Archbishop of Canterbury timidly pursued the subject. No doubt the Lady Elizabeth was virtuous and beautiful,
but she was far beneath him in station. She was not even the
daughter of a Duke or an Earl, though her mother, it was true,
was the Dowager Duchess of Bedford and a sister of the Count of
St. Pol. But such was surely not a wife for him, a Prince who
must marry in his sphere and for politic considerations. . . .

The King listened with affable courtesy, but when the voice faltered into silence, he replied simply that he would have her and none other.

The bewildered councilors besought him to change his mind.

With impervious good temper the King now disclosed that he had already acted on his choice, since it was his alone to make. He had married Elizabeth Woodville.[1]

Elizabeth Woodville! A mother of two sons almost as old as Edward's brothers. A widow of no importance. And a Lancastrian. Her husband had been killed fighting for Queen Margaret at St. Albans. Her brother Anthony had been captured by Warwick after fleeing from Towton Field. And her father . . . her father was that same Lord Rivers whom Warwick and his father and Edward had rated so arrogantly that long-ago evening in Calais. The woman's gross unsuitability for the throne exacerbated the injury Edward had done to Warwick's pride. What was even worse, Warwick learned that Edward had married her months ago—on that May-day excursion to Grafton Regis—and then permitted his friend and mentor to go on giving promises to Louis. The King of his own making had dared make a fool of him before the King of France. The King of England had committed *lèse-majesté* against the ruler of England. . . . It was a bitter awakening. That Edward had dissembled probably more in heedless procrastination than by design did not cushion the blow.

Nevertheless, the Earl of Warwick made an attempt—a first, reflexive effort—at keeping his stride unbroken and encompassing Edward's marriage within the periphery of his pre-eminence. He sufficiently suppressed his rage to sponsor the presentation of the new Queen. With his young friend, the Duke of Clarence, he led Elizabeth Woodville into an assemblage of lords at Reading Abbey that they might pay their formal homage to her. But there was small comfort in this threadbare gesture. Nor was it sufficient consolation that both commons and peers immediately showed their dislike of the match and their scorn of the bride.

An ominous event followed hard after. One of the Queen's sisters was betrothed to Lord Maltravers, heir of the Earl of

Arundel. The Queen had many more eligible sisters, as well as ambitious brothers. Nobody knew better than Warwick how matrimonial alliances could elevate a family into greatness. Was Edward willfully creating in the House of Woodville a rival to challenge the sway of the Nevilles? Would the Woodville connection with the Count of St. Pol, an adherent of the Count of Charolais, push Edward in the direction of Burgundy against France?

These thoughts drove their stings too deep for Warwick to accept with haughty equanimity the graceless action of his sovereign.

Let Edward try in vain to be ingratiating. He could but too well afford to be so! Edward was young, young, while middle-age crept apace upon the Earl, consuming the moments God had allotted him in which to do *faicts grands et dignes d'estre renommés*. There was no strain upon Edward to maintain his right to rule: by grace of God and Warwick he was the King, wore a crown, enjoyed without lifting a finger the bliss of giving commands and receiving homage. The Earl owned only what he had hard earned, the authority of his greatness, and he must labor constantly to keep that authority in force. This daily strain could not bear the shock of Edward's careless stroke. Not in the man did the wound burn nor even in the governor, but in the legend. Warwick's vision of himself which all England, all Western Europe, had accepted and amplified, had been assailed. The lessening of himself in others' eyes the Earl could not endure, whatever the considerations of policy or self-interest.

It was an age in which symbols of all kinds meant much. Just as the unknown world closely swathed the known and irradiated it with endless intimations of God's presence, just as the Church accustomed men to seeing the divine in a thousand symbolical gestures and physical representations, so too did the great men of the earth, nursed in allegory and romance, play as well as live their parts, emulating the devices of Holy Church and consciously accepting the passionate, adventurous, high-stomached role with which lesser creatures endowed them. Needs must Queen Margaret don peasant's costume and seek the Duke of

Burgundy in a cart to express the "tragedie" of fallen greatness; needs must she pour out to the ladies of the Burgundian court the high perils and misfortunes she had endured in England: fearsome robbers taking her and her little son captive—one lad among them touched to the heart and gallantly bearing Queen and Prince to safety on his steed—a Scots archer grudgingly lending her a penny for her offering at Mass. Needs must Philip himself enact King Arthur and Charolais assume the posture of imperial Caesar. England was a grimmer, colder land, the grandiloquent chivalry of Edward III's court long ago extinguished in the greed of the French wars, in the blood of civil strife, and in the rising bourgeois world of ambitious merchants and grasping country gentry.* But if the English were less romantic than the upper classes on the Continent, Warwick was as sensitive to the symbolical representations of his position as Margaret of Anjou or Philip, not only because by temperament he was given to dramatizing himself but also because the very heart of his power —unsupported by crown or authorized prerogative—lay in what others thought of him.

Warwick was not Wolsey, who for all his power was only a minister and must abide any fiat of his master's will. Nor was he the Last of the Barons, eager to rally his fellow peers in order to reduce the King's power. He was more powerful than Wolsey and more ambitious than the barons of old. He must assert—not rights, not principles—but his legend. The modern politician must accept a thousand checks upon his impulses and follow a line hammered out by conflicting masses of opinions and by pressure of competing interests. Warwick had to preserve the illusion of heroic being. Besides, the impact of experience was then felt and acknowledged more nakedly than it is today. The mechanics of modern life, the force exerted on individual conduct by the intricacy and claustrophobic closeness of social existence, have

* The classes who eagerly supported for their own gain Henry VIII's rule and Henry VIII's spoliation of the Church had not suddenly acquired their itch for a place in the sun in his reign or even in his father's. The merchants and gentry of Edward's new monarchy were aiming at what their grandsons would achieve. As early as 1461, an Italian observer was amazed by the outspoken aspirations of the Londoners. See *Cal. Mil. Papers*, I, p. 74.

dulled and lowered man's emotional responses. In the fifteenth century, not only was life more terrible, more exciting, more tightly stretched between violent contrasts of piety and cruelty, luxury and squalor, pleasure and pain, fairyland and hell, but it was enjoyed and suffered with exposed nerves and a desperate acquiescence in God's will. Today men confine themselves to the middle notes of their sensory orchestra; Warwick's age played the wild gamut of strains from piccolo to doublebass. And princes were still more sensitive than ordinary men. They are passionate and high-strung, says Chastellain, "and their affairs are great and perilous." It is not surprising, he concludes, that they often live in hostility.

Casting aside the outward relationship of sovereign and subject, the Earl of Warwick confronted the King in the royal chambers and hurled his ire in Edward Plantagenet's face. He scathingly exposed the political stupidity of the marriage—the just resentment of nobles and commons, the frittering away of the chance for an Anglo-French entente. He assailed the too-forgetful young man with all the debts of blood and risk and toil he owed the House of Neville. He bitterly enlarged upon the indignity which the King of England had dared inflict on the man who had made him and kept him a King.

Then he stalked from Edward's presence. Taking with him a number of discontented nobles, he shortly afterward quitted the new court and rode northward for Middleham Castle.

Years before—no more than three weeks, in fact, after the Battle of Towton (March, 1461)—a shrewd envoy of the Duke of Milan had reported to his master that if the Yorkists could solidly establish their rule, then recriminations would eventually break out between Edward and Warwick, and the House of Lancaster would in the end prove victorious.[2]

A part, at least, of this remarkable prophecy had now come true.

Part Four

Louis' Man

(1464-1468)

Edward IV. Artist unknown.

Elizabeth Woodville, wife of Edward IV. Artist unknown.

Henry VI. Artist unknown.

René, Duke of Anjou and King of Naples and Sicily, father of Margaret of Anjou.

John, Duke of Calabria, brother of Margaret of Anjou.

Philippe de Commynes (Museum of Arras).

Louis XI.

Louis XI by Fouquet.

Philip the Good and Charles the Rash (Museum of Arras).

Antoine, Bastard of Burgundy. Musée Condé, Chantilly.

Warwick's Navy. Note pennant at left with the Bear and "Ragged Staff." (From contemporary manuscript entitled "The Pageants of Richard Beauchamp, Earl of Warwick.")

Middleham Castle from the South.

The Battle of Barnet from a
contemporary miniature. Edward is shown overcoming
Warwick, though actually
Warwick was cut down by
anonymous Yorkists while
fleeing the field.

I

Eyes Across the Channel

BUT BEFORE Warwick rode away from Reading, there was a reconciliation, of sorts.

In the first flame of anger, he hurried off a letter to his friend, King Louis, to report his quarrel with Edward and to announce that he was sending his secretary, Robert Neville, with a message that would please the King of France. The violent language of this letter stimulated Louis to the conclusion that Warwick wanted to make himself King. "He can do so, too," Louis told the Milanese ambassador, adding he meant to help Warwick because the English earl was one of the three best friends he had in the world.

When Warwick's rage had cooled a little, however, he had Lord Wenlock compose a more "official" missive to the Seigneur de Lannoy for transmission to the King of France. Wenlock explained that Edward's marriage, which had surprised everybody, was displeasing to the nobles and to most of Edward's own council as well. Since there was no telling at the moment how Edward felt about treating with France, it was thought that Warwick should not attempt a diplomatic journey till the King's mind was known. Wenlock made plain that the arrest of Philip of Bresse and tales of Louis' machinations against Burgundy had certainly helped to spoil Warwick's game. Nevertheless, Edward's council had no wish to believe evil of the King of France, and they were sending him a man named Pierre Puissant, who had told a number of these tales, so that Louis could discover what was being said about him.[1]

While Warwick was putting himself right with the King of France, at Reading men were working behind the scenes to reconcile Edward and his one-time guide and mentor. Both as an Archbishop and as Chancellor, Warwick's brother George was well placed to use his glib tongue in patching up the quarrel, and he was probably aided by the genial Lord Hastings, Edward's Chamberlain and Warwick's brother-in-law.

Warwick was the party who had to be worked upon; for the King, despite his mighty subject's bitter language, was clearly anxious to show his unabated affection for the Earl and even his good will toward the Earl's friend, the King of France. Edward meant to be independent, but in his optimistic fashion he hoped to keep the friendship of the man who had hewed his path to the throne.

He sought to propitiate the Earl by heartily endorsing the mission of Warwick's secretary, providing him with friendly letters to the King of France and to the Duke of Burgundy; and since he was hastily negotiating a renewal of his mercantile pact with Philip, he went out of his way to request Warwick's agents, Lord Wenlock and Thomas Kent, to "devise a gentle letter in French to our cousin, the French King, for prorogation of the same"— an unusual gesture of respect for Louis' rights, for though the King of France was entitled to pass upon the Duke of Burgundy's treaties, the English had not usually scrupled to indulge such niceties in their dealings with Philip. Finally, to make clear to the realm his undiminished confidence in Warwick, Edward gave the Earl a commission to prorogue until the following January the Parliament scheduled to meet at York in November.[2]

Warwick was sufficiently mollified to accept these tenders of the King's esteem. He ordered Robert Neville to tell King Louis that matters between himself and Edward were by no means settled, but when he rode haughtily away from Reading with his train of followers, he had permitted the quarrel to be surfaced over.

On his way into Yorkshire he spent some time at Warwick Castle. While there, he was asked to intervene in the affairs of nearby Coventry.

Some months before, an involved legal quarrel between two citizens of the town—Will Huet and Will Bedon—had been referred to the King, for in those days the royal council found time to concern itself with all manner of troubles in the realm. Edward himself was present when it was decreed that the two men should accept the arbitration of the Mayor of Coventry. The Mayor decided that Huet must ask Bedon's forgiveness and give him forty shillings toward his costs and expenses, the sum to be increased to ten marks (more than three times as much) if Huet balked at the judgment. Huet, it turned out, used such "seditious unfitting language" about the award that he was committed to prison. After the Mayor reported his action to the Earl of Worcester, the King wrote from Reading on October 4 to give his emphatic approval.

But now Huet's friends came running to Warwick Castle and "laboured unto my lord of Warwick for favour and ease to be had in the said decree at my lord's instance." Warwick was the great lord of the region. His wishes carried enormous weight in Coventry; the loyalty of Coventry might also be of much importance to him. He was in no mood to weigh the latter consideration or to respect the dignity of the Mayor. Jumping at the chance to cross the King's will, he brought such pressure to bear that the city fathers were quickly forced not only to forgive Huet but to make Bedon repay him a third of the ten marks which Huet had finally disgorged. This momentary rush of feeling cost Warwick the hearts of the Coventry magistrates. Should they afterward have to make a choice between the Earl and the King, they would choose the King, if they could.[3]

A little later, the Earl expressed his feelings more privately in the founding of a chantry in the parish church of Olney, Buckinghamshire. A chaplain was endowed to celebrate divine service for the "good estate" of the Earl, his Countess, their forbears, and, as was customary, of the King, but the soul's health of the Queen went unregarded.

Richard Neville had reason to think himself ill-used in the brash and awkward manner with which Edward had made his sally of independence; but he had left himself unarmored against the shock by failing to sense that the times which had given wonderful birth to his greatness might be altering. Yet he soon began to recover from his state of taut nerves and blind resentment. Riding through villages to the accompaniment of caps in the air and cries of "Warwick! Warwick!", feasting devoted knights and squires of the North Country in his great halls of Middleham and

Sheriff Hutton, remembering Edward's eagerness to placate the Nevilles, he was not long in deciding that he was strong enough to proceed as if nothing had happened. After all, perhaps Edward's marriage had been only an irresponsible act of passion.

The news Robert Neville brought him from across the Channel also acted as an anodyne. Warwick's secretary had been warmly received by the Duke of Burgundy as well as by the King of France. Philip had not bothered to say much about Edward, but he had spoken at great length of the Earl of Warwick, expressing his lively regret that Warwick had been unable to cross the sea and affirming that he was still confident of being able to make peace between England and France.

Philip had also contributed to Warwick's plans in quite a different way. Heeding the pleas of his merchants, he had published an edict on October 26 prohibiting the importation of English cloth into his dominions. English opinion was outraged. In January (1465), Parliament vindictively passed a sweeping ordinance against imports from Burgundy. The louder the London merchants inveighed against Philip, the better looked Warwick's chances of bringing about an alliance with France.

As for the King of France, he showed his esteem for the master in the way he treated the man, warming him with a flattering informality that left a glow of gratification on all that Robert Neville had to tell. Neville had delivered to the French court the man who had made malicious remarks about Louis, and the King insisted that Warwick's secretary sit with his council so that he could hear with his own ears the fellow's abject denial of these libels. Louis protested his unalterable friendship for the Earl of Warwick; he made very clear, so far as Warwick's quarrel with Edward was concerned, who *he* thought should be the ruler of England. The King's estate, Neville reported, was never better. His lords had forgotten their disaffection and were flocking to the royal court; even the Duke of Brittany was humbly swearing his loyalty.[4]

This news crowned Warwick's resurgent confidence. By the time the Christmas season of 1464 rolled around, Warwick had convinced himself—weighing the repentance of the King of England and the friendship of the King of France—that he had lost nothing at all. But henceforth he was increasingly concerned with what happened across the Channel, and he followed Louis' fortunes with as much assiduity as he studied the shifting currents of affairs at Westminster.

King Louis, for his part, was avidly interested in the state of Edward's realm. At the beginning of 1465 he sent a member of his household to test the atmosphere of the English court, while a French herald brought private messages to the Earl of Warwick.[5] By this time, Margaret of Anjou, leading a straitened existence with her little court at one of her father's castles in the Duchy of Bar, had got the stirring news of the rift within the cause of York. In regal style she wrote to ask for aid from the King of France, taking care to let him know that she now felt sure of regaining her kingdom whether or not he would help her. With a smile Louis showed the letter to the Milanese ambassador: "Look how haughtily she writes," he remarked.[6] Perhaps this occurrence subtly planted in his mind a bizarre conjunction—Warwick and Queen Margaret. But at the moment he was indulging in quite a different flight of anticipation. "I wanted to be linked with King Edward for his own good and to be his firm friend," he confided to the Duke of Milan's envoy, "but he did not have enough sense to do the right thing, and on this account he has come to a serious parting of the ways with the Earl of Warwick, which could easily be his undoing." [7]

But the fact was, King Louis had slid much closer to the brink of civil strife than King Edward. The picture Warwick's secretary had drawn of Louis' unchallenged might was far from accurate. Even as Robert Neville was sojourning at the court of Burgundy, a French embassy had arrived headed by Louis' Chancellor. He bluntly demanded the release of the Bastard of Rubempré, accused the Count of Charolais of harboring evil suspicions against his sovereign, and declared that Charolais was treacherously conspiring with the Duke of Brittany. Duke Philip adamantly refused to give up the Bastard, but in defending his son he preserved a mild temper despite some hot retorts from the French Chancellor. Charolais' alleged suspicions? Well, if his son was suspicious, he certainly did not inherit that quality from him, for he wasn't in the least given to suspicion. It must come from his mother, who was the most suspicious lady the Duke had ever known! Even when the Chancellor accused the Duke himself of bad faith because he had defaulted on his promise to wait for King Louis at Hesdin the preceding month, the old Prince merely laughed and remarked, "I don't break my word, except to ladies!" Next day, Philip permitted the furious Count to speak in his own defense. Kneeling before his father on a square of velvet, Charolais passionately denied Louis' charges of treason—he'd have spoken much more bitterly still, Commynes thought, except that he was in awe of his father. Finally, Charolais pledged his loyalty to the King, and Duke Philip showed his willing obedience by sending Louis an embassy.[8]

But the Count of Charolais went heatedly to work to develop a plot against the King of France. He was soon thick with the Duke of Brittany, who began angling for English support, and he had no difficulty finding other allies. Like a breeze that suddenly brings to life a drooping stand of corn, a thrill of excitement ran through the feodality of France, long resentful of Louis' moves to geld their feudal powers. At last! At the end of the year King Louis, aware of Brittany's double-dealing, secured from a convocation of the Estates at Tours a condemnation of Duke Francis' perfidy; but that Christmas there had been an important meeting of conspirators in Paris; and most of the great lords who solemnly echoed Louis' commands at Tours had already joined the Duke of Brittany in the plot which the Count of Charolais was engineering. The last obstacle in Charolais' path was removed in February ('65), when his father became so senile that the Count finally took over the government and promptly sent the Croys and other enemies fleeing to the refuge of King Louis. For his remaining two years, Philip spent most of his time in a small chamber playing with bits of glass, sharpening needles, and re-tempering old swords—worn out not by the exercises of Mars but by the wars of Venus. On hearing what Charolais had done to the Croys, he snatched upon a boar-spear and tottered from his room, crying that he would teach his son to lay hands on his old servants. But the ladies of the court quickly surrounded him and soothingly conveyed him to his quarters, like an old bull being herded back to his field by the patient cows among which he had once so ramped and raged. Charles threw himself on his knees before his father and won the feeble old man's forgiveness.[9] By this time he was driving on preparations with the other mighty malcontents of France for an armed rebellion, which was to be glossed with the euphemistic title of the League of the Public Weal.

Early in March, as King Louis left Poitiers to go on a pilgrimage, his malcontent young brother Charles made a bolt from court and joined the Duke of Brittany. A few days later, a cavalry force under Brittany's orders attempted a sudden swoop for the King. Warned of the ambush just in time, Louis found refuge in a castle. Quickly he set about gathering men. Before the end of April, he launched a powerful army against the Duke of Bourbon, who had begun hostilities prematurely.

A month before, the Earl of Warwick had returned to Westminster to find that the Woodville connection with Burgundy was already making itself felt at the English court.* In order to emphasize his Queen's distinguished lineage, Edward had requested Duke Philip to send over her mother's brother, Jacques de Luxembourg, Seigneur de Richebourg, to represent the Duke at Elizabeth's coronation. When the Lancastrian Count of Charolais assumed control of the ducal government, many people probably jumped to the conclusion that Burgundy's friendship with Yorkist England was a thing of the past; but the Count was too deeply involved in the League of the Public Weal to harbor any thoughts of breaking with King Edward. Jacques de Luxembourg arrived in England in March, not only to talk about coronation arrangements but to offer an alliance with Philip's son. He was lavishly entertained by the Woodvilles, received from the King

---

* The Queen's mother was of the House of the Counts of St. Pol, which was politically allied with the Duke of Burgundy. This House was now represented by her two brothers, Louis de Luxembourg, Count of St. Pol, and Jacques de Luxembourg, Seigneur de Richebourg.

more than £100 worth of jewels to deck his person, and was cheerfully dubbed "Lord Jakes" by the Londoners.

But Warwick was welcomed by Edward as if there had been no break in their relationship. As of old, he immediately took charge of current diplomatic affairs. Lord Hastings joined him on a commission to treat with Luxembourg. Warwick had no difficulty finding ways and reasons to frustrate an alliance with the Count of Charolais. Edward amiably accepted this failure, though when he bade Lord Jakes farewell, he told him that if Charolais needed any help—there being no doubt against whom such help might be necessary—he would be glad to furnish it.

Still, the remark could be counted as no more than a friendly gesture in speeding the Queen's uncle on his way, and Warwick found no cause to complain of his treatment by the King. By this time the Earl's eyes were anxiously turned toward France. Fighting was already in progress; the political situation was obscure; the Count of Charolais had not yet made a move. Warwick proposed to cross the Channel in order to explore this tangled skein of affairs and negotiate where it seemed most advantageous. Edward readily agreed. The Earl received a broad commission to treat virtually for what he could get from the Duke of Burgundy, the Count of Charolais, the Duke of Brittany, the King of France. He was again associated with Lord Hastings, but the lesser members of the embassy were Warwick's men. So, after four years during which he had been on the verge, time and again, of heading a diplomatic mission abroad, Warwick finally came in person to negotiate with Continental princes who had learned to regard him as the joint-ruler of England.

It was a disappointing debut. The Duke of Brittany, preparing to march against his sovereign with Louis' young brother, Charles, Duke of Berri, was too busy to bother with diplomacy. The Count of Charolais did send ambassadors, but they were authorized to come no nearer Calais than the Burgundian territory of Boulogne. Warwick and his colleagues rode over from Calais to talk with them. Neither party was eager for a treaty, and Warwick had no difficulty blighting negotiations. After all, if Margaret of Anjou's devoted friend, Piers de Brézé, was leading the van of Louis' army, Margaret's brother, the Duke of Calabria, was gathering forces to support the Count of Charolais, and Edmund Beaufort (calling himself Duke of Somerset since the execution of his brother Henry in '64) was Charolais' friend and companion-in-arms. Early in June Warwick learned that the Burgundian host had crossed the Somme (June 6) and was marching southward to encounter the royal army.

King Louis managed to send one of his councilors to Calais, but nothing came of the mission. Like the Count of Charolais, Louis undoubtedly realized that if he negotiated any sort of agreement with King Edward now, he would be accused of selling out the realm to the English. As for Warwick, committed though he was to Louis' cause, he could have little stomach for signing a treaty with a monarch so precariously situated as the King of France at this moment appeared to be. Yet, determined to do what he could for Louis, he sent him a sworn assurance that he had nothing to fear from England.

Warwick returned to London on July 22, six days after the King of France and the Count of Charolais had fought a bloody, swirling, inconclusive battle. The Earl reached the capital in the nick of time to ride out to Islington and formally arrest Henry the Sixth, who had been captured some days before, skulking helplessly in Lancashire with only a handful of attendants. Richard Neville could not resist the opportunity of staging a little drama to remind the capital who was responsible for the triumph of York. The legs of the drooping, slack-eyed King were bound by leather thongs to his stirrups, and then victor and vanquished made their way through the city to the Tower.

But Warwick experienced little elation this summer. Louis was now in desperate straits. It was rumored that certain English lords were dickering with the League of the Public Weal. Warwick did what he could. He sent word that the Yorkist government was offering no aid or encouragement to the rebellious Princes. To bolster his friend's political position, he persuaded Edward to empower Robert Neville to discuss "divers secret matters" with Louis and then he hurried Neville off to Normandy.[10]

For all King Edward's amiability, Warwick sensed that his fortunes were bound up with those of the King of France.

II

Louis Fights:
The Woodvilles Climb

B Y EARLY summer, King Louis had overrun most of the
territories of the Duke of Bourbon. Bourbon himself was
almost in Louis' grasp when the King learned, at the beginning of July, that the Burgundian host of the Count of Charolais
had driven through Picardy and was sweeping upon Paris. Louis'
brother Charles, Duke of Berri, and the Duke of Brittany were
moving eastward to meet the Burgundians, and an army under
Margaret of Anjou's brother, the Duke of Calabria, was marching
westward from Lorraine.

Breaking off his campaign, Louis hurried northward with most
of his army, hoping to avoid the Burgundians and throw himself
into his capital. When he learned, however, that the Count of
Charolais, balked before Paris, had crossed the Seine and was
blocking his road at Montlhéry, the King decided to fight. But
treachery hung in the air. The commander of his left wing, the
Count du Maine, Margaret of Anjou's uncle, showed little desire
to assail the rebels, and there were others whom the King suspected. What about Margaret of Anjou's staunchest friend, Piers
de Brézé, whom he had treated so harshly on first coming to the
throne?

Louis accused him of secretly favoring the League.

"Oh, they have my seal [i.e., promise]," he told the King cheerfully, "but my body remains here!"

Louis was shrewd enough to sense Brézé's loyalty and gave
him charge of the advance guard and scouts.*

---

* Louis himself, not many years later, confided this story to his intimate
councilor, Philippe de Commynes, who, on this day of battle, was riding by
the side of the Count of Charolais.

With grim humor, Brézé confided to intimates that, whether Louis really wished to fight or not, he himself would place the two armies so close together that a battle could not be avoided. Valiantly he led the opening charge and was among the first to perish—one of the few truly chivalric figures of the age.

Louis had about fourteen thousand men; the Count of Charolais, probably twenty thousand and an artillery train superior to the King's. On July 16, the two armies collided among bright fields of beans and grain on a slope below the castle of Montlhéry. The Count du Maine treacherously turned tail and fled with almost a third of the royal host, hotly pursued by the Count of Charolais. But Louis—the nervous, subtle King who distrusted the chancy issue of battle—stormed to the front of the conflict and heroically rallied his broken ranks. The Bastard of Burgundy charged at the King, missed a mortal thrust and killed Louis' mount. Fighting like "mad, furious dogs," the French finally forced the Burgundians to retreat, many of them fleeing all the way to the Seine. When night fell on this wild, confused battle, Louis was stoutly holding his position, deprived by du Maine's betrayal of a decisive victory at great odds. The Count of Charolais, slightly wounded in a fierce melee, drew his broken forces together within the shelter of his "wagon-laager" and camped on the field; but the King, fearful of further betrayals, led his army through the night to Corbeil and so, in a few days, to Paris. Then he rode off to Normandy to strengthen the garrisons of key strongholds, gather men and supplies, and meet with Warwick's envoy.

Meanwhile, the morning after the battle of Montlhéry, when Charolais learned that the King of France had retired from the field, he suddenly perceived that he could claim a victory. Then it flooded through his passionate being, never to recede—the delicious sense that he was a master of warfare, a modern Caesar. This seductive vision would eventually lead him, through disastrous defeats, to snow-covered fields outside the town of Nancy, where a Swiss halberd would smash his face into a bloody ruin and wolves would gnaw his despoiled and naked corpse.

When Louis returned to his capital toward the end of August

with several thousand well-armed Normans and hundreds of carts of wheat, he found the banners of the Dukes and Counts of the League waving before the walls of Paris in a great semicircle.

The leaguer of the lords made an impressive sight, but their supplies were beginning to run low, few of the men slept under tents, and most had worn through their shoes. They suffered severely in the unusual heat of this summer—it was so hot that, amidst all his troubles, Louis begged the Duke of Milan to send him enough cool Florentine silk to make two pairs of hose. Francesco Sforza was loyally sending him more than that: Sforza's son had crossed the mountains with a stout army, set up head-quarters at Lyon, and was beginning to attack the lands of the Duke of Bourbon. In the daily skirmishing before the walls of Paris, the royalists, often led by the King himself, got the better of their adversaries, and Louis' cannon broke up rebel attempts to storm one or another of the gates.

But Louis' plight was desperate. Some of his officers, along with certain Parisians, were negotiating with the rebels behind his back. His soldiers were grumbling for pay. There were deser-tions to the banners of the League. The Princes talked of sum-moning the Estates and haling Louis for judgment before this body—a fate which would write a quick finis to his reign and life and put his brother Charles on the throne as a puppet to do the anarchic wills of the magnates.

Louis talked of taking refuge with Sforza's son. A wild scheme coursed through his mind, that he might pursuade his rebels to call off their war with him and attack the English, who, he was sure, would do them all in. Yet, despite ravaging suspicions and attacks of nervous despair, he tenaciously hung on, waiting for quarrels and hunger to ruin his enemies. Then, with the game in his hands, he was again undone by treachery.

By the beginning of September the Princes of the League were reduced to parleying with the King, and a series of short truces were taken while negotiations went on. The rebel terms were astronomical—every Duke and Count had ready his list of offices, money, or territory that he meant to get his hands on. Louis' brother Charles demanded no less than a third of the realm;

and the Duke of Calabria had to be outfitted with an army to conquer Naples (ruled by King Ferrand, the ally of Louis' loyal friend, the Duke of Milan). The King refused to consider this wholesale pillage of his prerogative and his treasure. Vigorously he set to work with all his arts and wiles to sow discord among his enemies. The stratagem showed signs of succeeding. As September waned, the collection of feudal egotists outside the walls of Paris were bickering among themselves while their armies grew daily more ragged and surly.

But on September 23, a royal officer delivered Pontoise to the Bretons. The Dukes of Bourbon and Brittany sent their men swarming into Normandy, and in a few days Rouen was treacherously surrendered.

With Normandy gone, the King had no choice but to treat. It looked as though the French crown were to become as feeble as in the days of the tenth-century Capets. In attempting to break the power of the nobles and give France a strong central government, Louis had moved too far, too fast, and too exuberantly. The lords had the fox in a trap.

But Louis was never greater than when the water was up to his neck—as he himself said of his friend, the Duke of Milan. He was instantly all geniality in his negotiations. Confident of his powers of personal cajolery, he concentrated on charming the Count of Charolais—remarking wryly to the Milanese ambassador that since his brother Charles of Berri had become a good Breton, he for his part was going to make himself a good Burgundian! The Milanese ambassador feared that the King "will lose so many feathers he will be incapable of flying"—but the young Italian had not sounded the bottom of Louis' powers.

Finally, the King arranged an interview with Charles of Charolais, casting himself in the role of a humble suppliant. One morning Louis had himself rowed up the Seine to Conflans. He found the Burgundian chivalry drawn up on the river bank in the full panoply of martial pride. Besides the oarsmen, there were only four or five men with Louis in the boat. The King was dressed, as usual, in a cheap, haphazard costume that was anything but royal. The little craft drew in to the bank where the

Counts of Charolais and St. Pol waited to receive their sovereign. Louis was thinking of the indiscretion he had committed the previous November, when he had sent his Chancellor to the court of Burgundy with an arrogant declaration that the Count of Charolais was conspiring with the Duke of Brittany. The Count had restrained himself in denying the charge, but as the French delegation was departing, he plucked the Archbishop of Narbonne by the sleeve and hissed in his ear, "Recommend me very humbly to the good grace of the King, and tell him that he's given me a fine dressing down here by his Chancellor but that before a year has passed he'll repent it."

Louis was remembering these words as he gazed at the ranks of armed men and the stiff figures of Charolais and St. Pol.

"My brother," he called to Charolais (whose first wife had been Louis' sister), "do you guarantee my safety?"

"My lord, yes," Charolais replied. "Yes," echoed the Count of St. Pol and the other nobles.

The King stepped ashore. Charolais and St. Pol knelt in punctilious courtesy. Louis graciously raised them up. The lips beneath the long ominous nose were smiling now and the hooded eyes twinkling. "My brother," he began affably to Charolais, "I know that you are a gentleman and of the House of France."

"How so, my lord?" Charolais asked, grim and suspicious.

"For this reason. When I sent my ambassador to Lille last November and this fool spoke so eloquently to you, you sent me word by the Archbishop of Narbonne that I would repent the words that the Chancellor had said against you, before the end of a year." Louis laughed, shook his head ruefully. "You have kept your promise, and in much less than a year's time!" Smiling a sunny smile, he added, "And with such people do I like to deal, who keep their promises."

In spite of themselves, Charolais and St. Pol melted, laughed . . .

By making himself a good Burgundian and caressing the Duke of Bourbon, Louis soon brought Charolais and the Duke to see that the demands of many of the lords were clearly exorbitant. In October Louis signed treaties that put an end to the League of the Public Weal. The Count of Charolais received the Somme

towns, without repayment of the 400,000 crowns they had cost
Louis. His friend, the Count of St. Pol, was made Constable of
France. Young Charles of Berri was given the dukedom of Normandy to compensate him for the bad luck of having been
born later than Louis. Most of the other lords received titbits
of one kind or another. The Duke of Calabria got little more
than empty promises for his enterprise of conquering Naples. His
sister, Margaret of Anjou, descended on Paris in an attempt to
persuade the triumphant lords to back the cause of Lancaster,
but though she declared that the quarrel between Warwick and
Edward would ensure her success, Louis received her coldly and
the feodality of France was busy reckoning its gains.[1*]

These grants and privileges soon turned to ashes. The lords
had let the genie out of the jar, and they would never get him
in again. Charolais had fastened the Count of St. Pol on Louis'
back, but it was not long before St. Pol had been converted into
Louis' friend and was zestfully working against Burgundy. By
the time that inseparable pair, the Dukes of Berri and Brittany,
left Paris, they were already quarreling about Normandy. Instantly Louis seized their division as an excuse to launch his
forces on the province; most of the dukedom was soon in his
hands, and early in 1466 Charles was forced to take refuge at
the court of Brittany. As for the Count of Charolais, in less than
a year he and Francis of Brittany were trying vainly to form
another League against the advancing power of King Louis.

By the end of 1465, the Earl of Warwick had received word
that his friend, the King of France, had fully recovered himself
and was eager to push on negotiations with England, to their
mutual profit. This piece of good news closed what appeared on
the surface to be a very satisfactory year. Warwick had kept his
pre-eminence in the public eye; Edward had affably accepted his
conduct of foreign affairs; his brother George was now Archbishop of York as well as Chancellor. At Newcastle in December,
the three mighty Nevilles, in exclusive charge of negotiations with
the Scots, had concluded an agreement to prolong the truce
between England and Scotland until the last day of October,
1519. Taking his ease this winter season in the great hall of

Middleham Castle, could Warwick not conclude that he had successfully reasserted his dominance of the realm?

On the contrary, it had been an exasperating, an ominous year. The final crushing of Lancastrian resistance in the North had deprived him of his military leadership. The War of the Public Weal had prevented him from exerting his power as a statesman. He had lost his vocation, his means of keeping bright the Warwick legend, at the same time that King Edward was every day making it clearer that his marriage to Elizabeth Woodville was more than a heedless act of passion.

The Woodville brood were reaching for the high places of the realm; the court had become a silken nest of Lord Rivers' offspring. The Queen's coronation, which Warwick had avoided by his diplomatic journey in May, had been notably more splendid than Edward's own. The list of those who were made Knights of the Bath on this occasion numbered two of the Queen's brothers and several Woodville friends and connections but no conspicuous adherents of the Nevilles. Lord Grey de Ruthyn, Elizabeth's cousin by marriage, was given the earldom of Kent, which had been held by Warwick's uncle, little Fauconberg (deceased without issue); and Sir Walter Blount, once Warwick's devoted officer but now the King's man, had become Treasurer of England and been made Lord Mountjoy. The Queen herself was given money, lands, an elaborate London establishment, and the custody of the most valuable royal ward in the realm, the young Duke of Buckingham. Sir John Woodville got himself a marriage prize—scandalously mercenary even for that day—by wedding the Dowager Duchess of Norfolk, who was old enough to be his grandmother, but very rich.

The Woodville connection with the Count of St. Pol was already giving the court a Burgundian coloring of chivalric flourishes, which augured that the Woodvilles would be pushing for still more important ties with Burgundy. Not only had Jacques de Luxembourg headed a delegation of Burgundians at the coronation, but the Queen's eldest brother Anthony, Lord Scales, who was attracting all eyes in the tiltyard, had ceremoniously challenged the Grand Bastard of Burgundy to a joust.

Warwick felt Edward grow colder to his greatness, felt his power depressed by the Woodvilles' soaring. He had deluded himself in supposing that he could continue to act as if nothing had happened. Bitterly he put all such comforting illusions behind him. The Woodville marriage had signified Edward's declaration of independence, which for Warwick meant a declaration of war. He would have to fight to regain what he had lost, to demonstrate that his dominance in the realm rested on more than Edward's good will. His hopes of what his good friend King Louis might do for him and the injury Edward had visited on his pride in flouting the French marriage both pushed him in the same direction—he would publicly prove his power and reestablish his mentorship by forcing Edward, one way or another, to make an alliance with France.

Early in January, 1466, the Earl of Warwick surreptitiously sent his herald to King Louis with a very secret message: Although there is open war between France and England—the herald confided to the French King—my master says that you may confidently push on with your reconquest of Normandy and with reducing your realm to order, for in this uncertain time England will attempt no offensive against France or make any kind of aggressive move. This, concluded the herald, my master certifies on his honor.[2]

III

Burgundy or France?

1466—Warwick's life apparently followed the same pattern as that of other years. Out of the North he came, to stride through the Woodville-encumbered halls of Westminster, to conduct the King's foreign policy—once again crossing the narrow seas—and then in the autumn to retire into his northern fastnesses, the international statesman become the hardy Marcher lord. But underneath the pattern there was increasing strain and bitterness; the split with Edward widened, its edges showing sharp and jagged. In the little western enclave—France-Burgundy-England—within an enormous world, most of it a dark unknown stretching westward and southward and eastward from the edges of Europe, tensions were tightening between the ambitious, flamboyant, aggressive princes struggling for mastery, King Louis and Duke Charles and Edward of York and Warwick.

The Earl of Warwick came to Westminster early this year, not many days after he had secretly dispatched to the King of France a message which, by any terms, was treasonable correspondence. But not in Warwick's view. He was an independent power and he had shifted his alliance, privately as prudence at the moment dictated. "Potenti principe" King Louis gratifyingly called him in diplomatic documents—mighty Prince.[1]

He was gracious to the Woodvilles, so gracious that a learned young cleric, fast rising in Edward's service, believed that he had quite accepted them into his scheme of things. The birth of Queen Elizabeth's first child, a daughter, in February, was what brought him to Westminster. Richard Neville stood sponsor at the baptismal font, along with the baby's two grandmothers, and George Neville performed the ceremony. At the splendid entertainment which celebrated the "churching" of the Queen, the Earl of Warwick represented the King (by tradition, barred from the feast). He shared his table with a visiting Bohemian nobleman, and before the banquet was over, he conducted his guest to an ornate side-chamber in order that the Bohemian might not miss an impressive sight. In haughty grandeur, sitting on a golden chair, the Queen dined alone at table, her mother and her ladies all kneeling in silence before her while she ate without deigning to speak a word to anyone. Was there a wry smile on Warwick's face? The German in the visiting party who recorded the scene does not say, but he was struck by the arrogance of the King's beautiful consort.[2]

Warwick could not resist indulging himself in emulative ostentation. After the King spread a banquet offering a choice of fifty courses to the visiting Bohemians, the Earl swathed the hall of his town house in rich hangings and set sixty courses before them. Shortly before he came south, George Neville's enthronization as Archbishop of York had given the Nevilles an opportunity for an entertainment which was to become the most famous banquet of fifteenth-century England. Warwick himself acted as Steward for the occasion; brother John, the Earl of Northumberland, as Treasurer; Lord Hastings, their brother-in-law and Edward's Chamberlain, as Comptroller. A huge assembly of the great ranged themselves about the banquet boards. Though the Duke of Clarence, who was becoming a close friend of the Earl's, was not present, Richard, Duke of Gloucester (now in his fourteenth year), was seated with Warwick's two lovely daughters and his Countess. There was drink by the tun. More than half a hundred cooks prepared thousands of sheep and cattle, hundreds of swans and egrets and other delicate birds, thirteen thousand sweet confections, and an array of those artful sculptures in pastry called "subtleties." But there was nothing subtle about the banquet itself. If, by Burgundian standards, the feast was somewhat barbaric—it was held, after all, at Cawood Castle in the rude North—it was a lively reminder of the undiminished puissance of the House of Neville.[3]

Spring brought round the season of diplomacy. This year, the Count of Charolais made the first move. The acid disillusion of beholding King Louis' swift and menacing rebound from his defeat by the League leached away enough layers of Charles' sentimental Lancastrianism to permit him to dispatch across the Channel a hint that the future Duke of Burgundy might be willing to marry Edward's sister Margaret.

Once again Warwick set out with Lord Hastings for Calais to treat with France and Burgundy. He was commissioned to negotiate with Charles over the usual subjects, the Burgundian edict against English cloth, and truce, and intercourse of merchandise; but there were also two marital propositions on the agenda: the marriage Charles had suggested between himself and Margaret of York, which Warwick had already countered by insisting that King Louis, too, was to be given an opportunity of offering for her hand, and a marriage of Charolais' heiress, Mary, to the King's brother George, Duke of Clarence, for whom Warwick had begun to develop quite different plans—as Edward was aware.

On April 15, Warwick and his party rode from Calais to Boulogne to deal directly with the Count of Charolais. It was apparently the first meeting of the two men.

Warwick found himself in the presence of a man who was neither so tall nor so straight-backed as his father Philip, with a face that was rounder than Philip's and crowned by a shock of thick, black hair, though he had his father's large red mouth and straight nose. His eyes were remarkably clear and bright (perhaps because he drank but little wine). He had a powerful torso with thick-set shoulders that hunched forward in a muscular stoop—the body of a man hardened to physical toils and accustomed to wearing steel. A violent temper and a strong will to be reasonable were continually at war within him. He radiated suppressed passion, a rigorous earnestness. He never stopped working: night and day he was in council. The chivalric Chastellain was rather shocked by this pedestrian attention to business, which did not, he thought, befit such a prince.

This was an attitude of the past. Probably never before in medieval history had there been three men of power who, in mortal rivalry, drove on their affairs so dynamically as Louis, Charles, and Richard Neville. Their concentration on day-to-day problems of government, their enjoyment of business for its own earthly sake, reveal the workings of that secular spirit, that idea of life-as-job which would begin to infiltrate Western Europe less than a century after their deaths.

Charles of Burgundy and Richard Neville were too self-willed to own much sense of humor, and probably neither of them realized that, in some ways, their situations were much alike. Certainly the western world had never before beheld such a pair. Each burned to pluck down his overlord and to taste the bliss of absolute rule; and each was seeking the aid of a foreign monarch to secure his heart's desire. Warwick saw a tough, haughty prince whose bright gaze made no attempt to conceal his dislike; a prince, enviable in his independence, who was seeking to queer Warwick's diplomatic game by allying himself with King Edward at King Louis' expense. Charles of Charolais saw a proud English earl, enviable in his knightly fame, who put on all the airs of a prince and who was working hand-in-glove with King Louis to ruin the House of Burgundy.

At first sight the two men hated each other . . . politically, viscerally.

Surrounded by their splendid trains, furred and jeweled in the ostentation of their pride, they greeted each other with hauteur. Their talk soon became heated by lowering looks and sharp retorts. They came to quarrelsome exchanges. When Warwick rode back to Calais three days later, negotiations had been shattered by their enmity.[4]

But the ambassadors of the King of France came riding into Calais with offers that showed Louis' eagerness to put high cards in Warwick's hand. In late May, Warwick signed an engagement with the French that sent him back to England in confident spirits. A truce by land and sea was to endure until March of 1468, with a peace conference scheduled for the coming October. Louis promised that during the truce he would give no aid to the Lancastrians, and the King of England was to give none to the Count of Charolais or Francis of Brittany. Louis also had enticing suggestions for further negotiation—that he pay Edward 40,000 gold crowns a year (about £8,000) during the life of whatever final agreement they reached and provide a match for Margaret of York with an appropriate Continental prince of his choosing, Louis arranging the marriage at his own cost and furnishing the dowry.

Warwick found Edward perfectly willing to ratify the truce, and the King duly promised to consider Louis' proposals for the agenda of the October conference.

Yet, the year was already going sour, and would go sourer.

The advance of the hungry Woodvilles had been accelerated. One after another, four more of the Queen's sisters were betrothed to the principal young magnates of the realm. The Queen even dared, by bribing the Duchess of Exeter with 4,000 marks, to snatch the Exeter heiress from Warwick's nephew George, son of John Neville, and affiance the girl to the elder son of her first marriage, Sir Thomas Grey. In the spring, the Queen's father had become Treasurer of England, and on Whit Sunday, Edward created him Earl Rivers. The appointment to the treasurership of this handsome, pushing squire's son—prototype of the "new men" in Henry VIII's reign—displeased the nobles, and his elevation to an earldom displeased the nobles and the commons too (who were no less snobbish than their betters); but the unpopularity of the Queen's kindred was small comfort to the Earl of Warwick, reading Edward's intention to use the House of Woodville as shears to clip the wings of the Nevilles.

And as the summer passed, the King began to indulge in some diplomacy of his own. Though he had promised not to support Louis' malcontent vassals, he welcomed word from Brittany that Duke Francis and Louis' brother Charles both wanted to sign treaties with him and promptly dispatched safe-conducts for their ambassadors—this only five weeks after he had ratified the truce with France. Not many days later he sent off two of his councilors to Castile to conclude an accord obviously aimed at the French King. When Warwick reminded him of the October conference, he showed no intention of accrediting envoys to meet with Louis' representatives.

But Richard Neville, too, was playing a double game. He had begun actively to seek allies in England. Edward's sharpened aggressiveness may have resulted partly from the intense interest the Earl was taking in the royal family.

George, Duke of Clarence, now seventeen, was a handsome, loquacious, spoiled youth, fretfully ambitious—like many another King's brother, including Louis'—but weak of will and shy of talents. Born the son but not the heir of York, he could not find, in all the lands and honors King Edward generously heaped upon him, the means of enduring this galling distinction. He was still heir-male to the throne, but only so long as Elizabeth Woodville, of a remarkably fertile family, continued to produce daughters. Even before his royal brother's marriage, he had been discontented with his lot; Edward, easily reading Clarence's shallow character, did not attempt to conceal his preference for his loyal youngest brother, Richard, Duke of Gloucester. The arrival of the Woodvilles exacerbated Clarence's discontents. Sulking and fuming at court, he retorted their upstart pretensions with petulant arrogance.

Years before, the Earl of Warwick had taken pains, as became a prudent statesman, to cultivate the friendship of the Duke of Clarence. The radiance of personality that all the world acknowledged did not fail to make its impress upon the willful young Duke, who, feeling himself unappreciated by his elder brother, hastened to warm himself in the friendship of the mighty Earl. Now, Warwick found it easy to draw tighter the silken cords, in intimating that Clarence's wrongs would be fully recompensed when Warwick had ousted the Woodville caterpillars of the commonwealth.[5]*

Warwick also held a claim on the affections of Richard of Gloucester. Whereas Clarence was abounding in health and in surface charm, Richard, three years younger, was frail and undersized and solemn. This apparently unlikely lad, whose dominant passion was his devotion to King Edward and who fiercely willed himself to become strong in order to do his brother service, was graciously accepted into Warwick's household at Middleham Castle, at the age of twelve, as an apprentice in knightly conduct. Here Richard learned the use of weapons and the code of knightly behavior; practiced polite conversation and music-making with the Earl's wife and two young daughters; and admired the prowess of the Earl of Warwick, shedding from his cloak as he strode into the great hall of Middleham the aura of his triumphs over the Lancastrians. In the three years Richard spent in Warwick's household he had become devoted to his Neville cousins and the life of the North. Translated from this happy period of training on the hardy moors to the chambers of Westminster palace and the terraces of Greenwich, Richard could not feel at home among the crowding Woodvilles and their ornate, cold civilities.

In the summer of 1466, as this earnest lad and his unstable brother were being shouldered by the ubiquitous kindred of the Queen in their royal brother's halls and coldly eyed by Elizabeth Woodville as the rivals of her family for her husband's favors, the Earl of Warwick treated them to all his charm. He sketched for the young princes the picture of an England happily rid of the Woodvilles in which the three scions of York would live happily ever after with their three Neville cousins, as Providence had obviously intended for the weal of the realm. To the impressionable Duke of Clarence, Warwick held out a more glittering inducement—the hand of his lovely elder daughter Isabel, whose dowry would stretch to half the great estates of her mother's Beauchamp and Despenser heritage. Apparently Warwick also dangled a fine marriage before Richard, though it is not clear whether he proposed his younger daughter Anne or held out the prospect of a Continental match, to be arranged with the help of Warwick's friend, the King of France.

A tale about Warwick's tampering with the two lads was soon circulating abroad. On one occasion, the story ran, the Earl lured Edward's brothers to a secret meeting in order to draw them farther into his net of intrigue and lay plans for Clarence's marriage to Isabel. When the King discovered what was going on, he dispatched men of his household to fetch the pair back to court. As soon as they returned, he commanded them to appear before him.

Why had they slipped away from the royal presence without permission? he demanded. Who had advised them to do this?

It was their own idea, they replied.

Abruptly Edward inquired if either of them had entered into an undertaking of marriage with one of Warwick's daughters. They protested that they had not, but the King had penetrated the truth, and he gave them a stiff lecture on the duty they owed him to seek no marriage alliances without his permission.

George of Clarence dared to argue. Why should he not affiance himself to Warwick's daughter? It was an excellent match.

In a burst of anger Edward swore that he would punish his brothers rigorously if they disobeyed him. Then he ordered them into another chamber, where four of his household knights stood guard over them for a time, in order to give them a taste of what was in store if they ventured to ignore his command.[6]

Distorted tales of what was happening in England constantly circulated on the Continent in these years; but this much of the story is probably true:

Edward soon discovered Clarence's intention of marrying Isabel and told him emphatically that he was to put the match out of his mind. The prohibition served only to drive Clarence and Warwick into deeper secrecy. Richard of Gloucester, however, drew away from them. He would have nothing more to do with their plans when he realized that they meant to enforce their wills upon the King by any means they could find.

George Neville, Chancellor and Archbishop, had happily jumped into Warwick's contest with the King and was now intriguing at the papal court for Clarence and Isabel's marriage dispensation, required since they were cousins. With the encouragement of his brother he was also working, without Edward's knowledge, to secure a Cardinal's Hat. George had entered the Church to seek an eminent place in the world. He was a precocious lad; he belonged to the most powerful family in the realm; he shot into high position like a rocket. Scarcely in his twenties, he was made Chancellor of the University of Oxford, and when the Yorkists came to power in 1455 after the first battle of St. Albans, he was able to pluck the bishopric of Exeter from the hands of Master John Hals, who had already been provided to the See by the Pope. Accumulating benefices, he pushed the

King's clerk, William Scrop, out of the wardenship of St. Leonard's Hospital, York. Before he was thirty, he became Chancellor of England.

He was a thorough worldling, clever and cultured, if not erudite. He corresponded learnedly with professors; he collected manuscripts; he employed a Greek scribe to copy out classical masterpieces for his library. Even Chastellain, accustomed to the polish of Burgundian etiquette, was impressed by George Neville's stately bearing and elegance of language. "Moult reverent et facondieux [eloquent]," Chastellain found him, adding that he was a "bel et modeste prelat," which reveals how George's ready gift of acting and supple personality could deceive even a sophisticated observer. As he left the court of Burgundy in 1463, he could not resist a vivid gesture—if Duke Philip would do him the honor to receive him as a fellow-crusader, he would serve him at his own cost for the whole journey with three hundred soldiers! George Neville, in short, was ambitious, exuberant, slippery as mercury, fond of secret courses; but the test of action would show him to be more willful than strong-willed, and inclined to be timid in a crisis.[7]

John Neville, Earl of Northumberland, was a much less satisfactory ally. Warwick's two brothers were rather like the halves of his own character. Whereas George possessed the taste for splendid experience and the flair for drama, John exemplified Warwick's endurance and will-to-work. He was a man of plain nature, a tough and valiant soldier. The "pack horse" of Warwick's campaigns in the North, he had served his brother devotedly. Unfortunately, he was also doggedly loyal to King Edward and was averse to intrigue. No matter what the Earl said about the Woodvilles, he could not shake John's allegiance to his sovereign.

With the nobility as a whole the Earl was on very good terms. Civil war and attainders had reduced the number of peers to fewer than fifty, of whom a goodly share were closely connected with the Nevilles and most of the rest had grown accustomed to Warwick's leadership. The rise of the Woodvilles tightened his hold on the lords' affections. Many were affronted by the

King's marriage and resented the favors showered on the Queen's kindred. Warwick played upon their displeasure, working to isolate Edward from his nobility while appearing to seek no more than the deflation of the Woodvilles. He secured a valuable ally in Thomas, Lord Stanley, a shifty, ambitious baron wielding great influence in Cheshire and Lancashire, who was soon to become his brother-in-law. He was likewise cultivating two peers with pronounced Lancastrian leanings, the Earls of Oxford and Shrewsbury. Though the strains of the past year had forced him into open dislike of some of Edward's court favorites, especially Lord Herbert, who had married his heir to a sister of the Queen, Warwick was still hoping to win over his brother-in-law Lord Hastings, who was the King's Chamberlain and boon companion but strove to be on good terms with everybody.

Among the commons Warwick could count on an immense popularity. He had fired their imaginations and he took pains to court their applause. He never outgrew his pleasure in the huzzahs of the lowliest villagers, and perhaps he sensed that ordinary folk were the true custodians of the Warwick legend. At his London inn there might be as many as six oxen roasted for a breakfast; anyone who was acquainted with a member of his household was permitted to carry away as much meat from the Earl's kitchens as he could thrust upon a long dagger.[8] The Earl was especially popular with the lower classes of London, the seamen of Kent, the yeomen of the North, and the humble artisans of towns and villages.

While Warwick conned his resources and King Edward tried his own hand at foreign affairs, the Count of Charolais, in the late summer, made another move. Alarmed by what King Louis' truce with England might portend, he had fired off a wrathful accusation that Louis was offering territory to the English in return for an alliance aimed at smashing Burgundy. The King of France returned an elaborate denial, but Charles was not soothed. He began to fear that Warwick had stolen a march on him. Hastily he got in touch with King Edward, displayed a lively interest in Margaret of York, and asked for a pact of amity and mutual defense. Edward leaped to close with his offer, and on October 23 a treaty of friendship was signed. A Burgundian embassy was to come to England shortly to continue negotiations.

Furthermore, the King found excuses to avoid commissioning representatives to meet with the French at the October diet which had been arranged. The best Warwick could do was to insist that envoys be sent to King Louis. Edward's treasury did not pay their expenses nor did Edward's chancellery issue them commissions; but the King probably clothed their diplomatic nakedness in a letter of accreditation and some vague instructions. Warwick's private instructions to his men were anything but vague. According to what Louis revealed to the Milanese ambassadors, Warwick made angry promises to commit England to an attack upon Burgundy.[9]

Then, before the Burgundian embassy arrived in England, the Earl of Warwick quitted London, accepting as an excuse for his departure a commission to go to Newcastle and negotiate breaches of the truce with the Scots. Edward had pushed him another step along the bitter road of their rivalry. The coming of the Burgundians in December marked the first occasion on which Warwick failed to conduct an important diplomatic negotiation. In ignoring Charles of Burgundy's envoys, he had let slip the mask of treating in King Edward's interest.

The roads were still in the grip of winter when the Earl of Warwick rode south, some time during the early weeks of 1467, to continue the struggle for mastery with his sovereign. Now he was coming to the capital as the overt advocate of France. The negotiations with the Burgundians had so far accomplished nothing, Warwick's friends on the royal council having made the most of Charolais' coyness on the subject of the marriage and his hedging over the issue of English cloth. In these circumstances, Warwick quickly secured from Edward a grant of safe-conducts for a French embassy. In March, the envoys whom the Earl had sent to King Louis escorted across the Channel an impressive delegation headed by the Bastard of Bourbon, Admiral of France.

Westminster became the scene of a high diplomatic duel between the French and the Burgundians. Warwick and his brother

George, the Chancellor, and his adherents on the Council dilated upon the princely offers of the King of France; the Burgundians and their Woodville friends extolled the advantages of closing with the Duke of Burgundy. Each side sought to win public opinion in the capital and to enlist the support of the merchant class. Edward listened amiably to both parties. Warwick grew impatient. Despite obvious indications that the realm had little use for France, the Earl was still confident that he could secure from King Louis terms which Edward could not refuse and which Edward's subjects would gladly embrace. At the beginning of April, Warwick proposed to go himself to France to clinch negotiations.

Though economic and political circumstances seemed, on the surface, to favor the Burgundian cause, the issue was more complex than it first appeared.

Trade with the Low Countries had long been the keystone of England's overseas commerce. Chaucer's merchant talks about it as the first article of business.* The Dutch and Flemish cities had become the chief merchandise exchanges for the products of northern and central Europe, Italy, France, and Spain; and the skilled artisans of the Low Countries were dependent upon English wool for their famous cloth manufactures—"Alle Naciouns afferme up to the fulle/ In al the world ther is no bettir wolle."

But though the trade in wool—"cheef tresoure in this land growyng"—remained the basis of foreign commerce, it had been declining for more than half a century, partly because of the continuing business depression which followed upon the visitation of the Black Death (1348–51), partly because of the political upheavals of the times, but also because England had been rapidly expanding her cloth-making industry, absorbing large amounts of wool in the home market and exporting cloth in increasing quantities. This trade began to pose such a threat to the textiles of the Low Countries that Philip of Burgundy had intermittently

* "He wolde the see were kept for any thyng/ Bitwixe Middelburgh and Orewelle." That is, he wanted the route between the Dutch port of Middelburg and the English port of Orwell kept free of pirates.

prohibited the importation of English cloth. His latest edict, of 1464, still in force, had caused the cloth-exporting Merchant Adventurers indignantly to forsake Bruges for Utrecht (a fief of the Empire) and had provoked Parliament into a sweeping embargo on the importation of goods from the Duke's dominions. As the rich import-export trade with Burgundy withered, the merchants of London used bitter language of Duke Philip, and the rumblings of their discontent had not escaped the Earl of Warwick.

Politically, too, Burgundy was not popular. The English had never forgiven Philip for making peace with Charles VII at the Congress of Arras in 1435, for this desertion of his alliance with England had signed the death warrant of the English conquest in France. Nor was Philip's son Charles, Count of Charolais, much liked or trusted. English merchants and travelers in the Low Countries could see Margaret of Anjou's devoted adherents, the Dukes of Somerset and Exeter, riding in the Count's train; and Somerset and Margaret's brother had fought for his League of the Public Weal. Though Charles of Charolais now talked of a close alliance and a marriage with the House of York, he was clearly being driven by his fear of King Louis—a fact that Warwick would take care to dwell upon—and he showed no signs of jettisoning his Lancastrian friends or sentiments.

On the other hand, since 1463 the King of France had been acting like the figure in a morality play labeled "Friendship," and the fair, broad land of France, though still suffering from the depredations of the Hundred Years' War, offered potentially abundant markets for English merchants. France could use cloth and wool, hides, leather, tin, and other raw materials. England looked to Normandy for apples and fine Caen stone; she needed the woad of Picardy and Toulouse for the dyeing of cloths, and salt from the Bay of Bourgneuf. The thirst of the English upper classes could be properly quenched with no other wine than that of Gascony, and the loss of Guienne to the French in 1453 had cut off a thriving trade, English imports of wine from Bordeaux—sometimes as much as 15,000 tuns a year—being paid for by the export of cloth and foodstuffs.[10]

In the political market King Louis was making a high bid for the friendship of England—abandonment of the House of Lancaster, an annual subsidy in return for a long truce, a fine marriage for Margaret of York to be made at his own expense. If Francophobes at the English court declared that Louis was courting England only until he had gobbled up the Count of Charolais and the Duke of Brittany, the Nevilles could cast as much doubt on the good faith of the Count and Duke.

The possibility that Philip's son would bring himself to embrace the House of York seemed so unlikely to Sir John Paston that in this spring he agreed to pay six marks for a horse he had purchased if the Count of Charolais married Margaret within two years and otherwise but half that price.[11] The Earl of Warwick had a certain amount of evidence, as well as the insistence of an imperious will, to sustain his belief that he could drive through a treaty with the King of France.

But Warwick had long been out of touch with what went on in King Edward's mind. Edward had no difficulty perceiving that the French alliance had become Richard Neville's touchstone of supremacy in the realm, and he had no wish to strengthen the ties between his mightiest subject and King Louis. Furthermore, he had a remarkably good ear for public opinion. Beneath the surf of angry slurs upon the ruler of Burgundy, he had sensed what Warwick would not hearken to or discounted—the deep, unchanging tide of anti-French feeling. If Charles and Philip were disliked, Louis was loathed. Eager though merchants were to expand trade, they were, most of them, skeptical of Louis' enticements and swayed by the same prejudices as other folk. The Agincourt fever still burned; in the taverns of London men talked of reconquering the French provinces so shamefully lost in the reign of Henry VI; the Yorkists had promised a renewal of the war as the prime undertaking of their government. Besides, there was a traditional belief that the ulcer of domestic discontents could be lanced by the sword of foreign war; the invasion of France would offer the proper outlet for the restlessness of old soldiers, the smoldering bellicosity of former Lancastrians, the greed of gentry and nobles whose incomes were being squeezed during this period between rising wages and falling prices.

Though Edward was aware that the Count of Charolais was no very willing ally, he was playing a shrewd and patient game, waiting for Louis' offers to drive Charolais firmly into his arms. Yet in his dealings with the Earl of Warwick he was more slipshod than shrewd and much too optimistic.

Edward immediately complied with Warwick's proposal to go to France, complied so willingly that, for the first time in his life, he wrote Louis an autograph letter, promising to send the Earl across the Channel to discuss a treaty. On May 6 Warwick and three of Warwick's followers were issued a broad commission to negotiate for peace or a perpetual truce. Warwick's enemy, Lord Herbert, graciously desired the Earl to convey half a dozen dogs on his behalf to the dog-loving King Louis.

But Edward was walking a tightrope. In the middle of April he had sent three of his own men to Burgundy to treat with the Count of Charolais for the marriage and an alliance; on May 25 he extended his truce with Louis' rebellious vassal, the Duke of Brittany; and he and his courtiers were making elaborate preparations to welcome Antoine, the Bastard of Burgundy, coming to joust with the Queen's brother, Anthony Woodville, Lord Scales, in a tournament obviously meant to advertise the friendly connection between the Woodville court and the house of Burgundy.

On May 27, the Earl of Warwick set out from London on his journey to the King of France, whom he had been trying to meet for the past five years. The Earl took with him a princely retinue of some two hundred attendants—trumpeters and heralds and ushers and grooms, household officers, knights and squires, an honorific guard of archers. This cavalcade, accompanied by the French ambassadors, paused at Canterbury to hear vespers and went on to Sandwich the same evening. Next day Richard Neville took ship for Honfleur, where he was presented with the keys of the city. Then he sailed up the Seine to greet at last the lodestar of his fortunes, Louis of France.

IV

The Meeting of Friends

URING the past sixth months King Louis had displayed
prismatic shifts and flashes of fears, stratagems, fantasies.
He had been a little suspicious of the offers of Warwick's envoys. Their talk of a long truce and of English willingness to help Louis conquer Burgundy seemed extravagant, particularly since they bore no commission from King Edward to
negotiate a treaty, and Louis was beginning to realize that what
Warwick wanted might not be what Edward was willing to grant.
But when he received Edward's autograph letter in April, he
permitted his hopes to blaze up. One day he plucked the Milanese
envoys aside, swore them to silence, and proceeded to spin a fine
tale. Solemnly he disclosed a "secret understanding" which the
Earl of Warwick had arranged between himself and the King of
England. They were to live forever after as brothers-in-arms. Edward would renounce all his claims on France and help Louis to
exterminate the Count of Charolais. The Burgundian dominions
were to be divided between the two kingdoms, and there would
be appropriate matrimonial arrangements. Louis added that Edward had written him a letter in his own hand, promising to send
the Earl of Warwick to conclude everything—which mixed at
least a little metal of truth in the glittering alloy of this fiction.[1]

But by the month of May, when Louis had learned from his
ambassadors across the Channel that Edward was deeply interested
in the Burgundian negotiations for the hand of Margaret of York,
he began to consider what might be done in case the English King
disregarded Warwick's urgings and allied himself with the Count
of Charolais. He soon had a plan in mind that might possibly be
even richer in returns than an alliance with King Edward.

One day during the past February he had had a stimulating dinner conversation with his old antagonist, the Duke of Calabria,
Margaret of Anjou's brother. Since Louis enjoyed baiting people

he despised and the Duke was too headstrong to conceal what he felt, they soon fell to quarrelsome exchanges glossed by a pretense of joking.

When Louis deliberately introduced the Earl of Warwick into the conversation, John of Calabria said hotly that Warwick was a traitor to his true sovereign, King Henry. Blandly Louis continued to praise the Earl. The Duke snarled that he was nothing but a dissembler, *un homme rusé*, whose treacheries had been the chief cause of Queen Margaret's misfortunes.

Louis replied that he had better reason to speak well of Warwick than of others, including some of his own relatives—an obvious hit at the Duke, who had been one of the leading spirits in the War of the Public Weal. Warwick, the King went on, had always been his friend and had exerted his influence to prevent England from going to war with France. Warwick's friendship was well worth preserving.

In a passion Duke John flung back: "If you are so fond of Warwick, you should try to restore my sister to the English throne. Then you would be even more certain of English friendship."

Louis concealed his interest in this wrathy outburst behind a half-jesting insult. What security would the Lancastrians give for their good intentions? Would they offer Margaret's son, Prince Edward, as a hostage? And even if they gave security for an alliance with France, would they keep their word?

John cried furiously that if young Edward made such a promise and did not keep it, he and his friends would fly at him and tear out his eyes! [2]

The piquant joining of Warwick's name with Margaret of Anjou's in a remark about restoring the House of Lancaster was probably not the first time such an idea had presented itself to Louis' mind; he may well have thrust his praise of the Earl upon Queen Margaret's brother in order to test the Duke's feeling. In any case, Louis now began to cultivate this apparently bizarre and unlikely stratagem. Unburdened by sentiment himself, he saw no reason why Queen Margaret, whom Warwick had called an adulterous bitch and ousted from a throne, and Richard Neville, whose father, brother, uncle, and cousin had lost their lives at the hands of her adherents, should not join causes if it was to their interest to do so. Louis had learned that strong-willed people, such as the Earl of Warwick, will pay any price to secure what they regard as essential; and he delighted in helping such people to descry—for his own benefit—the true colors of their necessity.

Louis had Queen Margaret send him one of her councilors. As he moved from Chartres toward Rouen with this agent of Lancaster in his train, he was publishing to the realm that the great Earl of Warwick was coming to him in order to negotiate on behalf of King Edward and that he hoped to conclude a treaty which would nullify the machinations of the Count of Charolais against the realm of France.[3]

When he learned at Rouen that Warwick was on his way up the Seine, he took horse and hurried to greet him, though he had been ill of a fever and was vomiting blood. The King and the Earl met at the village of La Bouille.

Warwick found himself hailed like a Prince and caressed like an intimate.

When the Earl had an opportunity to scrutinize his host, he beheld unprepossessing features and an unkingly figure. Louis had a jutting, irregular, coarse face, dominated by a pendulous nose that gave him his sardonic look. His eyes were deep-set, hooded, veiled. He had a loose, wry mouth and a long chin. His short coat of cheap gray cloth—if he was wearing his usual dress—emphasized the contrast between the bulkiness of his body and his spindly legs. His speech was rather thick and he talked too fast. He was now forty-four, six years older than the Earl. He looked like one of the burgesses of his good towns, a shrewd, close-fisted merchant on whom years of bargaining and secret deals have left their mark.

Yet, though his appearance might seem to be a most unlikely instrument for projecting charm, Louis was a King and a remarkably intelligent man and a great actor. He would embrace the Earl, he would touch his arm familiarly as they conversed, his face would light up and his words would tumble over each other to express his pleasure, and in a repertory of gestures he would convey that he felt himself talking to an equal, a fellow ruler of men, a friend.

Louis insisted upon returning to Rouen overland so that Warwick, continuing the journey by water, might enjoy, *solus*, a solemn state entry into the city which Henry V had captured in 1419 and which the Duke of Somerset had lost in 1449. The Earl was welcomed to the capital of Normandy by the municipal magistrates and by clergy bearing crosses, banners, holy water. Like a King, he was escorted in a great procession to the cathedral of Notre Dame to make an offering. Then he was conducted to his lodgings in the convent of the Dominican friars. Louis established himself close by in a dwelling from which a gallery led to the Dominicans.

For the next twelve days the French and English diplomats conferred. Warwick was publicly feted at a variety of regal entertainments, and Louis treated his guest to the still more stimulating hospitality of a series of secret tête-à-têtes. The King of France had brought his baby daughters and his Queen—"my wife" was the plain term he liked to use—to Rouen that they might behold the celebrated Earl, and the usher who conducted this distinguished guest to the court receptions was the Duke of Bourbon, a Prince of the Blood. There was an opulent scattering of presents: for Warwick, a cup of gold garnished with precious stones, which cost Louis more than 2,000 livres; for Warwick's retinue, pieces of plate and gold coins specially minted for the occasion; for the servants, a lavish outpouring of tips. Louis insisted that his English guests take what they liked from the famous textile shops of Rouen, and the envoys hastened to enrich their wardrobes with silks and satins. This munificence was not only good diplomacy but good business: the ambassadors would be walking advertisements of the handsome goods which English merchants might import from France.

In this atmosphere the official negotiations proceeded with velvety ease, while behind the scenes Louis and Warwick conferred in private.* Daily Louis slipped down the gallery to the Dominicans and led his friend into a secluded chamber, where they could unbosom themselves without protocol or fear of eavesdroppers. No longer dependent on the clumsy medium of messengers and missives, Warwick was free to pour out to Louis the treacherous ingratitude of King Edward and to make clear that he was still master of the realm.

What listener could better draw forth such disclosures than the King of France? Like a ragged and ungainly fir tree that at Christmas blossoms into the magic of colored lights and balls, his forbidding features were transformed by the animation of his interest, the glow of his sympathetic attention, as he nodded and threw up his hands in vivid agreement and interjected expressions of condolence and encouragement. After Warwick's struggles with Edward, Louis' exquisite mingling of familiarity and admiration was balm to a bruised warrior.

In these talks they shaped the outline of the treaty, which was elaborated in the official diplomatic sessions. Louis was desperately anxious to forestall the marriage of Margaret of York and the Count of Charolais; Warwick was looking for terms which would make it impossible for Edward to avoid accepting a French alliance. Their collaboration, therefore, was completely harmonious, and Louis readily offered proposals that went beyond anything he had previously suggested.

* Warwick's knowledge of French: As far as writing French is concerned, Lord Hastings, who was presumably no better educated than Warwick, was able to indite a missive to Lannoy (see p. 164); Lord Wenlock could draw up official correspondence in that tongue (see p. 126); Warwick's officer, Whetehill, managed a letter to King Louis (see p. 156). Caxton remarks in his preface to *A Boke of the Hoole Lyf of Jason* that King Edward understands French. When Edward and Louis met on a bridge over the Somme at Picquigny in 1475, they conversed together in French for some time. Though nothing is known of Warwick's proficiency in speaking French, there is no reason to suppose that he was less adept at the language than his contemporaries; as Captain of Calais he had had ample opportunities to practice the tongue in his negotiations with the Burgundians in the '50s and he had afterward talked with many French envoys. That he could write French readily is proved by a postscript he quickly added to a missive that French envoys in England had written to King Louis (see p. 342).

For an alliance against Burgundy, the King of France was willing to submit the question of the rightful ownership of the duchies of Normandy and Guienne to the arbitration of the Pope, who was to be given four years to make his decision, during which time Louis would pay King Edward 4,000 marks annually for a truce. Margaret of York was to be provided with a suitable bridegroom, probably Prince Philip of Bresse, son of the Duke of Savoy (who was now in Louis' favor). To this offer were appended economic inducements: when the Kings of England and France had joined to dispose of the ruler of Burgundy, Louis would transfer all the fairs of Flanders to his own dominions—English merchants to have the power of choosing their locations!—and he would grant those merchants greater privileges than his own traders enjoyed.

But the French King had other matters to discuss besides the treaty. Once that was arranged, he broached a delicate subject.

What would Richard Neville do if Edward dared, after all, to reject the friendship of France?

Warwick made it vehemently clear that he meant to assert his authority at any cost.

Louis ventured to press on. Might there not be a better way? Might it not be simpler for the great Earl to get rid of Edward altogether and restore King Henry, whom he could be certain of controlling? That the House of Lancaster would gratefully accept Warwick's aid, Louis had no doubt. In fact, there was now at his court an emissary of Queen Margaret's, whom he had summoned with just such a possibility in view. . . .

But the Earl was totally uninterested in the idea. The House of Lancaster was finished; and he was confident of his ability to make King Edward acknowledge his power. Louis let the subject drop. At least, it had been planted in Warwick's thoughts.

There was another matter, however, in which the Earl was deeply interested—the particular meaning which the French alliance would have for Richard Neville. Kindled in his mind as long ago as the Seigneur de la Barde's visit in 1462, this vision had achieved an urgent focus in the bitter years following King Edward's marriage. Warwick wanted what he could never have in

England: a dominion to rule in his own right, a chance to exercise in his own name his capacity to wield affairs.

King Louis well knew what, at bottom, made his charm so operative upon the Earl, and he was ready with a proposal, much more enticing than the lordship of Normandy which he had once hinted might be Warwick's. The extermination of Burgundy would yield numerous principalities, Louis pointed out. Why should not Warwick become a Prince, perhaps the ruler of Holland and Zeeland? *

The suggestion found its mark. Henceforth, fighting his way through the darkening tangle of his enterprises, Richard Neville never took his eyes from this bright prospect.

The exhilarating conversations between Warwick and King Louis came to an end on June 16. Tidings had probably arrived at Rouen which gave fresh impetus to Anglo-French affairs— Philip the Good was dying. He expired on the fifteenth,† and the man who hovered over his deathbed in agonized grief, his son Charles, the mortal enemy of Louis and Warwick, was now the Duke of Burgundy. It may be that even worse news, borne across the Channel by fast messenger, had reached Warwick's ears.

In the final days of the conference, the Earl decided not to sign the treaty. Instead, he and Louis came to the conclusion that it would be better to let a French embassy present Louis' offers at Westminster. Though Warwick had succumbed to the King's charms, he had not lost his wariness. He was fully empowered to negotiate an agreement with the King of France, but in fifteenth-

---

* Ironically enough, it was perhaps Duke Philip himself who put into Louis' head the idea of using Holland and Zeeland as a reward for English aid. While Louis, then Dauphin, was living at Genappe under Philip's protection in the late '50s, Philip accused Charles VII of marrying Margaret of Anjou to Henry VI with the promise that Henry was to have Holland and Zeeland in return for helping to make war on Burgundy (Beaucourt, VI, p. 216).

† Among the elegies which the Burgundian court poets hastened to compose was one in which the Duke was pictured as bidding farewell to all that he loved; it contained these touching lines:

"Adieu mon bastard Anthoine
Et tous mes enffans naturelz."

century diplomacy no international pact was binding until it was ratified by both monarchs. In the end, Warwick refused to risk a rebuff that would publish to the realm his loss of influence over Edward.[4*]

Laden with Louis' handsome bid for English friendship and Louis' gifts and Louis' secret picture of the future, Warwick set out from Rouen on the sixteenth in the company of a high-ranking French embassy. They sailed from Honfleur on June 23, the ships having been revictualed at the expense of the ever-thoughtful King of France. In a rush of optimism Louis announced the mission of his envoys to the lords spiritual and temporal and his "good towns."

In early July a Norman official reported to one of his friends that Warwick had safely returned home and added, in the best vein of his kingly master, "You may be sure that everyone there trembles before him, whatever others may say."[5] One, at least, who did not tremble was a pleasure-loving, sometimes incautious, but shrewd and resolute young man named Edward Plantagenet.

When Warwick set foot in England, he learned, if he had not already got word, that a shadow had fallen upon the might of the Nevilles. People dared mouth the rumor that in France the Earl of Warwick had come to terms with Queen Margaret; the Burgundian faction at court were wearing looks of triumph; and while the Earl had basked in the smiles of the King of France, the King of England had ousted his brother George from the chancellorship.

V

The Parting of Foes

AS THE struggle between the King and Warwick grew increasingly intense, George Neville, Archbishop of York and Chancellor of England, had permitted himself, clever though he was, to act more and more openly as his brother's agent rather than the King's servant. He had used his office, through which passed all important documents, to obstruct good relations with Burgundy by niggling devices and to forward his brother's affairs in every way possible.

Some months before Warwick departed for France, King Edward was given further reason to suspect the loyalties of his Chancellor. A papal emissary arrived in England—too mysteriously. Indiscreetly ignoring the court, he paid no calls, except a furtive visit to the Archbishop of York's manor, The Moor, in Hertfordshire. This strange conduct apparently aroused the King's curiosity and led him to discover that George Neville was secretly intriguing not only to be made a Cardinal but also to secure a papal dispensation for the marriage of George of Clarence and Warwick's daughter, Isabel.

Then came the Woodville-sponsored visit of Antoine, the Bastard of Burgundy, who was to break a lance with Queen Elizabeth's brother, Anthony, Lord Scales. The very day after Warwick sailed from Sandwich, the Bastard's little fleet, masts and rigging bedecked with pennons, was ceremoniously met at Gravesend by Garter King of Arms. The following morning, Antoine received a splendid welcome to London and was lodged at the palace of the Bishop of Salisbury, one of Edward's specialists on Burgundian affairs. Three days later (June 2), King Edward made a ceremonious entry into his capital with Lord Scales riding before him holding the sword of state. The Bastard and his party were invited to attend the opening session of Parliament next day.

George Neville was so disturbed that his powers of dissembling forsook him. Unable to contend with this elaborate display of friendship for Burgundy and fearful of what it might betoken in his brother's absence, he sent word at the last moment that he was too ill to deliver the Chancellor's customary address to the Parliament and angrily immured himself in his palace.

Affairs of state moved forward without him. The Bishop of Lincoln improvised a speech for the inaugural session of Wednesday, June 3. When the Commons presented their Speaker on Friday, the Queen's father made the response ordinarily delivered by the Chancellor.

On the following Monday, Edward took horse with Warwick's enemy, Lord Herbert, rode to the Archbishop of York's palace near Charing Cross, demanded in his royal person that George Neville forthwith surrender the Great Seal of his office, waited until it was placed in his hands, and imperturbably rode away, to deliver it in a few days to Robert Stillington, Bishop of Bath and Wells.

After that dramatic humbling of the Nevilles, Edward and his capital gave themselves up to the delights of the tournament. On Thursday, June 11, the Bastard and Lord Scales tilted with lance and sword till the Bastard's horse rammed its head into Scales' saddle and deposited its master on the ground. Next day the two champions, on foot this time, hammered each other so furiously with battle-axes that the King broke off the combat and made Scales and the Bastard swear to "love together" forever as brothers-in-arms.[1] On Sunday the Bastard and his company were feasted by the King and Queen in Grocers' Hall, the location of the banquet emphasizing the trade connections between Burgundy and England. Other festivities followed, while negotiations went on at Westminster. The news of Duke Philip's death caused the Bastard to depart hastily on June 24, but one of the ducal councilors remained to continue diplomatic conversations.

Such was the cold news that struck the Earl of Warwick, while still heated by the flattering regard of King Louis. For the moment he crushed down his rage in order to drive on the business of the French embassy—"so subtle and imaginative was he above all men," as a contemporary chronicler observes.[2]

No one appeared from court to welcome Louis' envoys but George, Duke of Clarence. They were domiciled in the Burgundian atmosphere of the Bishop of Salisbury's palace, just vacated by the Bastard. When Warwick had seen the ambassadors settled, he betook himself to Westminster to report their arrival to the King. Edward politely agreed to see the envoys next day, but when Warwick launched into an account of Louis' hospitality and Louis' good will toward England, Edward did not trouble to conceal his lack of interest.

On the morrow the Earl and the French ambassadors were rowed to Westminster in barges which Warwick had had specially decorated. His faithful disciple Clarence was at the landing stage to greet them, as were representatives of the King—his Chamberlain, Lord Hastings, and two of the Queen's brothers, Lord Scales and Sir John Woodville. Young Clarence did his best to take the chill off this unpropitious welcome by greeting the envoys warmly and himself ushering them into the palace. The King received them in great state, surrounded by his chief councilors and more Woodvilles. He coolly listened to Jehan de Popincourt's general statement of King Louis' proposals, withdrew to consult briefly with his advisers, then made answer that as he was otherwise engaged he would appoint negotiators to consider their terms. Earl Rivers brought the interview to an end by calling for the traditional diplomatic collation of wine and spices. That afternoon the King departed for Windsor, plague having broken out in London.

Richard Neville, forced to watch this bitter comedy in silence, now fully understood that his brother's fall meant that Edward had chosen Burgundy against France and proclaimed his independence of the House of Neville. As he was rowed down-river with the disconsolate envoys, he could no longer contain his anger.

"Did you not see the traitors who are about the King!" he burst forth.

The Admiral of France replied as Louis would have wished: "My Lord, do not heat yourself. You will be well avenged."

"Know ye," Warwick rushed on, "that these are the men by whom my brother has been ousted from the office of Chancellor!" The Admiral would have no difficulty understanding that he meant the Woodvilles.[3*]

Warwick and Clarence saw to it that the ambassadors were honorably entertained and were able to procure an invitation from the King for them to stay with him at Windsor. At the end of six weeks, however, the French took their leave. All that they had secured for King Louis was a pointedly modest gift of hunting horns, leather bottles, and some mastiffs with collars and leashes, and Edward's vague promise to send an embassy across the Channel. During this time, Edward had signed a treaty aimed at France with Henry of Castile and renewed his treaty of amity and defense with Charles of Burgundy.

Warwick grimly emphasized his adherence to the cause of France by persuading his brother John, Earl of Northumberland, and John's Countess to join him in escorting Louis' envoys to Canterbury, whence the Earl rode on with them to Sandwich. On the day Warwick left London, his sovereign called together the royal councilors to announce that since Charles of Burgundy had made their agreement binding on his heirs, he intended to do likewise.

From Sandwich, Richard Neville rode into Yorkshire with a storm of wrath in his heart. The labors, the hopes of the last three years had been dashed in a moment. Edward had sent him to France merely to get him out of the way; Edward had toyed with his policy only to expose him to the world as the dupe of the King he had created. The Burgundian alliance finished what the Woodville marriage had begun. He had deluded himself in thinking that he could set the clock back to pre-Woodville times. To regain his sway, he must rule in despite of, not through the King. Only the use of naked power would avail him now. If Edward had made it impossible for him to regain the days of 1461, he would go back even further, to 1459–60. It was time to resume the life of adventure.

VI

"Master or Varlet"

THERE was the Kingmaker at Middleham Castle; there was the King at Westminster. The distance between Yorkshire and London symbolized the gulf between them. Power in England was sundered in twain; the York-Neville compound of government had split into its original elements.

Though medieval ideas and institutions would long linger, Warwick and Edward had brought the medieval English monarchy to an end in 1461. The regime they established would last, through the Tudors and Stuarts, to the Revolution of 1688. Warwick was the commanding figure of its birth and the first difficult years of its growth, but Edward was now stamping upon this kingship his own individual style, a style accented by his engaging bonhommie, his responsiveness to the interests of townsmen, his appreciation of luxury and of learning,[1] his vigorous confidence, and his close relationship with the city of London—whose support, a Milanese ambassador had noted early in 1461, "enormously increases the chances of the side that it favours."

Edward's convivial habits and his zestful sensuality were manifestations of his character but they did not sound the bottom of it. His hearty, easy-going manner hid from some of his contemporaries, and from many later historians, his steely earnestness of purpose. Behind the façade of jousts and feasts and hunting parties in the greenwood, he was bending all his powers to establish a strong kingship, independent of baronial control and sensitive to the popular will.

What power behind the throne had directed the choice of Burgundy over France and weaved an industrious web of diplomacy stretching from Spain to Denmark? There was none. Edward had become his own chief minister. His favorites and the Woodvilles were only what he had made them; they were, in fact, the first burgeoning of a Renaissance court nobility.

The royal council was the principal instrument of government —executive, judicial, and even legislative. Warwick, however, had chosen to exert his power directly through the King; consequently, though Edward's advisers numbered several of Warwick's supporters, Edward had begun to dominate his council in a manner that foreshadowed the Tudor age. Lords occasionally sat at the council board, but the daily work of governing was performed by able, learned clerics, forging careers in the royal service. They advised Edward on policy and they executed the policies determined upon, but the King did the determining as he pleased. He was transforming the royal council—once the battleground between baronial pretensions and the King's prerogative—into an agency of his own will.

Yet for all his shrewdness in statecraft, Edward had handled his relations with Warwick sloppily, and he had known from the beginning of his reign that his relations with Warwick were the prime business of his regime. Though the Earl would probably not have been content, under any circumstances, to decline from master to first servant of the Crown, Edward had needlessly exacerbated Warwick's temper by the awkward and disingenuous manner in which he had revealed his intentions. He was disingenuous out of laziness and perhaps out of bad conscience rather than out of malice, but he was disingenuous all the same, maladroitly feeding a flame he had no other desire but to extinguish.

His deep-grained dislike of facing up to unpleasant situations—except on the field of battle—had led him to these procrastinations and palterings, and now his natural exuberance convinced him that, somehow, all would still be well. In his facile optimism he underestimated the intensity of the Earl's feelings and the height of his expectation, just as he overestimated the usefulness of the Woodvilles and the stability of the realm.

Neither man was able to appreciate the resources or the inflexibility of purpose of the other. But Warwick was the one who had been challenged, who was burning with a sense of injured merit and thwarted destiny.

Edward's blow had opened a gap between the shape of the facts and the shape of the Warwick legend and had forced an unbearable cleft in Warwick himself between the public and the private man. His personality had been organized around his sense of himself as a figure of state. He had identified his *self* with his position in the world, and that self could only reach avidly to regain its identity.

Perhaps Warwick was too obsessed with this quest to realize how miserable Richard Neville had become in these last three years, how his natural warmth of disposition, his grace of character, his love of work and eager embracing of experience, had all been contorted, shrunk, by the spoiling touch of adversity, had been forced into parodies of themselves to satisfy the imperious demands, not so much of ambition, as the word is ordinarily used, but of imagination. He had become the fierce prisoner of his vision of himself, the victim as well as the subject of the Warwick legend. He was a little like Macbeth—the staunch, indefatigable warrior driven to the ruin of all joy by dreams. But it was the airy dagger that Warwick grasped, plunging it into his own character.

The fall from dominion ate upon the nerves of the Kingmaker, but in the history of Richard Neville the real descent was the fall from happiness and the waste of talent and energy. His life was now a fever. He forsook all the enjoyments of ordinary men to pursue into whatever jungles and gulfs it might lead him the image of his destiny which he himself had invented.

So he rode into Yorkshire, Antaeus-like, to regain strength from the earth which had nurtured him, to regain assurance by standing upon the bedrock of his power, his lordship of the North.[2]

From his strongholds of Middleham and Sheriff Hutton, the Earl of Warwick explored the sinews of his strength and scrutinized events. Though brother John, the Earl of Northumberland, persisted in holding aloof, brother George, eager to retaliate against the King, soon joined the Earl in the North to exercise his nimble brain in plotting. George of Clarence was also eager for mischief. In London, Warwick's agents reported on the progress of Edward's negotiations with Charles of Burgundy and tested the popular temper, listening to the gossip in alehouses and the talk of merchants. Warwick sent his secretary, Robert Neville, to explain to King Louis the failure of their hopes and to reiterate his determination to master King Edward.

This withdrawal into the North surrounded Warwick with the atmosphere of his great years. Messengers clattered into the court-yard. Neville relatives and connections by marriage, Yorkshire barons like Fitzhugh and Scrope of Bolton, knights and squires of the Yorkshire dales, rode in to affirm their devotion. There was a continual coming and going of retainers and friends with their menies of armed followers. The great halls at Middleham and Sheriff Hutton were filled with men happy to follow the banner of the Lord of the North. From moorland castles and villages, a restlessness spread slowly to the Midlands and other parts where Warwick or his adherents had a following.[3]*

Meanwhile the tide of King Edward's policy had set full for Burgundy. Envoys plied back and forth to treat of the alliance and the marriage. On September 30, Margaret of York appeared before a Great Council at Kingston to announce that she was content to marry the Duke of Burgundy. Edward continued dick-ering for a military alliance with Charles's ally, Francis of Brit-tany, who was begging for an armed force to help him against Louis. The King also showed his aggressive confidence by further jabs against the Nevilles. He had intimated to the Pope that he would welcome the elevation of Thomas Bourchier, Archbishop of Canterbury, to the College of Cardinals, the eminence which Warwick's brother had been intriguing so hard to achieve. When the King received word of Bourchier's election, he sent the papal notification to George Neville in reckless mockery.[4] Nor did he scruple to demonstrate that the royal confidence in the Earl of Warwick could be shaken. In the course of besieging Harlech Castle, the last foothold of Lancaster, Lord Herbert captured a messenger from Margaret of Anjou. This man—perhaps at a hint from Herbert—dared to assert that overseas he had heard reports of the Earl's favoring the party of Queen Margaret. Ed-ward asked Warwick to come in and clear himself of the accusa-tion. But when the Earl showed his rebellious mood by an angry refusal, the King contented himself with sending the accuser un-der guard to Sheriff Hutton, and Warwick had no difficulty showing the emptiness of the allegation.

As Warwick kept close watch upon the kingdom from his eyries in the North, circumstances began to turn against the King with the oncoming of winter. Edward was finding Charles no enthusiastic ally. As the Duke continued to evade coming to terms about English cloth and put off signing the marriage treaty, Edward was driven to revoke the edicts of Parliament prohibiting the importation of Burgundian goods. Merchants and artisans were loud in their complaints; threats were uttered in London taverns against the men who had counseled the King to this capitulation. Indignation mounted when it was learned that Charles, the ally to whom English interests were being sacrificed, had signed without warning a six months' truce with France. Edward decided not to face Parliament till the following year. Mutterings of discontent grew into a ripple of disorder sweeping over the land. The realm was being betrayed, ran the rumors. The Woodvilles had estranged the King from his true lords and were delivering the kingdom to the thraldom of Burgundy. The London magistrates, nervously aware of growing tension between Neville adherents and Woodvilles, forbade all citizens to accept badges or liveries from any lord, on pain of losing their citizenship.

From reports crossing the Channel, the Milanese ambassadors at the French court drew the conclusion, "In England things are upside down and in the air." King Louis complained bitterly that Warwick had not fulfilled his promises, but after talking with Warwick's secretary, he let it be known that his friend the Earl had retired to his estates to raise troops. Struggling to prevent the Anglo-Burgundian marriage alliance, he dispatched the Count of St. Pol, once the friend of Duke Charles, to the court of Burgundy in order to hold Charles in empty negotiations until— Louis assured the Milanese envoys in a burst of optimism—the Earl of Warwick had arranged his affairs. The Duke of Burgundy, his humor not improved by the sight of St. Pol, told him grimly, "Though I am French—or Burgundian—[the King of France] has turned me English despite me." Grudgingly, "contre coeur," the lover of Lancaster was pushing himself toward the unpalatable marriage with the House of York.[5]

George Neville, the while, was secretly working for the papal dispensation required for the marriage of Clarence and Isabel.

One of his emissaries to the Curia met with a rebuff, but the slippery Archbishop had other strings to his bow. He began to worm his way into the confidence of James Goldwell, Edward's own representative at the papal court. George of Clarence—a spoiled, rash seventeen-year-old—was also zealously bestirring himself, hating the Woodvilles and itching for glory. In his halls he dispensed hospitality to the gentry of Gloucestershire and Somerset and dabbled in the affairs of the magnates to enlarge his following. He was flirting with John Talbot, the Lancastrian Earl of Shrewsbury, and gave his patronage in particular to the powerful Vernon family of Derbyshire, supporters of the Earl. Some followers of Lord Grey of Codnor, who was a friend of the King's, and a party of Shrewsbury's retainers fell into a quarrel which resulted in the violent death of one of the Vernons. Clarence immediately began meddling in this promising hornet's nest, hoping to inflame the House of Talbot against the King.[6]

The hot partisanship of the Duke of Clarence and the Archbishop of York did not move the Earl of Northumberland. Caught in a conflict of loyalties, he stationed himself on the Scots border and doggedly went about his duties as Warden of the East March. Still, numbers of lesser men acknowledged no higher authority than Warwick's and would march when he beckoned. A bold knight of the North, Sir John Conyers, related to Warwick by marriage, rallied a following of Neville tenants and well-wishers under the pseudonym of Robin of Redesdale and sent word to the Earl that he and his men were ready to take arms under the banner of the Ragged Staff. Warwick hastily returned his thanks but asked that each man remain quietly in his home; he would let them know when it was time to be stirring. His ardent friends, the commons of Kent, took matters into their own hands on New Year's Day (1468), assailed a manor of Earl Rivers, killed his deer and ravaged his acres, and were forestalled from completely pillaging the estate only by the flight of the servants with their master's valuables.[7]

As King Edward moved toward Coventry to keep his Christmas, he found so much disorder that he was forced to appoint several commissions of oyer and terminer to investigate and repress these outbreaks. Aroused now to the Earl of Warwick's disaffection, he took the unusual step of surrounding himself with a guard of two hundred elite archers; and he peremptorily summoned the Duke of Clarence to join him in Coventry for the holidays, certainly not for the pleasure of his brother's society. He had with him most of the Woodville clan, his court favorites, and his council. At Coventry he stood between Warwick in the North and Warwick's strength in the Midlands and Kent. The citizens of the town pointedly showed their loyalty by presenting Edward's unpopular Queen with a hundred marks (£66).

This critical Christmas season brought to the Earl of Warwick an emissary from his friend, the King of France. In early December Louis sent Robert Neville back to England with William Menypeny, a Scot high in Louis' service. They hoped to reach Warwick unobtrusively by slipping into a northern port; but contrary winds forced them to land at Sandwich and pass through London.

There Menypeny found friends and picked up some happy tidings to retail to his master. Warwick's household council was in the capital, reporting events and disseminating anti-Burgundian propaganda, and with his council were two of Warwick's agents, Lord Wenlock and Master Thomas Kent. Immediately Wenlock and Kent asked Menypeny if it was true that a Burgundian embassy had visited the Duke of Brittany and then journeyed to the court of France. Menypeny was able to confirm the report since he had himself seen the Burgundians at Honfleur. Wenlock and Kent told him that this was the best news in the world for the Earl of Warwick's cause. King Edward, they said, had heard of these suspicious dealings set on foot by Charles of Burgundy. There were reports that Charles was working with Margaret of Anjou's family to reconcile Louis and his disgruntled lords and that a scheme was afoot to marry one of Louis' daughters to Margaret of Anjou's son. It looked as if Edward's supposed friend and ally was conspiring with Louis to bring about the restoration of his beloved House of Lancaster to the English throne. This juicy intelligence—in which there was not a word of truth—Warwick's agents had taken care to spread abroad, and, according to Wen-

lock and Kent, the citizens of the capital "were about as frightened as any people ever were, and in all the London taverns and
everywhere in the country men were saying that there was nothing for it but to cut off the heads of those traitors who had advised their King to abandon treating with you"—Menypeny
wrote Louis—"and take an alliance with the Duke of Burgundy."
Menypeny strongly advised his master to work on the Pope in
order to block the marriage dispensation which Margaret and
Charles required (since they were both descended from Edward III) and to spin out negotiations with Duke Charles. "The
marriage broken," Menypeny went on, "there is not a woman or
child in England who will not rise up in wrath against the Duke
of Burgundy, and you can wholly destroy those who on this side
of the water have held to his party."

Wenlock and Kent advised Louis' emissary to present himself
openly to King Edward on his way north. "For many reasons"—
doubtless to allay any suspicions his journey to the Earl of Warwick might arouse and to attempt to deepen Edward's misgivings
about Burgundy—Menypeny decided to follow this counsel.

The moment the Scot made known his arrival in Coventry, Edward summoned him to an audience.

What was the news from the court of France? he first wanted
to know. Menypeny reported Louis' prosperity and strength in
glowing terms.

Edward next inquired, Do you have any letters for me from
your master? Menypeny fended off this awkward query by explaining that he was traveling to Scotland purely on private business.

The next question was worse—Do you have, by chance, any
letters for my lord of Warwick?

Menypeny thought it prudent to admit that he had.

Do you know anything of their contents? the King pursued.

Menypeny replied that he did not know exactly what the messages said. He supposed they expressed no more than King Louis'
astonishment that England had failed to respond to the proposals
his ambassadors had put forward the past summer.

Edward was content to drop the subject of the letters. He told

Louis' agent mildly that by the advice of my lord of Warwick he intended to send an embassy to France very shortly in order to negotiate with King Louis. As for Louis' troublesome brother Charles and the disaffected French nobles—suddenly he raised his voice and swore his favorite oath: By the mercy of God! he would help Louis against his brother. The man was a fool, a mere dupe of those lords who aimed at governing France as they pleased. With that vigorous comment, King Edward amiably dismissed Menypeny to continue his journey northward to the Earl of Warwick. The Scot happily concluded that the King did not trust the Duke of Burgundy and the Duke's friends; but though Edward probably felt a genuine contempt for Louis' feeble brother and malcontent nobles in general, Menypeny had missed the point of his calculated outburst. The men of the royal household must have realized that the fool of whom the King was thinking was his own brother George.

On January 7 the King abruptly ordered the Earl of Warwick to come to Coventry.

Richard Neville, pushing himself toward the brink of action, shooting out schemes in all directions, sent back a hot, curt answer: he would not enter the court until the mortal enemies of him and his policy, Lord Herbert and the Woodvilles, had been dismissed from it.

But he was tormented by conflicting, uncertain second-thoughts. To gain time—as well as to underline his position as an independent power—he hurried off an embassy to the King. In the crucible of his passionate pride all the far-reaching and ambiguous issues had become fused into a simple ultimatum, formidable, naive, and deadly: "It is a matter," he told Menypeny fiercely, "of being either master or varlet."

As the bitter days of January passed, he was calculating his resources. After he had sent pleas to his obstinate brother, Northumberland agreed to talk matters over if he came to the Marches. He had even made veiled overtures to the King of Scots, who now returned word that he was willing to meet Warwick somewhere along the Tweed. Menypeny offered to help persuade James III and his advisers to support the Ragged Staff. The Earl's garrisons in the West March constituted a small but expert standing army. Assembling men in Yorkshire, Warwick prepared to start for the border on January 17.

But Edward at Coventry preserved an enigmatic silence. Was he secretly summoning a force? If the King moves northward, Warwick declared to Menypeny, I will spring to arms at once! The words betrayed an attack of irresolution. Menypeny divined it. Reporting all these matters to King Louis on January 16, he noted dryly that Warwick "is very long in his doings and a little cowardly, but the hour has come when he can no longer dissemble." That, however, was a matter of opinion and Menypeny wrote with the objectivity that comes from one's own neck being in no danger.

At this moment, brother George, finding the issue perilously doubtful, hastily took matters into his own hands. Who could make peace more gracefully than an Archbishop? Through mutual friends he managed to arrange a secret meeting with Earl Rivers at Nottingham. A compromise was patched up. Warwick would be warmly received at court, if he would come in a mood befitting his allegiance.

When the Archbishop urgently commended these terms to his brother, Warwick was ready to listen. He realized that he had revealed his enmity before he was quite ready to act on it. The King was forewarned and on guard, whereas he himself had not yet been able to marshal all his forces. The understanding arranged by the Archbishop would permit him to return to court with his dignity unimpaired, while he awaited a better opportunity to unfurl his banners.

Signifying his willingness to meet Edward's desire for a reconciliation, he sent word to his intimates that the moment had not yet struck. Before he departed for Coventry, he wrote Louis reassuringly that he had drawn over Edward's brother Clarence to his cause and added, in the royal style Louis had encouraged, that he had consented for the moment to treat for an accommodation. The missive was carried by a messenger whose verbal report was so confidential that Louis was asked to speak to him "seul à seul."

As Richard Neville set out for Coventry, he embarked upon a double life. Erecting an effigy of himself in the great world, he went underground to perfect the means of regaining the mastery of the realm.

He received a hearty greeting from the King. Genially Edward brought his old friend and his favorites together. The Earl graciously went through the form of being reconciled with Lords Herbert, Audeley, and Stafford of Southwick. The Woodvilles were kept discreetly in the background. For his good service in promoting this reunion, George Neville had some manors restored to him which he had lost in a recent act of resumption.* The Earl of Warwick was received with great respect at the council board.

Edward, overoptimistic as usual, persuaded himself that Warwick would now accept his sovereign's authority and acquiesce in the choice of Burgundy over France. On this assumption the King briskly asked him to lend his name to the bond which Duke Charles demanded as security for the payment of Margaret of York's dowry.† At the same time he pressed the Earl to help find four thousand archers, which Francis of Brittany was demanding in order to defend himself against King Louis.

Warwick would have nothing to do with either proposal. Assuming the tone of an impartial adviser, he told Edward that he had been misled by false councilors, that the Dukes of Burgundy and Brittany made him fine offers only because they were afraid of the King of France. Edward, outwardly conciliatory, vaguely agreed to hold another council meeting on foreign policy in London, to begin on February 27. It was only a gesture, but Warwick, too, was only gesturing.

As he rode to the capital for this meeting, he took pains to diffuse his affability upon the admiring throngs that greeted him when he passed through towns and villages. "There is no man,"

---

* That is, an act decreeing that certain crown lands, bestowed by the King, should be returned to the royal holdings.

† Charles was asking—and received—200,000 gold crowns (£41,000)— 50,000 crowns down and the remainder in three yearly installments; the dowry equaled about two-thirds of a year's revenue of the English Crown.

King Louis heard from Menypeny (whose private business in Scotland had suddenly evaporated), "who loves you more loyally than does the Earl of Warwick and I comfort myself in another thing—that nobody is so well loved in England as he is now; for [wherever he goes] it seems to the people that God has descended from the skies, and they all cry in one voice, 'Warwick! Warwick!' " [8]*

Edward did not bother to attend the foreign policy meeting, and its deliberations came to nothing. The King arrived in London in the middle of March to announce that Charles of Burgundy had signed the marriage treaty. Not long after, he concluded an alliance with Francis of Brittany and loosed a fleet in the Channel to prey on French shipping. He was lighting the old Agincourt flame. Parliament met on May 12 to the beating of war drums.

While Warwick watched impassively, Robert Stillington, the Chancellor, sounded the summons to arms against the French. Having secured treaties with the chief powers of Europe, Stillington told the Lords and Commons, the King of England had negotiated an "amity and confederation" with the Dukes of Burgundy and Brittany, "the mightiest princes that hold of the crown of France," in order to cross the Channel and recover his ancient right from his "great rebel and adversary, Louis, usurpant King of the same." The Dukes of Burgundy and Brittany had sworn to risk "their own persons" in this enterprise and declared that never had a King of England enjoyed a better opportunity of getting back his own. The Chancellor finished by warning his hearers that if they did not carry the war to French soil, King Louis would soon be mounting an attack on England. The Lords eagerly embraced the prospect of military adventure and plunder, and the Commons, fired by memories of Harry the Fifth, voted a war grant of two Fifteenths and two Tenths, a sum of £62,000.[9] Despite this enthusiasm, Warwick still did not admit to himself that his sovereign had read the feelings of the realm better than he. Edward, on the other hand, blithely overlooked the fact that in order to wage war abroad he had first to make sure of his power at home.

The Earl held himself firmly to his course of outward acquiescence in the new shape of things. When the Lady Margaret left London on June 18 on the first stage of her bridal journey, the Earl of Warwick headed her great train of lords and ladies. He escorted her to the monastery of Stratford Langthorne in Essex, where the Queen and Margaret's three brothers were awaiting her. Several days of feasting followed—Warwick and Clarence drinking cheek by jowl with the Woodvilles, with young Richard of Gloucester who had annoyingly ranged himself on the King's side, and with the convivial but strong-willed monarch who had once been a Neville protégé.

But having a King of France for one's most ardent supporter, a King's brother of England soon to be one's son-in-law if all went well, and with the handsome, arrogant Earl Rivers and his kin surely marked for death in one's mind, it was perhaps not hard to play a gracious part. Already there was trouble in the air.

VII

Mine and Countermine

KING EDWARD had his Burgundian alliance, his Burgundian marriage, and a war grant for his invasion of France. As Margaret of York sailed for Sluys, the Earl of Warwick appeared to have been decisively worsted by his sovereign.

But Warwick was only awaiting opportunity in order to counterattack. In the last six months of 1468, opportunities appeared; and Warwick turned to his advantage every circumstance and force he could manipulate to undermine Edward's triumph. Across the water, the King of France used all his powers in the same cause, the two friends linked by the passing and repassing of secret messengers. From June to December the Yorkist realm quivered under repeated shocks; and beneath the surface of these roils was waged an unacknowledged war of intrigue and counter-intrigue.

Even before Margaret of York began her wedding journey, the kingdom was shaken by alarms. Aroused by the split in Yorkist ranks, Queen Margaret and her followers were hopefully sending emissaries into England. Early in June one of them was caught at Queenborough with incriminating letters. When hot irons were applied to his feet, he accused almost a dozen prominent citizens of London and a man named Hawkins, a servant of Richard Neville's trusty agent, Lord Wenlock. Hawkins in turn involved a former Lord Mayor, Sir Thomas Cook, and declared that Lord Wenlock was up to his neck in Lancastrian plotting.

But Edward knew that Warwick had no reason to love the House of Lancaster, though he failed to perceive how much the Earl might profit from these ominous rumblings. Demonstrating his confidence in the Nevilles, the King permitted Wenlock to accompany Margaret to Burgundy and included Warwick, Warwick's brother John, Earl of Northumberland, and Warwick's friend, George of Clarence, on the commission of oyer and terminer appointed to investigate the conspiracy. The accused were indicted of treason in sessions enlivened by the irreverent wit of the youthful Duke of Clarence. When the Mayor, "a lumpish man," dozed off one day, Clarence "said openly in his derision, 'Speak softly, sirs, for the Mayor is asleep.' " [1]

Before the treason trials came on, King Louis did his bit to keep the English realm in turmoil by outfitting Jasper Tudor, the Lancastrian Earl of Pembroke,* with three ships and sending him off to make a descent on Wales. He rallied enough men to march inland and burn Denbigh, but his little force was routed by Lord Herbert's brother and he barely escaped back to France. The news of Pembroke's invasion, feeble though it was, made Edward so suspicious of a widespread Lancastrian plot that Sir Thomas Cook, who had been freed on bail, was immediately returned to prison; and on August 3 the King peremptorily requisitioned every ship in every port of the kingdom. But the trials of the accused uncovered no real evidence of a Lancastrian conspiracy, and all but three of them got off with fines. Hawkins and another man were executed; a London draper, likewise condemned to death, was saved at the very foot of the gallows by a royal pardon which the Archbishop of York delivered with his own hands—a gesture which did not hurt the popularity of the Nevilles among the substantial city burgesses. Warwick took care to let the other accused citizens know of his sympathy for their unmerited sufferings; and this group—wealthy merchants, most of them—henceforth gave their allegiance to the Earl rather than to the King.

Warwick's bid for popularity was made the easier by the fresh accretions of ill will that the greedy Woodvilles earned on this occasion. Months before, Sir Thomas Cook had incurred the

---

* He was the half-brother of Henry VI; their mother, Katherine of France, widow of Henry V, had entered into a secret liaison with a Welsh adventurer named Owen Tudor and had borne him three children. One, Owen, became a monk; the other two, Jasper and Edmund, were created Earl of Pembroke and Earl of Richmond. Edmund had died in 1457; his wife, Margaret Beaufort—niece of the Duke of Somerset who fell at the first battle of St. Albans—had given birth to one child, Henry Tudor, who would one day defeat Richard III at Bosworth Field and become Henry VII.

enmity of Earl Rivers by refusing to let Rivers' wife have a valuable tapestry at her own price. Upon Cook's arrest, Rivers plundered Cook's town and country houses of thousands of pounds' worth of goods; and though Cook was found guilty of nothing worse than misprision of treason and received a pardon, he was kept in prison until Rivers had mulcted him of £8,000 in fines and Rivers' haughty daughter had extorted a further 800 marks under the color of an archaic privilege called "Queen's gold." Then Earl Rivers drove from office Justice Markham, famed for his honesty, who had dared direct the jury to find Cook guilty of misprision only.[2]

A few weeks later, the King himself stirred up fresh sentiment against the Queen's kindred by clumsily trying to thrust his brother-in-law, Sir Richard Woodville, into the office of Prior of the Order of St. John of Jerusalem, after the brothers had already elected Sir John Langstrother. Like Cook, Langstrother was not long in making his way into the Neville fold.

At this very time, a story was going the rounds that the Queen had cruelly procured the death of the gallant Earl of Desmond —executed in Ireland a few months before—in revenge for his telling King Edward, when they were merrily conversing during a hunt, that it might have been better for the realm if Edward had married a King's daughter.[3]

Nobles and commons alike hated the Woodvilles and chafed at their influence over the King. One day during this summer a court jester ventured to remind Edward of what people were thinking. He appeared in a fantastically cut short coat, absurdly long boots, with a marsh pike in his hand. When Edward asked him to explain his costume, he replied, "Upon my faith, sir, I have passed through many countries of your realm, and in places that I have passed the Rivers been so high that I could hardly 'scape through them except by searching the depths with this long st ff." [4]

While the Lancastrian scare was still agitating the government, there arrived tidings in London that enabled Richard Neville to embroil King Edward in a far more dangerous situation than Queen Margaret and the Earl of Pembroke had been able to create. Up the Thames came flying a ship with news that the King of Denmark had seized four English vessels in the Sound as they were on their way to Danzig. It was claimed that the Hanseatic League had instigated and taken part in the seizure.

Of the fifteen lords and merchants who owned a share of the ships and cargoes, the most prominent were the three Nevilles. The Earl of Warwick had taken a strong nationalist line ever since his Calais days, when he had cheered the merchant classes by sacking an Easterling fleet and plundering unpopular Italian merchants. He had at his side an expert on foreign trade, Master Thomas Kent, a royal councilor but Warwick's man, who for more than two decades had been conducting a campaign to force the Hanseatic League to accord better terms to English merchants.* When, in these wracking days of July, the injured traders and indignant Londoners besieged the royal council with petitions demanding retaliation against the Hanse, Warwick took the lead in advocating harsh measures.

The issue was grave, for trade with the Hanseatic League was of great importance to English mercantile prosperity. Not only did the towns of Cologne, Lübeck, Hamburg, and Danzig import large quantities of English cloth, but whereas the cloth imported by the Low Countries had to be left unfinished in order to give work to Dutch and Flemish artisans, the cloth destined for Germany was finished and thus required the services of English dyers, shearers, and other workers. In return the Hanse exported bulk products from the Baltic—timber, pitch, and tar, for shipbuilding; potash for the processing of cloth; furs, bowstaves, wax, and other raw materials.

The Earl of Warwick sprang into action the very day the news arrived. He and his brother George and Thomas Kent pressed the royal council so hard for a sweeping retaliation, other lords and merchants were raising such a clamor, and London was at the

---

* In London the Germans had long been privileged to maintain their "Steelyard," virtually a legatine compound of wharves, warehouses, and dwelling places, and they were represented on the London council by an alderman. For more than half a century, English merchants had agitated, with small success, to be given comparable privileges in the Hanse towns.

moment so upset by the treason trials of some of its leading citizens, that King Edward gave in to this pressure, though the Archbishop of Canterbury warned against the folly of breaking with the Hanse.

On this same day—Friday, July 28—officers suddenly descended on the Steelyard, sealed up its doors, and sent its inmates to prison; and royal orders went out to all the towns in the kingdom to arrest merchants of the Hanse wherever they might be found. The Easterlings were told brusquely that unless the Hanse could prove its innocence, the inhabitants of the Steelyard would have to pay £20,000 in compensation for the loss of the ships. The Germans protested that they had had nothing to do with the capture—which is apparently true—but in late November they were haled before a meeting of the council and informed that they had been adjudged guilty of the piracy and must produce the £20,000 or lose their goods. When the stubborn merchants refused to pay, they were returned to prison, all except the men of Cologne. These merchants had had nothing to do with the English troubles in the Baltic and chose now to break with the Hanseatic League rather than share the burden of reparations. Consequently they were released from prison, given possession of the Steelyard, and confirmed in their old privileges.

The case dragged on into 1469, with the rest of the Hanse towns united in bitter determination to resist English demands. The King of Denmark sent word that he alone was responsible for the seizing of the ships, in legitimate retaliation for depredations committed by English fishermen in Iceland the year before. Most of the princes of western Germany, the King of Poland, the Duke of Burgundy himself, even the Emperor and the Pope tried to intervene in favor of the Hansards. Nor were they lacking friends in England. Through native agents committed to their interest they stirred up the cloth-workers of Gloucestershire to petition Edward's council in their behalf; and from Bruges the Merchant Adventurers, headed by William Caxton (soon to become immersed in the new art of printing), likewise begged the government to avoid a rupture.

By this time the council was split between the Neville faction and the intimate adherents of the King. The Hansards found allies in the Keeper of the Privy Seal, Thomas Rotherham, who owed his rise to Woodville favor; Master William Hatclyf, the King's physician and secretary; and other royal servants. Edward wished himself well out of the business, but relations were almost beyond repair and Edward probably hesitated, in the midst of other troubles, to provoke Warwick and the Londoners. In the summer of 1469 an attempt to negotiate with the Easterlings under the auspices of the Duke of Burgundy came to nothing. English vessels no longer plied the northern ocean on their way to the Baltic lands; the Hanse merchants, except for the insurgent Cologners, quitted London. A savage sea-war broke out, with England getting the worst of it.

It was Warwick's war. At first he gained much from it, though in the end, by an ironic turn of fortune, it would cost him everything. He genuinely believed, as Captain of Calais, in a strong naval policy. His agent, Thomas Kent, had probably convinced him that English interests and English public opinion demanded a firm stand against the tough, stubborn Germans. In his homeland of Yorkshire he had imbibed from an early age a prejudice against these indefatigable traders, who were very unpopular with the citizens of York. His stand was ardently backed by the majority of London merchants and the men of the eastern and southern port towns. But elsewhere in England there were plenty of people who looked sourly on the Earl for ruining trade with the Germans. Unlike the Italians, who incurred popular hatred for importing useless luxuries, the Easterlings dealt in solid, plain goods which were sold cheap; and the cloth they exported had kept many a weaver and dyer at work. Though timber and potash and tar continued to come into England via the Low Countries and though the men of Cologne diffused English cloth throughout Germany, trade soon began to fall off. But if Richard Neville had lost hearts as well as gained them by this policy, he had scored an undoubted triumph over his sovereign. With the fleets of the Easterlings furrowing the seas to pounce upon English sails, there was small chance that Edward would be able to mount an invasion of France, and there was nobody whose services he would need more than those of the greatest naval warrior in England.[5]

Meanwhile, throughout the summer of 1468, Richard Neville's friends kept the pot of trouble boiling. No sooner were the treason trials completed and the Easterlings clapped into prison than disturbances of a different kind threatened. Though some of those who had accompanied Margaret of York to Burgundy were dazzled, like young John Paston, by the marvelous pageantry and luxurious entertainments that Duke Charles had ordered to celebrate his wedding, others returned to England grumbling about the mean hospitality they had received. "The Burgoners showed no more favour unto Englishmen than they would unto a Jew. For meat and drink was dear enough as though it had been in the land of war, for a shoulder of mutton was sold for 12d. And as for bedding, Lyard my horse stood in the house and the yeomen sometimes lay without in the street. For less than 4d a man should not have a bed a night. Lo! how soon they could play the niggards!" [6] As far as the English merchants and artisans in the cloth-trade were concerned, Charles himself was the greatest niggard of all, for even his sumptuous fetes and his pleasure in discovering that the bride he had taken against his will was a very pretty girl did not soften him to "enlarge" English cloth.

In August the simmering brew of anti-Burgundian feeling in the English capital foamed up into a plot to take vengeance on the Flemish weavers and other Flemish artisans living across the river in Southwark. Whether or not Warwick's agents had dropped a hint to kindle the conspiracy, the four or five hundred craftsmen —goldsmiths, skinners, tailors, cordwainers—who were plotting the riot were undoubtedly numbered among the Earl's partisans in the city. They planned to cross the Thames early on the morning of August 31, rouse the Englishmen of Southwark, drag all the Flemings out of bed, and hack off their thumbs and hands —or heads, some said—so that they could never again take the bread out of honest English mouths by the labor of their dexterous fingers. On the very eve of this night of knives, the plot was disclosed to the Mayor and Aldermen. Swiftly rounding up the ringleaders, the city magistrates secured confessions and consigned the men to prison to cool their heads.

Across the Channel, Warwick's ally, the King of France, was likewise busily engaged in undermining the Anglo-Burgundian alliance. The preceding April he had assembled the Estates General to procure a condemnation, aimed at the Duke of Burgundy, of any lords who should ally themselves with those ancient enemies of the realm, the English. He had vainly tried every stratagem he could think of to block the marriage of Margaret and Charles, including stories impugning the lady's chastity. Once the wedding was accomplished, Louis shifted his tactics. Suddenly he launched his armies on the weakest link in his circle of enemies, the Duke of Brittany. As towns and castles fell to the royal arms, Francis frantically implored King Edward to send the archers he had promised. Edward got them ready as fast as he could, despite the distractions which were harassing him this summer. Lord Mountjoy and the Queen's brother, Lord Scales, signed contracts September 10 to lead the expedition. But on the same day, Francis capitulated and concluded a treaty with Louis, which included a secret renunciation of his English and Burgundian allies. The herald who brought this unsavory news to Charles of Burgundy thought for a moment that he was going to be hanged for his pains. The Duke exploded in a violent fit of anger, hastily took the field with an army and moved southward to Péronne.

Louis, excited by his success with Francis, leaped to the hazardous conclusion that now was the time to work his subtle arts upon Charles. He rushed into arrangements for a personal interview and rode off with only about fifty followers to meet the Duke at Péronne. Not many hours after the town gates had shut behind him, on October 9, there arrived a Burgundian force which included a number of Louis' notorious evil-wishers. In alarm, Louis secured permission from his host to shift his lodgings from a comfortable house in town to the dilapidated castle, which was no more than a hall and a ruined tower.

These crumbling stones provided no protection against the blow which now descended—a *coup de théâtre* which was none of Louis' stage managing. Couriers galloped into Péronne with the news that the citizens of Liége had risen in revolt and captured their Prince-Bishop, the Duke of Burgundy's kinsman and ally. Their rallying cry was, "Vive le roi!" Emissaries of King Louis had been seen urging on the insurgents.

These tidings sent Charles into a red rage. Crying out that the King had come to Péronne in order to betray him, he gave instant orders for the town gates and the castle entrances to be shut. Suddenly Louis discovered that he was a prisoner, guarded by a force of Burgundian archers. The too fervent Liégeois, by mistiming their rising, had delivered the King of France to the fury of his greatest enemy. Most of the next day and night Charles closeted himself with his advisers in intense consultations. Rumors ran through the town and reached the King in the castle that the furious Duke was set upon a fearful revenge. Louis was terrified, but with the water again up to his neck, he coolly exerted all his wits and his wiles to win over influential advisers of the Duke.

The third night, Charles' rage reached its climax. Refusing to undress, he paced his chamber, occasionally hurled himself on his couch only to rise and pace again, breaking out in fiery menaces against his royal guest. So we are told by the shrewd young man who paced with the Duke, his chamberlain, Philippe de Commynes, who skillfully let Charles' wrath burn away, then managed to turn his mind from bloody thoughts. Himself a man of politic ways, Commynes admired the captive fox even though he served the passionate lion. He got word to the King that if he was to escape from deadly peril, he must accept without demur the Duke's peace terms and agree to help punish the Liégeois.

When Charles arrived at the castle to confront his prisoner with his demands, the proud prince bowed his knee but his shaking voice and twitching limbs revealed his terrible struggle to control himself. To everything that he proposed, the King of France— forewarned, as Commynes modestly notes, by a friend *—softly

* Louis, ever seeking able councilors, did not fail to follow up whatever promises he made Commynes at Péronne. On the night of August 7–8, 1472, Commynes fled Charles' court and took service with King Louis, receiving lands, favors, a noble wife, the lordship of Argenton, and what was most important to him, the King's intimate confidence.

said *yes* and *yes* again, and, like a man gingerly fingering an explosive with a minimum of pressure, said very little more. Territorial concessions, recognition of the Anglo-Burgundian alliance, agreement to help Charles punish Liége—he accepted everything. But his manner so mollified Duke Charles that he managed to slip into the treaty a promise from the Duke of Burgundy, signed and sealed, to give no aid to an English invasion of France. Then Louis rode with Charles to Liége. The Duke of Burgundy gained much by Louis' predilection for personal interviews. In forcing the King to witness the savage sacking of the town which had revolted at his instigation, Charles inflicted a terrible humiliation on his overlord, and by the Treaty of Péronne he strengthened his pretensions of independence.[7]

But the genie was again out of the jar.

Now Louis turned his arts against King Edward, having heard —probably through the Earl of Warwick—that the English King was planning a strike. Louis let it be known far and wide that he meant to take up arms in behalf of the House of Lancaster. Rumors promptly flew across the Channel that Margaret of Anjou was poised at Harfleur with a French fleet.

King Edward had decided to employ the ships and men which Lord Scales had assembled for the aid of Brittany, on an expedition to Guienne, a "feeling-out" raid to test the temper of this province which had been so long in English hands. But when he heard the reports of Queen Margaret's imminent descent upon England's shore, he sent Scales to sea, toward the end of October, with orders to intercept the French fleet. Buffeted by storms, Queen Elizabeth's brother futilely cruised the Channel for several weeks, then brought his battered ships back to port. By late autumn (1468), Louis and Warwick, between them, had wrecked Edward's hopes and his peace of mind. While the Earl kept the pot of trouble bubbling in England, Louis had hamstrung the English King's vaunted war pacts. By force, he knocked Francis of Brittany loose from his English and Burgundian friends; by treaty, he bound the Duke of Burgundy not to aid an English invasion; by guile, he caused Edward to waste on Scales' inglorious expedition some £18,000 of his war chest.

Edward began to consider ways of placating the Nevilles. He had already rewarded the Earl of Northumberland's loyalty by bestowing on him the manor of Wressel, near York, which had once been a seat of the Percies. At the beginning of September he granted his malcontent brother, George of Clarence, the reversion of the office of Chief Justice in Eyre, Keeper, and Steward of the King's Forests this side of Trent. A month later, he refrained from supporting the young Duke of Norfolk, one of his great adherents, when the Duke incurred the wrath of the Earl of Warwick and the Archbishop of York.

The Nevilles, sensitive to every means of increasing their influence, were winning golden opinions in East Anglia by taking the side of the Paston family in their great quarrel with Norfolk over the title to Caister Castle. To the King's face, they sharply upbraided the Duke for his covetousness, George Neville declaring that "rather than the land should go so, I will come there myself." Norfolk, intimidated, could only mutter that he would try to reason with his wife, who, he said, had her heart set on the place. "Ye would marvel," an anonymous correspondent wrote to Sir John Paston on October 28, "what hearts my lords hath gotten, and how their language put people in comfort."

By this time Edward was driven almost to the point of reinstating George Neville in the chancellorship. Rumors of this move were widespread, but, in the end, he grimly forbore making so signal a concession.[8] Still, the Archbishop of York had the consolation of knowing that his clever fingers could reach as far as Rome—he had won over James Goldwell, the King's own representative at the Vatican, to work for the marriage dispensation for Isabel and Clarence.

Later in the autumn the kingdom was shaken by another Lancastrian alarm. The King, his nerves frayed by these spasms of restlessness, leaped angrily into action. Yeomen of the Crown galloped the roads to lay hands on suspected plotters. Knights, some nobles, two of Edward's household men, even a quartet of bishops, were suddenly put under arrest. London was shaken by rumors of a vast conspiracy to assassinate the King. There was talk of Warwick's going hastily to Calais to forestall a Lancastrian coup. Among those clapped into prison was John de Vere, Earl of Oxford, whose father and brother had been beheaded in 1462 for plotting with Queen Margaret. Oxford saved his skin by a confession that cost two men their lives.[9] Upon his release, he was ready to do Edward any mischief that lay in his power. It was no coincidence that he was soon in the thick of the Earl of Warwick's designs. To broaden the base of his power, Richard Neville had long been cultivating old Lancastrians. He had already won over the Earl of Shrewsbury and his brother-in-law Thomas, Lord Stanley. He sealed his friendship with Oxford by giving him his sister Katherine in marriage.

As the troubled year drew toward its end, the Earl of Warwick was feeling his way toward the moment for action. However much men might huzzah for a French war, the grant of £62,000 was beginning to press uncomfortably on their pocketbooks, at the same time that they were increasingly exasperated by the greed of the Woodvilles, the unease which persisted in the realm, and the failure of the King's ally and brother-in-law to revoke the Burgundian edict against English cloth. "Many murmurous tales ran in the city a'tween the Earl of Warwick and the Queen's blood." [10] Beneath the surface of disturbances moved hidden currents of intrigue. Edward permitted his sheriffs to retain a portion of royal fees in order to repay their labors in detecting unrest and conspiracy. In these months of 1468 the King's Italian factor, Gerard Caniziani, dispensed more than £2,000 for "certain secret matters concerning the defence of the kingdom." Warwick's agents worked to undo these secret matters, to stir up discontent, and to nourish the Earl's strength in all quarters of the realm and beyond the seas.

The most successful countermine of Warwick's that has come to light is the Boon affair.

At the time when Edward was about to launch his raid on Guienne, he wished to sound out the chief nobleman of the region, Jean V, Count of Armagnac, who had been one of the leading spirits in the League of the Public Weal. For this enterprise Edward chose a tough adventurer from Dartmouth named John

Boon. At the end of October (1468), Boon was given a packet of letters, written by the King, to deliver to Armagnac.

But John Boon was a secret agent of the Earl of Warwick.

Warwick bade him delay his journey until King Louis had been warned of the plot by a herald of the Earl's. Not daring to remain in London, John Boon betook himself to Exeter. A month later, he got word from Warwick that when he had delivered his letters to the Count of Armagnac, he was to make his way to the court of King Louis, who would be waiting to hear a report of the results of his mission.

In the early days of 1469, Boon set sail from the Cornish port of Fowey. Landing at St. Sebastian, he got in touch with one of Armagnac's men and was conducted to the Count's town of Lectoure. A member of the Armagnac household took King Edward's letters to his master. Very shortly after, however, the gentleman returned to the Red Lion Inn, where Boon was lodging, and handed him back the letters, seals unbroken. The Count, Boon was told, refused to look at the letters or their bearer, and ordered Boon to get off his lands at once, declaring that he would have nothing to do with the King of England.

Boon then betook himself to King Louis' court at Amboise, as he had promised Warwick. Finding the captain of the castle at tennis, he asked to speak with the King, saying that he was the man my lord of Warwick's herald had brought word of. That night, late—"entre chien et loup"—the captain introduced Boon into the castle of Amboise by a postern gate. He was led along a gallery and into a gloomy bedchamber, lit by a single candle on a mantel over a high fireplace.

"There is the King," said the Captain.

On a bench sat a man dressed in crimson velvet with a black hat pulled low over his face. When Boon had knelt and done his reverence, the man ordered him to be seated on a bed, and asked him to recount what had happened on his mission. When Boon had told his story and delivered up King Edward's letters, he was dismissed with the word that further services would be required of him. The next evening he was brought into the same dark chamber at the same hour. This time the man in the room was wearing a yellow gown and a tawny hat. He took Boon familiarly by the hand, bade him repeat his story since he'd been slightly ill the previous evening and could not remember the details. When the Englishman finished, King Louis said, "On your life, you will tell no one that you have already been on your mission to the Count of Armagnac. You must do me a service." Boon was to pretend that he had not yet visited the Count but had come directly from England to Amboise.

For the third night he was brought to the chamber; this time he found the King in the company of four of his household lords, including the wily Jean du Lude and Tanguy du Chastel, with whom Warwick would one day negotiate at a critical moment of his life. While the lords sat on the bed and read over King Edward's letters, Louis familiarly pulled John Boon down beside him on the bench. "Here are the knights in all the world in whom I have the greatest trust," Louis whispered to Boon—and then deceived them the next second by remarking aloud, "This is the man who brought the letters. I want them to be resealed and delivered by him to the Count of Armagnac, and I wish a copy of them made." He then told Boon, *sotto voce*, that he should go off for a while under pretense of carrying the letters to the Count.

When Boon came to the castle next day, he bluntly told the gentleman who conducted him that he did not like the King of France's way of doing business. He had no certainty that he had actually spoken to the King. When the gentleman tried to reassure him, Boon retorted that he knew the King's face and voice and the man who had hidden his face with the black hat was not the King. At this moment Louis himself appeared in the gallery. On learning the cause of the dispute, he gave Boon one of his winning smiles, said he was pleased that the emissary of his cousin, the Earl of Warwick,* had been clever enough to pene-

* The flattering appellation "cousin," by which Louis was wont to address Warwick, was rather far-fetched, but accurate. Warwick's father's mother, Joan Beaufort, was the daughter of John of Gaunt, son of Edward III. Edward III's mother, Isabel of France, was the daughter of Philip IV, elder son of Philip III. Louis XI was descended from the younger son of Philip III, Charles of Valois. Thus Warwick and Louis were cousins five times removed. Louis called the Earl "cousin" even in official documents (see, for example, DeMaulde, "Un Essai"–fully cited in note 24, p. 392).

trate his little game. The truth was, he had been uncertain of Boon's identity and had therefore hidden in an adjoining chamber, the first evening, while M. du Lude played his part.

Heartened by the King's flattery and the jingling of the King's coins in his pocket, John Boon bought himself a horse and some French clothes and went off to while away several months in the vicinity of the Armagnac lands. As had been previously arranged, when he returned to the French court in August, 1469, he was met by Jean du Lude—not for nothing called by Louis "Jean Cleverness (Jean des habilitez)"—who gave him a packet of papers. "Here are the letters," said du Lude, "in which M. d'Armagnac makes his reply to the King of England, touching what you know. Take them and deliver them to the King (Louis) when he asks you for them." John Boon pocketed the forgeries, saying he understood what was going forward.

He found the King hunting at Niort. "Art thou come, John Boon?" was all Louis said at that moment, but the next evening at supper he had Boon brought before him and commanded M. de Craon to undo the packet, remarking, "You can attest that you had the letters before I ever saw them"! When the King was riding back from an interview with his brother Charles,* a few days later, he summoned John Boon to his side to instruct him in his official story, promising to send him a good man who would know just how to word the deposition. Boon was to say that after he had delivered King Edward's letters to the Count of Armagnac, he had been sent off to Bordeaux while the Count conferred with the Duke de Nemours ("who is even worse than Armagnac," Louis told Boon) and other members of his faction. When Boon returned to Lectoure, the Count gave him letters for the King of England (those provided by M. du Lude), called Edward his sovereign lord, and swore to help him win Guienne with fifteen thousand men.

---

* By the Treaty of Péronne, Louis had been forced to grant his brother the province of Champagne, dangerously adjacent to the lands of the Duke of Burgundy; but an artfully casual question of Louis' had elicited from Duke Charles the careless remark that if Louis' brother turned down Champagne, Louis might compensate him as he pleased. In 1469 Louis succeeded in persuading his brother to accept the province of Guienne instead.

Feeling himself in very deep water, Boon muttered that he did not know whether he could play his part to the royal satisfaction. "Oh, act it boldly," Louis told him jovially.

That evening Boon's deposition was taken by Guillaume de Cerisay, who, like some of the other men Boon had met, would one day have important dealings with the Earl of Warwick. The next day John Boon had his moment in the limelight. He was led before the King and a high assemblage of nobles, and Cerisay read out, as the proof of Armagnac's treachery, Boon's statement, a copy of the letters written by King Edward, and the pseudo-reply of the Count of Armagnac fashioned by the pen of Jean Cleverness.

Not long after, the King remarked to Boon that if the Count swore that he had written no letters to the King of England, Boon would of course have to offer to meet him in single combat. In terror, Boon replied that this went far beyond his daring. But Louis laughed and explained that he would only have to offer. This Boon obediently did, before the Chancellor and the royal council.

On the basis of Boon's accusation, Louis ordered an attack on Armagnac a few years later, and the Count met his end on the dagger of one of the royal archers. As for Boon, he was still being actively employed by Louis, it seems, when Warwick next came to France (spring, 1470); but shortly after, he fell under the terrible displeasure of the French King and was accused of treachery. There is a hint that Boon's wife—perhaps given him by the matchmaking Louis—became one of the King's mistresses. At any rate, Boon was condemned to have his eyes put out.

But his luck did not entirely desert him. Somehow the hangman in his horrible operation missed one of Boon's pupils; and Warwick's agent, who, like Rosencrantz and Guildenstern, learned what it meant to be the tool of a King, was still able to see—"especially when the weather was clear." He made his escape from France, only to be caught on the sea by a fellow-townsman of Dartmouth, John White. Though Boon offered 2,000 scutes for his freedom, White delivered him to the King of England. No more is known of him until Warwick, Louis, and Edward had all come to the end of their stormy rivalry. In July of 1485 he was a prisoner in the castle of Craon, between Angers and Rennes. With Louis safely in his grave, he poured out the story, in all its mazy details, of how the King of France had used him to hunt the Count of Armagnac to death. The adventurer disappears from history on a domestic note—"married and living near Mantes." [11]*

The Earl of Warwick, having joined with King Louis to shake Edward's grip on the English realm and vitiate Edward's Burgundian alliance, was now ready to fly at higher game. As the winter of 1468–69 turned to spring, he was preparing to prove by force that the House of Neville rather than the House of York was the arbiter of English destiny.

Richard Neville was now forty years old. His daughter Isabel was seventeen and Anne, four years younger. His Countess would never give him a son to carry on his name and hold whatever he might achieve. Perhaps the lack of a male heir drove him the harder to make a memorable impact upon his times. Isabel, as the wife of Clarence, might someday—by one means or another—be Queen of England. Anne remained unbetrothed, though many girls of her age and station were already married. A few years earlier, Warwick apparently hoped that she might become the bride of Edward's youngest brother, Richard of Gloucester, but Richard was firmly attached to the King. Neither Warwick nor his frail younger daughter yet had a glimmering that she would one day soon bear in her fingers the most splendid dowry of the age.

In the past four years of checks and humiliations, the Earl had spent more time with his wife and daughters than in his days of ruling the realm. But as he sat with them on the dais of the great hall at Middleham or Sheriff Hutton or Warwick Castle, his mind was restlessly turning over plans and hopes; and he was often closeted with messengers, secretaries, advisers. No scrap of information has survived to suggest that Warwick was a devoted father and husband; on the other hand, not even those chroniclers most hostile to him have hinted that he neglected his family or was unfaithful to his wife. His vitality was expressed otherwise than in the ordinary affections of man. He had admirers, followers aplenty, but apparently no real friends. Richard Neville was consumed by Warwick. His passion and his energy were poured into works and ambitions, were diffused to the world in the radiance of his role-playing.

He was no longer young. He felt his identity shrunken by enforced idleness, by the loss of authority, by the wear and strain of dissembling and plotting. He could wait no longer. The dissatisfactions rampant in the realm and the loyalties he had attracted to his cause had generated the best opportunity he was likely to have. He meant to burn out the nest of Woodvilles and royal favorites; he meant publicly to impose his will upon King Edward. Just how far he would proceed against the King, if he were successful, he did not yet know.

Behind this vision of the future, there glowed an even more splendid prospect—a Continental dominion which he would rule in his own right. In England, however complete his triumph, he must always exercise regal sway through the King, Edward or another. But his whole being cried out his capacity and will and merit to rule in his own right. Why should not the man who had made a King and rescued a realm from disorder himself enjoy a princely crown? This was the dream that had shaped all of his doing and thinking since he had first hearkened to the mellifluous suggestions of King Louis.

Richard Neville could find himself again only in the daring Captain of Calais, writ large upon the realm. His horizon was bounded by the reign of Henry VI on one side and by the ramparts of his will on the other. It was the 1450s, the broken times of opportunity, which had brought him glory. Now he would himself break the times to recreate the opportunity.

Part Five

"Setter-up and Plucker-down of Kings"

(1469-1470)

I

The Failure of Success

THE YEAR 1469 began quietly. Emerging from the winter of his discontent, the Earl of Warwick shone with his old warmth and charm. King Edward responded by bestowing the goodly manor of Penley on the Archbishop of York in early February; three weeks later he added a number of estates to Warwick's swelling domains. The Earl's sunny temper seemed to have charmed the realm out of its mysterious restlessness.

There was not much talk of an invasion of France, for which the Commons had taxed themselves £62,000 the preceding summer. In early April a Burgundian embassy appeared in London to give the King of England formal notification of his election to the Order of the Golden Fleece. Some observers thought that their real mission was to concert plans for an attack on France, but others believed that Charles of Burgundy had decided to reconcile King Edward and King Louis.

Foreign trade was finally recovering from the doldrums of Henry VI's last years. Though the Burgundian edict against English cloth was still unrepealed, thousands of cloths were again making their way—by one means or another—into the markets of the Low Countries. The Hanse merchants, except those of Cologne, had angrily left England, and the ships of the Easterlings were beginning to swoop on English merchantmen; but the Cologners, now in sole possession of the Steelyard, were promising a brisk trade. In the Kentish ports, shipwrights and sailors were hard at work. The Earl of Warwick was preparing to send a fleet to sea in order to dominate the Channel. About the time that the Burgundian ambassadors arrived in London, Warwick crossed to Calais, commissioned to survey the boundaries of the English territory.[1]

He left behind him a great and swelling secret, known by this time to hundreds upon hundreds of his followers but betrayed by none.

During the late winter he had sent word to Robin of Redesdale (Sir John Conyers) that the time for action was close at hand. While, at Westminster, he amiably discussed with King Edward plans for a sea offensive against France and the Easterlings, messengers were making their way across moorland tracks from castle to castle and village to village. Neville tenants and retainers began to look to their arms. Badges of the Ragged Staff were affixed to jackets and bonnets. Supplies were assembled—there was plenty of Neville money flowing. If Warwick made a fresh attempt to win over his brother John, it was repulsed. He could only hope that, at the moment of action, the Earl of Northumberland would not have the heart to take up arms against his kin.

The rising was to appear spontaneous and popular, but Warwick had impressed on his chief followers that he wanted an army, not a mob. He had not forgotten the hatred Queen Margaret's unruly host of northerners aroused. Sir John Conyers had no trouble finding experienced captains and veteran troops, men who had won their scars battling the Lancastrians and the Scots under Warwick's banner.[2*]

Far-off at Calais, Richard Neville was playing his role to the hilt. On April 21 he rode over to Ardres to pay a friendly visit to Edward's brother-in-law, Duke Charles, and Charles' guest Sigismund, Archduke of Austria. On the twenty-sixth, he "came with a great company" to St. Omer to spend three days with Charles and Sigismund. Then, in the full bloom of courtesy, he accompanied Charles to Aire in order to pay his respects to the Duchess of Burgundy, Edward's sister Margaret. If the galloping of messengers through Yorkshire dales and suspicious whisperings in the halls of northern castles happened to reach Westminster, who could associate these signs of restlessness—in a region often restless—with the Earl of Warwick? [3]

In early May, Warwick crossed to the Kentish harbors. At Sandwich men were rebuilding his flagship, the *Trinity*. By this time, or shortly after, Warwick's brother, the Archbishop, had in his hands the marriage dispensation for Clarence and Isabel. All was going very well indeed.

But when the Earl reached London—if not earlier—he received bad news. Some of Robin of Redesdale's men had sprung to arms days before their rising was scheduled. Warwick's brother, the Earl of Northumberland, speedily gathered an armed force, and while Warwick exchanged compliments with the Duke and Duchess of Burgundy, John Neville was routing the rebels. But he had found himself unable to proceed harshly against Warwick's friends and his own kin. Robin and his lieutenants were able to slip away into Lancashire.

Warwick's masquerade did not falter. He sent messengers northward. Secretly he received Robin's couriers. The situation began to clear. Robin's captains and followers had not lost heart; they were preparing to join him in Lancashire. Warwick dispatched word to Robin to go forward with their enterprise.[4*]

By this time he had joined the King at Windsor. On May 13 Edward held a chapter meeting of the Order of the Garter, wishing to honor his brother-in-law Charles, as Charles had honored him. Warwick and Clarence and Lord Wenlock dutifully joined with their fellow members in electing Warwick's enemy, the Duke of Burgundy, to their most noble order.[5]

There was talk of Edward's coming down to Kent to inspect the fleet and pay a visit to Calais. Did Warwick conceive that he might hold the King captive in this great stronghold across the sea? There is no knowing. Even as it appeared that Edward had made up his mind to cross the Channel, word came that a new insurrection was brewing in the North.[6]

Another Robin had popped up, this time in the East Yorkshire district of Holderness, to lead a riotous protest against a purely local grievance, a tax on corn which for generations had been exacted by St. Leonard's Hospital, York. But soon Robin of Holderness and his men began clamoring for the restoration of Henry Percy to the earldom of Northumberland—Percy having been a prisoner in the Tower since the death of his father at Towton. Warwick had no sympathy for this cause. Only the year before he had headed a commission which approved the hospital's claim.[7] And he had no desire to see the Lancastrian Percies become the rivals of the House of Neville in the North. The rising struck even more strongly at the interests of Warwick's brother John, now owner of the Percy estates and Percy title. Once again the doughty Earl of Northumberland gathered an armed fellowship, met the rioters at the very gates of York, routed them, and cut off the head of their leader.

Under cover of this diversion, Robin of Redesdale had been marshaling his army. Now he openly appealed to the commons for support and spread his banners.

While Richard Neville cocked his ear to the growing thunder in the North, he was still counseling with the King at Windsor. What would Edward do? How would John Neville act? Messengers came and went. The King abandoned his journey to Calais. Warwick assured him that he need have no fear of Louis XI; the Earl's fleet would sail immediately to menace the coasts of France.[8]

Edward decided to go North himself to investigate these repeated outbreaks and restore order. Reassured by Warwick's willing service and Northumberland's loyalty, he optimistically concluded that there was no need to raise a large army. About June 6 he set off in leisurely fashion to visit the shrines of Bury St. Edmunds and Our Lady of Walsingham, in East Anglia, before joining the main body of his troops at Fotheringhay. Except for his brother Richard and a few trusty captains, the chief figures of his entourage were Woodvilles—Earl Rivers and his sons, Anthony, Lord Scales, and Sir John Woodville. The royal retinue was demonstrating the chief complaint that Robin of Redesdale had raised against the King's government.

Weeks before, Warwick and his advisers had drawn up a "popular" petition which was to serve as the rallying cry of the rising. It began ominously—comparing King Edward with Edward II, Richard II, and Henry VI, all deposed monarchs. The realm was being ruined by the Queen's omnivorous kindred and the King's blood-sucking favorites, Herbert and Stafford and Audeley. With these tyrants governing as they pleased, no man's goods or life was safe—an obvious reminder to Londoners of the sufferings of Sir Thomas Cook. An appeal was made to the conservative religious opinion of the North in the charge that King Edward had pocketed contributions made by the clergy for a papal crusade, "for the which cause this land standeth in jeopardy of [the Pope's interdict]." The general displeasure Edward had aroused by tinkering with the money system, in 1464, was reflected in a complaint against the King's changing "his most rich coin." [9] Like the Calais Earls in '60, Warwick was aiming for the support of the masses rather than the nobles. The petition demanded that the King punish his evil councilors, cease loading his poor subjects with taxes, and take the advice of the true lords of his blood—i.e., Warwick and Clarence. But whether Edward was to be chastened, or removed, was left ambiguous.

Behind this façade of traditional protest lay a demand unlike any that had previously been raised in England. For centuries the magnates had made use of accusations of royal misrule to pare the prerogatives of the Crown by a series of "constitutional" limitations. The great insurgent lords of the past—Simon de Montfort, Mortimer, Bolingbroke (Henry IV)—had all, in varying degrees, made a case against the monarch of their day on the grounds that he had violated these limitations.*

But Richard Neville was not interested in the rights of the barons or in constitutional arguments; he had no desire to use the royal council as a check upon the King. He did not desire to limit but to wield the King's prerogative. His claim to do so had no basis in law or, like Bolingbroke's, in lineage. It was almost an article of faith, a golden aureole projected by his record of achievement and his popularity. He it was who had rescued the realm by bringing the House of York to the throne, and therefore he, rather than the King, was the true representative of the Yorkist cause, was the ultimate source of Yorkist *virtu*. This was the grand assumption which, he hoped, the Warwick legend had

---

* Limitations subscribed in Magna Carta and developed in later charters and agreements which kings were persuaded, or forced, by their baronage to accept. These limitations had to do mainly with the subjection of the king to the law, with the right of the barons to advise their sovereign, and with the powers of the royal council, through which (as well as through Parliament) such baronial rights were exercised.

warmed English hearts to accept. At bottom, Warwick based his right to power upon his uniqueness as an individual. He is perhaps among the first of modern political adventurers.[10]*

This claim Warwick well knew he could not urge directly; he had to use the idiom with which the age was familiar. He apparently did not conceive that he ran the danger of getting what he asked for rather than what he wanted.

Still, though he had not ventured to raise the issue of deposition in Robin's petition, he decided to test the temper of the realm regarding a change of monarchs. The bond of shared perils, losses, triumphs between the King and him was long since canceled by Edward's ingratitude; his daughter Isabel offered him the chance of becoming the founder of a royal dynasty; and he would unquestionably find it easier to rule in the name of his weak son-in-law than through a revengeful, if helpless, Edward.

In London and elsewhere Warwick's agents began to spread the rumor that the King was a bastard and that George of Clarence, the legitimate heir of the Duke of York, was therefore rightful ruler of England.[11] Warwick was reviving, not inventing, rumor. Five years before, when Edward shocked his subjects by marrying Elizabeth Woodville, this slander had been bruited as an explanation of the King's unkingly choice. In the surf of gossip rode the lurid tale that when the Duchess of York learned of her son's marriage, she fell into a frenzy, cried that he was unworthy of the throne because she had conceived him in adultery, and offered to submit proofs of his bastardy to a public inquiry.[12]

At Sandwich, Warwick was ostensibly occupied with his command of the sea. Before the end of May some thirty vessels were furrowing the Channel; he was readying others to follow; and he had arranged a ceremony to mark the refitting of his flagship, *Trinity*. The news which reached him was mostly good. With a small cavalcade Edward was making his way slowly through East Anglia, unaware of what was really happening in the North. Robin of Redesdale, having assembled a well-disciplined host of some five or six thousand men, was about to march southward. But Robin's host were raising no cries against the King himself, and the rumor of the King's bastardy appeared to be causing very little stir.

Men and weapons were pouring into Sandwich. Warwick's agents in London were buying "harness"—armor, helmets, brigandines *—from the armorers.[13] The roads of Kent were full of riders and retinues. On June 7 George of Clarence arrived in Canterbury with a large train of servants and retainers, remained two nights, and went on to Sandwich. That same seventh of June, King Edward and his fellowship had halted briefly at the Archbishop of York's manor of The Moor in Hertfordshire. The King suggested that it might be well for the Archbishop to ride north in order to look into the disturbances in his See. George Neville smoothly agreed to come as soon as he had fulfilled a trifling engagement. The moment the King departed for the east coast, George was on his way. Reaching Canterbury a few hours after Clarence had left, he rode on to Sandwich with Thomas Kempe, Bishop of London, and the prior of Christ Church Abbey, Canterbury.

On the twelfth of June there was holiday in Sandwich. The Archbishop of York blessed the refitted *Trinity* and said High Mass on board in the presence of Warwick, Clarence, and an array of their supporters. What mariner could fail to recall the sea triumphs won by the Captain of Calais—in happier days before Woodvilles cumbered the earth?

Two days after this burnishing of the Warwick legend, an unexpected guest arrived at Christ Church Abbey—Cicely, Duchess of York. Next day she set out for Sandwich, letting the monks know that she was going to see her son George. Had she caught wind of Clarence's schemes and was she hurrying to implore him to remain loyal to his brother? John Stone, the monk-chronicler of Christ Church Abbey, simply records that she returned to Canterbury on June 19 and left for London on the twenty-first. Next day, Warwick and Clarence rode into Canterbury, spent the night, and went off the following morning to Queenborough Castle.[14]

---

* Canvas or leather coats covered with iron rings or plates; loosely, any kind of corselet.

A week later the Earl was in London. The capital was growing uneasy. On the twentieth, the Mayor had forbidden the guild of armorers to send arms out of the city without a special license. The King still lingered at Fotheringhay, assembling a modest array of troops. Robin of Redesdale's host was driving southward —well-officered, well-provisioned, and keeping good order. Seizing the opportunity offered by the King's lethargic progress, Warwick sent word to Robin to swing westward around Edward's force and cut him off from London. In a blaze of confidence the Earl wrote two letters to Coventry on June 28, one for the Mayor, the other addressed to his friends and well-wishers.[15] He announced that the Duke of Clarence was about to marry his daughter Isabel, after which he and Clarence would join the King, and he commanded the city fathers to prepare an armed band to accompany him.*

On July 4 Warwick came to Canterbury, together with his brother George, Clarence, and his new brother-in-law, John, Earl of Oxford. A few days later the Earl and his friends crossed to Calais with a great train of followers. Isabel had apparently made the journey in secret some time before.

There was a brief, anxious wait for news. Was Calais to be the springboard of attack or a refuge? In a few days a ship slid into the harbor, bearing hopeful tidings. Robin of Redesdale had succeeded in cutting the King's army off from London. Edward had got no farther north than Newark, was beating a hasty retreat to Nottingham Castle. His favorites, William Herbert, Earl of Pembroke, and Humphrey Stafford, created Earl of Devon on May 19, were reported to be marching from the west to the King's aid.

On July 11 the Archbishop of York married Isabel Neville to the Duke of Clarence in the presence of several Knights of the Garter and a splendid company of lords and gentry.[16] Then, sensitive to the pattern of his greatness, Warwick sought to re-

---

* Nevertheless, Coventry remained loyal to the King. When Edward sent a demand for troops on July 10, the city promptly dispatched him fifty men (*Coventry Leet Book*, II, p. 343). However, most of the citizens were probably unaware of Warwick's intentions, which he had purposely left vague.

enact the great days of 1460. He launched a manifesto from Calais, summoning the faithful men of Kent to his banners. By means of an open letter attached to Robin of Redesdale's petition, Warwick, Clarence, and the Archbishop announced that they meant to lay this just complaint before the King and called on their friends to join them at Canterbury on July 16.[17]

Again, Warwick sailed in martial array across the Channel to right the wrongs of England. The men of Kent responded as of old. A growing army, bright with red jackets and ragged staves, streamed up the road to Canterbury. By July 20 Warwick was marching on London at the head of many hundreds of armed men. This time there was not even a pretense of resistance, but the city did not repeat its tumultuous welcome to the Calais Earl. Though the mass of citizens doubtless cheered themselves hoarse, the Mayor and his brethren gave the Earl no more than the polite greeting which Warwick's power dictated.

Skillfully Richard Neville dissembled his intentions and swathed the general state of affairs in a fog of obfuscation. He and the Duke of Clarence were marching to join their sovereign—that was all he gave out. As a result, the royal councilors at Westminster, unable to get word from the King, remained helplessly at their posts, and the city docilely agreed to lend Warwick a thousand pounds, on poor security. By this time messengers were coming thick. Edward's favorites, the Earls of Pembroke (Herbert) and Devon (Stafford of Southwick) were converging on Banbury with stout fellowships of Welsh pikemen and West Country archers. Robin and his army were fast approaching Banbury. Edward was still far to the north at Nottingham, apparently waiting for Pembroke and Devon.[18*]

Warwick quickly pushed ahead a mounted band to support the northern rebels. Then he and Clarence marched northward out of London. The critical moment had struck. It found Pembroke and Devon quarreling about billets for their men. Devon angrily pulled back his archers some ten miles from Banbury. At Edgecot, the Earl of Pembroke and his Welsh pikemen were suddenly assailed by the host of Robin of Redesdale. Lacking archers, the Welsh were severely punished by the guns and the arrows of the Northerners, but Pembroke's men put up a fierce struggle. William Herbert and his brother Richard fought with magnificent courage, hewing great gashes in the enemy line. Stafford of Devon, spurred by messages from Herbert, was coming up with all speed.

But before he could arrive, Warwick's advance force charged onto the field to clinch the victory for Robin. The Herberts were taken captive and haled to Northampton, where Warwick and Clarence established their headquarters. Warwick followed the bloody tradition of party strife. William Herbert and his brother were beheaded the morning after the battle.[19]*

It was soon learned that King Edward, marching to join Pembroke and Devon, had been deserted by most of his men when they heard the news of Edgecot. In order to avoid the appearance of using force, Warwick sent his brother, the Archbishop of York, to greet the King—but George Neville and his escort were clad in steel.

The Archbishop found Edward nearby at Olney with only a small following. Days before, Earl Rivers and his two sons had been sent—or had fled—to seek shelter from the storm. Lord Hastings and Edward's youngest brother, Richard of Gloucester (now sixteen), were the only men of note with their sovereign. The Archbishop smoothly suggested that Edward permit himself to be escorted to his faithful lieges, the Earl of Warwick and the Duke of Clarence. The King had been badly outgeneraled but he was now aware of the role he must play. He matched the Archbishop's bland smiles and agreed. Hastings and young Richard were amiably dismissed to go whither they would. Richard was considered to be of no importance; the genial Lord Hastings, though Edward's Chamberlain, was also Warwick's brother-in-law, and Warwick still hoped to win him over.[20]

At Coventry, Richard Neville, forty years of age, confronted the twenty-seven-year-old King. The triumphant Earl felt no necessity to indulge in recriminations. He had richly expressed himself in action. Captive Edward could plainly see how foolish he had been to suppose that he could rule without the man who had made him King. There is no record of what passed between the two, but hints in the chronicles and the subsequent course of events indicate the style of their new relationship. Warwick was content to maintain the formal courtesies. He had an urgent need to use Edward's authority, and preserving the fiction of the King's kingliness was, for the moment, the easiest way of getting what he wanted—provided that Edward was willing to play the game. Edward played the game. All pliancy and ease, he immediately assumed the role Warwick offered, preserved an unruffled demeanor, and did what he was bidden as if it were his dearest wish. In a day or two the Earl prudently deposited his prisoner, however complaisant, behind the stout walls of Warwick Castle.

Once again Richard Neville had leaped to the top of golden hours. This time, no one could doubt that he was the "conduiseur du royaume." The humiliations, the suppressed bitterness, the galling inaction of the past five long years, he swept away at one great stroke. He had consummately hoodwinked and outmaneuvered the King. Avoiding the risk of alienating public opinion by opposing his sovereign in open battle, he had quietly taken into his hands a monarch helpless and abandoned. His Northerners in their march had left behind no trail of outrage and pillage, and he saw to it that they returned speedily and unobtrusively to Yorkshire. "As astute as Ulysses," an Italian observer then in London called him. He had scored as full a triumph as he could have dreamed.[21]

Vigorously Warwick began to gather in the fruits of success. Earl Rivers and Sir John Woodville, captured along the Severn, were executed outside Coventry on August 12. A mob in Somerset slew the Earl of Devon for him. Warwick hastened to inform Louis the Eleventh of his victory. He helped himself to the chief offices in South Wales which had belonged to the Earl of Pembroke. He bestowed the treasurership of England, left vacant by the beheading of Rivers, upon Sir John Langstrother. He appointed a dozen of his followers to offices in the customs service. For the moment he withheld the Great Seal from his brother George, however, because Edward's Chancellor, Stillington, remained docilely in London with the rest of the royal council, attempting to keep up an outward show of government-as-usual. Warrants, orders, proclamations—Edward cheerfully signed whatever was put before him. Warwick had an absolute grip on the royal prerogative.

He secured a privy seal from the King ordering Parliament to convene in the Neville stronghold of York on September 22. He knew that he must have some sort of parliamentary confirmation for his seizure of power. His swift and easy triumph seemed to assure his ability to dominate Lords and Commons.

The examples of the past suggested what this Parliament might be called upon to do. After Edward II and Richard II had lost power, after the Yorkists had taken Henry VI at Northampton in 1460, the summoning of Lords and Commons had signaled the fall of the King. If Warwick hoped to plant Clarence upon the throne, however, he was careful to conceal his design. Doubtless he planned to push Parliament as far as it would go, but was prepared to accept a settlement that would securely fetter Edward to a Neville regime. He would then be exercising by the consent of Parliament the mastery of the realm that he had formerly exercised by the grateful acquiescence of the King. The Warwick legend would be legalized.

But before August was ten days old, something had gone wrong. The realm was not following the example of obedience set by the captive King and his bewildered council. There were no signs of revolt against Warwick's government. The realm was acting as if Warwick had destroyed government altogether. Wild tales were upsetting people's minds. Some men were openly demanding the release of the King. Others, thinking that Edward was dead, were eagerly resorting to whatever violence would satisfy their private ambitions. The lawlessness of Henry VI's last days was suddenly reborn. Warwick had been able to ambush the King, but the King's moral authority was proving insusceptible to ambush.

London was transformed into a hive of fear and rumor. Warwick's numerous well-wishers among the lower classes read the Earl's triumph as license to do as they pleased. The mob stirred ominously—pillage of the wealthy and death to the Flemings!

As the city magistrates and the royal council struggled to keep order, a letter came from the Duke of Burgundy promising aid if the city remained loyal to his brother-in-law and threatening vengeance if the citizens failed in their duty. This missive and the presence of Burgundian ambassadors—known friends of the King's—strengthened the hand of the Mayor. Warwick himself, much as he hated to show favor to Burgundy, could not afford to have his cause tarred with violence. In the King's name he proclaimed that severe punishment would be meted out to any who dared act against the King's amity with the Duke of Burgundy and his subjects.[22]

The London mob subsided, but by the middle of August England had fallen into such a queasy state that Warwick could no longer maintain the pretense that all was well. He dispatched the Duke of Clarence and his brother George, the Archbishop, to the capital to try to stiffen the authority of the royal council.[23] The Earl himself conveyed King Edward by secret night marches to his stronghold of Middleham Castle, in Wensleydale. He was putting himself perilously far from the center of affairs, but Yorkshire was the heart of his power and he had to keep his grip on the King at all costs. By this time he had little else to show for his great labors. Mysteriously, maddeningly, his triumph was crumbling around him. He was not defied. He was not attacked. He was ignored. The realm would not recognize the commands of a captive King; it would not acknowledge Warwick to be more than the King's captor.

What was to prevent a man with retainers at his back from doing as he pleased? The King's loyal supporter, the Duke of Norfolk, took the occasion to beleaguer Caister Castle, claimed by the Paston family, and despite the efforts of Clarence and the Archbishop of York to help the Pastons, Norfolk pressed his siege until young John Paston capitulated.[24] Trouble was stirring in the West between the Berkeleys and the House of Talbot. In London and elsewhere men raised their voices against the summoning of Parliament. The kingdom pitched and rolled in mounting swells of restlessness. Suddenly a Lancastrian rising erupted on the northern border, provoked by Humphrey Neville of

Brancepeth, a distant kinsman of Warwick's who was perhaps misled by the Lancastrian support Warwick had enlisted.

At the moment he got word of Humphrey Neville's insurrection, Warwick, at Sheriff Hutton, was receiving increasingly gloomy news from his brother in London. With the realm quaking on the verge of anarchy, there was nothing for it but to cancel the meeting of Parliament. This admission of his failure to control the realm so galled the Earl that he dispatched no less than four royal messages of explanation to the Council, striving in vain to put a good face on a bad matter. It is easy to imagine with what secret pleasure King Edward, immured at Middleham, obediently put his seal to these confessions of his gaoler's weakness.*

Meanwhile, Warwick had confidently sent out a call for armed men to help him put down the Lancastrian rising. But he soon received another jolt: even in Yorkshire the Ragged Staff had lost its magnetism. The Neville retainers and friends and tenants who followed Robin of Redesdale had returned to their homes thinking that the cause they had fought for was triumphant. Had not the worst of the Woodvilles and the King's favorites been removed for good and all, and was not the King willing to do what the Earl asked? They were confused and troubled by their sovereign's captivity, which was not the end for which most of them had risked their necks, and not even for Warwick would they again spring to arms until they understood what was going on.

The Earl hastily summoned his brother George from London,

---

* The way in which Warwick issued commands through the King is illustrated in the first message, a letter Edward addressed to the Council on May 30: the bearer of the missive would explain certain matters "concerning our parliament, which by us and our cousin of Warwick and other of our Council in these parts is not thought expedient to be kept at our city of York . . ." Three days later, Warwick wrote to the Council in his own name. On September 4 he sent still another order to countermand Parliament, this time under Edward's privy seal, admitting "great troubles in divers parts of this our land not yet appeased," but in his final communication, also under the privy seal, he commanded the Council to excuse the canceling of Parliament simply on the grounds that county elections could not be held in time. (Scofield, I, pp. 501–02 and notes 1, 2, and 3, p. 502.)

but the Archbishop of York had neither good news nor hopeful counsel to offer. Warwick found himself caught between bitter alternatives. To give Edward even a show of liberty would confess his own impotence and risk losing the King altogether. But as long as he continued holding the King captive, he was powerless to check the Lancastrians or restore order in the realm. He could cut through the dilemma with a sword—kill Edward, try to proclaim Clarence King. . . . But whatever chance of success this savage course might have had directly after the battle of Edgecot, it was now only a hideous expedient of despair, and Warwick was too responsible and too self-confident to plunge England into chaos.

Quickly he chose the risk which at least offered a course of action. He sent the Archbishop off to Middleham to bargain with the King. Edward was impeccably good-humored. In return for a little more liberty, he readily agreed to support Warwick's campaign against Humphrey Neville. Amiably he assured the Archbishop that he harbored no ill-will toward the House of Neville and would seek no retaliation. The shrewd young King, kept secretly in touch with affairs through Burgundian agents and his own followers, knew that his hour was approaching.[25]

Warwick permitted him to enter York in royal state, to talk freely with those who thronged to pay him homage, and then to take up official residence at Pontefract Castle. Now men willingly took arms to put down the Lancastrians. Seeking to reassert his power, Warwick drove northward in a whirlwind campaign that before the end of September had extinguished the Lancastrian revolt and captured its leaders. On September 29 the King rode up to York to witness the execution of Humphrey Neville and put his seal of approbation on Warwick's efforts.

Edward returned to Pontefract. A few days later, the chief lords of his court suddenly appeared, having been summoned secretly by the King—the young Duke of Buckingham, the Earls of Arundel and Essex, Lords Mountjoy, Dynham, Howard, and others. At the same time, Lord Hastings and Richard of Gloucester came riding in at the head of a stout band of armed men.

John, Earl of Northumberland, likewise put himself at the King's side. Blandly Edward informed the Earl of Warwick that he was returning to his capital.

There was nothing Warwick could do to prevent him. Edward set off in royal state with a force of about a thousand men. In a forlorn attempt to keep up appearances, the Archbishop of York rode Londonward also. Halting briefly at his Hertfordshire manor, he was joined by the Earl of Oxford, and the pair then spurred on in order to appear in the King's retinue when he entered the capital. They were soon stopped by a royal message: when he wanted them, the King announced, he would send for them. Having thus declared his independence, Edward rode into London, ceremoniously escorted by a delegation of officials and citizens, and before the middle of October he was once more ensconced at the palace of Westminster.

"The King himself," Sir John Paston reported to his mother, "hath good language of the Lords of Clarence . . . [and] of Warwick . . . saying that they be his best friends; but his household men have other language."

Though nobody reported Warwick's words on the subject of Edward, Sir John and the rest of the realm could have little doubt of Warwick's feelings. Paston added, "What shall fall hastily I cannot say." [26*]

Warwick's defeat was the more intolerable because it had worn the guise of victory. For one exultant heartbeat he had held everything in his hand. Then the King's power and the King had slid through his fingers as if he were paralyzed and the realm bewitched. Edward had proved himself to be more deeply engrafted in the hearts of his subjects than Warwick had estimated. Yet no protests had been raised against the bloody rooting out of Woodvilles and royal favorites; no rising, no conspiracy even, had been stirred against Warwick's rule. But somehow the Warwick Legend—and goddess Fortune—had not supported the weight which Richard Neville had put upon them.

In fact, he had presented the realm with an anomaly that it refused to understand; he had leaped beyond the political thinking of his age and found himself alone.

But having won such a quick and overwhelming and tangible success, how could he accept a defeat so elusive and unreasonable? He could not fail to realize the hazards of the political vacuum in which he was now suspended; he could not forget the military prowess of his Northerners and Kentishmen. He was a man— abler than most men, groping like all men, given to illusion and created to err, a man of a changing time and himself a changeling in his time, gifted with the capacity to make an impact upon men's minds and unusually sensitive to the power of that impact, a man struggling to play a high role on the world's stage, driving his life by the airy prompting of a dream.

Onward, then!

The lion was loose, but had not he himself let the beast go? Next time, he would be wiser.

II

"Fair Stood the Wind"

THE NEXT two months are a murky interlude in Richard
Neville's history. He and Clarence apparently moved about
the North and the Midlands with large bands of armed
men. With the King holding the capital, he was laboring desperately to keep his grip upon the country.[1]

In London, Edward made no attempt to gather an army, but he
imperturbably flaunted his independence. He emphasized the Burgundian alliance by taking the oath of the Order of the Golden
Fleece and he sent an embassy to invest his brother-in-law with
the Order of the Garter.[2] He dismissed Sir John Langstrother
from the office of Treasurer. He stripped Warwick of the offices
in Wales which the Earl had seized and gave them to his loyal
brother Richard, who was made Constable of England. Anthony
Woodville reappeared at court wearing his dead father's title
of Earl Rivers. Warwick and Clarence were excluded from
commissions of array. Even those humble Neville supporters who
had been rewarded with posts in the customs were, most of them,
replaced by appointees of the King.

But Warwick made his power felt in the spasms of restlessness
that were soon shaking the divided kingdom. Young Richard
of Gloucester successfully quelled a rising in Wales, but there
were stirrings in other parts of the realm.[3] If the Earl of Warwick
had been unable to govern without Edward, neither would Edward be able to govern without coming to terms with the Earl
of Warwick.

It did not take Edward long to see the point. Before the end
of October, the Earl and the Duke of Clarence received invitations to attend a Great Council at Westminster. Warwick was not
to be drawn so quickly. He demanded assurances and guarantees.
Messengers sped back and forth through the no man's land between the capital and the Neville strongholds. Not till early De-

cember did Warwick finally agree to ride to London. Arriving with a powerful retinue, he and Clarence found the capital bristling and watchful—the gates heavily guarded, bands of armed men patrolling the wards at night. It was the turbulent '50s all over again.

But Warwick and Clarence were cordially welcomed to the council chamber; Edward appeared as amiable as ever; the atmosphere of Westminster was redolent of a love feast. It was agreed that grievances on both sides should be buried in oblivion. Warwick and all his followers were granted pardons covering any kind of offense committed before October 11. The Earl made good his protest against excessive taxation by securing a remission of part of the grant Parliament had made in 1468. As for the "evil councilors" singled out in Robin of Redesdale's petition, most of them had been forever removed, and the justice of their taking off was tacitly acknowledged in the King's readiness to make all the concessions. The reconciliation was sealed by the matrimonial union of Neville and Plantagenet: Edward's eldest daughter Elizabeth was betrothed to the Earl of Northumberland's son George, who was created Duke of Bedford.

But John Neville was the King's follower, not Warwick's; and the betrothal had been arranged months before. This symbol of Warwick's success was as hollow as the rest of it. He had won almost all that he had asked for, but he had utterly failed to get what he wanted—the mastery of the realm. Behind the confident mien he exhibited in the council chamber, he was leading a taut, strained existence. He could guess what bitter words the Queen was pouring into her husband's ear and what hard resolves lay behind Edward's smiles. In his own chambers he had to listen to the discontented bluster of his shallow son-in-law. Edward was vigorously knitting up loyalties and rallying powerful supporters—Richard of Gloucester, the Dukes of Norfolk and Suffolk, the Earls of Essex, Kent, Arundel, Worcester, Lords Hastings and Howard and Mountjoy, and other magnates. Warwick knew that the apparent victory he had negotiated was no more than a shaky truce, and he meant to strike first.

The fever of action raced in his blood; the memory of his

tantalizing near-triumph burned along his nerves. If he could not
rule England through Edward, he needed only to aim higher. He
must set the pliable Clarence on the throne, Clarence who would
one day make him the grandfather of a line of Kings. He had
failed because he had not dared enough. Middle age had not
worn down his buoyancy nor blurred the outlines of his imperious
vision. The life of adventure still beckoned. As the year 1470
came in, he was impatiently scanning the uneasy realm for a sign,
a clue.

Early in January a disturbance erupted in Lincolnshire.[4*]
Richard, Lord Welles, who had been feuding with Sir Thomas
Burgh, gathered an armed following and attacked Burgh's manor.
The place was razed to the ground; goods and chattels were
carried off; and Burgh was forced to flee to London. King Edward took an immediate interest in this outrage because Burgh
was his Master of the Horse and Lord Welles had been an ardent
Lancastrian. Fearing the hand of the King, the Welles family
began working for popular support by spreading rumors that
Edward was coming into the country to hang great numbers of
the commons.

This was opportunity enough for the Earl of Warwick, who
happened to be a second cousin of Lord Welles. Secret messages
were dispatched to Lincolnshire. At the first hint, Welles and his
son, Sir Robert, jumped at the chance to secure the support of
Warwick and Clarence. By the beginning of February, plans for
an insurrection were being actively concerted. Warwick remained
in London, attending the royal council, showing himself well-
content with the new-found peace between himself and his
sovereign. In order to build up Clarence's royal stature in the eyes
of the rebels, he left the burden of conspiring to his son-in-law.

Clarence dispatched his chaplain and another priest into Lincolnshire, exhorting Welles to muster his followers secretly and
to make no move until the Earl of Warwick left London. Warwick sent messages to persuade Welles that the object of the
rising must be to set the Duke of Clarence upon the throne. Busy
with his plotting, the Duke slipped in and out of the capital,
avoiding the palace of Westminster.

But Warwick had enemies—among the great merchants of the city as well as at court—and some of them were quick to note this surreptitious activity. Rumors began to sift through London that the Duke and the Earl were conspiring. Placards appeared one morning on the Standard in Cheapside and in other public places, denouncing them for traitors. When Warwick indignantly protested his innocence to the King, he found Edward apparently willing to believe him and the agitation died away.[5]

By this time King Edward was preparing to march into Lincolnshire. Wooing rebellious hearts by a fresh offer of pardon, he announced that he would leave London on Sunday, March 4; he sent out summonses for troops to meet him at Grantham on March 12; and he peremptorily ordered Welles and Welles' brother-in-law, Sir Thomas Dymmock, to appear before him. They duly came in at the beginning of March, emboldened by their confidence in Warwick's power. This prompt submission won them a speedy pardon, but Edward detained them in London, for some of the commons of Lincolnshire were now riotously demanding the restoration of the feeble King languishing in the Tower.

This Lancastrian clamor helped to screen Warwick's intentions. Lingering in London until the end of February, he took leave of the King with a promise to join him on the march into Lincolnshire. Edward readily agreed to send the Earl and Clarence commissions of array for the counties of Warwick and Worcester, even though men at court were muttering that Warwick's offer to support the campaign was a bad omen.[6]

Clarence dispatched word to the Welleses to unleash their rising on Sunday, March 4. To give the rebellion a little extra momentum by delaying the King's march, he wrote to Edward that he would be in London on Tuesday, March 6, and hoped to have a word with his brother. Edward obligingly put off his departure—but he was not the Edward of '69; this time he had a stout army and he was ready for anything.[7] On Tuesday afternoon the brothers enjoyed an amicable interview at Baynard's Castle, their mother's home, in the course of which Clarence explained that he was on his way westward to join his wife. They demonstrated their friendly relations by going together to St. Paul's to make an offering. Then Edward rode out of London at the head of a strong band of lords and men-of-arms of his household.

The next morning Clarence conferred secretly with Sir John Langstrother, Welles, and Dymmock, after which he sent word to the King that he had decided to join the Earl of Warwick in helping to put down the rebels. Then he rode into the Midlands as fast as he could spur his horse.

At Coventry, Warwick was slaking his hungry energies in a swirl of activity—mustering men, listening to reports from his agents, dictating a flow of communications. Messengers were carrying appeals to his friends in the North to foment a new insurrection. He had secured promises of support from Lord Stanley and the Earls of Shrewsbury and Oxford. He was dispatching daily words of encouragement to the Welleses and sending out men to report on the King's movements.

As the week passed, the news continued good. On the previous Sunday (March 4), Sir Robert Welles had had published in all the churches of Lincolnshire a summons to arms in the name of Warwick and Clarence. Word arrived that the rebel host had entered Lincoln and would shortly be moving on Grantham. Warwick assured the messenger that he and Clarence would soon be on the way with a powerful fellowship, laying his hand on a book and swearing his oath. On Friday, March 9, came letters written by the King himself the day before, thanking them for their support and enclosing the commissions of array for Worcestershire and Warwickshire.

By this time, Scrope of Bolton, Sir John Conyers, and Lord Fitzwalter had succeeded in stirring a rising in Yorkshire. Edward was approaching Fotheringhay. Sir Robert Welles had reached Grantham. Sending Welles a ring, Warwick urged him to hurry his army on to Leicester and let the King pass into Lincolnshire. Warwick and Clarence would join the rebels at Leicester on Monday night (March 12) with twenty thousand men, and once again Edward would be cut off from his capital. On Sunday, March 11, the Earl, still at Coventry, sought to allay any suspicions his sovereign might have developed by sending an assurance that he and Clarence were marching to join the royal army.

What Warwick did not know was that the King had had Welles and Dymmock fetched from London and had threatened them with death unless Sir Robert Welles immediately submitted. Welles was allowed to send off a terror-stricken plea to his son. What Warwick knew too well was that he had not been able to muster twenty thousand soldiers—or even a quarter of that number. He was discovering that men showed small desire to risk their lives in order to clap a crown on the head of the Duke of Clarence. Even the town of Coventry, however enthusiastic it might pretend to be now that it was Warwick's headquarters, had loyally sent off its usual quota of forty men to swell the royal army.

Early Monday morning (March 12) came a frantic message from Sir Robert Welles: in an attempt to save his father's life, he was reversing his march in order to fall upon the King's host.

His plan shivered to pieces, Warwick remained in Coventry anxiously awaiting news. It arrived on Tuesday the thirteenth—brought by fugitives from battle. King Edward had suddenly come up with the rebels a few miles outside of Stamford and routed them. Sir Robert Welles and the advisers Clarence had sent him were fleeing for their lives. Not many hours later, John Down, an esquire in the royal household, appeared with letters written in Edward's own hand. Announcing his victory, the King desired Warwick and Clarence to dismiss the men they had arrayed and join him at once.

They would do so, they assured Down. They would ride to the King in all speed. But after a hasty consultation they set out with their small army for Burton-on-Trent. Down ventured to remark, "Meseems you take not the right way towards the King." They got rid of him with the vague answer that the route they were following would do the King better service.

It was a gloomy journey that Warwick took with his son-in-law through Burton and onward to Derby. The Earl got few

huzzahs from the villages along their road. No lads rushed to join
the banners of the Ragged Staff. Warwick's soldiers were beginning to wear the look of men who feel a traitor's noose about their
necks. Numbers of them were disappearing behind hedgerows
or slipping away under the cover of night.

The news was all bad. The Earl of Shrewsbury joined the royal
army. John Neville, still faithful to his King, had quickly broken
the northern rising. And King Edward, marching northward on
a route some twenty-five miles to the east of Warwick's, was
moving fast enough to block the road to Yorkshire.

How much did Edward know? On Saturday, as he was making
for Chesterfield, Warwick sent two men to the King with
promises that he and Clarence would meet the royal host at
Retford. But next day, Sunday the eighteenth, Garter King of
Arms came riding into Chesterfield. Formally he delivered two
privy seals of summons to the King's presence. Sir Robert Welles
had been captured and confessed everything. Warwick and Clarence were commanded to appear at once in humble wise in
order to answer grave charges against them.

Warwick sought to bargain, or at least play for time. He returned word that he and Clarence must be assured of pardons
for themselves and their followers. On the same day the King fired
back two more privy seals of summons, with the terse observation that he had already offered pardons. The Earl and his son-in-
law remained that night at Chesterfield, desperately seeking a
way out of the trap that had suddenly closed round them. On
Monday morning, Warwick sent the King a request for safe-
conducts. Edward replied grimly that even his ancient enemies,
the French, would not ask for such sureties as Warwick and
Clarence were demanding. If they were innocent, he would be
as glad as they; if guilty, he would remember his long-cherished
affection for them and minister "rightwiseness with favour and
pity."

Warwick realized that the game was played out. Before dawn
on Tuesday—only two weeks from the day Clarence had ridden
into London to hoodwink his brother—the pair took horse with
what remained of their followers and galloped hard for Man-

chester and the promised aid of Lord Stanley. They were soon met by messengers from that shifty lord—with the greatest regret he protested that he was powerless to help them. There was nothing for it but flight.

Fortunately, King Edward had had to break off his pursuit for lack of food and horse fodder and hurry to York to gather provisions. As royal messengers coursed the roads with proclamations offering money rewards for the capture of the King's "great rebels," Warwick and Clarence made their way safely to Warwick Castle, where their ladies were anxiously awaiting news of them.[8] Isabel, who was to have been made Queen of England, found herself a hunted fugitive. She was eight months pregnant and in no condition to travel. But there was no help for it. With her mother and her sister Anne she was soon journeying toward the south coast. Warwick sent messengers ahead to round up ships in the Devon ports and to get word to his uncle's bastard, Thomas of Fauconberg, who was commanding a flotilla in the Channel.[9]

Warwick reached Exeter about April 10, five days ahead of the King's advance guard. He was able to lay hands on a goodly number of ships. Quickly he embarked the ladies and several hundred faithful followers. His vessels thrust their prows into the Channel and set sail for the haven of Calais, which was in the charge of Lord Wenlock. Ten years after the disaster at Ludlow, the Earl was again an outlaw; the life of adventure had come full circle.

Sweeping up additional ships in the harbors of Devon and Dorset, Warwick coasted toward Southampton, where a number of his stoutest craft were berthed, including the *Trinity*. But Earl Rivers, commanding at the port, had been forewarned and was not caught napping as he and his father had been, a decade before at Sandwich. Warwick's little navy was so sharply assailed by Rivers' fleet that the Earl was soon forced to break off the engagement, losing a few ships as he did so. But he got safely away and on April 16 he was standing in to Calais harbor. . . .

Guns cracked. Cannon balls splashed about the fleet. Despite the Earl's signals, the fire continued until he ordered his vessels to heave to. Barely half a day before, a messenger had arrived with Edward's stern orders against admitting the fugitives; and the garrison had decided to remain loyal to the King, at least for the moment.

Unable to believe this reversal of destiny, Warwick cast anchor and tried to parley. Wenlock sent courteous messages but remained firm. Calais would not admit its Captain. At this moment Isabel began her labor. It was a difficult one; the Countess of Warwick and Anne grew frightened; there were no herbs or even wine to ease Isabel's suffering. Warwick, alarmed for his daughter's safety, sent a boat begging some wine, and Wenlock obliged with two casks. Isabel gave birth to a dead child. Anne and her mother prepared the little body for burial, sailors slipped it into the water, and the infant disappeared as quickly as had his father's hopes of becoming a King.

But the sea was Warwick's element. He shook off the months of too hasty plotting, of rash venturing soon brought to disaster. He was not daunted by his rebuff before Calais. Boldly he set his ships to furrowing the Channel in search of Breton and Burgundian prey. In a few days he was joined by a stout squadron under the Bastard of Fauconberg, who had broken away from the royal fleet. From their anchorage before Calais, Warwick and the Bastard ranged the Narrow Seas, their haul of prizes growing daily. Soon they had brought in upward of half a hundred Burgundian and Breton merchantmen and fishing boats.

Lord Wenlock managed to send Warwick a secret message quite different from his official pronouncements. Calais, he pointed out, was a mousetrap. Once Warwick entered, he would be besieged by the Duke of Burgundy on land and an English fleet by sea. Far better for the Earl to retire into France to recoup his fortunes. When the proper time came, Wenlock promised, he would give a good account of himself for his master.

Warwick had already dispatched word to King Louis.[10] He now gave orders to his captains to sail along the Norman coast. Earl Rivers and Lord Howard came down on him as he got under weigh. In a bitter sea-fight which cost the lives of several hundred men, he held his own against the royal fleet, encumbered though he was with booty. Some of his captures were wrested from him but he inflicted so much damage on his assailants that he was able to break away without being pursued.

Flaunting his rich train of prizes, he coursed westward through the Channel, the birthplace of his greatness. He was never more himself than at this moment, an independent force, cruising beyond the bounds of the politics of his day. On his starboard— the white cliffs of England, for the moment Edward's England but harboring thousands who would rally to the Ragged Staff. On his port bow—France and his friend King Louis who had acknowledged the spell of Warwick as warmly as any. If he was to master England again, he must accept the limitation of his times and work through a king. Otherwise, he was a free agent— unconstrained by obligations of the past, the proprieties of worldly place, the fading myth of chivalry, and the tyranny of the conventionally possible. He steered by the pole star of his legend.

He had captured but he could not govern through King Edward. He had put forward but he could not enthrone his weak son-in-law. There was another monarch available, however, and he had a second daughter to make him the grandfather of kings if Isabel could not. And there still glimmered the prospect of ruling in his own right a Continental dominion, when he and the King of France had destroyed Charles of Burgundy.

About the first of May, Warwick turned his fleet into the mouth of the Seine and cast anchor at Honfleur. He was greeted by his old friends, the Admiral of France and the Archbishop of Narbonne, who had been instructed by their sovereign to give the Earl of Warwick a kingly welcome. Warwick immediately dispatched word to Louis that he proposed to uproot the man he had placed upon the English throne and restore the House of Lancaster.[11]

III

The Return of the Native*

AND WHO was more excited than King Louis by the turn of fortune's wheel which suddenly cast the Earl of Warwick upon his shores?

He had been miserably puzzled by the welter of events across the Channel. On learning of Warwick's triumph in August of '69, he commissioned the Earl's friend William Menypeny to treat with the Neville government; but before Menypeny departed, news arrived that Edward was again his own master. There followed vague tales of civil strife, of which Louis could make nothing. On receiving word that Edward and Warwick had composed their differences, he nervously jumped to the conclusion that the Earl had betrayed him and called out the *ban* and *arrière-ban*. Nonetheless, he sent Menypeny across the Channel, empowered to treat with both Edward and Warwick. In mid-March, the Scot returned with the comforting news that England was again in the throes of war. In April, Louis rejoiced over tidings that Warwick had killed Edward in battle. Suddenly he learned that the Earl was a fugitive. Then came word that Warwick had been welcomed at Honfleur, followed hard by a message from Warwick himself. With his friend Louis' help, he was ready to restore King Henry to the English throne and he sought an immediate interview.[1]

The King of France was thrown into one of his nervous crises of elation, fear, suspicion, hope. The wild fluctuations in England since he had entertained Warwick at Rouen had made him doubtful of the Earl's real motives. With horrible speed the Duke of Burgundy learned that the great rebel of his ally Edward and the spoiler of his subjects' shipping had been welcomed to Normandy with all his Burgundian booty. Scarcely had Louis been jolted by Warwick's arrival when he was bombarded by the enraged Duke with accusations of bad faith and demands for Warwick's arrest.

Louis did not want war with Burgundy on these unfavorable grounds; besides, he was short of money and he needed time to work Francis of Brittany loose from his alliance with Charles.

But Louis of Valois was not the man to decline the marvelous gambit which fortune had thrown in his hands.

He plunged. He sent a messenger posting to Warwick with the declaration that the King of France would do all in his power to accomplish the desires of his friend. He dispatched two of his officers to the tattered little court of Margaret of Anjou with an invitation to her and her son to join him at Amboise in order to close with the opportunity offered by the Earl of Warwick. He also sent a hasty message to Charles of Burgundy, promising that Burgundian goods would be restored and making the lame excuse that when he extended a safe-conduct to Warwick he did not know that the Earl had taken prizes from the Duke's subjects.

But these words, he knew, would never satisfy the Duke. Day and night Louis was "closely closeted and in secret councils" over Warwick's affairs. "It seems," reported the Milanese ambassador, "that they give him plenty to think about." [2] For there were Warwick's ships and Warwick's telltale prizes riding at anchor in the mouth of the Seine; there were Warwick's seamen hawking their plunder in Norman towns and villages—all terribly visible to prying Burgundian eyes. And there was Warwick insisting upon making an open appearance at the court of France!

Yet, despite these perils, Louis insisted upon treating Warwick, not as a suppliant but as an independent potentate. On May 12 he hurried off two of his most trusted officers, William Menypeny and Jean Bourré, with a set of instructions to the Admiral and the Archbishop of Narbonne for negotiating with his guest. The instructions shout Louis' agitation. They fall all over themselves —explaining, cajoling, re-explaining, promising.

The King could not speak to the Earl of Warwick nor show him favor while he was flaunting his Burgundian prizes, for Louis would be breaking the treaty of Péronne, which he had sworn to uphold. Therefore he begged Warwick to send his prizes and fleet to the Channel Islands. Or even to Guienne, for the King was sure that his brother Charles, Duke of Guienne, would gladly

offer Warwick a safe-conduct. Then if the Earl wished to speak
with the King, Louis would make a pilgrimage to Mont St. Michel
and meet him nearby at Granville. Or Warwick could send his
ships to Cherbourg or Granville, far from Burgundian eyes. Besides, if there was urgent need of communication he could dispatch messengers to the King and he would have a quick reply,
just as if they were talking together. In any case, Louis could
say nothing till he had word from Queen Margaret—a copy of
his letter to her he enclosed for Warwick's inspection. After he
had heard from her, that would be the time for Warwick and
Clarence to speak with him at Granville. The Queen, he thought,
would do what he wished.

But if Warwick insisted on an interview before going off with
his ships, he and Clarence, making a pretense of accompanying
their fleet, could secretly come over land to Falaise, where the
King would meet them. The Admiral and the Archbishop were to
say that Louis would exert all his power to help Warwick recover
the kingdom of England, either through the agency of Queen
Margaret or by whatever means he wished. For the King loved
Warwick better than he loved Queen Margaret and her son. Indeed, he had hitherto always held himself aloof from them for
love of Warwick, acting as if he had never seen them. *Any*
means that Warwick wanted to employ—the King would support him.

But Louis could not break the treaty of Péronne. The ships
had to be moved before any other step was taken. Warwick was
now in the very worst place he could possibly be. Flemings and
Burgundians came there every day; the Count of St. Pol—Elizabeth Woodville's uncle—was governor of the region; the actions
of Warwick's seamen, any comings and goings between Warwick
and the King, would be reported daily to the Duke of Burgundy.
From the Channel Isles Warwick could send his ships to Cherbourg and Granville, as he would. If he wished to leave his ladies
ashore, Louis would see them properly cared for at Carentan or
Bayeux or Valognes or if he preferred to send them to Amboise
they would have no worse a hostess than the Queen.

There was a final item, less weighty. Either Clarence was feel-

ing the heat and had begged a gift or Louis was feeling the necessity of giving a little pat to his ego: Menypeny and Bourré were
to bring some silk cloth for Warwick's son-in-law.[3]

For all his agitation, Louis did not fail to make his central point
emphatically clear: he was Warwick's ally, not Margaret of
Anjou's. If he helped the House of Lancaster, it would only be
at Warwick's request and as a means of returning Warwick to
power. There was certainly Louis' usual vein of self-interest in
this declaration: he probably had more confidence in Warwick's
power than in the Queen's; more confidence in Warwick's gratitude, since the Earl had no royal claim to lean on; more confidence in Warwick's devotion to a French alliance. Yet it may be
also that beneath the layers of his intricate calculations lurked a
genuine affection.

The Admiral and the Archbishop did their best to carry out
their instructions, but Richard Neville stood squarely on the
dignity which Louis had accorded him. He must speak with the
King before he did anything else. When Menypeny and Bourré
reported their difficulties, Louis began dispatching furious messages:

He already knows very well that Warwick wants to see him,
but they have ignored the main point, *the ships*—"Never will I be
at my ease until I know that all their vessels have departed and
that not a single one remains!" They must be hidden in Lower
Normandy, Barfleur or Granville or Cherbourg, anywhere to get
them out of the Burgundians' sight. And the booty must be
given up—he will see that Warwick is recompensed. The Earl
must be told firmly that the King of France cannot do a thing for
him while his men and ships remain at Honfleur. As for the English ladies—"You enrage me!" he wrote to poor Menypeny and
Bourré, "for having let the ladies remain in that neighbourhood!"
They must be escorted at once from such dangerous territory,
temptingly close to Charles' borders and swarming with officers
of the Count of St. Pol. "I beg you, plead so convincingly with
Warwick that without fail he will remove the ladies to Lower
Normandy." When the fleet has been shifted, Louis adds, "I can
say that it is M. the Admiral who harbours it . . . and not I."[4]

Warwick, however, stood adamant. He knew that his seamen, outcasts and outlaws, needed the jingle of coins in their pockets to keep their hearts up; he could guess that the bellicose gestures of the Duke of Burgundy must sharpen Louis' eagerness to come to terms. He would not move his ships nor do anything else until his great business with the King of France had been given its due precedence. With aplomb he dispatched the Bastard of Fauconberg to sea to bring in more prizes and even borrowed the fast, heavily gunned carvel of the Admiral of France to raid the coasts of the Low Countries.

Infuriated by Louis' gesture of conciliation, Charles of Burgundy fired off a sulphurous communication to his overlord, announcing that he meant to attack Warwick and Clarence, *wherever they were*, by land and sea. In the same hot vein, he wrote to the Parlement of Paris that the King of France had broken the treaty of Péronne because he knew all about Warwick's seizures at sea before he sent him a safe-conduct. Reports were soon reaching Louis that Charles was rapidly assembling troops and a fleet and encouraging the Duke of Brittany to unleash his sea-rovers.

Yet, by the beginning of June, Warwick had had his way. Leaving their ships at the mouth of the Seine, he and Clarence rode for the Loire valley with as impressive a retinue as they could scratch together. Three or four miles from Amboise, they were greeted by all the great lords who were in attendance at court. Before they reached the royal castle, there came the King of France himself on foot to give Warwick (and Clarence) a warm and intimate embrace; and at the castle door there was the Queen of France, big with child, presenting herself like a good housewife to be bussed by her husband's dear friend. The husband escorted the guests to their chambers, saw that they were comfortably settled, and then closeted himself with them for a long private talk. During their four days' sojourn, the King bent his greatness to do Warwick all possible honor. He feted him with banquets and joustings and balls. An acrobat in Warwick's train, Louis—a connoisseur of agility—rewarded with a gift of twenty crowns. Daily he waited upon his guests, coming to their apartments rather than summoning them to his. In long conversations he and Warwick (and Clarence) planned their great design.

When the English lords rode away on June 12, the "enterprise of England" had been hatched. Warwick would reseat King Henry on his throne with the aid of a fleet and troops and money provided by King Louis. In return, he promised a treaty of peace and an alliance against Burgundy. Margaret of Anjou's son, Prince Edward, would marry Anne Neville and accompany his father-in-law on the expedition. Clarence? Clarence would be taken care of, somehow.

Richard Neville chose to rely on Louis' arts before he ventured into the presence of the passionate and revengeful Margaret of Anjou. "The Earl of Warwick does not want to be here," the Milanese ambassador noted, "when that Queen first arrives, but wishes to allow his Majesty to shape matters a little with her. . . . That done, [he] will come back to give the finishing touches to everything, and immediately afterwards . . . he will return to England." [5]

But the enterprise did not turn out to be quite so simple.

The Duke of Clarence rode off to Normandy, while Warwick went only to Vendôme to await Louis' signal that his honest-brokering had done its work. But in a day or two messengers came galloping with the news that an Anglo-Burgundian fleet was visiting fire and slaughter upon the Norman coast. Giving Louis carte blanche to deal with Margaret of Anjou, Warwick hurried back to his ships.

Charles of Burgundy had unleashed his powerful fleet on June 11, and the next day he gave orders to arrest French merchants at Antwerp Fair and elsewhere in his dominions. Meeting at sea a fleet under Earl Rivers, the Burgundians anchored at Chef-de-Caux on June 13. Admiral Borselen demanded that the English pirates and their stolen goods be surrendered. When the demand was refused, the Anglo-Burgundian naval force demonstrated before Honfleur and Harfleur, demolished houses on shore, killed some inhabitants, burnt a few of Warwick's ships. Then they sailed westward along the coast to descend on St.-Vaast-la-Hougue, crying "Vive Bourgogne et le Roi Edouard!" as they tore down French ensigns and burned more houses. Finally they established a blockade of the Bay of the Seine.

Even as Louis fired off orders for the strengthening of coast defenses, he struggled to avert open war. He sent another contingent of his advisers into Normandy to help round up Warwick's plunder. He dispatched commands to Bourré and the rest that the Burgundy booty must be recovered without fail and restored to its owners. Warwick, now as anxious as the King to appease Duke Charles for the moment, pledged his word to relinquish all prizes. Louis continued to harass Jean Bourré with injunctions—

"You know that the Bretons and Burgundians have no other ends but to find means of breaking the peace under the colour of M. de Warwick's remaining there, and thus to begin war; which I do not at all wish to see begun under this colour." Therefore, Bourré, Menypeny, the Admiral were urged to "work upon M. de Warwick so that he sets out for England as quickly as he can, and to effect this, tell him all the causes and reasons you can think up." But manage all gently, tactfully, Louis added—"in a manner that he does not perceive that it will be for other ends than his own advantage." Then Louis disclosed to Bourré as frank a statement of those ends as he was perhaps capable of making: "You know how I desire M. de Warwick to return to England, as much for the good it would do me to see him come out on top—or at least that by his means the realm of England might be embroiled in strife—as also to avoid the problems which could arise on account of his remaining there." [6]

With the booty on its way back to its owners, Louis sent an embassy to the Duke of Burgundy to protest against the depredations of his fleet and to report their master's arrangements for the return of the prizes taken by the English. But Charles was in no mood to listen with sweet reasonableness to emissaries from the King of France. The passing years had shown his character to be like an eroded upland, each year's tempest scoring it more harshly, gashing it more deeply into a few dominant contours—a rigorous insistence upon the forms of greatness, hatred of the King of France, belief in his military genius, ambition to erect his domains into a kingdom. He had forgotten that he was a Frenchman, Chastellain confesses sorrowfully. The haughtiness of his bearing, the sharpness of his reproofs, lost him hearts. The noblemen of his court were held in a straitjacket of ceremonies and duties, including a grand audience three times a week, during which Charles lectured them at length. He wished to keep his lords like serfs in great fear, Chastellain reports, and King Louis, who saw the way things were going, won over numbers of them. "So there was the King, very much to be feared for his trickery, the acutest in the world. And there was Duke Charles, to be feared for his great courage; when it would come to war with the French, he held himself strong enough, with his Edward, to withstand all men, his heart having been exalted by the glory he'd won at the expense of the French at Montlhéry. . . ."

Charles received Louis' envoys with fierce pride. The dais he sat on, specially built for the occasion, was the highest that had ever been seen. Over his head gleamed a canopy of cloth of gold. His chair of state, the dais, the steps leading to it, were draped in black velvet. From this eminence Charles glared upon the ambassadors as they accused him of breaking the treaty of Péronne in attacking the Norman coast. Then they began to explain the King's offers of restitution and reparation. But the Duke of Burgundy furiously interrupted them. Louis it was, he declared, who had broken the treaty by supporting the Duke's mortal enemy, Warwick. He wanted to hear no talk of reparations. The interview was brought to an end by an angry outburst—"Among us Portuguese," cried the Duke, "we have an old custom, that when those we have held to be our friends make friends with our enemies, we consign them to all the hundred thousand devils of hell!" [7]

But though Charles remained bellicose, his ships were not equipped to maintain a long blockade. Toward the end of June the Burgundians drew off to refit. Earl Rivers' fleet was forced to make sail for the coast of East Anglia in order to encounter a marauding flotilla of the Hanse. Warwick seized the opportunity to remove his ships to the safer anchorage King Louis was urging. On the 29th his fleet made for Barfleur and La-Hougue on the

Cotentin peninsula, and the next day the Admiral followed to Chef-de-Caux with his warships and supply vessels. The Earl established his headquarters at the inland town of Valognes, which was but a short ride from these ports.

Meanwhile, King Louis at Amboise had been exercising all his arts upon Margaret of Anjou. The Queen readily signed a thirty years' truce, which included Louis' promise to take the part of Lancaster against King Edward, but that was as far as her readiness went. Although her wise old Chancellor, Sir John Fortescue, immediately set to work to draft an agreement granting Warwick the governance of England under King Henry, the Queen insisted upon giving full sway to her dignity. Her passions had not been cooled by misfortune nor the memory of her wrongs softened by nine years of exile. Touch the base and bloody hand of Warwick, author of all her woes, calumniator of her son's good name? Never!

Louis indefatigably cajoled, soothed, flattered, and preached the gospel of political necessity. Finally, Margaret relented so far as to agree to permit the Earl of Warwick to place her again upon a throne. But the marriage of her son to Anne Neville—that she would not hear of. It was not to her profit and it was even less to her honor, she declared haughtily. Louis persevered. The birth of his heir, the future Charles VIII, on June 30 gave him the chance of honoring Margaret's son by making him godfather to the infant. Transferring negotiations to her family province of Anjou, he summoned her father, King René, and his own brother Charles to his aid and swathed her in the good advice of her relatives and their councilors. At last she allowed herself to be persuaded—except for one point. She would not dream of trusting her son to Warwick. Only when he had conquered most of England would she and the Prince of Wales cross the sea. Louis the Go-Between heaved a sigh of relief and sent word to the Earl that all was ready for his appearance at Angers, the capital of Anjou.

This time the Earl of Warwick came out of Normandy without his son-in-law, now an embarrassing encumbrance. But he was accompanied by his Lancastrian ally, John, Earl of Oxford, who had managed to elude King Edward and slip across the Channel. Warwick's cavalcade and the Queen's party both arrived in Angers on July 22. That very evening Louis took Warwick by the hand and led him into the presence of the Queen he had derided and dethroned. Richard Neville went humbly down on his knees—England and the crowning of his daughter were well worth a genuflection. Margaret salved her pride by keeping him there a good quarter of an hour while he begged her pardon for the wrongs he had done her. Finally she brought herself to forgive him with a show of graciousness and he did formal homage to the House of Lancaster. He had already agreed, once England was won, to repeat this act of contrition in a public ceremony at Westminster. The Queen then greeted the Earl of Oxford, but with genuine warmth, for he and his family had suffered "much thing" for her cause.

During the next three days, Richard Neville and Margaret of Anjou settled the details of their alliance under King Louis' benevolent auspices. Louis would support in style the Queen, the Neville ladies, the Prince of Wales and his bride, Anne Neville, until Warwick had England firmly in his grip. Henry VI's half-brother Jasper, Earl of Pembroke (the Lancastrian Earl, that is), and the Earl of Oxford would accompany Warwick's expedition. Warwick secured for Clarence as good a bargain as could be expected: he was to receive back all his lands, to be given the vast estates of the Duchy of York, and in case Prince Edward and Anne had no lawful heirs, he was to succeed to the throne. Through Warwick's two daughters, the House of Neville had won a surer hold on the succession than the House of Lancaster. At least in theory.

On July 25 the betrothal of Anne Neville to Edward, Prince of Wales, was solemnized in the cathedral of Angers. The high contracting parties then took their oaths on a piece of the True Cross, called the Cross of St. Laud d'Angers, which was reputed to have a terrible power: anyone perjuring himself on this cross would die within the year.

The Earl of Warwick swore "to uphold the party and the quarrel of King Henry." The Queen swore merely to treat Warwick as a true and faithful subject and never to reproach him for deeds past. Then, arrayed in canons' robes, the King of France and his young brother Charles, Duke of Guienne, took the oaths which gave substance to the pact. True to his word, Louis allied himself not with the House of Lancaster but with the Earl of Warwick, "showing the great love that he had unto him, and that he was bound and beholden to the said Earl more than to any other man, and therefore he would do as much and more for him than for any man living." Louis and Charles went surety for Warwick's promises to Queen Margaret and swore to help Warwick in every way possible to reseat King Henry on the English throne.

Margaret of Anjou—and the world—need not suppose that she had made a *mésalliance!* If she was a Queen and represented the royal house of Lancaster, Richard Neville was the friend and ally of King Louis and commanded the resources of the kingdom of France. Louis called them both cousins, but he was aiding his first cousin, Margaret, only because his cousin five times removed, Richard, had decided to support her.[8]

It is almost impossible to discern what true feelings flickered behind the sinuosities of Louis' politics. But if he genuinely cherished any human beings, Francesco Sforza, Duke of Milan (died 1466) and Richard Neville, Earl of Warwick, were the two. Sforza, tough and canny soldier of fortune, had won a dukedom by his sword and kept it by his wits. With the same means Warwick had put his own king on the throne and made himself master of England. Both were adventurers who had leaped beyond the bounds of caste and custom. And what was Louis if not an adventurer? He too had broken with the past and the mental limits of his time. The whole cumbersome, inefficient machinery of feudalism he passionately longed to sweep from the face of France so that he might shape a national realm under a strong central government. By trying to go too fast, Warwick had come a cropper; for the same reason, Louis had almost been crushed by the League of the Public Weal. Despite his lineage, Louis was a *novus homo*, a man of the coming age of power, a man in touch with the realities of politics, as one day soon Machiavelli would enunciate them. Warwick had won Louis' admiration; Louis had won Warwick's loyalty. For the Earl, too, had probably sensed this kinship, had shaken off the traditional English hate of France not only because of the rewards Louis might be able to offer but also because in King Louis he found a man, like himself, who ignored the shackles of his time and reached for what he dared to call his own. They shared the bond of craftsmen; they were plying the same trade in a world that was not quite ready for their wares. Yet Louis was a King anointed and Warwick could be only a maker of Kings. But as long as they had common interests as well as common aspirations, the difference did not seem to be significant.

Their contemporaries on the Continent recognized this kinship and labeled them birds of a feather. Warwick was just the man for Louis, noted Chastellain, the Burgundian chronicler; and Thomas Basin, Bishop of Lisieux, the King's bitter foe, linked the two as prime dissimulators. In the propaganda war now being waged between France and Burgundy, Duke Charles' ballad-makers jeered

> Le Roy avoit bien rencontré
> En Warvic proppre compaignon;
> Eux deux, leur cas considéré,
> Furent d'une complexion.[9]

> (The King had met indeed
> In Warwick his true kin;
> This pair—who runs may read—
> Were brothers under the skin.)

Neither of them recognized any bar to the marriage of Anne Neville and the Prince of Wales, but this union shocked the age, accustomed though it was to considering marriage as a matter of policy. To Chastellain, the lover of chivalry, it was a brutal and treacherous business and showed that Warwick's honor weighed but little with him. Even Commynes, that trenchant realist and admirer of Louis' statecraft, was jolted; to him, the marriage illustrated how cynical the ways of statecraft could be.[10]

What were the feelings of Warwick's Countess? Of Anne herself? She was a girl of fifteen. She had spent most of her short life in the comparative seclusion of Warwick and Middleham Castles, far from the sophistication of King Edward's gay court, far from the political battles of Westminster. Suddenly, in late March of 1470, she had been uprooted from her quiet life, had become a hunted fugitive, hurried across England and tossed on the seas. Landed in Normandy, she had found a momentary peace in a religious house. Then, when her father returned from the French King's court, she was informed that she was to become the bride of a youth she had been taught only to hate.

Richard Neville could doubtless guess his daughter's bewilderment and fear. At Angers he had an opportunity to observe the husband he had thrust upon her. Prince Edward, reared on the bitter milk of his mother's hatred, was apparently an arrogant and swaggering youth. Three years before, a Milanese ambassador had written of him, "This boy, though only thirteen years of age, already talks of nothing else but of cutting off heads or making war, as if he had everything in his hands or was the god of battle. . . ." [11] Warwick could guess, too, the coldness with which Anne would be welcomed into the household of Margaret of Anjou.

Yet he never hesitated. The marriage of his daughter was the price he must exact for his alliance with Lancaster, the pledge he must have of Lancastrian good faith. No doubt he loved his daughter well, but to him, as to Louis, she was a part of his repertory of power. And what better gift than greatness could a father bestow upon a daughter? She could hold her head high, Earl's child though she was. For if she was wedding the heir to the English throne, her dowry was nothing less than England itself, and she was sponsored by the greatest King in Christendom. Warwick was giving his daughter what he himself desired above all things. Besides, to strike back at Edward, to regain the seat of power, he would have bartered his soul as well as his daughter.

On the day of the betrothal, Louis wrote to Bourré with great satisfaction and a dash of irony, "Today we have made the marriage of the Queen of England and of [Warwick]." [12] He immediately sent for the Lady Anne, for her father wanted the wedding made sure and the marriage consummated before he risked his neck in England. But a dispensation was necessary, and even the King of France could not produce one in a twinkling. Warwick, impatient to set about his enterprise, put his trust in Louis to see to the accomplishment of the marriage. While waiting for the dispensation, Anne and her mother would become part of Queen Margaret's household at Amboise.

On the last day of July, the Earl set out for Valognes to ready his fleet . . . and console the Duke of Clarence. He was unaware that while he was becoming a good Lancastrian, his son-in-law had been listening to a daring young lady who had managed to cross the Channel, ostensibly to join Isabel's household but actually to bring an urgent plea from King Edward that brother George return to his family allegiance.

At Valognes, Warwick plunged into a whirl of business. He was stirring the hearts of his old friends, the men of Kent, and by the aid of Kentish seamen he passed messengers into England. The Earl of Shrewsbury and Lord Stanley once again sent secret assurances of their support. Warwick's brother George, the Archbishop, was confined under guard at his manor of The Moor and could do little at the moment; but brother John had undergone a change of fortune and Warwick was striving to turn it into a change of heart. Despite John Neville's dogged loyalty, King Edward had restored the great earldom of Northumberland to the Percy heir, young Henry, who ever since the battle of Towton had been a prisoner in the Tower. He had sought to compensate John Neville by elevating him to the dignity of Marquess of Montagu, but how could a mere title compare with a princely earldom?

The newly made Marquess was now supposed to be holding the North for Edward, together with the newly restored Percy Earl. Warwick sent fervid pleas to his brother, playing upon his discontent, begging him to come to the succor of his House —even as King Edward was doing with Clarence. The Earl was also urging his adherents in the North to raise at least a token insurrection in order to draw Edward away from the southern coast. His clerks had made copies of a manifesto, signed by himself and Clarence, which his agents were spreading through the Kingdom.

Warwick reminded the commons how "uncourteously" he

had been treated, and all because he had wanted to advance the weal of the Crown and to remove the oppressions of the poor. Now England was being victimized by certain covetous and seditious persons, to the imminent destruction of people and realm, which was "like to be aliened and governed by strangers and outward nations." Wherefore he and Clarence would soon be returning to reform the government and deliver the kingdom from the thraldom of these outward nations. He did not mention that the return was to be made in French ships, under the auspices of a French alliance tighter than ever was Edward's with Burgundy. Nor was any reference made either to King Edward or to King Henry. Warwick preferred, for the moment, to keep secret his conversion.[13]

August began to wane. Yet, though a rising in the North, duly fomented by Warwick's friends, had drawn King Edward and his chief supporters into Yorkshire, and though the Courtenays, Lancastrian exiles, had succeeded in returning to Devonshire to prepare Warwick's way, the Earl still remained at Valognes. About the middle of August a great Burgundian fleet, joined by some English vessels, had once again descended upon the Bay of the Seine, doing more damage at La-Hougue, making descents near Honfleur and Harfleur, and clapping a tight blockade upon the Norman coast.

Warwick's men were growing sullen and restless. Even before the Burgundian fleet swooped down, he had twice had to pry money out of Jean Bourré to quiet them. They knew that a hangman's noose awaited them in England if their expedition went awry. Their Burgundian booty had been taken from them. In the port towns they met with hostile glances and muttered curses; there must have been brawls aplenty with the Norman populace. For the French, high and low, had no use for these English pirates. Laborers rounded up to strengthen coast defenses blamed Warwick and his men for their toil. The Count of St. Pol, Constable of France, refused to see King Louis as long as his sovereign supported these traitors to King Edward.

In this atmosphere of hostility and uncertainty, with the Burgundian armada looming offshore day after day, the temper of

Warwick's men worsened. They slouched discontentedly through the streets of Valognes, showed an unruly mood in taverns. No sooner had Warwick squeezed 4,000 crowns out of Bourré for them, than they were irately demanding another round of wages. All his charm and eloquence and force of will could scarcely keep them in hand. On August 21, Warwick ordered them to proceed from Valognes to Barfleur and prepare to board ship. Instead of obeying the order, they gathered in angry crowds. Then they were shouting and milling in the streets in open mutiny. They were sick of promises. They would not fight for Warwick unless he gave them more money.

The Earl managed to quiet them for the moment. Having already pawned most of his own goods, he turned once more to the King's officers for money. Bourré and Tanguy du Chastel were in a sweat of perplexity—if they again opened the King's purse, Louis might round upon them for disobeying his orders; if they refused Warwick, their sovereign might deal with them even more harshly because they had jeopardized the expedition. Bourré flooded Louis with anxious messages—for all decisions fell upon the King, who had chosen to surround himself with able servants rather than responsible ministers. Pay Warwick what he needs, Louis tersely ordered Bourré. By another distribution of coins and exercise of all his powers of command, Warwick got his men in hand and set them to work readying the fleet to sail.

As August drew to a close and the Burgundians still cruised the coast, Louis, in a fever of impatience, made a pretense of going on a pilgrimage to Mont St. Michel and then slipped over to Avranches. On the first of September he set out for the coast and probably met with Warwick a day or two later. It was the last time these bedfellows of ambition would ever see each other.

The Earl's men and ships waited in the harbor, prepared to sail at a moment's notice. The escorting squadron of the Bastard of Bourbon, Admiral of France, was equally ready. Offshore lay the Burgundian fleet, also waiting.

Then, as the great venture threatened to grow overripe with delay, a storm shattered the blockade. On September 9 the Earl of Warwick and the Admiral put to sea in some sixty ships, accompanied by the Duke of Clarence and the Earls of Pembroke and Oxford.

On the night of September 13 Warwick's little army was landed at Dartmouth and Plymouth. There was no opposition. Warwick learned that King Edward still lingered in Yorkshire. Jasper Tudor rode off to win the Welsh to his banners. Horsemen galloped the roads to rouse the partisans of Lancaster and the friends of Neville.

King Louis, the meanwhile, neglecting no possible support, was busy bribing and beseeching Heaven's divine intervention. He offered at Notre Dame de la Délivrance a great taper, six sacred vessels, and his own image in wax; to Notre Dame de Celles he vowed himself. Neither in this world nor the other did Louis expect to get something for nothing: he was equally as buoyant but not so sanguine as his friend the Earl.

Warwick spread his banners and marched to Exeter. Lancastrian Devon rose to his support. He issued a proclamation which trumpeted his loyalty as if he had never had a Yorkist thought. It was worded as coming jointly from the Duke of Clarence, the Earls of Pembroke and Oxford, and himself. All men, save King Henry's "capital enemies," were pardoned whatever trespasses they had committed against the House of Lancaster, provided that they joined the four lords in delivering Henry from captivity, as that "most noble Princess, Margaret, Queen of England," had bidden them do. Concerned to make a good impression on the people, Warwick stringently warned his followers against breaking the peace by brawling and announced the death penalty for robbery or rape.[14]

As he moved northeastward to encounter King Edward, he was joined by the Earl of Shrewsbury and Lord Stanley with several thousand men at their backs. Barons and knights came in with their retainers to swell his numbers. He entered Coventry with so large a host that the townsfolk numbered them at thirty thousand men.[15] Twice he had met small bands of Yorkists and beaten them from his path, but these engagements mattered little compared with news from the North which he was awaiting.

About the time his army reached Coventry, it arrived—great good news, all that he could have hoped for.

As soon as Edward received the tidings of Warwick's arrival, he gathered up his forces and hurried south from York, summoning the Marquess of Montagu to join him on the march. John Neville obediently set forth from Pontefract with an army larger than Edward's own. But when he was within a few miles of the royal camp at Doncaster, the Marquess suddenly halted his men and proceeded to harangue them. King Edward, he declared, had forfeited his allegiance by taking his earldom from him and fobbing him off with a Marquisate and only "a'pie's nest to maintain his estate with." [16] He urged his troops to throw in their lot with Warwick, Lord of the North and their leader of old. Most of the men agreed to follow the Marquess against the King. Forewarned barely in time to get away, Edward and his brother Richard, Lord Hastings, Earl Rivers, and a small band of trusty followers fled through the night toward the coast of East Anglia. Soon word came that the King and his companions had sailed from Lynn for the shores of Burgundy (October 2).

By this time Warwick was marching with all speed for London. His unruly Kentish followers had thronged to the capital the moment they heard of his landing and were mobbing the hated Flemings and Dutchmen of Southwark, burning their beer houses, threatening to storm across the river into London itself.

The great town was in a tumult. When word of the King's flight arrived on Monday, October 1, a throng of Warwick's adherents, Lancastrian die-hards, debtors and criminals issued from the sanctuaries, led by Warwick's retainer, Sir Geoffrey Gate. They broke open the prisons and released a rabble of felons as well as political prisoners. Encouraged by this violence within the city, the Kentishmen, reinforced by the watermen, resumed their pillaging and burning in Southwark. Though the Mayor was able to keep them out of London, Queen Elizabeth and her mother fled in the night from the Tower to the sanctuary at Westminster. Next day, Edward's Chancellor and other high ecclesiastics of his council took refuge at St. Martin le Grand. On Wednesday, the

Tower was delivered up to the Mayor and Sir Geoffrey Gate.
They led a shambling, blinking King Henry—"not so cleanly kept
as should seem such a Prince"—to the spacious apartment which
the Queen had just redecorated for her approaching confinement.
On Friday, October 5, George Neville, Archbishop of York,
having overawed his guards and gathered a band of armed men,
entered the city in state and installed himself in the Tower.

The following afternoon the Earl of Warwick rode into the
capital with his Lancastrian-Neville army, accompanied by the
Duke of Clarence (whose father had died fighting Queen Margaret), the Earl of Shrewsbury (whose father had died fighting
Warwick), and Lord Stanley (who accommodated himself both to
King Henry and to King Edward). At the Tower, Warwick
knelt before the "royal-woolsack" (Chastellain's phrase), which
he had tumbled from its shelf. Henry was arrayed in a long gown
of blue velvet, conveyed to St. Paul's to make an offering, and
placed in the Bishop of London's palace. Clarence found accommodation at "The Erber," once the home of Warwick's father. Warwick chose to emphasize his position in affairs by lodging with the King. A week later, Henry was duly exhibited in a
procession to St. Paul's, with the Earl of Warwick bearing the
royal train and the Earl of Oxford, the sword of state.[17]

All the French King's horses and all that King's men had been
able to put humpty-dumpty together again.

And for Richard Neville, the chief of Louis' men, the intoxicat-
ing wheels of greatness and destiny had been spinning as, even for
him, they had never spun before. In less than eighteen months
he had fomented three insurrections, captured the King who
had defied his mastery, fled that King's sudden resurgence of
power, allied himself with two other Kings, driven Edward from
the throne in a stroke, and restored the House of Lancaster which
he had spent most of his manhood fighting. It was an enterprise of
will and energy such as few men have experienced.

Yet, though this vast stir, this mighty impact upon the times, had
magnificently expanded his legend, what meaning it had for England and what actual power it had brought Richard Neville remained to be discovered.

Part Six

The Lancastrian

(1470-1471)

I

The Grand Alliance

SO BEGAN what was officially called the "Re-Adeption" of
Henry VI. It might have been more truly named The Return of Warwick. The adventurer had won a marvelous
triumph. But it was a triumph on terms. Some of the terms, like
his obligation to King Louis, were known and stringent. Other
terms were vague, but might be even more stringent. These were
to be read in the faces of the Lancastrians who surrounded him;
these were to be guessed in the enigmatic silence which settled
over the realm.

The adventurer was aging now. If hard experience of men and
the buffets of fortune had not dimmed his vision of himself, they
had taught him something of the power of circumstance and the
constraints of fact which hedge the human will, however imperious. Even the hero of his own saga was aware that he had
come to the last of his possible choices and courses. From the moment he landed in France he had concentrated all his thinking,
poured all his energy into his drive to overthrow Edward and
fight his way back to power. Now domiciled in the regnal seat
at Westminster, he confronted the fearful odds he had accepted
as the price of his option to govern.

His victory had been almost too easy. Montagu's sudden coup
which had driven King Edward from England had left the temper of the kingdom untried, his own strength unmeasured. If Edward returned—but could there be any doubt of it? Plantagenet
was no less highhearted than Neville; he was the first soldier of
Europe; he had his Charles as Warwick had his Louis; and if
Warwick had accumulated five years of humiliation to spur his
revenge, the fall from a throne was the most ignominious plunge
in the world. *When* Edward returned, much would depend on the
rule which Warwick was able to give England.

Part of the problem of good governance was basic and obvious. Men had grumbled under Edward because he had not been able to put an end to disorder and had had to summon citizens time and again to take arms "at their own cost"; because he had taxed the commons, permitted Woodville extortions, and gathered money where he could under the color of receiving voluntary "benevolences"; because he had hurt foreign trade by his failure to bring the Hanse to terms and get rid of the Burgundian edict against cloth.[1] These discontents Warwick must allay in order to secure popular support for the Neville-sponsored House of Lancaster. But with hundreds of hostile Yorkists crowding the sanctuaries and Edward safe in Burgundy the prospect for peace was not promising; and with the treasury empty, money must be found somehow to keep the government going and meet military needs.

Yet this was only the beginning of his problem. Committed to King Louis, he had to carry the French alliance on his back; he must persuade the merchant class to hate the Duke of Burgundy, whose trade they depended on, at the behest of the King of France, whom they loathed. He had to convince Lancastrians—before Queen Margaret and the Prince arrived—that their loyalty to King Henry should embrace Henry's rescuer; he had to teach his own followers to translate their devotion to him into allegiance to Lancaster. And there was Clarence, who had learned to think of himself as rightful King and was now little more than his father-in-law's appendage. Clarence was weak but could be dangerous; he was already quarreling with Warwick over his eclipse;[2] and the sight of him in the halls of Westminster was not likely to please the enemies of York. Beyond these formidable difficulties loomed the shape of the future, once Prince Edward was established as his father's regent and Margaret of Anjou reigned in England. Warwick could have little doubt that it was going to be easier to perpetuate the triumph of Lancaster than to perpetuate his own share in it. He was struggling for a success that might well be the ruin of him. His chief assurance against this prospect lay in his personal alliance with the King of France.

Warwick's actions indicate that he was well aware of the terrible problems that ringed him round. Henceforth he would be constricted by deficiency of power rather than of perception. This understanding, rashly bought but courageously fronted, not only marks a new phase of his life, but it ties him poignantly to the common fate of man. When he begins to struggle, in awareness, with his circumscribed lot, he earns compassion if he does not attain to the dignity of tragedy.

While the realm was sunk in silence, Westminster swarmed with place-hunters—Neville adherents who had risked their necks in '69 and '70; old Lancastrians, eager to dilate upon their sufferings under the usurper Edward and ready to show the scars of Towton or Second St. Albans; dependents of Oxford and Clarence and Shrewsbury and Stanley . . .

Amidst the clamor, Richard Neville felt his way gingerly in search of firm footing. Resisting the pressure to placate his new friends at any cost, he determined to ease the change of regime by retaining the base of Edward's government. The Justices of King's Bench and Common Pleas, the barons of the Exchequer, the Sheriffs, Edward's Attorney-General and his sergeants-at-law, were all promptly reappointed. At the same time, Warwick sought to give a properly Lancastrian color to King Henry's rule by parceling out offices to well-known adherents of Queen Margaret. The Bishop of Coventry and Lichfield became Keeper of the Privy Seal; Sir Henry Lowys was appointed Comptroller of King Henry's household; Sir Richard Tunstall's long years of faithful service were rewarded with the lord chamberlainship and with the rich sinecure of Master of the King's Mints; the wealthy London grocer, Sir John Plummer, who had suffered persecution along with Sir Thomas Cook in '68, became Keeper of the Great Wardrobe. A certain number of minor offices—customs inspectors, parkers, constables and stewards of royal castles, keepers of royal forests—were also doled out.

Warwick was sparing in his distribution of plums. He gave his chief allies, like Oxford, a taste of patronage; he gave the King some old friends for intimate officials so that the royal household had a Lancastrian look; but the only office which carried any real power with it, the Privy Seal, was in the hands of an ecclesiastic, the Bishop of Coventry, who was doubtless amenable.

As a sop to the ill-content, Warwick was careful to keep the King visible and easy of access: and disappointed Lancastrians assuaged their feelings by thronging to pay homage to Henry and eat a meal or two on his royal bounty. After all, it would not be long until Queen Margaret and the Prince returned, and then . . .[3]

Meanwhile, the Earl of Warwick fastened a tight grip upon authority. He justified his assumption of the royal prerogative by taking the title of King's Lieutenant of the Realm, using Queen Margaret's agreement to this as his warrant; he resumed his old offices of Great Chamberlain of England and Captain of Calais and closed his hold on the navy by appointing himself, a little later, Lord High Admiral. Brother George, the Archbishop of York, once more became Chancellor, and Warwick's ally, Sir John Langstrother, resumed the treasurership, which Warwick had given him in 1469. Following Edward's lead, the Earl constituted a royal council, mainly composed of ecclesiastics, which was entirely subordinate to his will but which was also as able as he could make it, for he did not hesitate to employ bright young career men, like Dr. John Russell and Dr. Henry Sharp, who had been fast rising in Edward's service. It was a Neville regime in a Lancastrian costume.[4]*

George of Clarence was permitted to do no more than hover at the edges. He recovered his estates; he sat in council; and Warwick permitted him to make at least one minor proclamation in his own name.[5] But he had no real authority, and Warwick hesitated so long even about giving him back his lieutenantship of Ireland that the order was not signed till December and the patent itself did not pass the Great Seal until February. As for John Neville, the Marquess Montagu, though his *volte-face* had overthrown King Edward, he was simply restored to his wardenship of the East Marches and told to stay in the North and maintain order. He was still felt to be so tainted with Yorkist leanings that when Parliament met, Warwick required him to make a speech of apology for his allegiance to Edward, which he excused as being solely due to fear.

Warwick's chief allies, the Earls of Oxford and Shrewsbury and Lord Stanley, and the two great Lancastrian lords returned from exile—Courtenay of Devon and Tudor of Pembroke—received no places in the government, nor did they become members of the royal council. Warwick was able to show plenty of good reasons why, in this topsy-turvydom of shifting estates and changing local authorities, they should stay on their lands and win hearts for the new regime. The Earl of Devon needed no urging; he apparently refused to have anything to do with Warwick. Jasper Tudor came up to Westminster about the first of November. He brought with him his nephew, Henry Tudor, whose father had been Earl of Richmond. But how could Warwick restore that lordship to young Henry, with Clarence, already jealous and sulky, determinedly signing himself Lord and Earl of Richmond? In less than two weeks Jasper and his nephew returned to Wales; all they had to show for their journey was a commission to take into royal custody the holdings of the late William Herbert, the Yorkist Earl of Pembroke.[6] Fortunately for Warwick, war and execution had pretty well disposed of most of the bitterly partisan Lancastrian houses. Ironically enough, the two greatest remaining lords—Edmund Beaufort, calling himself Duke of Somerset, and Henry Holland, calling himself Duke of Exeter—were the pensioners of Charles of Burgundy, now host to King Edward.

In his treatment of the enemy faction, Warwick's statesmanship showed at its best. He was relieved of dealing with Edward's hottest adherents, who had fled overseas with their master, and the principal Yorkist ecclesiastics had taken sanctuary. The chief partisan magnates who remained—the Duke of Norfolk, Henry Bourchier, Earl of Essex, and a few other nobles—were carefully watched for a short time, but upon evincing a willingness to accept the new shape of the world, they were restored to freedom and took their usual places in the Lords when Parliament was summoned.[7*] Warwick strongly exerted himself to reconcile these men to his government, and he so far won over the Earl of Essex, he believed, that Essex—Yorkist of Yorkists—became a member of the royal council.[8]

In the turmoil of Warwick's return, Edward's councilor-diplomat-physician, Master William Hatclyf, had been captured in flight. The Pastons took it for granted that he would be executed, for the Lancastrians hated him as a turncoat—he had been Margaret of Anjou's physician—and being a friend of the Hanse merchants and a leading negotiator of the Burgundian alliance he was no friend of Warwick's. But the Pastons were wrong: Hatclyf suffered nothing worse than a brief imprisonment.

Warwick issued a general amnesty, which specifically included Edward's Chancellor, Stillington, Bishop of Bath and Wells, who had taken refuge in St. Martin's, and even a member of the hated Woodville clan, the Queen's brother Sir Richard, had no difficulty securing a pardon for himself. Warwick protected the Yorkists who had sought sanctuary by issuing an emphatic proclamation that, on the pain of death, no man was to "defoul" holy places by vexing or injuring their inmates because of "cause or quarrel, old or new." [9] Even Elizabeth Woodville, lying pregnant in the sanctuary of the Abbey, was treated with chivalrous consideration. She received supplies of food, and as her lying-in approached, Lady Scrope was given a paid appointment to attend upon her.[10] On November 2 Edward's Queen gave birth to her first male child, who was christened with his father's name.*

England now owned two Kings, two Queens, two Princes of Wales named Edward—and one Warwick striving to twine the white rose and the red around the Ragged Staff.

A single execution the Earl did allow, but that the whole realm clamored for. Edward's Constable, John Tiptoft, Earl of Worcester, had earned for himself the name of "Butcher of England." In Italy he had acquired some of the new ideas of statecraft to which Machiavelli would give expression a quarter of a century later. As Constable, he had condemned many men to death; xenophobic Englishmen muttered that he "judged by law of Padua"; and he horrified a kingdom that took disembowling for granted by impaling the quarters of some of Warwick's followers executed in the spring of 1470. To Caxton, who printed some of his works, he flowered in virtue and intellectuality; to the commons, he was an Italianate villain (though the term itself would

---

* The future Edward V, deposed and succeeded by Richard, Duke of Gloucester (Richard III).

not become current till the days of Shakespeare). He is a Renaissance figure, harsh and erudite, combining that sensitivity to the beauties of literature and insensitivity to human suffering which baffles our understanding of the Elizabethans.

The Earl of Worcester had been caught hiding at the top of a tree in Huntingdonshire forest. Warwick gave the pleasure of presiding over his arraignment to John, Earl of Oxford, whose father and elder brother Worcester had consigned to death in 1462. On Monday, October 15, 1470, he was quickly found guilty of treason, condemned to be led on foot from Westminster to Tower Hill and there beheaded. He began his last journey on Wednesday, but the streets were so packed with men and women yelling execrations and struggling to tear him to pieces that the officers were forced to take shelter for the night in Fleet Prison. The next afternoon the impassive Earl, as brave as rigorous, was conveyed to Tower Hill by a powerful armed guard. Coldly ignoring the jeers and curses of the bloodthirsty crowd, Worcester declared on the scaffold—when an Italian friar reproached him for his cruelty—that he had governed his actions by the good of the state, and he requested the headsman to perform his office in three strokes in honor of the Trinity.[11]

In the circumstances, it is hard to see how Warwick's policy could have been bettered. His talent for managing affairs showed brighter now, under the stress of enormous difficulties, than ever it had in easier times. To keep the most ardent Yorkists out of England or gently neutralized; to keep the extreme Lancastrians isolated from power at Westminster; to end factional strife by wooing the moderates of both parties—these were the means by which he struggled to win through a maze of hazards.

Only the outlines of Warwick's government survive; the living, day-to-day substance of it must be imagined—the shambling King, blinking bewilderedly at him; the covert glances, the rustling whispers of former enemies which followed him through the chambers of Westminster; the exchange of swagger, scowls, muttered threats between old Lancastrians and Neville servants; the jealousies that flared, on both sides, at any fancied mark of favor to the other party; and, always with him, the harsh necessity of solving the problems of today without digging a grave for tomorrow.

The tensions at Westminster were reproduced throughout the realm. In the North, Richard Neville's friends and his brother John, Warden of the East March, were still dominant; but the region harbored many Lancastrians, bitter foes of the Nevilles for three decades, who were now ruffling up their spirits and flaunting their allegiance to the good old cause. There was a third element, ominously enigmatic, represented by Henry Percy, Earl of Northumberland. The Percys had long been the rivals of the Nevilles for the lordship of the North; Henry Percy's grandfather and father had died fighting for Queen Margaret against the Yorkists; yet Henry himself had been given back his titles and estates by King Edward and had sworn to be his liege man. Now Percy and his retainers sat mum, waiting.

Warwick's rule exudes an atmosphere of uneasy silence, of curious emptiness: the whole realm—weary of strife, resentful of disorder, suspicious of change—was as mysteriously quiescent as a slick, slate sea with dark clouds piling on the horizon. At Westminster, Warwick seems to walk alone through a cardboard palace housing a cardboard King, the governor in a government of shadows, perhaps himself a shadow—though real enough in the prodigious energy with which he grappled with his problems, seeing to everything himself. Yet of all this activity, how much made any impact beyond the walls of Westminster Palace? how much was but an evanescent prelude to the real drama, waiting in the wings?

Ten days after arriving in London, Warwick sent out summonses for a Parliament to meet on November 26. By this time in the century the Commons had got the habit of protective docility; there was little need of rigged elections and none of coercion. The burgesses and knights of the shire were accustomed to endorsing the military triumph of one party over the other, as they had done in '55 and '59 and '60 and '61. Half a century before, they had emphatically stated that, though they expected to be consulted about legislation and to control money supply, they had no wish to wield any executive power; and now they were less inclined than ever to meddle in what had become a very hazardous occupation. As for the assemblage of temporal lords, their thin and divided ranks would make no trouble.

The silver-tongued George Neville, Chancellor, opened the sessions with an address. He had hit on a strikingly apt text with which to inaugurate King Edward's first Parliament of 1461—"Amend your ways and your doings"—and this time he again found in Jeremiah a thesis of impeccable appropriateness: "Return, O backsliding children . . ." [12] Though the records of this Parliament were destroyed, the scanty comments of the chroniclers can be presumed to supply the major articles of legislation. Henry VI was declared true King of England. The succession was established upon his heirs male and, those failing, upon the Duke of Clarence and his heirs male. In effect, the throne was more firmly secured for the line of Neville than for either York or Lancaster; for by Christmas the Earl learned that his daughter Anne had been wedded in early December to Margaret of Anjou's son. The attainders of the Lancastrian lords were reversed. Edward was declared an usurper and attainted, along with his brother Richard of Gloucester. But Warwick stopped the condemnations there—the most moderate parliamentary reprisal of the century. Though Lancastrians were doubtless angrily disappointed, the Earl stuck to his policy of moderation, avoiding the wholesale turning over of estates that engendered confusion and bitterness, and hoping for the eventual adhesion of even the most partisan Yorkist lords. The Earl was confirmed in his lieutenantship of the realm. George of Clarence, acknowledged to be the true heir of York, was recognized as Warwick's "associate," a term which Warwick left empty of meaning.

One of his most harassing difficulties he did not dare submit to Parliament—his desperate shortage of money. He was collecting customs and the wool subsidy, claiming the grant of the Parliament of 1453 as his warrant to do so,[13*] but these would be slow to come in, as would the yield from crown lands and perquisites and from the annual fees paid by the King's towns.* As soon as he entered London he borrowed £1,000 from the city council for the defense of Calais and £100 from various aldermen for his own use; but the London magistrates were now demanding repayment of the £1,000 he had borrowed in the summer of 1469. Most of the expenses of the Household and the ordinary costs of running the government he seems to have met somehow out of his own pocket.[14] But badly as he needed money, he carefully refrained from asking the Commons for a grant, knowing that there was no quicker way of hardening their hearts; nor did he even venture to ask the Convocations of the clergy for the usual grant of a tenth.

After a short session, Parliament adjourned for the Christmas season; it met again in February, but only because Warwick needed its confirmation of his treaty with King Louis.

Queen Margaret and her advisers in France doubtless spent these days in drawing up their own plans for the future, and there must have been plenty of Lancastrians in England who were cogitating on the subject for the benefit of the Queen and the Prince. One of them was George Ashby, close upon fourscore years of age, who had been for four decades a clerk of the Signet, first in Henry's service and then in Margaret's, and who had been cast into Fleet Prison shortly after the triumph of the Yorkists. Now he was writing a poem of advice to Prince Edward. Though it was execrable as verse, old George Ashby reverenced poetic talents greater than his own: in his invocation he links Gower and Lydgate with their master, Geoffrey Chaucer, as "Primier poetes of this nacion,/ Firste finders to oure consolacion/ Off fresshe, douce englisshe . . ." His lengthy didactic piece blends conventional maxims of kingly morality with some shrewd counsel on ways and means of governing, but in the midst of the

* In the end, it appears from the Exchequer receipts that Warwick received only the town fees, collected by the sheriffs, and the revenues from the Duchy of Lancaster (see Ramsay, II, p. 360); but there was undoubtedly some income from customs. The sum total of these yields was probably not more than the meager sum of £15,000—about a quarter of King Edward's yearly revenue. It may be that Warwick found a few thousand pounds in Edward's treasury.

poem there suddenly flash out verses which are aimed against the Earl of Warwick: Almighty Jesus was disobeyed, he writes,

> . . . in heaven by Lucifer unwise
> And in earth by Judas in his false guise.
> Have not ye now need about you to look?
> Since god was deceived by high wiles' crook [trickery].
>
> Be well aware of falsehood in fellowship,
> And namely of corrupt blood and suspect,
> Abiding in power, might, and lordship . . .

He then exhorts the Prince to remember old servants, who have never flagged in their faith and have suffered great pain, and he ends the stanza with an unmistakable jab at Warwick:

> And be ye ware of the Reconciled
> That hath deserved to be reviled.

George Ashby, though prudent with years and experience, seems to have felt confident that once the Queen and Prince appeared at Westminster, he could publish this attack with impunity.[15]

There had been a chance, however, or the illusion of a chance, that Warwick's enemy, Charles of Burgundy, might provide him with the means of gaining time to strengthen himself against Queen Margaret's faction at home and of preventing a Yorkist invasion from abroad.

The moment Charles learned that Edward had landed on his shores and his enemy Warwick ruled in London, he realized that King Louis was now in a position to hurl the might of England and France against Burgundy. The Duke's mind had not yet hardened into that final pattern of imperious ambition and recklessness which was to earn him the title of "Charles the Rash"; with all the means in his power he sought desperately to avert the fatal combination of his two greatest foes.

He saw to it that Edward and his party were supplied with funds and arranged for them to be fittingly entertained at Bruges, but he carefully avoided meeting his brother-in-law. He ordered his subjects to make no retaliation against marauders from Calais.

As early as October 11 he hurried off to London a declaration that, having been long a lover of Lancaster, he rejoiced in the re-establishment of Henry VI. He followed this up with letters to some English lords, in which he protested that he had stayed clear of the royal quarrels of Britain and that St. George himself knew the Duke of Burgundy to be a better Englishman even than they were since he had always worked for the good of that realm and was descended from the House of Lancaster.

Meanwhile he had quickly worked out a formula to justify his insistence upon amity with the regime which had ousted his brother-in-law, and he immediately posted Philippe de Commynes off to Calais to apply it. As Commynes neared the port, he was met by subjects of the Duke fleeing from bands of English soldiers. When he finally entered Calais, after first sending for a safe-conduct, he learned that the raiders were a force of several hundred troops which Warwick had dispatched the moment he seized power. Commynes learned, too, that in less than an hour after the news of the Earl's triumph arrived, white roses had entirely disappeared and every man was wearing Neville livery or an emblem of the Ragged Staff. He found the door of his lodging decorated with white crosses—device of France—and pinned to his chamber door were rhymes proclaiming that King Louis and Warwick were one.

Lord Wenlock courteously invited Commynes to dinner that evening. He found the baron in the company of the leading officials of Calais. Wenlock was wearing a golden Ragged Staff on his bonnet, and every man in the room sported the same emblem in gold or cloth. Wenlock made a brief, frank explanation of Warwick's political turnabout, summing up his defense of his master with the statement, "He is doing great things." Commynes was less impressed by the honesty of the others, all of whom—even the ones he had previously thought to be Edward's most loyal supporters—were loud in their denunciations of the fugitive King: some of them out of fear, Commynes decided; others out of policy. But Commynes was equally disingenuous, as he himself notes, for he kept repeating at every opportunity that King Edward was dead; and having thus attempted momentarily to deflect from his master the odium of harboring the Yorkists, he went on to urge Charles' formula. Even if Edward were not dead, the Duke of Burgundy considered his alliance with England unbroken, for he had made his treaty with the King and the kingdom, not with Edward himself, and whomever the English regarded as their monarch was quite satisfactory to the Duke. All he cared about was preserving the alliance, which he expected the English to observe as scrupulously as himself.[16]

This point of view powerfully appealed to the wool merchants of Calais, most of whom were agents or partners of the great London firms which dominated the association of the Staple. War with Burgundy would cram their warehouses with rotting wool and crowd their books with debts owing to the growers and middlemen. And nobody knew better than Lord Wenlock himself that war with Burgundy would immediately stop the wages of his garrison, which were paid by the Wool Staplers from the custom and subsidy they collected on behalf of the government. Word of Commynes' stand was speeded to London. The Wool Staplers there were quick to bring pressure on the Earl of Warwick. Meanwhile, Wenlock, waiting for his master's decision, called off the raiders and paid lip-service to Commynes' doctrine.

Besieged by the anxious tasks of establishing his rule, awaiting an embassy from the King of France, Warwick played for time. On October 25 he wrenched himself away from affairs in the capital to come down to Sandwich, probably for a brief conference with Wenlock.[17] The Earl had decided to refrain for the moment from overt hostility to Burgundy. Wool once more began to make its way to Calais—not the customary great autumn shipments wafted by a convoyed fleet, but enough to show that the Earl gave some sort of temporary assurance to the Staplers. Throughout the rest of the year and the early months of 1471 Warwick temporized, going so far as to send a minor official as an envoy to the Duke.[18]

Richard Neville was eager to remain on good terms with the mercantile class, and the Merchant Adventurers, the great cloth-purveyors to Burgundy, were no less eager than the Wool Staplers for a continuance of good relations. He could not have failed to see that a solid agreement with Charles would enhance his popularity and might keep Edward immobilized long enough for him to establish himself firmly in England.

But he knew that Charles hated him, that Charles was showing himself friendly out of fear, and that however much the Duke was pleased by Henry's return to the throne, he would do everything he could to pull down the man who ruled in Henry's name. Furthermore, Richard Neville was committed by knightly oath and political necessity to the King of France. Louis held his daughter and Louis held the Queen under whose warrant he acted as the locum tenens of Lancaster; and he had long ago staked his claim to direct the destinies of England upon the rightness of a French alliance. Most of all, Louis offered the only insurance against the day when Margaret of Anjou and her son might forget their gratitude to the deliverer of their House.

King Louis undoubtedly appreciated that the Duke of Burgundy's desire to remain friends with England might do much for the survival of Warwick's regime; but he was impatient to devour the fruits of his scheming; he was perhaps doubtful that Warwick's rule would take deep root; and in his mind there lurked the suspicion that the surer Warwick became of his position, the more likely he was to desert the unpopular cause of France and ally himself with Burgundy for the same reason that had moved Edward to that choice. Louis would not wait. While he could, he would use Warwick's triumph to extirpate at last the hated House of Burgundy.

Two days after the Earl of Warwick reached London (October 6, 1470), he had hurried off an exuberant message to Louis: "Please to know that by God's help and yours, for which I don't know how to thank you enough, this whole realm is now placed under the obedience of the king my sovereign lord, and the usurper Edward driven out of it!" [19] He repatriated without ransom the French prisoners he found in England. He re-established friendly relations with Louis' ally, the King of Castile. He promised to French and Spanish merchants restitution of goods seized by English pirates. To honor King Louis' aid, he even had coins struck bearing the insignia of France,* and he worked to drum up a warm welcome for the French ambassadors, who would soon be arriving to conclude the all-important alliance.

They did not appear until December, for their master was in one of his intense periods of contriving stratagems. He received the first news of Warwick's success with extravagant joy—spread the tidings over his realm; proclaimed public rejoicings, holidays, processions; announced his thirty years' treaty with Queen Margaret; gave fervent thanks to God, the Virgin, and the Saints. As Chastellain puts it, he weltered in roses ("se baignoit en roses").[20] Not for an instant, though, did he lose his grip on practical details. He hastened to send supplies to Lord Wenlock at Calais and to make ready a fleet to hold the Channel passages. On November 13 he commissioned a great embassy to England.

But he had learned how to delay for an advantage even when he was most impatient to proceed. Before letting his envoys set forth, he took precautions against any change of heart on the part of the Earl of Warwick. He saw to it that Prince Edward put his seal to a secret engagement, in which Margaret's son promised to make war on Charles of Burgundy until all the Duke's dominions were conquered and to persuade his father to accept the obligation. In the treaty, Louis was called "Roi de France," a title which neither Lancaster nor York had ever acknowledged. Then, assembling princes and notables at Tours on December 3, Louis declared the Treaty of Péronne canceled by the Duke of Burgundy's hostile acts of the preceding summer and by his perfidious alliance with the Yorkists. Immediately he launched his armies against the Duchy of Burgundy and sent powerful forces into Picardy. By December 10 St. Quentin was his. Only then did he permit his embassy to cross the Channel: Warwick was confronted by a war already begun.

As another means of holding the Earl to his commitments, Louis permitted Prince Edward and Anne Neville to marry when the

---

* These were gold angels, showing on the obverse a ship and fleur-de-lis and the French white cross and on the reverse St. Michael, patron saint of France.

dispensation arrived, but he would not let Margaret of Anjou, the Countess of Warwick, and the young couple depart from Amboise until he learned how his envoys had been greeted.[21]

The Earl of Warwick did his best to stage-manage a resounding welcome for them; and if they were not overwhelmed with public exhibitions of joy as they rode through the streets of London, their ardent reception at Westminster and Warwick's obvious eagerness to do them all honor made a deep impression. Words failed them, they were quick to write, how honorably they had been received by King Henry, Warwick, the other lords, and the people, all of whom gave a marvelous demonstration of love and affection for King Louis.[22] On the receipt of this report, Louis sent off his Lancastrian guests in the middle of December to begin their journey back to England. At his orders they were royally welcomed to Paris and shortly afterward went on to Rouen and Dieppe.

As soon as Warwick received notice that they were on the way, he drew £2,000 from the treasury to prepare an escort of ships and men with which to fetch them from France. In the end, however, he remained in London, keeping a strained watch upon the kingdom while he began his negotiations with Louis' ambassadors. England was growing uneasy. Even as the Earl was talking with the French about committing thousands of troops to the enterprise against Burgundy, rumors were running through the realm that Edward would soon return; and Warwick needed no rumors to tell him that when Charles heard of Louis' embassy, he would fight back with the most powerful weapon at his command, the martial vigor of his brother-in-law, Edward of York.

In December Warwick dispatched powers of assembling troops for defense against the Yorkists. Commissions of array for the whole realm were issued to himself, Clarence, the Earl of Oxford, and Lord Scrope of Bolton. Marquess Montagu was appointed to array Nottinghamshire and the four northern counties. Later, Warwick included the Earl of Pembroke, along with himself and Clarence, in commissions for South Wales and the county of Hereford. So uncertain was allegiance that Warwick was forced to confine to this puny circle of adherents the authority for creating an army.

In the meanwhile, he had begun his talks with the French, a negotiation which was to occupy almost three months and which stood at the very heart of Warwick's rule. In order to avoid the appearance of rushing into Louis' arms, he kept the conversations private and informal, appointing no official commission to treat, and he labored at the task of persuading merchants, lords, clerics of the council that the friendship of King Louis was the key to England's peace and prosperity.

Louis had chosen for his envoys a group of his most trusted councilors who were also old friends of Warwick's.* He had provided them with elaborate instructions; and these instructions are couched in his best style since they were designed to be shown to the Earl of Warwick.

After a brief mention of the truce, amity, and intercourse of merchandise agreed on at Angers, Louis pounces on the issue which really matters to him. His ambassadors have not only the power but the duty of concluding with the King of England and with Warwick a special alliance against the Duke of Burgundy, the agreement to be so tightly drawn up that neither party can make a truce with that Duke without the express consent of the other nor cease to make war until the whole conquest has been achieved. To render this treaty unbreakable, letters and seals are to be used, the most precise and binding that can be devised. The conditions of the joint war effort are to be exactly determined —the division of the conquered lands between the victors, the payment of soldiers (each side to pay its own troops, Louis suggests, since the English are to share in the spoils), plans of campaign (Louis offers a choice of three joint operations), numbers

---

* The embassy: Louis de Harcourt, Patriarch of Jerusalem and Bishop of Bayeux; Tanguy du Chastel, Governor of Roussillon; William Menypeny, Seigneur de Concressault, and Ivon, Seigneur du Fou, royal chamberlains; with Dr. Nicole Michel and Guillaume de Cerisay, Registrar of the Parlement of Paris, as secretaries. Warwick was well acquainted with all of them, except possibly Dr. Michel. Du Fou, de Cerisay, and Tanguy du Chastel had all played a part in John Boon's story. Menypeny had been Warwick's companion in the critical winter of '67–'68 (see pp. 244–246).

of men each party is to contribute, the day on which simultaneous attacks are to begin. In order to avoid delay, the ambassadors have full power to bind their master to whatever treaty Warwick agrees to, since the King intends to do exactly as the Earl counsels. Furthermore, Louis is eager to get his hands on any evidence in the English archives of "machinations and enterprises" against the King of France that the Duke of Burgundy has undertaken with King Edward; he particularly wants letters signed by the Duke or sealed with his seal.

Despite his urgent pushing, the King of France was well aware of the difficulties Warwick faced in persuading the English nation to swallow the alliance against Burgundy, and he sought to make the dose as palatable as he could. He charged his envoys to consult with Warwick about the particular magnates of England "who must be gained and cherished for the good of all these matters" so that the ambassadors might arrange the means which Warwick thinks should be employed, be it to give them lands out of the conquest or to provide other persuaders. Above all, Louis was concerned to win the merchants, the staunchest upholders of the Burgundian connection. Upon learning of Warwick's triumph, he had arranged to establish two free fairs at Caen in order to attract English traders; he had proclaimed that English merchants and all followers of Warwick's party were to be benignly welcomed to France, treated with as great favor as his own subjects, and excused for two years from all dues, customs, tolls on whatever they chose to import or export. In short, they were to enjoy better treatment than Louis' own merchants. Finally, as a tangible illustration of the commercial advantages awaiting the entrepreneurs of England, Louis, bustling entrepreneur that he himself was, sent along with his ambassadors Jean Briçonnet and the son of Jean de Beaune, two wealthy merchants of Tours, with 25,000 crowns' worth of merchandise— spices, cloth of gold, silks, linens—to sell and distribute to English merchants as proof that the marts of France were fully able to supply the wants of English traders. Such a politico-economic *démarche* was entirely novel.

But the instructions always return to the Earl of Warwick. The

King of France holds the Earl to be the best friend that he has in the world—even his "very father"!—and the Earl can be certain that Louis, as long as he lives, will sustain him, his people, and his cause, without abandoning him no matter what happens. Every promise he made Warwick at Angers he will stand by. He has written to remind King Henry of the great services the Earl has done the House of Lancaster, emphasizing that Warwick represents the very foundation of Henry's power and exhorting him above all things to love and cherish his deliverer.

But the King of France knew well that the Earl of Warwick needed more encouragement than this effort to keep Lancastrian gratitude warm or the assurance that if the worst came to the worst, Louis would give him honorable refuge. Louis charged his envoys to suggest that the Earl, for his personal share in the Burgundian conquest, should take the "countries and lordships" of Holland and Zeeland. This seductive shape of the future had long ago brought Warwick to commit his fortunes to the cause of France. Now, Louis must have realized, a Continental dominion had also become in Warwick's mind an escape-hatch from whatever hostility Queen Margaret and her friends might be able to make good against him.[23]

The instructions mirrored fairly the terms Warwick had accepted in France—gave him all that he himself could ask for—provided lavish inducements to win the good will of nobles and commons. Yet before Warwick could commit himself officially even to negotiating, he had to have some assurance that he could take the realm with him into the embrace of the King of France.

Almost immediately there was trouble. Warwick found himself besieged by indignant merchants, clamoring that they were being robbed of their livelihood by this French pair, Briçonnet and de Beaune, with their fancy merchandise. Those costly bales had been admitted duty-free as part of the diplomatic luggage of the French ambassadors. No wonder, cried the merchants, that the French were able to undersell honest men! Too clearly, Warwick was made to see that London was not yet ready for such new ideas. He was forced to inform Louis' envoys that no more merchandise was to be sold, unless he gave special permission.[24]

This was only the start of the Earl's difficulties with the prejudice of his countrymen. As soon as he began canvassing public
opinion, he was driven to the conclusion—if he had not accepted
it from the beginning—that he would have to secure the confirmation of Parliament for his foreign policy. Though treaty-
making was the prerogative of the King and his council, Warwick
saw that, without the authority of Queen Margaret and Prince
Edward to back his diplomacy, he dared not force the French
alliance on the realm by simple fiat. But would the most that
Parliament was likely to accept—even a dull and docile and shorn
Parliament—be enough to give Louis satisfaction?

With the Lords and Commons in recess for the holidays, Warwick toiled at his task of consulting, explaining, propitiating. To
the French envoys he showed himself confident of success. But
they could see his difficulties for themselves, and from first to last,
they were deeply impressed by the sincerity of Warwick's
struggle to meet his obligation to the King of France.

The Earl was popular among large sections of the gentry; he
could exert an influence on numbers of the parliamentary knights
of the shires. Old soldiers and some of the nobles would respond
to the scent of plunder, little matter if it were French or Burgundian. The spiritual lords, who, as a whole, always favored
peace, would support the truce with France. If what Warwick
wanted did not cost the Commons anything and did not outrage
their accustomed political attitudes, they would probably be sufficiently willing or apathetic to follow the government's lead. But
when Warwick went into the city of London, he met a tide of
popular feeling—feeling that was anti-French, pro-Burgundian,
averse to novelty, suspicious of Warwick himself who now
seemed to be the very weathercock of change and "newfangled-
nesse." Some of this feeling could be disregarded or borne with
till time mollified it; but among the substantial merchants and
money-men—a class to which the Yorkist regime had given a new
importance in the realm—Warwick found a hostility that could
not be ignored.

These men and their exclusive, capitalist guilds controlled the
power of London, as their fellows in most English towns now

constituted a governing oligarchy. They were constantly having trouble with associations of journeymen and craftguildsmen, who resented this political dominance and chafed against restrictions which prevented all but a few from rising in the world. These workmen and shop-owning artisans were the very folk who cheered Warwick in the streets of London.

The Earl's popularity with the discontented lower classes did not endear him to the oligarchy, particularly after the threat of violence which had been raised by Warwick's short-lived victory over Edward in the summer of 1469. Temperamentally and commercially, these businessmen were opposed to wild political adventuring, which Warwick now stood for on a spectacular scale; they had had their fill of Warwick's special friends the *boreales bobinantes*—the roaring Northerners—who came rampaging down upon them when Warwick crooked his finger; they resented the fat Church Establishment, of which Warwick had felt obliged to pose as the protector; they were deeply committed to King Edward by the debts he owed them, by the favor he had shown them, by the soft, insistent pressure of their wives, who were ardent partisans of this handsomest and most impressionable of Kings. The Warwick who had put Edward on the throne and stood guard over the kingdom—yes. But the new Warwick of these past few years, with his mob-followers and his uprisings and his switches in allegiance—no. *That* Warwick reminded them all too feelingly of the bad old days of Henry VI. In fact, they had only to look out the windows of their warehouses on Thames Street to see those bad old days before their eyes—

The tall cranes—a marvel to foreigners—stood idle on idle wharves. Ships swung silently at their moorings. Warehouses were crammed with goods that could not be exported; others were empty of the goods which the traffic of the seas, now stilled, had once borne up the Thames waterway. The other ports of the realm were feeling the same blight. The great trade in cloth and wool had slowed almost to a standstill; imports of wine into the port of Bristol were only a trickle; the brisk movement of miscellaneous products, raw and manufactured, into and out of the country, had almost ceased. Merchant strangers were as hard hit as native dealers. The great mart of Duke Charles' dominions was about to be cut off; of the once thriving Hanse traders only the men of Cologne carried on a sadly diminished trade.[25]

And what remedy was being proposed by the Earl of Warwick —who had driven out the Easterlings and was pushing the people of England into war with their best customer, Burgundy? Having lost them all their other markets, he would deliver them over to King Louis. If they could trade with both France and Burgundy, well enough; but to be at the mercy of the fearsome and wily King of France—he and his bales of glittering samples! It was like being asked to give up a fat white porker in order to grab for a greased black pig on a dark night.

Burgesses from the other English towns, coming back to London for the session of Parliament which was to open at the beginning of February, probably felt much as their London fellows. Besides, the whole proposition was a piece of new-fangledness. In the preceding decades the representatives of the towns had themselves proposed the economic legislation of Parliament. Now the Earl of Warwick was asking them to accept something that in form as well as substance was as new as Louis' ill-fated trade exhibition—namely, an elaborate political and economic program of enactments sponsored by the government.

Warwick continued to toil at his Herculean task. He was aided by his merchant friends Cook and Plummer and probably by some of the Calais Wool Staplers who had become his adherents. He preached the wonderful concessions offered by the King of France, the wide horizons of trade that loomed to the south, the provisions for new fairs, the lifting of money-consuming restrictions. When Parliament reconvened, Warwick demonstrated his respect for merchant opinion by assembling at St. Paul's special meetings of parliamentary representatives from the towns.[26]* Inviting the burgesses to thrash out their doubts about his program, Warwick labored to "sell" the treaty of mercantile intercourse with France—a legislative procedure that was notably ahead of its time. But to his own age, the novelty and the nakedness of Warwick's bidding for support was probably disconcerting, if forceful. He was pressing very hard.

Meanwhile, the Earl was also working to meet his military commitments. Scraping together every penny he could find, he was outfitting a fleet in the Kentish ports; he was talking soldier-contracts with his friends and retainers, approaching veteran captains who could raise mercenary troops, stirring imaginations by promises of booty to be picked up in the Low Countries. In order to hold public funds ready to his hand and to keep his financial operations to himself, he arranged for the transfer of sums from the cumbersome and tradition-bound Exchequer to the coffers of the Great Wardrobe, which was in the charge of his city friend, Sir John Plummer, presumably an efficient businessman.[27]

On the night of Tuesday, February 5, a few days after Parliament had reassembled, the tense and weary Earl of Warwick rode to the lodgings of the French ambassadors. He could be sure of friendly welcome; perhaps by this time he was beginning to think that these men were the best friends he had. They had reported Warwick's labors to their sovereign in the rosiest possible terms. Soon after landing in England they wrote to Louis that Warwick and his associates were ready to embrace the alliance against Burgundy. Christmas and Epiphany came and went without their having further good tidings to offer and so they offered none. On January 19 Menypeny broke the silence by reporting that the King of France would soon secure the full measure of his desires. The ambassadors were now putting the final touches on the truce and the intercourse of merchandise, and the Earl of Warwick was making ready an army. Yet there was a glaring omission in this news—Warwick's army was all very well, but where was the unbreakable alliance against Burgundy? [28]

Now, on this night of February 5, the Earl of Warwick told the envoys that everything was all right: the treaty would go through. The royal council and Parliament would be willing to accept a truce which would run for a minimum of ten years and would continue in force for five years after either party chose to denounce it. Though this was much thinner fare than the fat thirty years' truce Margaret of Anjou had signed, Louis' envoys were well content; they had learned something about English Parliaments.

Warwick's biggest news was that he had secured acceptance for the military treaty against Burgundy, including all the provisions about an unbreakable agreement and the sharing of the spoils that Louis had laid down in his instructions. Warwick had got round a direct declaration of war against Burgundy by presenting the alliance with France as being aimed at the usurper Edward and his adherents, chief of whom was of course Duke Charles. The intercourse of merchandise, Warwick reported, was still being discussed by the special assembly of parliamentary burgesses but would soon be passed in precisely the form which King Louis had requested.

The Earl then sketched a glowing picture of his military preparations. His ships were ready to sail, a fleet so powerful that, with the support of the French, it would dominate the Channel. On the morrow he was dispatching orders to Calais to begin the war against Burgundy; in less than a fortnight he was sending two or three thousand men to reinforce the garrison; he himself would follow shortly with a great host, including eight or ten thousand elite archers—soldiers worth double the number of ordinary troops, Warwick assured the envoys.

Louis' emissaries hastened to write these happy tidings to their master. What had delayed matters, they explained, was the necessity of having the treaty approved by Parliament; but now the documents were being drawn up for presentation to the Lords and Commons, and the envoys expected to complete their work and head for home in a few days.

Warwick called at their lodgings next morning to read over this report; on finishing, he picked up a pen and added a postscript: "Sire, I promise you that all which is written above will be held and accomplished in every detail, and so have I promised the ambassadors; and I will see you very shortly, if God pleases, for that is my whole desire. Entirely your humble and loyal servant, R. Warrewyk." So much importance did Louis' representatives attach to this passionate avowal that they sent their master only a copy, for fear that the precious document "written word for word in the hand of M. de Warwyk" might miscarry on the road.[29]

But a whole week went by and nothing happened, except behind the scenes. Not until February 13 did Warwick even formally commission the English negotiators, a group of nine royal councilors. Four of these men were of the inner circle of government—Warwick himself; his brother George, Archbishop and Chancellor; the Duke of Clarence; and Sir John Langstrother, the Treasurer. Four were ecclesiastics, civil servants rather than men of party. And there was the powerful Yorkist peer, Henry Bourchier, Earl of Essex, whom Warwick had persuaded to join his regime. Three days later, on February 16, the treaty with France received the confirmation of Parliament, was signed by the English commissioners, and approved by the French ambassadors.[30]

It was by no means the alliance which Warwick had promised on February 5. The document merely provided for intercourse of merchandise and elaborated the ten years' truce Warwick had outlined to the envoys. During this period the Kings of England and France agreed to give no support to each other's enemies or rebels. A diet was to be held within three years for the purpose of settling all differences between the two realms so that a permanent peace could be concluded. The subjects of each Prince might trade, travel, and reside freely in the other's country and would be given the rights of citizens, these privileges being governed by minutely specified conditions. Finally, Louis and Henry pledged themselves to be the friends of friends, the enemies of enemies (except for their allies named in the treaty—and neither party named the Duke of Burgundy).

In the end, the Earl of Warwick could not perform what he had promised. He had not dared to submit for parliamentary approval an alliance aimed against Burgundy; perhaps even his subservient council had refused to be a party to it. The French envoys signed the treaty because they knew that Warwick had given them all that England would yield and that only Warwick's unremitting labors could have secured so much, and when they returned to France they did their nervous best to make their master content with what the Earl had achieved.[31]

After all, despite the lack of a declaration of war, Warwick was pressing on the assembling of an invasion army and he had announced that he himself would lead it. Did he consider that the clause, "enemies of enemies," gave him sufficient backing for the enterprise? Was a secret codicil to be appended to the public treaty? There is no knowing, but Warwick was probably depending upon Queen Margaret and Prince Edward to swing the country against Burgundy by royal proclamation. Though he had so far only half-heartedly attempted to arrange their crossing, on the very day the treaty was signed Sir John Langstrother was sent to France to escort them home and Lord Wenlock at Calais was ordered to join Langstrother in dispatching the business.[32] Meanwhile, Warwick continued to gather troops on the basis of rearing war against the usurper Edward and his allies.

But the Earl could never hope to produce the ten thousand archers he had optimistically promised to the French ambassadors. To employ such a force for forty days, including its officers and its supplies, would cost, at the standard wage of six pence a day, at least £30,000, a sum which was double the total revenue Warwick had so far collected. He was so barren of money that he had been forced to persuade the French envoys to deliver to him 17,000 crowns' worth of poor Briçonnet's merchandise, and he apparently tried to squeeze extra shillings out of this sum by fixing the rate of exchange at four crowns, instead of five crowns, to the pound. He was resorting to a more dangerous expedient, his commission of array for the whole of England. Such commissions were based on the old custom that every able-bodied male subject was required to spring to arms to defend his sovereign, when summoned by properly empowered officers of the King. But for many long decades now, this authority had been used only to raise troops for service within the kingdom, as Lancaster and York had in turn used it in order to gather an army to put down "rebels." Nevertheless, Warwick employed his commission in an attempt to eke out the numbers of his invasion force. He sent a mandate to the town of Coventry to supply a band of archers for service on the Continent, and the town dutifully set about raising a troop of forty men whose two months' service they would have to pay for themselves. This unpopular device Warwick probably confined to a few towns over which he felt he had a powerful hold—only the demand on Coventry survives—and perhaps to some regions in Yorkshire, though there were not many parts of the North wealthy enough to supply men at their own cost. For the rest, he was probably contracting for troops with nobles and captains who were willing to forgo a cash payment in advance on the promise of plunder for their men and lands for themselves. Thanks to the men of Kent, loyal as ever, he had managed to ready a sizable fleet under the Bastard of Fauconberg. And he must have hoped that by leading this expedition himself, he could allay Louis' disappointment over the numbers he was bringing with him.[33]

He knew that he had tried to move too fast, to push the English people too far. But what else could he have done with neither time nor circumstance on his side? He had been forced to jolt the realm with novelties; a Neville-sponsored House of Lancaster; Warwick as ruler of the realm under the aegis of Queen Margaret; an alliance with France, a violent upheaval in trading policies and habits, an attack on Burgundy.

The Burgundian chronicler Chastellain, a stickler for tradition, a lover of the past, was shocked and bewildered by Warwick's regime. The King, he wrote indignantly, was as mute as a crowned calf—was no more than a shadow on a wall. The King was a subject, and a subject was governor and dictator of the realm! [34] The English were not nearly so old-fashioned as Chastellain; they were a practical people, and the civil strife of the past two decades had rubbed the luster off kingship and the sheen from feudal memories. Tough, vigorous, and materialistic, the middle classes were lustily beginning to reach out toward a new world of capitalist enterprise and political power. But this world was still half a century in the future. In their stubborn way the English were traditionalists, too. Some two decades later, an

Italian diplomat observed scornfully, "If the king should propose to change any old established rule, it would seem to every Englishman as if his life were taken away from him. . . ." [35]

At the heart of Warwick's government gnawed the same canker that had blighted his success in the summer of 1469. The English were not prepared to understand the position of a man who ruled without reigning. They knew nothing of Mayors of the Palace. Even the magic of the Warwick legend could not transform the anomaly, could not overleap this barrier of habit. In vain Warwick struggled to impose on the age his claim to govern because of the talents he had proved and the power he had achieved. Doubtless many Lancastrians darkly believed that Warwick meant to keep the Queen and the Prince forever out of England. Doubtless many Yorkists could see the Earl only as a baron who had once supported the right cause and was now supporting the wrong one. Other folk were uneasy, vaguely resentful—for the English have always tended to look askance at a man who, they feel, too brashly tries to exceed his station.* The fact was, when Warwick spoke, they did not sense along their nerves the unmistakable thrill which signals the voice of Crown Authority.

If Warwick did not precisely understand this attitude, he could feel its effects, even as he could discern the shape of the future glimmering in the hostility of Somerset and Exeter. His broad promises to Louis, the ambiguity of the treaty, the haste to scramble together an army for service overseas despite the imminent threat of a Yorkist invasion—these desperate expedients reveal the gamble to which Warwick had committed himself. He hoped to lead an attack on Burgundy before Charles could launch Edward at England. Then the Duke would be too hard pressed to do much for his brother-in-law. Even if Edward succeeded in crossing the sea with his handful of followers, Queen Margaret and her lords, combined with Clarence and Montagu, should be able to deal with him. If, however, the sun of York rose again in England, or should the victorious Lancastrians turn upon the House of Neville, Warwick would be Lord of Holland and

* Sir Winston Churchill makes this point in his *History of the English-Speaking Peoples,* vol. II.

Zeeland, Captain of Calais, ally of King Louis, with an army and a fleet at his command. The alliance with France against Burgundy, which had well-nigh strained his government to the breaking point, offered nonetheless the one means by which he might hope to assure himself against either the restoration of Edward or the regime of Queen Margaret.

Already, clouds of wrath were gathering. Two days before the treaty was signed, a pair of apparitions had materialized in England, apparitions of the past who were ominous for Warwick's future. These were Henry Holland, Duke of Exeter, and Edmund Beaufort, Duke of Somerset, brother of Henry, who had been executed after the battle of Hexham (1464). Ignoring Warwick and his government, Somerset rode straight into the southwest to reclaim the Beaufort estates and confer with his fellow-Lancastrian, John Courtenay, Earl of Devon. Henry Holland went to Westminster to pay his homage to King Henry and then took up residence at his house in Thames Street; but there is no mention of his paying his respects to the King's Lieutenant. These two lords hated Warwick as bitterly as men could hate. To Somerset, Warwick was the author of his house's ruin, the butcher of his father and his brother. The Duke of Exeter was even more dangerous. "Cruel and fierce," an Italian observer had called him years before.[36] In the '50s he had savagely feuded with the Nevilles in the North, had been superseded by Warwick in the command of the navy, and had been humiliated at sea by the refusal of his sailors, in the spring of '60, to fight against the Captain of Calais. When the Tower yielded to the Yorkists in July of '61, Warwick saw to it that the servants of Exeter, who was King Henry's Constable of the Tower, were promptly charged with treason and put to death. In the Low Countries, Exeter had grimly begged his bread, barefoot, until Duke Charles discovered him and gave him a pension.

All this Warwick knew. But what Warwick did not know was that when Charles of Burgundy had at last, early in January, been willing to listen to Edward's pleas for help, Somerset and Exeter had begged him equally hard to support the House of Lancaster. In his perplexity, the Duke of Burgundy hit upon a piece of strategy, which, whatever else it accomplished, was designed to put an end to his mortal enemy in one way or another. Promising Edward his secret aid in mounting an invasion, he gave Somerset and Exeter permission to return to England, but only after they swore an oath to him to work against the Earl of Warwick.[37]

There were other matters of which Warwick was unaware. The Duke of Clarence, brooking ill the scowls of Lancastrians and jealous of the superior authority of his father-in-law, was being secretly exhorted to return to his family allegiance by his mother and sisters in England and by sister Margaret, Duchess of Burgundy. Warwick could see well enough that the Duke was malcontent and yet he was soon forced to aggravate Clarence's dangerous humor. He was committed to turning over to Margaret of Anjou some lands of hers now in Clarence's possession, and though he offered his son-in-law ample compensation in estates and annuities, the tetchy Duke was furious—his sense of outrage can be read in the wording of the letters patent which reimbursed him.

Though Warwick was probably aware that Clarence might prove false, he did not penetrate the state of mind of his brother John, Marquess Montagu. Through his commissions of array, the Marquess held an authority in the North superior to that of his rival, Henry Percy, the new Earl of Northumberland. He had received the profitable custody of the estates of the Earl of Worcester and Lord Clifford during the minority of their heirs, and Warwick was now about to regrant him the manor of Wressel, in Yorkshire, which Edward had bestowed on him in 1468. But John Neville could not forget that he had betrayed his sovereign, nor did it soothe his agony of mind to reflect that he had so acted in order to avoid betraying the hopes of his brother. The Marquess was now stationed at Pontefract with a strong force of soldiers, his heart torn by a conflict of loyalties.[38]

At the end of February, 1471, the Earl of Warwick rode down to the south coast to welcome Queen Margaret, his Countess, and the Prince and Princess of Wales. Days passed but no sails appeared. Warwick sent word to King Louis that he was about to

embark with his army. The slipping away of time grew dangerous. But Warwick could not leave England until the Queen
and the Prince appeared to proclaim the war against Burgundy
and hold the realm in his absence.

The Earl must have gazed long across the gray, wintry seas. The
Bastard of Fauconberg's keels were furrowing the Channel; Louis
had assembled a fleet; but Breton freebooters and war vessels of the
Easterlings and Burgundian carvels were also loose on those waters. Beyond, at Honfleur, lay the Queen whom Warwick was
awaiting with impatience and with dread. In the past, she had
harmed her cause by many a rash and impulsive decision. Now, as
after the second battle of St. Albans, she hesitated when she should
have acted. A warning had reached her from Bruges that she
should delay her departure because a fleet was being assembled
in Dutch harbors to transport Edward back to England. In vain
Langstrother and Wenlock urged her to sail. She was fearful for
the life of her Prince, mistrustful of Warwick. At last she said
that since the French ambassadors were momently expected, she
would cross the sea in the vessels that brought them home. And
while she temporized, the passing of each day silently, fatally
fretted the life-span of her cause, her husband, and her son.[39]

Louis' war against Duke Charles was going splendidly. A part
of his forces were overrunning the Duchy of Burgundy. His
troops in Picardy had seized and heavily garrisoned the great
Somme town of Amiens. Charles had advanced to the Somme,
but his army hovered impotently in the neighborhood of Amiens.
Louis remained with a powerful host at Beauvais, waiting for
Warwick. With his usual thoughtfulness, he had given orders to
ship 160 pipes of wine to England—100 for King Henry, 40 for
Clarence (it was wise to soothe Clarence), and 20 for the Countess
of Warwick.[40] The English of Calais were ravaging the Duke's
county of Boulogne. Daily there were reports—premature reports—that Warwick's host had landed.[41]

With mounting uneasiness, Richard Neville gazed upon the
Channel waters, at his back the enormous silence of the realm of
England. Early in March the harassed Earl returned to London.
Even as he rode, King Edward and some eighty score English

and Burgundian troops lay aboard ships in the port of Flushing, waiting for the weather to change. Duke Charles had provided money and a few hundred men. The Easterlings furnished fourteen ships, after Edward promised to settle his quarrel with the Hanse towns on terms favorable to them. The Germans thought Edward's chances worth the gamble. Besides, they were hoping for revenge upon their enemy, the Earl of Warwick.

When Richard Neville arrived in the capital, he found that Mayor Stockton had chosen to take to his bed. Sir Thomas Cook stepped into the breach, but Cook was hastily packing up his goods. London and the realm grew tense with rumors of Edward's imminent arrival. A hopeful stir and buzzing emanated from the sanctuaries of the city, crowded with Yorkists. Warwick continued to assemble men for his invasion force, daily expecting word that Margaret of Anjou had landed. Outwardly calm, he persuaded the French envoys to put off their departure in order to greet Queen Margaret.

The Earl had constructed an apparently tight cordon of defense against invasion. The North, filled with Neville adherents and old Lancastrians, should be safe enough, and Marquess Montagu lay at Pontefract with a stout force, ready to block the road southward. Warwick's Yorkshire follower, Lord Scrope of Bolton, and the Earl of Oxford were patrolling the eastern counties. The Bastard of Fauconberg's fleet cruised off the south coast, and the men of Kent were as loyal as ever. The Duke of Clarence rode off to the southwest to rally his following; the Earls of Devon and Somerset were there too, and the region was traditionally Lancastrian. Jasper Tudor, Earl of Pembroke, had gathered up the reins of power in Wales. Where could Edward and his tiny following land without being instantly set upon and overwhelmed? Warwick took the final precaution of putting under arrest in London such Yorkist stalwarts as the Duke of Norfolk, the Archbishop of Canterbury, Lords Cromwell and Mountjoy, the young Stafford Earl of Wiltshire; and, in the end, he lost his trust in Henry Bourchier, Earl of Essex, whom he had made a royal councilor, and ordered him into custody too.[42]

The wind changed.

About March 14, a messenger lashed his horse into London—
Yorkist vessels had appeared near Cromer, in Norfolk; a scouting party was quickly frightened back to its boats; then King
Edward had steered his little fleet northward toward the Humber.

Hastily the French ambassadors set out for the seacoast and
embarked that very night. Warwick sent an urgent message with
them: he was ready to cross the Channel with an army the
moment that Queen Margaret appeared in England. The envoys
barely got the message, and themselves, back to the Continent.
Breton pirates plundered part of their flotilla, seizing thirty
horses which had been meant for a present to King Louis. Easterlings fell on the ships carrying the remains of Briçonnet's merchandise, and in the fight young Jean de Beaune lost his life.[43]

Warwick committed King Henry and the capital to his brother
George, the Chancellor. Sending messages to the chief Lancastrian and Neville lords, he hastily gathered all the men he
could find and rode hard for Warwickshire to begin raising an
army.[44] The great host that was to have fallen upon the dominions of the Duke of Burgundy was suddenly only a fume of words,
an evanescent dream.

II

Barnet*

T HE EARL of Warwick did not send out commissions of array. Parchment stamped with the seal of King Henry's Re-Adeption had suddenly lost its meaning. It was a matter now of what primal loyalties could do. The rival of King Edward, Lieutenant of King Henry, and ally of King Louis, was reduced to the tough, simple trade of rallying retainers and arming tenants, by which he had first ascended to grander levels of experience.

In a few days, tidings reached Richard Neville at Warwick Castle that Edward of York, his brother Richard, Earl Rivers, Lord Hastings, and a force of some two thousand English and Burgundians had landed at Ravenspur, at the mouth of the Humber, and were attempting to move on York. Edward could not have chosen territory more hostile. This region of Holderness swarmed with loyal armed bands, constantly thickening on the flanks of the puny invasion force. Though Henry Percy, Earl of Northumberland, sent no word, John Neville, at Pontefract, had gathered a stout array of Warwick's Northerners, and the Earl of Oxford, with the Lancastrian adherents of the Eastern counties, was heading northward on the Newark road, accompanied by the Duke of Exeter and Viscount Beaumont. Rumor reached Warwick Castle that Edward had fled to sanctuary. Warwick sent off word to King Louis that the "usurper" had fallen into a trap.

Reporting the talk at the French court, the Milanese ambassador noted complacently, "It is a difficult matter to go out by the door and then try to enter by the windows. They think he will leave his skin there." But Louis was beginning to feel qualms. He quickly dispatched orders to halt the shipment of the 160 pipes of wine designed for his Neville-Lancastrian friends (but he was too late and most of the pipes were lost). He let it be known that English troops might not be required, after all; "And if they are unnecessary," reported the Milanese, "His Majesty would not wish to be under any obligation to them." Perhaps, despite his insistence on unbreakable obligations and his promises to press the war with Burgundy to the end, perhaps it would be better to wait and see. . . .[1]

News soon reached the Earl of Warwick that the rumor of Edward's flight to sanctuary had been false. Far worse—the Neville stronghold and capital of the North, York, had opened its gates to the invaders, and they had spent the night of March 20 within its walls. The thousands who menaced Edward's march in Holderness had lacked leaders of note. Some of their captains he had bought off. Others he had confused by his assertion that he came only to claim his dukedom. The farther Edward moved on his daring march, the more reluctant men were to oppose him, seeing that other regions had let him through. After he avowed to the citizens of York that he sought only his rights as the son and heir of Duke Richard, he had been allowed into the city— he and his brother striding boldly through the streets, the ostrich plumes of Lancaster mounted on their helms, shouting, "King Harry! King Harry!" Seven decades before, Henry VI's grandfather Bolingbroke, also landing at Ravenspur, had used this trick of claiming but his dukedom in order to push Richard II from the throne and, as Henry IV, found the dynasty of Lancaster.

Now Edward and his tiny army were driving southward, toward Pontefract. Richard Neville, his forces still streaming in, remained at Warwick Castle, awaiting news from his brother, Marquess Montagu. Too soon it arrived: somehow Edward has slipped around Pontefract to the westward, spent a night at Sandal Castle, where his father had met death, and was continuing his southward march at full speed. Though few men had so far joined the Yorkist banners, the invaders had safely made their way through the heart of Warwick's strength.

John Neville sent word that his force was pursuing the enemy. What had happened at Pontefract? Some thought that the Marquess had been fooled by Edward's clever march around his flank or that he had feared to attack the Yorkist army lest the Earl of Northumberland and his men, who had "sat still," might suddenly come to the invaders' support. Others believed Edward had sworn to the Marquess that he wanted only the dukedom of York and would remain loyal to King Henry. But the Earl of Warwick knew that his brother was too valiant and experienced a soldier to be daunted or fooled by Edward and his small fellowship. In the moment of decision, John Neville could not bring himself to fall upon the man he had long served and loved.

On March 25 the Earl wrote to his Derbyshire follower, Henry Vernon—as he was writing to dozens of other men at this hour—"In as much as yonder man Edward, the King's our sovereign lord great enemy, rebel, and traitor is now late arrived in the north parts of this land and coming fast on southward accompanied with Flemings, Easterlings, and Danes, not exceeding the number . . . of 2000 persons, nor the country as he cometh nothing falling to him, ye will therefore incontinent and forthwith after the sight hereof dispose you towards me to Coventry with as many people defensibly arrayed as ye can readily make, and that ye be with me there in all haste possible as my very singular trust is in you and as I may do thing to your weal or worship hereafter. And God keep you." [2]

Seizing the pen from his secretary, Warwick added a poignant postscript—"Henry I pray you fail not now as ever I may do for you. R. Warrewyk."

But the Duke of Clarence, beginning to advance from the southwest, was urging Henry Vernon to join *him*. He begged Vernon to keep sending news, thanked him for his reports on the whereabouts of "E late King," and asked him to find out what Shrewsbury, Northumberland, and Stanley meant to do. [3] Shrewsbury refused to heed Warwick's summons, as did Thomas, Lord Stanley, who kept himself busy besieging Hornby Castle. Nor would Jasper Tudor, Earl of Pembroke, follow the Ragged Staff; he meant to sit tight in Wales until Margaret of Anjou arrived. The Earl of Devon and the Duke of Somerset rode into London— but not en route to join Warwick. They merely sent word that they were awaiting news of the arrival of Queen Margaret. [4] Even in the face of Edward's invasion, these Lancastrian magnates would not identify Warwick's cause with King Henry's. The regime which the Earl had held together by the assertion of his will was cracking fast.

Yet Warwick still had reason to be sanguine. Clarence was coming up from the southwest with a strong fellowship. The Bastard Fauconberg had been ordered to bring his fleet into Sandwich and rouse the men of Kent. The moment Margaret and her son landed on the southern coast, they would be rallying troops to the attack. But it might even be that these powerful reinforcements were unnecessary; for Warwick now learned that Edward had halted his march at Nottingham. The Earl of Oxford, having reached Newark, was poised on the eastern flank and rear of the Yorkists. Montagu was advancing directly upon their rear. With Warwick's headquarters now at Coventry, he was only two days' fast march to the southwest of Nottingham. The convergence of the three armies would crush the invaders.

But Warwick had not perceived the opportunity quickly enough, or he hesitated. By the time he started for Leicester with a loyal host of several thousand Midland supporters, he had lost his grip on the forelock of time. Edward suddenly turned on his nearest foes, Oxford and Exeter. In the dead of night his scouts reached the outskirts of Newark. Roused by this startling news, the Lancastrian lords jumped to the conclusion that Edward's whole force was almost upon them. They routed out their men in a panic and fled from Newark at two o'clock in the morning. Edward at once resumed his southward march. Warwick, jarred by this news and uncertain of Montagu's and Oxford's whereabouts, pulled his army back behind the well-fortified walls of Coventry. Suddenly the fields outside the town were filled with the steel ranks of the Yorkist host. The chance of crushing the invaders had gone glimmering; the King's Lieutenant of the Realm found himself bottled up in a few acres of streets and houses.

A Yorkist herald arrived at Warwick's headquarters to deliver a formal challenge to combat. For three successive days this challenge was offered, and Edward drew up his host in battle array. But Warwick remained within the walls of Coventry.

Men's lives sometimes display a pattern of repeated motifs, forged by the interaction of circumstance and character. When

Warwick sought to retrieve defeat by means of a new idea—
thus tapping his creative, organizing talent—then he leaped from
failure to greater success: as he had done after his retirement to
Calais in the autumn of '56, after the disaster at Ludlow in the
autumn of '59, after the apparently decisive defeat at St. Albans
in February of '61, after his flight from England in April of 1470.
But upon his encountering a crisis which called for plain staunch-
ness of mind or required a swift military solution, this man who
had originally won his way to fame by a sword was at times
curiously paralyzed by a failure of will and imagination or by
some arcane suspension of vitality: as had happened when he
dallied in London in February of '61 while Queen Margaret's
Northerners swept over the realm, when he was thrown off
balance by the appearance of a Scots army at Alnwick in January
of '63, when he wavered agonizingly on the verge of armed revolt
in the winter of '67–'68, when he feverishly threw himself into
the Lincolnshire uprising of '70. Now, once again, he had let the
decisive moment slip; the bold act of leadership had eluded him
—while King Edward had darted through the midst of his enemies
and now stood confidently before the gates of Coventry, the
quarry daring the hunter to come forth.

Richard Neville doubtless gazed from the city walls upon the
invaders, a force somewhat smaller than his own. Beneath the
sun banner of the House of York stood the mighty figure of Edward, looking even taller than his six feet four inches beside his
slight young brother Richard. Most of the English in his ranks
were veterans of the Yorkist campaigns, had often fought under
Warwick's banner and brought him victory. And none knew
better than he the prowess of Edward of York. Edward's strategy
was simple—hunt down the enemy with all speed, bring him to
blows as soon as possible, fight until he breaks. Edward had never
lost a battle: he made time fight on his side, he was a peerless
warrior in the melee, he could not imagine himself defeated. Edward had been Warwick's pupil; Edward's fresh, vigorous regime
had been Warwick's creation. Gazing upon this Yorkist host,
Richard Neville was seeing the dearest and the best portion of
his past.

On April 1, the Yorkists, probably apprised of the approach of the Earl's reinforcements, drew off their army and marched southward to Warwick. Now proclaiming himself King, Edward flaunted his power by occupying the castle of his enemy and blocking the road to London. Then Richard Neville made a move. He sent a herald, offering to open negotiations. Edward would give no better terms than pardon with life only. This Warwick spurned. Perhaps he had parleyed only in the hope of immobilizing the Yorkists till his other armies arrived; it may be that his adventurer's sense of destiny had suddenly gone cold. Though Edward was now caught between the Earl's host and the force of the Duke of Clarence, advancing from Banbury, Warwick did not attack; he must have known, or feared, that his son-in-law was about to play him false. At this moment the troops of Oxford and Exeter and Marquess Montagu's army arrived at Coventry. They had scarcely passed through the gates when tidings came that the Duke of Clarence and all his men had gone over to the Yorkists.

Not many hours later appeared a messenger from Clarence, who was eager to refurbish his honor by reconciling his royal brother and his father-in-law. Warwick returned an angry, scornful refusal. But more messages came; they enclosed gracious offers from Edward himself of "divers good conditions, and profitable for the Earl if that he would have accepted them."

Warwick had no time to think, had time only to let his mind race over the glimpses of the future offered by Edward's favorable terms. Could he ever be sure that Edward would not someday take his revenge? Could he break his solemn oaths to the House of Lancaster, his fervent promises to the King of France, "without great disslander"? And then . . . there was always the assured refuge of Calais, the assured friendship of King Louis, the hope of being lord of Holland and Zeeland. In any case, what hope was there of taking himself and his men over to the Yorkists, with the vindictive Duke of Exeter and other Lancastrians scrutinizing his every move, weighing his every word, with wolfish suspicion? In a swirl of feelings, the Earl of Warwick harshly rejected Edward's offers.

Edward's answer was to lead his host once more before the walls of Coventry and dare the might of Neville-Lancaster to give battle. Warwick preferred to await a better opportunity, and his Lancastrian lords agreed. The countryside was now stripped of food and forage. The Yorkists would soon have to move or starve. And where could they go?

On Friday, April 5, Edward suddenly broke camp. His forces disappeared over the southern horizon, marching at full speed for London. While Warwick labored to get his army on the road, he sent urgent messages to his brother George, King Henry's keeper, and to the Mayor and Aldermen to hold the city at all costs until he arrived. By Sunday, Edward was reported at Daventry. Despite Warwick's best efforts to gain ground on the foe, the Lancastrians were two days' march behind. There was not much hope that London would hold out. Warwick's brother George had only a handful of lords by his side; the garrison probably numbered fewer men than the Yorkists in sanctuary; the citizens held the balance of power, and King Edward was popular with the ruling class and had a strong army at his back. The Earl of Warwick drove onward, shaken by Edward's advance through the heart of England and his unexpected dash for the capital, oppressed by the defection of Clarence and the doubtful allegiance of Montagu.

Not many men joined Warwick's banners, nor Edward's. As the rival armies toiled along the road to London—two streams of steel-capped archers, mounted knights, supply wains and artillery carts, with pennons and ensigns waving above them—the rest of the realm waited. Lords, squires, yeomen, townsfolk went about their daily business, indifferent to the claims of York and Lancaster, weary of the demands of Warwick. A few thousand fighters would decide the destiny of England.

While Richard Neville grimly rode southward through a silent kingdom, portents of which he was unaware were germinating in the western world. Columbus, a lad of some twenty years, was already seafaring; in Florence, Leonardo da Vinci was reaching manhood; Erasmus was a boy of five. In less than two decades Thomas More and Copernicus and Martin Luther would appear.

Even now, while the Pope, symbol of a bygone international christendom, called vainly for a crusade against the Turk, Louis XI was creating the first nationalist state in Europe. Great new forces were gathering strength as mighty institutions crumbled from within. The changing times in their working had cast up brilliant personalities to flash in the sunlight of power, but these, for all their flamboyant wills, were struggling in the grip of vast nether tides that would sustain some and pull others to destruction.

Messengers from the south managed to make their way to the Earl of Warwick. On Tuesday, the ninth, he learned that the Earl of Devon and the Duke of Somerset, hearing of Queen Margaret's imminent landing on the south coast, had turned their backs on London the preceding day in order to greet her. But the Earl had not yet tasted the full bitterness of the cup which he himself had done so much to brew. Late on Thursday night came the news he had feared: the Yorkists had triumphantly entered London at noon that day.[5*] Perhaps Warwick was also informed that on the evening before, George Neville had sent to Edward to ask his grace and, though consigned for the moment to the Tower, had been given a pardon for his capitulation.[6]

A few hours later, Richard Neville reached the sour dregs of his great adventure. A messenger from across the seas found his way to Warwick's headquarters. He reported that King Louis—Warwick's friend for life, the monarch who had insisted on the alliance against Burgundy which both parties were sworn never to break—Louis had signed a three months' truce with Duke Charles.

In the midst of his suspicion-ridden army, facing battle with the formidable young Prince who had outwitted him, surrounded by numbers of men who hoped for his death, Richard Neville glimpsed in the shock of this news the hard truth which his vision of himself had masked. In his passionate struggle to become a ruler, he had betrayed himself into the hands of rulers. For all his boldness, his diligence, his powers, he had fallen from the maneuverer to the maneuvered. He had become but a counter in the great struggle between Louis of France and Edward of England. The name "Warwick" had no power to hold back the remorseless tide of things rushing upon him.

And yet . . . the truce Louis had accepted made little difference to Warwick's affairs now. It was obviously a temporary expedient, the more understandable since Warwick himself had not been able to cross the Channel with an army. He would undoubtedly still find a princely welcome in France. . . .

No matter. Richard Neville had lived by symbols; it was the symbolic force of Louis' act that shook his nerves. The dream which had so long sustained him Louis had extinguished with a snap of his fingers. What were the pretensions of the Warwick legend in comparison with the assurance of a crown regal? Being a King, Louis could afford to toy with the alliance against Burgundy as he pleased. On that alliance Warwick had loyally staked everything, even at the cost of losing his hold upon the English realm. Another acrid thought must have pierced his mind—had he learned this news a scant week earlier, would he have refused Edward's offers? Time, as well as the King of France, was mocking him.

In a terrible agony of spirit, Warwick vented his bitterness and his rage upon paper, dictating a letter to King Louis such as few monarchs have ever received. Violently he excoriated him for his perjury and perfidy and treachery. Then he sent the messenger posting on the return journey. The letter, too, was a symbol. In thus gratuitously slamming the door upon his escape-hatch to the future, he was, at bottom, acknowledging that he had already despaired.[7*]

The harsh uncertainties of his position closed round him. What was to be done, now that Edward had regained his capital and captured King Henry? The Duke of Exeter and the Earl of Oxford, hot for Edward's blood, were willing enough to seek out the Yorkists; perhaps they could be trapped in London while the capital was observing Easter,[8] or if they tried to issue forth at the last moment, they might be crushed against the city walls. But the Bastard of Fauconberg was rousing the men of Kent; Queen Margaret and the Prince would soon be rallying the West Country adherents of the Duke of Somerset and the Earl of

Devon; and they would be joined by Jasper Tudor's Welsh levies. If Warwick waited just a little, three Lancastrian armies would converge upon London, and Edward would be caught in a vice of iron.

Richard Neville had little heart for such calculation. Where would he stand, afterward, if Queen Margaret commanded the decisive power which won the realm for Lancaster? The dazzling spiral of his adventures had tightened to a precarious point. He sensed that the time had passed for nice maneuvers and intricate stratagems. He would be truest to his vision if he boldly fronted the issue of battle, and in his heart he feared the revenge of Queen Margaret more than the sword of Edward of York.

He would play out the game as it had begun. He gave the word to advance banners. Early on Easter Eve, Saturday, April 13, the Lancastrian host rolled through St. Albans and took the road for Barnet. Word came from the scouts that Edward was marshaling his forces to march out of London. In the afternoon the Earl drew up his men on a rise of ground about a mile north of Barnet. His army was stretched across the great plateau, four hundred feet above sea level, which falls abruptly to the Middlesex plain just south of Barnet village. The left wing, commanded by the Duke of Exeter, was anchored on the edge of a sudden drop into a marshy flat, now called Dead Man's Bottom. The center, under Marquess Montagu, was astride the St. Albans-Barnet road; and the Earl of Oxford's right wing lay behind a hedge to the west of the road. Warwick himself, taking charge of the reserve, established his headquarters behind his brother's line. The Earl had been able to marshal some twelve thousand men; true to his faith in gunpowder, he had with him a large artillery train with which he hoped to dismay the ranks of Edward's army before they closed in hand-to-hand fighting. He was probably aware that Edward could muster no more than nine thousand soldiers and few guns.

As it was growing dark, Warwick's scouts were driven out of Barnet by the advance guard of Edward's army. Night shut down before the Earl could discover what battle positions the enemy troops had taken up. He concentrated his store of cannon to cover the road out of Barnet and kept his gunners firing into the darkness.

The first light of dawn gave him no sight of the enemy. It was April 14, Easter Sunday morning—by which day the great treaty between the Earl of Warwick and the King of France was to have been ratified. A thick fog had rolled up out of the valleys, blanketing the field. Warwick's guns would be of small use.

In the clammy grayness Lancastrian captains were arming themselves for battle. After long years of defeat, attainder, exile, they were moved to fight by hatred of Edward and a passion to vindicate a cause and a King. Their King was feeble-witted and their cause had nothing to offer the realm except a return to an unhappy past. Still, Exeter and his fellows represented a quarrel for which much had been risked and much lost. Beyond the wall of fog lay Edward Plantagenet, his brothers, and his chief lords, who represented a different shape of things. The realm as a whole had not thronged to the Yorkist banners, but it had not opposed Edward's march; and the capital had welcomed him joyously. With Warwick's help, Edward had forged a strong monarchy, based on middle-class support. Edward stood for a new direction in the destiny of England.

What did the Earl of Warwick represent? In this harsh dawn hour of arming for a desperate conflict, he could find in the extravagant course of his last years no greater meaning than was contained within the mortal integument of his own skin. He stood only for himself.

The fog made his armor clammy to the touch. The banners of the Ragged Staff hung limp in the heavy damp. A portent? He had always been upheld by the promise of tomorrow; but he had drawn so recklessly on the promise that it was now exhausted. Clarence had deserted him; Louis the Eleventh had mocked him; his brother George had fawned on Edward to save his own skin; his brother John, obeying the call of kinship, would fight at his side, but John's heart was in the other camp and he had the look of a man who has lost the will to live. There was bad blood between the Neville retainers and the old Lancastrians. Warwick's own men would stand by him, but they had little love for the cause in which they were risking their lives.

The Earl of Warwick strode from his tent into the dank gloom. For six years the course of his life had moved toward a final reckoning with the young man he had enthroned but could not dominate. He now faced that issue, stripped of everything but the will to fight for his life. It was nearly four o'clock. He was greeted by the knights and squires of his household. A page brought up his horse. Messengers were arriving from his captains.

Oxford and Montagu and Exeter had already roused their men to take up battle positions. Warwick rode toward the front of the line to seek his brother. He found Montagu giving final orders to his lieutenants. Ranks of fighting men stretched away into the fog. The Marquess drew him apart from their household knights and squires. Men's minds were uneasy, John Neville told his brother. To give them heart, Warwick this day must take the same risks as the commonest soldier in the field and remain on foot. In that age, as both men well knew, the heavily armed knights and lords had a good chance of escaping death in the fighting; but if their line broke, they were rarely able to get away, hampered by the weight of armor they carried.

Warwick agreed to his brother's demand. He ordered his war steeds to be led to the horse-park in the rear. Surrounded by the men of his household, he took up his command position behind Montagu's center ward. It was a little after four o'clock. Ahead, there was only a wall of fog, through which oozed the vague and muffled sounds of an enemy host preparing for battle. Montagu, Oxford, and Exeter sent word that they were ready.

Warwick signaled his trumpeters. Archers and gunners fired into the blankness of the fog. Close ahead, the trumpets of the Yorkists rang out. A great shout gave notice that they were coming on the run. Montagu issued the order to advance banners and plunged forward at the head of his troops. With a crash the two hosts came together out of the murk. Warwick could barely make out the wall of struggling men, his brother's flag in the center thrust against the sun banner of the House of York.

On either side the fog closed down, hiding what was happening on the wings.

In a few moments there arrived an alarm from the Duke of Exeter. His men had been suddenly attacked on the flank by a large Yorkist force storming up from the marshy bottom. Hastily Warwick sent off the bulk of the reserve to Exeter's aid. Messengers dissolved into the fog, materialized out of it. Exeter had managed to pull round his line to make a new front and was holding his own against the Yorkist right wing. A Boar banner showed it to be commanded by Edward's eighteen-year-old brother Richard, who had learned the rudiments of war at Middleham Castle under Warwick's tutelage. Then, from the other side of the field, great good news burst through the fog. The Earl of Oxford, finding no enemy before him, had fallen upon the Yorkist flank and smashed the left wing of Edward's army. Now Oxford and all the soldiers he could mount were spurring after the fleeing enemy. In the darkness Edward had drawn up his men in such a way that, unbeknownst to him, his right wing under Richard of Gloucester outflanked Exeter to the east while Lord Hastings' left wing was outflanked by Oxford. Quickly Warwick sent orders to the Earl to check his pursuit and swing round upon the enemy.

Meanwhile, directly ahead, the opposing center wards were locked in a fierce, swaying struggle. Here and there the weight of Montagu's power thrust back the outnumbered Yorkists; but before Montagu could achieve a break-through, Edward hurled himself into the battle with a detachment of his reserve and forced the Lancastrians to give ground. Again and again he hewed a path through the melee, Montagu's men recoiling before his mighty strokes. The shattering of Hastings' wing had not dismayed the Yorkist rank-and-file because the fog hid this unnerving collapse from their sight.

The surf of swords, spears, battle-axes twisted and shifted. Montagu sent a call for help. Warwick led forward a contingent of his precious reserve, cut his way into the fighting at their head; then his household knights and squire closed in front of him and he withdrew to bring up more men. Two hours of violent carnage

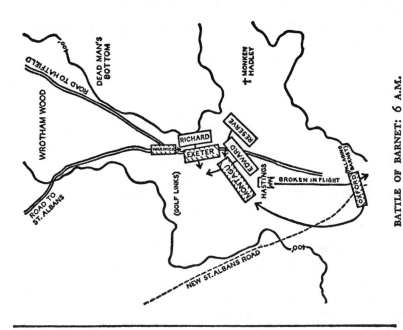

BATTLE OF BARNET: 6 A.M.

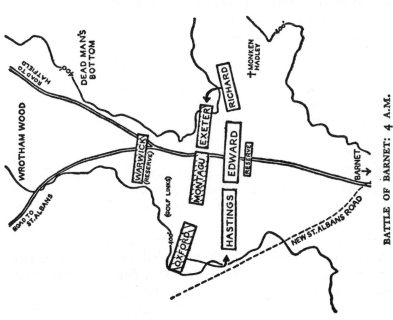

BATTLE OF BARNET: 4 A.M.

365

and the driving in of both flanks had wrenched the fighting about so that the lines were now running roughly north and south. There was no word yet from Oxford. The Lancastrian reserve was dwindling.

But Warwick—bringing up men to the front, plunging into battle, retiring to receive reports and give orders—had begun to glimpse victory. Exeter was pressing back the Yorkist left, foot by foot, toward the rim of the steep drop out of which they had climbed. When Oxford had rallied his men, he would strike the rear of the Yorkist center—

Suddenly, in the misty reaches on the right of Montagu's line, there were yells, a flurry of movement. The flank guard of bowmen were hastily loosing shafts. Horsemen drove into them, then recoiled before the arrow-fire. Now men were shouting "Treason! Treason!" Confusion spread down the line. . . . Out of the fog had ridden a cavalry force following a banner which seemed, in the uncertain light, to bear the Yorkist emblem of the blazing sun. But these were Oxford's men returning from the pursuit beneath Oxford's ensign of a star with streams. Unaware that the battle had shifted, groping his way in the fog, Oxford had collided with Montagu's right flank. Even as his men realized their mistake, they were met by a severe volley of arrows. Suspicions lurking in the minds of Lancastrians and Neville followers did the rest. With cries of "Treason!" Oxford and his men fled. The cries were taken up by Montagu's troops. Panic rippled down the line.

Warwick and his lieutenants struggled to bolster the wavering ranks. But before the Earl could restore order, Edward smashed with all his remaining reserve at the heart of the Lancastrian center. The great sun banner drove toward Montagu's pennon. Warwick called on the last of his reserve. He thrust up his visor to hearten them with cheering words, to urge stragglers back into the battle—if they held now, victory was theirs!

But Montagu's line began to unravel. News came that Exeter had been cut down. Weapons were beating about John Neville's banner as Warwick worked desperately to shore up the front. The banner disappeared. Word rushed through the ranks that Montagu had been slain. Men panted out conflicting stories to

Warwick. Some said that Lancastrians, calling him a traitor, had struck him down from behind. Others declared that he had become separated from his men and had fallen in the thickest press of the fighting.

Warwick had no time to listen. The trickle of fugitives was swelling to streams, fleeing past him heedless of his efforts to rally them. Throwing into the battle the last of his household men, he stood alone beneath his banner. Through the dust and fog, he saw Montagu's writhing line begin to fall apart. Warwick's voice was strengthless against the din. Men were flinging away weapons as they ran. Arrows began to whine about him. The glimpse of victory, like everything else, had been an illusion.

Even as his army began to break before his eyes, a ship carrying the Countess of Warwick was standing in to Portsmouth harbor; his daughter Anne, her husband the Prince, and Margaret of Anjou were landing at Weymouth.

Voices yelled in triumph. Yorkist banners broke out of the fog. In the blind reflex of survival, Richard Neville turned and began to run. Burdened by the weight of steel on his back and the weight of death upon his heart, he lumbered for the horse-park. The spacious reach of his great adventuring had contracted to a gasping fight for breath.

There he goes, a middle-aged man stumbling across a field.

A band of Yorkists sighted him, raced in pursuit. As he got his hand on a horse-bridle, an enemy caught him from behind. He was hurled to the ground. His visor was clawed up. A knife thrust in the throat extinguished Richard Neville and put a bloody finish to the Warwick legend.[9]*

While soldiers greedily stripped the rich armor from the body, a yeoman of Edward's household rode up—sent by the victor to save the Earl of Warwick's life. Next morning a humble cart bore the corpses of the Earl and the Marquess to St. Paul's cathedral. In wooden coffins, lying naked save for loin cloths, they were exposed to public view for two days, in order that all might know that the Kingmaker had met his end. Then Edward permitted the bodies to be borne to Bisham Abbey, where reposed Warwick's father and mother and brother Thomas. In Henry VIII's destruction of the abbeys, Warwick's tomb and bones were obliterated. Only the legend remained . . . distorted in Tudor chronicles, maimed in the hurly-burly of the youthful Shakespeare's Henry VI plays.

A few weeks after Barnet Field, jubilant Burgundians were taunting King Louis with jeering ballads—

> Or a-il bien son temps perdu
> Et son argent qui plus lui touche,
> Car Warwic est mort et vaincu:
> Ha! que Loys est fine mouche!
>
> Entre vous, Franchoix,
> Jettez pleurs et larmes:
> Warwic vostre choix
> Est vaincu par armes.[10]
>
> (Now time his schemes has eaten
> And his coin—yes, there's the sting:
> For Warwick's dead and beaten—
> Ha! *What* a sly dog is the King!
>
> Frenchmen, one to another,
> Rain tears and drip alarms,
> For Warwick, your sworn brother,
> Is crushed by force of arms.)

As for Louis himself, when a short time later the Milanese ambassador ventured to speak "quietly to His Majesty about English affairs, expressing . . . great sorrow at what had happened," Louis remarked with a sigh that it is impossible to fight against fortune.[11] He was busy with new schemes.

Richard Neville had been born into a violent world and by violence he had died—the maker of Kings at last undone by Kings. Louis had other resources. Edward had blood royal and genius and even, at the end, all the luck. Yet, though Warwick had missed his heart's desire, there must have been moments when he appreciated—for he was a man who watched himself living—that few men had explored so full a range of experience as he. He was of the world worldly, and perhaps as the knife flashed down, this fleck of perception mitigated the bitterness of death and the blankness of heaven.

Warwick left no enduring print upon the English state. He was an adventurer—a surcharged moment of human experience. It was men's imaginations that he stamped. But in the passing of time, he paid the price of becoming a legend by almost ceasing to be a man. Perhaps his wife and daughters, and at moments even he himself, felt that he paid that same price during his lifetime.

Epilogue

WITHIN six weeks of the death of its champion at Barnet, the House of Lancaster was no more. When the news of Warwick's end reached the south coast, his Countess took sanctuary at Beaulieu Abbey. Queen Margaret and her Prince, heartened by the rash assurances of the Duke of Somerset and the Earl of Devon, set out for Exeter to rally the Lancastrian adherents of the Southwest. By the time they moved on to Bath and Bristol, they had gathered a sizable army; but King Edward was now bearing down on them. Queen Margaret and her commanders hastily decided to slip into Wales in order to join forces with Jasper Tudor. In the race for the Severn crossings, Edward came up with the Lancastrians at Tewkesbury on the evening of Friday, May 3. Next day, he won a crushing victory. In the midst of the fighting, the Duke of Somerset rode up to Warwick's friend Lord Wenlock, accused him of treachery, and smashed his skull with a battle-axe. Prince Edward was slain in the field. Somerset and the other Lancastrian leaders were captured and executed. Queen Margaret was discovered hiding in a house of religion with her daughter-in-law, Anne Neville.

A few days later, it was the Bastard of Fauconberg's turn. Having assembled a mob of Kentishmen, he made an assault on London which was easily beaten off, and not long after he surrendered to Richard, Duke of Gloucester. On Tuesday, May 21, 1471, Edward entered his capital in triumph. During that night Henry VI was put to death in the Tower by the King's order. A few years after, Edward permitted Louis XI to ransom Margaret of Anjou. Louis received some return for his 50,000 crowns, however, by making her resign to him all her rights of inheritance from her father; and when she died, broken-hearted, in 1483, he promptly sent for her dogs. Louis was devoted to dogs.

The tide of English history rolled on in the direction toward which Warwick had set it going and from which he had then vainly sought to deflect it. King Edward, his dominion of the realm firmly established, turned his attention to settling scores with Louis XI. Allied with his brother-in-law, Charles, he finally invaded France with a great army in 1475; but the rash Duke of Burgundy, entangled in other military adventures, gave him no support. When Louis offered attractive terms, Edward promptly closed with them. In return for a long truce he received 75,000 crowns in hand and an annual payment of 50,000 crowns. Tribute, the English court exultingly called these sums; but Louis knew that Edward had, in effect, become his pensioner. Not long after, the King of France settled his long account with the Duke of Burgundy. Goaded by Louis and furiously seeking a Crown, Charles embroiled himself in a war with the Swiss which brought him the crashing defeats of Grandson and Morat. Early in 1477, Charles of Burgundy was slain pursuing to the end the role of Caesar which had captured his imagination the morning after the battle of Montlhéry.[1*] His heiress, Mary, married Maximilian of Austria in the hope of protecting her principality against the King of France, and the young couple appealed frantically for aid to Edward; but Louis kept the English King quiet by his annual payment of 50,000 crowns while he gobbled up the Dukedom of Burgundy and enlarged his northern borders at the expense of Flanders.

The two great antagonists died within a few months of each other in 1483. If Louis had somewhat the better of their duel of wits, Edward left to his successors a strong monarchy and a treasury surplus such as had not been known for centuries.

Warwick's Countess lived in obscurity until about 1490. George Neville, the clever Archbishop of York, got little good from his treacherous capitulation to King Edward. He was soon dabbling in conspiracy with the perpetually discontented Duke of Clarence, and in 1472 Edward sent him, a prisoner, to the dreary confines of Hammes Castle. Released in 1475, he died the following year, broken in health and in spirit. John Neville's son George, Duke of Bedford, was stripped of his dukedom in 1478 under the excuse of his lacking means to support the dignity; he died childless six years later.

Anne Neville did, indeed, become a Queen. Richard, Duke of Gloucester, married her in 1472, he and Clarence sharing the vast Warwick inheritance of their two wives. The following year Anne bore her husband a son, a frail child who died nine months after his father was crowned Richard III. Anne followed the boy to the grave a year later (March, 1485)—six months before Richard lost his life and Crown at Bosworth Field.

Anne's sister Isabel had succumbed eight years earlier, leaving a son, Edward, and a daughter, Margaret. When King Edward, pushed by the Woodvilles, finally had the feckless Duke of Clarence executed in 1478 for his interminable plotting, young Edward was permitted to retain the earldom of Warwick. The moment Henry Tudor won at Bosworth, he clapped Clarence's son behind bars, for the boy was now the heir of the House of York, and the little Earl of Warwick never drew a free breath after. When the Spaniards let it be known that they hesitated to permit Katherine of Aragon to marry Henry VII's elder son, Prince Arthur, while so dangerous a claimant to the English throne remained alive, Henry trumped up a charge of conspiracy against the lad and murdered him legally.

Clarence's daughter Margaret became a favorite of Henry VIII. He called her the most saintly woman in England and he created her Countess of Salisbury. In the end, however, he executed her eldest son, Lord Montagu, and sent the saintly Countess to the block when she was old and helpless. So ended Richard Neville's grandchildren, hunted to death by the Tudors because they were vessels of the royal blood of England. That they were descendants of the Earl of Warwick was of no importance.

Notes on Sources

The bibliography contains only those sources on which the fabric of the biography has been mainly constructed. Sources dealing with particular events or situations are identified in the notes to the chapters in which these materials have been used.

The notes to the text identify quotations and the sources of certain passages which seemed to be worth special notice. I have also commented on conflicting or uncertain evidence for important moments in Warwick's life, and I have noted those substantial conjectures and inferences not indicated in the text itself. Grants, commissions, and the like which are not identified are to be found in the *Calendar of the Patent Rolls, Calendar of the Close Rolls, Calendar of the Charter Rolls,* or *Foedera,* XI (see Bibliography).

I BIBLIOGRAPHY

MANUSCRIPTS:

Bibliothèque Nationale: Legrand Collections, MSS. français 6963–6990; Legrand's History of the Reign of Louis XI, MSS. français 6960–6962.
London Archives, Guildhall: Journal 7.
Public Record Office: Chancery Documents; Exchequer Documents.

OFFICIAL DOCUMENTS:

Calendar of the Charter Rolls, VI.
Calendar of the Close Rolls, 1454–61; 1461–68; 1468–76.
Calendar of Milanese Papers (Calendar of State Papers and Manuscripts, relating to English affairs, existing in the Archives and Collections of Milan, I, ed. by A. B. Hinds, London, 1912).
Calendar of the Patent Rolls, 1452–61; 1461–67; 1467–77.
Foedera, XI (*Foedera* etc., compiled by Thomas Rymer, London, 1727).
Lettres de Louis XI, Roi de France, 11 vols., ed. by J. Vaesen and others, Paris, 1883–1909.
Mandrot, *Dépêches (Dépêches des ambassadeurs milanais en France sous Louis XI et François Sforza,* ed. by B. de Mandrot, 4 vols., Paris, 1916–19).
Proceedings and Ordinances of the Privy Council of England, VI, ed. by Sir H. Nicolas, London, 1834–37.
Rotuli Parliamentorum (Rolls of Parliament), V.
Statutes of the Realm, II.

TOWN RECORDS:

Coventry Leet Book, II, ed. by Mary D. Harris, Early English Text Society, 1907–13.

York Civic Records, I, ed. by Angelo Raine, The Yorkshire Archaeological Society, 1939.
York Records (Extracts from the Municipal Records of the City of York, ed. by R. Davies, London, 1843).

CONTEMPORARY CORRESPONDENCE:

The Paston Letters, 4 vols., ed. by James Gairdner, Library Edition, London, 1910.

ALSO OF IMPORTANCE:

Cely Papers, ed. by H. E. Malden, Camden Society, 1900.
Plumpton Correspondence, ed. by T. Stapleton, Camden Society, 1839.
The Stonor Letters and Papers, 1290–1483, ed. by C. L. Kingsford, Camden Society, 1919.

COLLECTIONS OF SOURCE MATERIALS:

Chronicles of the White Rose of York, London, 1845.
Commynes-Dupont, III (*Mémoires de Philippe de Commynes*, ed. by Mlle. Dupont, Paris, 1840–47).
Commynes-Lenglet, II and III (*Mémoires de Philippe de Comines*, ed. by M. l'Abbé Lenglet du Fresnoy, London and Paris, 1747).
Ellis (*Original Letters*, 3 series, several volumes in each series, ed. by Henry Ellis, London, 1825, 1827, 1846).
Excerpta Historica, London, 1831.
HMC: Historical Manuscripts Commission Reports (*Reports of the Royal Commission on Historical Manuscripts*).

CONTEMPORARY NARRATIVES AND OTHER SOURCES DEALING WITH PARTICULAR EVENTS:

Chronicle of the Rebellion in Lincolnshire, 1470, ed. by J. G. Nichols, Camden Society, Miscellany, I, 1847.
Historie of the Arrivall of Edward IV in England, ed. by John Bruce, Camden Society, 1838.
Hanserecesse, 1431–76, II, vi, ed. by G. von der Ropp, Leipzig, 1890.
Samaran, Ch., *La Maison d'Armagnac au XVᵉ Siècle*, Paris, 1907.

SECONDARY SOURCES EMBODYING IMPORTANT SOURCE MATERIALS:

Beaucourt, VI (Beaucourt, G. du Fresne de, *Histoire de Charles VII*, VI, Paris, 1881–91).
Calmette and Périnelle (Calmette, J., and G. Périnelle, *Louis XI et l'Angleterre*, Paris, 1930).
Scofield, I (Scofield, Cora L., *The Life and Reign of Edward the Fourth*, I, London, 1923).

OTHER SECONDARY SOURCES:

Huizinga, J., *The Waning of the Middle Ages* (now available in Doubleday Anchor Books, Anchor A42, 1954).
Kingsford, Charles L., *English Historical Literature in the Fifteenth Century*, Oxford, 1913.

Power and Postan (*Studies in English Trade in the Fifteenth Century*, ed. by Eileen Power and M. M. Postan, London, 1933; 2nd impression, 1951).

ENGLISH CHRONICLES:

Chron. of John Stone (*Chronicle of John Stone*, ed. by W. G. Searle, Cambridge Antiquarian Society, 1902).

Chrons. of London (*Chronicles of London*, ed. by C. L. Kingsford, Oxford, 1905).

Croyland Chronicle ("Historiae Croylandensis," *Rerum Anglicarum Scriptorum*, I, ed. by W. Fulman, Oxford, 1684. English translation: *Ingulph's Chronicle of the Abbey of Croyland*, trans. and ed. by Henry T. Riley, Bohn's Antiquarian Library, London, 1854. All page references in this biography are to the English translation.).

Davies Eng. Chron. (*An English Chronicle of the Reigns of Richard II, Henry IV, Henry V, and Henry VI*, ed. by J. S. Davies, Camden Society, 1856).

Fabyan, Robert, *The New Chronicles of England and France*, ed. by Henry Ellis, London, 1811.

The Great Chronicle of London, ed. by A. H. Thomas and I. D. Thornley, London, 1938.

Gregory (*Gregory's Chronicle: The Historical Collections of a Citizen of London*, ed. by James Gairdner, Camden Society, 1876).

Six Town Chrons. (*Six Town Chronicles of England*, ed. by R. Flenley, Oxford, 1911).

3 15th Cent. Chrons. (*Three Fifteenth Century Chronicles*, ed. by James Gairdner, Camden Society, 1880).

Warkworth, John, *A Chronicle of the First Thirteen Years of the Reign of King Edward the Fourth*, ed. by J. O. Halliwell, Camden Society, 1839.

Whethamstede, John, *Registrum Abbatiae Johannis Whethamstede*, 2 vols., ed. by Henry T. Riley, Rolls Series, 1872–73.

Worcester, William, *Annales Rerum Anglicarum* in *Letters and Papers Illustrative of the Wars of the English in France during the Reign of Henry the Sixth*, II, pp. 743–93, ed. by J. Stevenson, Rolls Series, 1864.

FRENCH CHRONICLES:

Basin, II (Basin, Thos., *Histoires des règnes de Charles VII et de Louis XI*, II, ed. by J. Quicherat, Paris, 1855–59).

Chastellain, Georges, *Oeuvres*, ed. by M. le Baron Kervyn de Lettenhove, Brussels, 1863–65.

Commynes (*Mémoires de Philippe de Commynes*, 2 vols., ed. by Joseph Calmette, Paris, 1924).

Du Clercq (*Mémoires de Jacques du Clercq*, ed. by De Reiffenberg, 4 vols., 2nd ed., Brussels, 1836).

Haynin (*Les Mémoires de Jean de Haynin*, ed. by R. Chalon [Société des Bibliophiles Belges, Mons, no. 11], Mons, 1842).

La Marche (*Mémoires d'Olivier de la Marche*, ed. by H. Beaune and J. d'Arbaumont, Paris, 1883).

Maupoint ("Journal Parisien de Jean Maupoint," *Mémoires de la Société de l'Histoire de Paris et de l'Ile-de-France*, IV, Paris, 1877).

Roye, Jean de, *Journal*, I (*Journal de Jean de Roye connu sous le nom de Chronique Scandaleuse (1460–83)*, ed. by B. de Mandrot, Paris, 1894–96).
Waurin, Jehan de, *Anchiennes Cronicques d'Engleterre*, II and III, ed. by Mlle. Dupont, Paris, 1858–63.

II NOTES TO THE TEXT

I THE YORKIST (1428–1456)

1. THE EVE OF FAME

The known facts of Warwick's life up to the age of twenty-two (1450) are sparse:

1. Born November 22, 1428, nineteen days after his grandfather, the Earl of Salisbury, was killed at the siege of Orléans.
2. Married, before 1439 (the year of his father-in-law's death), Anne, daughter of Richard Beauchamp, Earl of Warwick.
3. Knighted at an early age.
4. Made Joint-Warden of the West Marches, on April 4, 1446, with his father for twenty years, the office to begin at the end of his father's term as Warden (in December, 1453).
5. Created Earl of Warwick, in his wife's right, by patent of July 23, 1449. For the estates he inherited, see *Calendar of Inquisitions Post Mortem*, Richard Beauchamp, Earl of Warwick.
6. When in London he lodged at the Grey Friars, Newgate.
7. On May 5, 1450—just before Jack Cade's rising—Warwick arrived in Leicester with more than 400 men. A month later (June 8), he was gathering another force at Warwick Castle in order to join the King at St. Albans in case the commons of Kent rose in rebellion. Apparently, however, he remained on his estates.

On November 25, he came to London "with a mighty people arrayed for war" (*Six Town Chronicles*, p. 137) to support his uncle, Richard, Duke of York, who had arrived in the capital two days before "with 3000 men and more" (*idem*).

1. Gregory, pp. 199–202.
2. Warwick's epithets for Margaret of Anjou: Chastellain, V, p. 467. Margaret's beauty and imperiousness: *Cal. Mil. Papers*, I, pp. 18–19; *Coventry Leet Book*, II, pp. 298–99.
3. *Proceeds. and Ords. of the Privy Council*, VI, pp. 163–65. *Paston Letters*, I, pp. 265–68.
4. *Rot. Parl.*, V, 240–41.
5. *Foedera*, XI, pp. 361–62.

2. ST. ALBANS

1. *Rot. Parl.*, V, pp. 280–82; *Paston Letters*, I, pp. 325–26. Edward of March with the Yorkists: *3 15th Cent. Chrons.*, pp. 151–52.
2. The numerous brief accounts of the battle of St. Albans differ in

detail but are in substantial agreement. Only one account emphasizes Warwick's contribution to the victory (in *Archaeologia*, XX, p. 519, and also in *Paston Letters*, I, pp. 327-31). An interesting contrast is provided by a report (*Paston Letters*, I, pp. 331-33) in which Sir Robert Ogle is given credit for breaking into the town. The statement in *The Great Chron.* (p. 187) and in the *Chrons. of London* (p. 163) that Warwick and the "Marchmen" stormed into St. Albans by surprise makes it probable that Ogle and his men were under Warwick's command. Abbot Whethamstede of St. Albans Abbey pictures the dead and wounded lying in the streets (Whethamstede, I, p. 353; also *Chrons. of the White Rose*, lii). I have conjectured the details of Warwick's action in the battle.

The derisive comment on the Earl of Wiltshire: Gregory, p. 198.

3. *Rot. Parl.*, V, p. 309; see also Scofield, I, p. 23, n. 2.
4. Events in London for the remainder of 1455: see particularly *Cal. Mil. Papers*, I, pp. 16-17; *Paston Letters*, I, pp. 335-37, 345-46, 352; *Great Chron.*, p. 188; *Rot. Parl.*, V, pp. 278-82; *Proceeds. and Ords.*, VI, pp. 261-79 (Warwick's presence at council meetings).
5. *Rot. Parl.*, V, pp. 295-300, p. 341.
6. *Paston Letters*, I, p. 377.
7. York and Warwick trapped at Coventry: *Paston Letters*, I, pp. 403, 408; *Rot. Parl.*, V, p. 347; *Chrons. of London*, p. 167; *Great Chron.*, p. 189; cf. *Coventry Leet Book*, II, pp. 286-92.
8. *Davies Eng. Chron.*, p. 74.

II THE CAPTAIN OF CALAIS (1456-1461)

I. "AS FAMOUS A KNIGHT"

Most of the material concerning Philip, Duke of Burgundy, the Dauphin Louis, and the court of Burgundy is taken from the Burgundian court chronicler, Chastellain (III). Compare Beaucourt (VI), du Clercq (II), and *Letters and Papers Illustrative of the Wars of the English in France during the Reign of Henry the Sixth*, I, ed. by J. Stevenson, Rolls Series, 1864.

1. Warwick's officers at Calais: see Ellis, series 2, I, pp. 124-26.
2. *Paston Letters*, I, p. 416.
3. *Cal. Pat. Rolls*, 1452-61, pp. 390, 412; *Cal. Close Rolls*, 1454-61, pp. 54-61, 240; *Proceeds. and Ords.*, VI, pp. 294-95; cf. *Paston Letters*, I, pp. 426-27.
4. I have conjectured details of the sea battle with the Spaniards from the general method of naval warfare of the day and from the letter of John Jernygan, one of the combatants, which supplies a number of touches and was written only three days after the battle (*Paston Letters*, I, pp. 428-29). The use of guns in Warwick's naval warfare is proved by a reference in Signed Bills, file 1477, no. 6640 (Scofield, I, p. 28, n. 1). See also *3 15th Cent. Chrons.*, p. 71; *Chrons. of London*, p. 168; *Cal. Pat. Rolls*, 1452-61, p. 443; *Foedera*, XI, p. 415.
5. *Paston Letters*, I, pp. 267-68.

6. Power and Postan, pp. 307–12.
7. *Davies Eng. Chron.*, pp. 83–84; Whethamstede, I, pp. 330–31; *Six Town Chrons.*, p. 147.
8. Beaucourt, VI, pp. 41–61.
9. Warwick's dealings with Burgundy: du Clercq, II, pp. 245–47; Chastellain, III, pp. 317–20, 337–39; *Cal. Mil. Papers*, I, p. 18; *Foedera*, XI, p. 410; Beaucourt, VI, pp. 124, 145–46, 182; n. 2, p. 260; pp. 427–28; cf. Scofield, I, p. 28.

    Arrival of the Burgundian embassy about June 3: *Paston Letters*, I, p. 428.

10. The Wenlock mission: Beaucourt, VI, pp. 261–63; du Clercq, II, pp. 329, 336; *Letters and Papers*, I, pp. 361–77; *Forty-Eighth Report of the Deputy Keeper of the Public Records*, pp. 427–29.
11. *Six Town Chrons.*, p. 147.
12. In the spring of 1459 Warwick was reliably reported as about to visit the Duke of Burgundy (*Letters and Papers*, I, pp. 376–77); I have conjectured the details of his visit from accounts of such ceremonies in Chastellain and La Marche and from illustrations in manuscripts depicting the Burgundian court.
13. *Paston Letters*, I, pp. 424, 426–27; *Proceeds. and Ords.*, VI, pp. 293, 294–95; *Cal. Pat. Rolls*, 1452–61, p. 424; Anthony Steel, *The Receipt of the Exchequer, 1377–1485*, Cambridge, 1954, p. 280.
14. *Davies Eng. Chron.*, pp. 78–79; *Chrons. of London*, p. 169; Whethamstede, I, p. 340; *Letters and Papers*, I, pp. 367–69.

2. DISASTER AT LUDLOW

1. Warwick's manifesto: *Chrons. of the White Rose*, pp. lxviii–lxix.
2. Warwick's steering to Guernsey: Waurin, II, pp. 196–97; whether or not the story is true, it reveals the attitude of the public toward him.

3. THE CALAIS EARLS

See C. L. Kingsford, "The Earl of Warwick at Calais, 1460," *Eng. Hist. Rev.*, XXXVII (1922), pp. 544–46, and Cora L. Scofield, "The Capture of Lord Rivers and Sir Anthony Woodville, 19 January, 1460," *ibid.*, pp. 253–55.

1. Fabyan, p. 635.
2. *Paston Letters*, I, p. 506.
3. Events in England: see also G. Baskerville, "A London Chronicle of 1460," *Eng. Hist. Rev.*, XXVIII (1913), pp. 125–26.
4. Coppini: Ellis, series 3, I, pp. 85–88; *Cal. Mil. Papers*, I, pp. ix–x, 23–24. Cf. Scofield, I, pp. 71–76.

4. "MARVELLOUS THINGS"

1. Manifestoes: *Davies Eng. Chron.*, pp. 86–90.
2. Warwick in London: see also "A London Chronicle of 1460" (note 3, Chap. 3, above); R. R. Sharpe, *London and the Kingdom*, London, 1894–95, I, pp. 299–301.

3. *Cal. Mil. Papers*, I, pp. 23–26; Vatican Transcripts, Portfolio 62 (Scofield, I, pp. 83–85 and n. 1, p. 85).
4. Battle of Northampton: details are scanty but sources show fairly substantial agreement; see particularly *Davies Eng. Chron.*, pp. 96–98; Gregory, p. 207 (Sir Wm. Lucy); "A London Chronicle of 1460"; *Chron. of John Stone*, p. 80; Waurin, II, pp. 224–28; *Cal. Mil. Papers*, I, p. 27; *Proceeds. and Ords.*, VI, p. 361.
5. *Cal. Mil. Papers*, I, p. 27.

5. THE CROWN

1. *Cal. Mil. Papers*, I, pp. 28–29.
2. Whethamstede, I, pp. 376–77.
3. Scene between Warwick and York: Waurin, II, pp. 244–47. Waurin is not always reliable in his details, and he may have worked up this conversation out of his imagination; but the account as a whole is in accord with the scanty information which is available on the subject of Warwick's and York's relations at this moment.
4. *Paston Letters*, I, pp. 521–22, p. 532.

6. "LIKE ANOTHER CAESAR"

1. *Cal. Mil. Papers*, I, p. 44.
2. *Ibid.*, pp. 21, 37–41, 57.*
3. *Croyland Chron.*, p. 423.
4. *Cal. Mil. Papers*, I, p. 46.
5. J. Anstis, *The Register of the Most Noble Order of the Garter*, London, 1724, II, pp. 166–68; G. F. Beltz, *Memorials of the Order of the Garter*, London, 1841, pp. lxvi, clxii.

* Though dated March 22, 1460, this letter was undoubtedly written March 22, 1461, as is shown by the general context and particularly by the reference to "the one newly chosen," which evidently refers to Edward IV.

7. WARWICK'S PROTÉGÉ

1. Gregory, pp. 211–14
2. Edward must have marched from the West to the Cotswolds via Coventry—*Coventry Leet Book*, II, p. 313. The dialogue is imagined.
3. Gregory, pp. 214–15.
4. The battle of Towton: only meager details are available despite the large number of accounts. See especially *Paston Letters*, II, pp. 5–6; *Cal. Mil. Papers*, I, pp. 65–77; Worcester, p. 777; Waurin, II, pp. 276–86; *Croy. Chron.*, pp. 425–26; du Clercq, III, p. 118; cf. C. Ransome, "The Battle of Towton," *Eng. Hist. Rev.*, IV (1889), pp. 460–66.
5. Warwick's remaining in the North: It appears, from an entry in the *Coventry Leet Book* (II, pp. 317–19), that Warwick paid a hasty visit to Warwickshire shortly after King Edward passed through Coventry on his way south. He may have accompanied Edward as far as Coventry, but the failure of the city records to make any mention of Warwick, the great lord of the region, in their account of Edward's

reception makes this unlikely. On June 18, six days after the King had arrived at Shene (Richmond), Warwick took north with him a band of soldiers furnished and paid by the city "for to resist kyng Herry & quene Marget that were, and alle other with theym accompanyed, as Scottes & Frenchemen, of theyre entre yn-to this lande etc." It looks as though Warwick hastily enlisted the citizens when he heard about the Lancastrian attack on Carlisle, soon after repulsed by his brother Montagu (see p. 115). It is possible that, except for this emergency, he might have gone on to London for Edward's coronation, but the probability that he did not come south with Edward and the general situation suggest that he would soon have gone back to the North in any case and that he had not intended to go on to London.

III MASTER OF THE REALM (1461–1464)

1. THE EARL AND THE KING

1. Waurin, III, p. 173.
2. *Cal. Mil. Papers*, I, pp. 100–02.
3. *Idem.*
4. See, for example, Waurin, II, pp. 298–99.

2. LABORS IN THE NORTH

1. Worcester, p. 779.
2. *Collection of Ordinances and Regulations for the Government of the Royal Household*, London, 1790, p. 131.
3. For a discussion of Warwick's whereabouts in the summer of 1464, see note 9, Chap. 5 below.
4. Warwick's siege of the Northumberland castles: Warkworth, pp. 37–38; Worcester, p. 782.
5. Warwick's method of fighting: Commynes, I, p. 214.
   Continental chroniclers' accusing Warwick of cowardice: hinted by Commynes in foregoing passage; Waurin, III, p. 35. Chastellain in one passage calls Warwick a coward (V, p. 486), but elsewhere he says that Warwick is one of the great men of the world "because of his intelligence, his valour, and his bright fortune" (V, p. 23)—even though he very much disliked the English. Cf. George B. Churchill, "Richard the Third up to Shakespeare," *Palaestra*, X (1900), Berlin, p. 58. For a brief contemporary account of the English method of making war, see Dominic Mancini, *The Usurpation of Richard III*, ed. by C. A. J. Armstrong, Oxford, 1936, p. 103.

3. WARWICK'S FRIEND THE DAUPHIN

1. The court of Burgundy: see particularly Chastellain, III and IV; Commynes, I; du Clercq, II; and Olivier de la Marche, *Mémoires*.
2. Commynes-Dupont, III, p. 200.

4. WARWICK'S FRIEND THE KING OF FRANCE

1. Chancery Diplomatic Documents (Foreign), no. 365P (Scofield, I, pp. 239–40 and n. 1, p. 240).
2. Davies, *York Records*, pp. 2–7, and Scofield, I, p. 240, n. 1.
3. Louis and Jean II of Aragon: *Lettres de Louis XI*, II, pp. 37–39; Commynes-Dupont, III, pp. 199–205; see, in general, J. Calmette, *Louis XI, Jean II, et la révolution Catalane*, Toulouse, 1902.
4. Chastellain, IV, pp. 274–75.
5. Lannoy's embassy: Mandrot, *Dépêches*, I, p. 264; Chastellain, IV, pp. 340, 381, 493–94; Commynes-Lenglet, II, p. 400; *Lettres de Louis XI*, II, pp. 117–18; B.N. MS. français 6970, f. 137 (Scofield, I, p. 277, n. 3); French Roll, 3 Edw. IV, m. 18 (Scofield, I, p. 277, n. 4); Warrants for Issues and Issue Rolls (Scofield, I, p. 278, ns. 1 and 3); *Chron. of John Stone*, p. 88.
6. English embassy of August–October, 1463: *Chron. of John Stone*, p. 89; B.N. MS. français 6970, f. 365 (Scofield, I, p. 299, n. 7); *Foedera*, XI, pp. 504, 507–09, 520; Chastellain, IV, pp. 279–399; *Lettres de Louis XI*, II, pp. 150–51, 163–64.
   Louis' imprudent remarks about the Scots: see a letter written from Scotland in 1464 by Louis' agent, William Menypeny (B.N. MS. français 6970, ff. 185–87, reprinted in Scofield, II, App. V).
7. See letter written by the secretary November 17, 1464—Commynes-Dupont, III, pp. 211–17.
8. Louis' wooing of Warwick: Commynes-Lenglet, II, p. 179, p. 413; B.N. MS. français 6970, f. 146 (Scofield, I, p. 322, n. 1); *Lettres de Louis XI*, XI, p. 31; Waurin, III, pp. 182–86; a letter from Whetehill to Louis—B.N. MS. français 6971, f. 388 (reprinted in Scofield, II, App. III).

5. THE FRENCH MARRIAGE

1. Warwick's knowledge that Louis wanted a treaty aimed at Burgundy: it does not seem likely that, with Louis in correspondence with Warwick in the early months of 1464 (see p. 121 and note 8, Chapter 4), the French King would have waited for Lannoy to broach this all-important matter. By the summer of 1464 even the court of Burgundy apparently had some knowledge of Louis' hostile intentions, as Warwick's agent, Wenlock, certainly did—Chastellain, V, p. 25. For an indication that Warwick and Lannoy discussed this subject, see Mandrot, *Dépêches*, II, pp. 212–13.
2. Lannoy's embassy: Mandrot, *Dépêches*, II, p. 10, pp. 31–32, 75, 80–81, 99; *Cal. Mil. Papers*, I, p. 109; Commynes-Lenglet, II, pp. 412–17; *Foedera*, XI, pp. 513, 518, 520–22; *Stonor Letters and Papers*, ed. by C. L. Kingsford, Camden Society, 1919, I, pp. 66–67; Household Accounts, Exchequer K.R., bundle 411, no. 13 (Scofield, I, p. 325, n. 2); B.N. MS. français 6960, f. 616 (Scofield, I, p. 327, n. 1).
3. B.N. MS. français 6970, f. 361, reprinted in Scofield, II, App. I.
   Lannoy's hint about the dukedom of Normandy: *Cal. Mil. Papers*, I, pp. 111–12; Mandrot, *Dépêches*, II, p. 148.

4. Edward's relations with Somerset: Worcester, p. 781; Gregory, pp. 219–23.
5. *Cal. Mil. Papers*, I, pp. 101–02.
6. Edward's and Warwick's letters to Louis: B.N. MS. français 6970, f. 323 (Scofield, I, p. 345, n. 3).
7. Mandrot, *Dépêches*, II, p. 75.
8. *Foedera*, XI, p. 526.
9. Warwick's whereabouts in the summer of 1464: Cora L. Scofield has brought to light an entry in the Account Rolls (see "The Movements of the Earl of Warwick in the Summer of 1464," *Eng. Hist. Review*, XXI (1906), pp. 732–37; cf. Scofield, I, pp. 344–47) which apparently proves that Warwick left London on June 17 with ninety attendants and went to Calais on embassy to the Duke of Burgundy, returning to London on August 5, and that again on August 10 he went off on a month's embassy to Philip, this time going beyond Calais and returning to that town on August 30.

This seems to be one of the rare cases, however, in which the reports of the chroniclers, and circumstantial evidence, are to be preferred to an official document. None of the Continental or the English chroniclers mentions Warwick's mission. Even more remarkable, the Milanese ambassador to the French court was with King Louis this summer and his sharp eyes and ears missed little; but though he knows all about Wenlock and Whetehill's embassy—as does Chastellain—like Chastellain he makes no mention of Warwick's crossing the Channel. Yet after Lannoy went to Calais to escort Wenlock and Whetehill to Louis and Philip at Hesdin, Warwick's presence at the port could scarcely have been kept a secret.

Furthermore, the English chroniclers place Warwick this June and July in Northumberland besieging the Lancastrian castles (Gregory, p. 227; two MS. chronicles cited in Warkworth, pp. 29–30 and 36–39; "Hearne's Fragment" in *Chrons. of the White Rose*, pp. 14–15 [including a specific affirmation that Warwick did not go abroad this summer]; Worcester, p. 782). Some of these accounts are convincingly detailed. In addition, a letter Wenlock wrote Lannoy on October 3 of this year indicates that Warwick had stayed in England all summer: ". . . the Earl of Warwick sends at once to the King [Louis] and M. le Duc [Philip] one of his servants with letters showing the cause of his remaining on this side of the sea . . ." (Waurin, II, p. 326, n. 1). In the face of this evidence, and considering the pointlessness of Warwick's journeying to Calais simply to hide himself there, it appears that the Account Roll is mistaken. There is such an indication in the entry itself. For Warwick's supposed second journey (August 10–30), the list of his expenses ceases on his return to Calais on August 30. But Warwick's allowed expenses would not have ceased until he returned to London. This curious discrepancy yields a clue: Richard Whetehill, who, with Lord Wenlock, did go on embassy to Philip and Louis this summer, was Lieutenant of Guisnes Castle; and *his* expenses would cease when he returned to Calais after a visit to the Duke of Burgundy. Hence, it seems likely that the expenses of the second journey are those of Whetehill and Wenlock; and if this explanation fits the second journey, it also explains the first. That is, after Wenlock and Whetehill returned to London following their negotiations with King Louis, Whetehill was then sent back to the court of Burgundy before finally returning to Calais.

It would appear that Warwick, unexpectedly baffled in his efforts to see Louis this summer, insisted that he outfit Wenlock and Whetehill for this journey with an impressive retinue—they being his representatives, as it were, as well as King Edward's—the bills to be paid, of course, by the royal treasury, whence would arise the error of stating that Warwick himself undertook the journey.

On submitting this hypothesis to Alec R. Myers, Senior Lecturer in Medieval History, the University of Liverpool, I received from him the following illuminating comment:

"As to Warwick's movements in 1464, I think that you are probably right. On the one hand the K.R. Memoranda Roll states very explicitly that for each journey 'idem Comes iter suum arripuit de dicta Ciuitate Regis London versus dictum Ducem'; on the other hand it is most strange that neither the English sources nor the French nor the Burgundian seems to refer at all to the presence of Warwick on either embassy. There appears to be no reason why Louis should not have mentioned Warwick's name in his correspondence about the first embassy; and it is extremely odd that a well-informed chronicler like Chastellain should not have referred to Warwick as leading the embassy to Philip, Duke of Burgundy. It therefore looks as though the Exchequer officials had been told that these were the details of the Warwick embassy and assumed in making up their accounts that it had taken place as planned. Perhaps this is one of those cases where the evidence of narratives is to be preferred to that of records; and it may have been decided at the last minute that Warwick would stay in the North after all."

10. Edward's negotiations with Brittany: *Foedera*, XI, pp. 531, 532, 535–37; *Lettres de Louis XI*, XI, p. 217; B.N. MS. français 6970, ff. 185–87 (Menypeny's letter from Scotland to Louis XI informing him of the English dickering with Brittany and of Montagu's refusal to take command of the archers because of Warwick's objection—reprinted in Scofield, II, App. V).

11. Edward's favors to the Nevilles: archbishopric—*Foedera*, XI, p. 533; *Cal. Pat. Rolls*, 1461–67, pp. 327, 329; grant of Percy lands to John Neville—*Cal. Pat. Rolls*, 1461–67, pp. 340–41; Warwick's present— Warrants under the Signet, file 1378 (Scofield, II, p. 417, n. 1).

6. WAITING FOR WARWICK

See particularly Chastellain, V; Mandrot, *Dépêches*, II; *Cal. Mil. Papers*, I; *Lettres de Louis XI;* Commynes, I; du Clercq, IV; Commynes-Lenglet, II.

7. QUARREL

1. Edward's disclosing his marriage: the dialogue is drawn from Waurin's detailed account, which may have imaginative touches but certainly agrees with the known facts and seems convincing—Waurin, II, pp. 326–28.
2. *Cal. Mil. Papers*, I, p. 76.

IV LOUIS' MAN (1464–1468)

1. EYES ACROSS THE CHANNEL

1. Warwick's first letter to Louis: *Dépêches*, II, p. 304. Wenlock's letter (written October 3, received by Lannoy October 13 and forwarded to King Louis next day): Waurin, II, p. 326, n. 1; cf. Scofield, I, p. 354, n. 3, and p. 355, n. 2.
2. Edward's mollifying Warwick: Warrants under the Signet, file 1379 (Scofield, I, p. 356, n. 3); Robert Neville's letter of November 17 (see note 4 below).
3. *Coventry Leet Book*, II, pp. 328–33.
4. Robert Neville's report: see his letter written on November 17 to Warwick's agent, Richard Whetehill, Lieutenant of Guisnes—Commynes-Dupont, III, pp. 211–17; see also *Dépêches*, II, p. 323.
   The enactment against Burgundian goods: *Rot. Parl.*, V, pp. 565–66.
5. Robert Neville's letter (note 4 above); also Calmette and Périnelle, p. 65, n. 2.
6. *Dépêches*, III, p. 40.
7. *Dépêches*, III, p. 51.
8. The Morvilliers embassy to Burgundy: there are three vividly detailed accounts which are in close agreement—Commynes, I, pp. 4–9; Chastellain, V, pp. 113–39; *Dépêches*, II, pp. 349–55. See also Commynes-Lenglet, II, pp. 417–20.
9. Du Clercq, IV, pp. 97–98.
10. Robert Neville's mission: *Dépêches*, III, pp. 283–303; Treasurer's account, Warrants for Issues, 5 Edw. IV, 1 March (Scofield, I, p. 386, n. 4).

2. LOUIS FIGHTS: THE WOODVILLES CLIMB

1. War of the Public Weal and Paris Besieged: *Dépêches*, III, pp. 72–388, IV, pp. 1–39; Commynes, I, pp. 11–88; Chastellain, V, pp. 211 and 227, n. 2; du Clercq, IV, pp. 149–237. See also Haynin, *Mémoires*, I; Maupoint, *Journal Parisien;* Jean de Roye, *Journal*, I; Commynes-Langlet, pp. 422–542; J. J. Champollion-Figeac, *Documents historiques inédits*, II, Paris, 1843–48.

The best accounts of the whirling, confused battle of Montlhéry are those of Commynes, who rode with Charles of Charolais, the young Milanese envoy Jean-Pierre Panigarola, who was at Louis' side, and the Burgundian adherent Haynin. Panigarola's letters give the best picture of Louis' desperate situation in Paris during the siege.

2. Panigarola to the Duke of Milan, January 23, 1466, in Arch. d'État de Milan, Potenze Estere, Francia (Calmette and Périnelle, p. 72, n. 2).

3. BURGUNDY OR FRANCE?

1. See, for example, Commynes-Lenglet, II, p. 413.
2. Mrs. Henry Cust, *Gentlemen Errant*, New York, 1909, pp. 36–39.
3. J. Leland, *Collectanea*, ed. by T. Hearne, London, 1715, VI, pp. 1–14.
4. Warwick and Charolais: Worcester, p. 784, and Commynes, I, p. 140 (who both confuse the year); du Clercq, IV, pp. 254–55.
   Description of Charles: Chastellain, VII, pp. 228–33.
5. The early relationship of Warwick and Clarence: this is inferred from Clarence's attendance at the interment of Warwick's father in Bisham Abbey, 1463 (*Collection of Ordinances and Regulations for the Government of the Royal Household*, London, 1790, pp. 131–33); from Clarence's linking himself with Warwick to present Queen Elizabeth to the peers of the realm at Reading Abbey, September, 1464 (Worcester, p. 783); and from Warwick's proved interest in Clarence's young brother Richard of Gloucester, who was trained in knightly conduct in Warwick's halls (see Kendall, *Richard the Third*, pp. 45–48), an interest which suggests that Warwick would not be likely to neglect Clarence, heir-male to the throne.
6. Waurin, II, p. 334.
7. George Neville's scholarly accomplishments: see R. Weiss, *Humanism in England during the Fifteenth Century*, London, 1941; James Tait, "Letters of John Tiptoft, Earl of Worcester, and Archbishop Neville to the University of Oxford," *Eng. Hist. Review*, XXXV (1920), pp. 570–74.

Chastellain on George Neville: IV, pp. 338, 374.
8. *Great Chron.*, p. 207.
9. *Cal. Mil. Papers*, I, p. 118.
10. Trade: see Power and Postan, pp. 28–31, 187, 211–13.
    The wool trade: see Power and Postan, Chap. II, "The Wool Trade in the Fifteenth Century." The quotations are from the *Libelle of Englyshe Polycye*, a contemporary rhymed plea for a strong naval policy and other measures to promote English trade.
11. Paston Letters, II, p. 305.

4. THE MEETING OF FRIENDS

1. *Cal. Mil. Papers*, I, pp. 118–20.
2. *Cal. Mil. Papers*, I, pp. 117–18.
3. *Lettres de Louis XI*, III, pp. 143–45.
4. Warwick and Louis at Rouen: I have conjectured what passed in their secret interviews from the terms which Louis offered (Worcester, p. 787), from the fact that Louis had sent for an emissary of Queen Margaret's and talked of treating with Warwick to restore King Henry (*Cal. Mil. Papers*, I, p. 120), and from the subsequent relationship of Warwick and Louis. For Warwick at Rouen see particularly Jean de Roye, *Journal*, I, pp. 170–72; Basin, II, pp. 178–79; Ch. de

Beaurepaire, "Notes sur six voyages de Louis XI à Rouen," *Travaux Académiques de Rouen*, Rouen, 1857, pp. 284-334; *Lettres de Louis XI*, III, pp. 143-49; Waurin, II, pp. 340-41. Cf. Calmette and Périnelle, pp. 83-87.

Ratification of treaties: In November of this year, for example, King Edward refused to ratify a treaty which his ambassadors had concluded with the Duke of Burgundy (see Scofield, I, pp. 432-33 and n. 1 of p. 433). For a discussion of treaty ratification in the fifteenth century, see J. G. Dickinson, *The Congress of Arras*, Oxford, 1955, p. 193.

5. B.N., Legrand collection, MS. français 6974, ff. 163-64 (Scofield, I, p. 426 and n. 1).

5. THE PARTING OF FOES

1. The tournament: for a detailed contemporary description, see *Excerpta Historica*, London, 1831, pp. 197-212.
2. Waurin, II, p. 344.
3. Warwick and French envoys in England: Worcester, p. 787; Waurin, II, pp. 345-50. Waurin's report of conversations may be partly imaginative but it is convincingly in character. Waurin, who dedicated his history to King Edward IV, probably secured his account from a member of the embassy.

6. "MASTER OR VARLET"

1. State of learning at Edward's court: See R. Weiss, *Humanism in England in the Fifteenth Century*; R. Mitchell, *John Tiptoft*, London, 1938; Kendall, *Richard the Third*.
2. For a good brief picture of northern England in Warwick's day, see R. R. Reid, *The King's Council in the North*, London, 1921, pp. 1-41.
3. I have conjectured the actions of Warwick's adherents here, but the account is supported by subsequent events, Warwick's popularity in the North, and the customs of the times.
4. Worcester, p. 789.
5. Milanese ambassadors: *Cal. Mil. Papers*, I, pp. 121-22.
   Charles of Burgundy's retort: Chastellain, V, p. 345.
6. Worcester, p. 788.
7. Sir John Conyers, the sacking of Earl Rivers' manor, etc.: Menypeny's letter to King Louis of January 16, 1468 (see note 8 below).
8. Menypeny and Warwick (pp. 266-72): the details come from two letters Menypeny wrote to King Louis, one on January 16, 1468 (Waurin, III, pp. 186-96) and the other on March 8, 1468 (P. H. Morice, *Mémoires pour servir de preuves à l'histoire de Bretagne*, Paris, 1746, III, pp. 159-60). These letters furnish the most intimate view we have of the Earl of Warwick in a moment of crisis.
9. *Rot. Parl.*, V, pp. 622-23.

7. MINE AND COUNTERMINE

1. *Great Chron.*, p. 206.
2. *Great Chron.*, p. 206.
3. See Kendall, *Richard the Third.*
4. *Great Chron.*, p. 208.
5. Warwick and the Hanse: *Hanserecesse*, 2, VI, *passim; Hansisches Urkundenbuch*, ed. by K. Höhlbaum, K. Kunze, W. Stein, Verien für Hansische Geschichte, 10 vols., Halle and Leipzig, 1876–1907, IX (Leipzig), *passim.* Cf. Power and Postan, pp. 91–138; Scofield, I, pp. 465–69 and 486–87. For the career of Thomas Kent, see *Hanserecesse*, II and III, *passim;* Power and Postan, pp. 104, 127, 130, 134.

   Unpopularity of Easterlings at York: *York Civic Records*, I, ed. by Angelo Raine, The Yorkshire Archaeological Society, 1939, *passim.*
6. Gregory, p. 238.
7. Louis at Péronne: The most famous and best account is Commynes, I, pp. 125–28, 131–34, 142–45; see also Chastellain, VII, p. 342; Commynes-Lenglet, III, pp. 17–46.
8. Nevilles and Pastons and rumors of the chancellorship's being restored to George Neville: *Paston Letters*, II, p. 325.
9. Oxford's confession: "Hearne's Fragment" in *Chrons. of the White Rose*, p. 20; *Plumpton Correspondence*, ed. by T. Stapleton, Camden Society, 1839, p. 20.
10. *Great Chron.*, p. 207.
11. The story of John Boon: Ch. Samaran, *La Maison d'Armagnac au XVᵉ Siècle*, Paris, 1907, pp. 162–172 and notes (Samaran's narrative of Boon's adventures); pp. 412–13 (Boon's deposition of 1469, the false story in which he was coached by Louis XI); pp. 413–20 (Boon's deposition of 1485, in which he tells in detail the true story). For King Edward's charging Boon to bear the letters to Armagnac: Samaran, p. 164, n. 2, and Scofield, I, p. 476, n. 2. Boon's capture by John White: Scofield, I, p. 477, n. 1.

V "SETTER-UP AND PLUCKER-DOWN OF KINGS" (1469–1470)

1. THE FAILURE OF SUCCESS

1. Mission of the Burgundian ambassadors: *Cal. Mil. Papers*, I, p. 128; Reiffenberg (Baron de), *Histoire de l'ordre de la Toison d'Or*, Brussels, 1830, pp. 4, 37–38, 40.
   Foreign trade: see Power and Postan.
2. The preparations for Robin's rising are conjectured: the efficient conduct of the rebellion suggests that it was planned months ahead.
3. Warwick and Duke Charles: Commynes-Lenglet, II, p. 193.
4. Warwick's communications with Robin are conjectured; what subsequently occurred indicates that they refurbished their plans after the abortive rising.
5. Commynes-Lenglet, III, pp. 99–101.

6. Edward and Calais and Warwick's fleet: *Paston Letters*, II, pp. 353–54 (May 22).

7. *Cal. Pat. Rolls*, 1467–77, p. 131.

8. Sailing of Warwick's fleet: *Cal. Mil. Papers*, I, pp. 129–30.

9. Warkworth, notes, pp. 47–51.

10. Warwick's claim to rule: While I was attempting to develop this comparison, I was fortunately able to submit the question of Montfort's, Mortimer's, and Bolingbroke's position to an authority on English medieval administrative history, Professor George P. Cuttino, of Emory University. Professor Cuttino's suggestions have been of the greatest aid to me in this matter. He has perspicuously analyzed this complex problem in a few words:

"At first thought, comparing Montfort, Mortimer, and Bolingbroke, I'd say that Montfort's opposition was most clearly 'constitutional' and the least personal. Bolingbroke's is still 'constitutional' but more personal. Mortimer's is extremely complicated by his position as Marcher lord, by the Despensers, by Isabella, and by Edward's copain, Piers Gaveston. He is certainly the least 'constitutional' and the most personal—and also the least attractive. The issues in all three cases have these points in common: acceptance of the Angevin administrative achievements; the question of who are the king's 'natural' advisers; the question of the power of the Council, both baronial and administrative; the insistence on the principle established by the Great Charter that the king is beneath the law. None of these appears to be paramount in Warwick's case . . ." (From a letter from Professor Cuttino to the author.)

11. Milanese ambassador to Duke of Milan, from Amboise, August 8, 1469 (quoted in Calmette and Périnelle, Pièces Justificative no. 30, pp. 306–08).

12. Dominic Mancini, *The Usurpation of Richard III*, ed. by C. A. J. Armstrong, Oxford, 1936, p. 75.

13. Shown by London's prohibition of sales—see note 15 below.

14. Comings and goings at Canterbury and blessing of the *Trinity: Chron. of John Stone*, pp. 109–10.

15. Mayor's prohibition: *London Journal*, 7, f. 195.
   Letters to Coventry: *Coventry Leet Book*, II, pp. 341–42.

16. *Collection of Ordinances and Regulations for the Government of the Royal Household*, London, 1790, p. 98.

17. Warkworth, notes, pp. 46–47.

18. Edward's apparent laxness in remaining so long at Nottingham: It may well be that the King had decided to avoid a resort to arms, confident of his hold on the kingdom and unwilling to give battle to the man to whom he owed his throne. The curious tale of *The Great Chron.* (see next note) supports this view, as does Polydore Vergil's *History* (ed. by Henry Ellis, Camden Society, 1844, pp. 122–24—a sixteenth-century translation of parts of the *Anglica Historia*). It is also supported by our knowledge of Edward's character: however lazy he might be at Westminster, he was always in the field a man who made time work for him and closed with his enemies with all possible

speed. It is hard to believe that the King—once Robin of Redesdale had put himself between the Devon-Pembroke forces and Edward's at Nottingham—would not have hastened to crush the rebels between his two armies if he intended to fight at all. His letter to Coventry of July 29—three days after Edgecot—likewise tends to support the foregoing hypothesis (*Coventry Leet Book*, II, pp. 345–46). It may be that Devon and Pembroke, under orders from the King, were preparing to retire westward at the time of their quarrel over billets or that they had not received Edward's commands. On the other hand, it is possible that Robin had cut all of Edward's communications so that he lingered at Nottingham because he was unaware of the Pembroke-Devon advance and completely out of touch with events.

19. Warwick's dissembling: In dealing with Warwick's purposes and reporting the battle of Edgecot, several sources display an unusual confusion which suggests that Warwick had deliberately and successfully beclouded his motives and his intentions. For example, "Hearne's Fragment" (p. 24) says that Warwick notified King Edward of the advance of the Northerners and also that Warwick—or the King himself, it is not clear which—dispatched a force to Edgecot which caused the defeat of Pembroke. The account of Edgecot given by an Italian observer then in London is equally confused (*Cal. Mil. Papers*, I, p. 131). The *Croyland Chron.* pictures Warwick as hastening to Edward for the purpose of soothing him in his distress (p. 447). The *Great Chron.* (pp. 208–09) relates the curious tale that Herbert of Pembroke, after writing to Edward to know if he wanted men, was ordered by the King not to stir till he was sent for, but Warwick intercepted the letter and altered it into a command to hasten to the King with troops—"which was done to the intent that all men should think that the King began the war . . ."

20. Warwick's hope of winning over Hastings: he conferred on Hastings offices in Wales a few days later (*Cal. Pat. Rolls*, 1467–77, p. 165—August 12).

21. The exemplary conduct of the Northerners: *Croyland Chron.*, pp. 447–48.
Italian observer: *Cal. Mil. Papers*, I, pp. 131–32.

22. Duke of Burgundy's letter and Warwick's proclamation: Waurin, III, p. 5; *London Journal*, 7, f. 199b.

23. *Cal. Mil. Papers*, I, pp. 131–32; see also Kendall, *Richard the Third*, p. 523, n. 10.

24. *Paston Letters*, II, pp. 366–81.

25. Edward aided by Burgundian agents: Commynes, I, p. 193.

26. The sources display wide disparities on the subject of how Edward escaped from, or was released by, Warwick. For a discussion of the evidence, see Kendall, *Richard the Third*, p. 523, n. 12.

2. "FAIR STOOD THE WIND"

1. See, for example, *Cal. Mil. Papers*, I, pp. 133–34.
2. Reiffenberg, pp. 61–62; Commynes-Lenglet, III, p. 99.
3. Welsh rising: see Kendall, *Richard the Third*, pp. 89–91.

4. The Lincolnshire Rebellion: my account is based mainly on the confession of Sir Robert Welles (in *Excerpta Historica*, London, 1831, pp. 282–84; also in Warkworth, notes, pp. 21–23) and on the *Chronicle of the Rebellion in Lincolnshire*, 1470 (ed. by J. G. Nichols, Camden Society, 1847), a detailed contemporary narrative, probably written to put forward King Edward's version of events but apparently accurate.

5. *Great Chron.*, p. 209.

6. *Paston Letters*, II, pp. 394–95.

7. Polydore Vergil, *History*, pp. 125–26; *Paston Letters*, II, p. 395.

8. King's proclamations: Warkworth, notes, pp. 52–56; *Cal. Close Rolls*, 1468–76, pp. 135–36 and 137.

9. Warwick's messages to Fauconberg and to the ports I have inferred from subsequent events.

10. Warwick's message to Louis: proved by Louis' instructions to his officers: Commynes-Lenglet, III, pp. 124–25; see also Calmette and Périnelle, P.J. no. 32, pp. 311–12.

11. Warwick before Calais, his captures, and his arrival at Honfleur: the "Rows Rol" of John Rous, par. 58; Commynes, I, pp. 194–96; Waurin, III, pp. 28–32; Haynin, p. 153; Calmette and Périnelle, P.J. no 32, pp. 311–12; "Hearne's Fragment," p. 26.

3. THE RETURN OF THE NATIVE

This chapter is based mainly on the following sources:
Basin, II.
Cal. Mil. Papers, I.
Chastellain, V.
Commynes, I.
Commynes-Lenglet, II and III.
"Enquête faite en 1471 sur une descente opérée dans le pays de Caux par les Anglais et les Bourguignons," *Mémoires de la Société des Antiquaires de Normandie*, 3rd Series, vol. 3(XXIII), Part I (supplement), Paris, 1858, pp. 11–14.
Haynin.
Jean de Roye.
Lettres de Louis XI, IV.
"The Manner and Guiding of the Earl of Warwick at Angiers," *Chronicles of the White Rose*, pp. 229–36.
Waurin, III.
Also Pièces Justificatives and other sources cited in Calmette and Périnelle.

1. *Cal. Mil. Papers*, I, pp. 132–35; *Foedera*, XI, p. 650; French Roll 9 Edw. IV, m. 2 and Signed Bills, file 1501, no. 4321 (Scofield, I, p. 507, n. 4); Jean de Roye, I, p. 235; Calmette and Périnelle, P.J. no. 31, pp. 308–09.

2. *Cal. Mil. Papers*, I, pp. 136–37.

3. Commynes-Lenglet, III. pp. 124–25.

4. *Lettres de Louis XI*, IV, pp. 110–14.

5. *Cal. Mil. Papers*, I, p. 139.

6. *Lettres de Louis XI*, IV, pp. 121–22.
7. Chastellain, V, pp. 448–56.
8. Warwick's oath; Louis' attitude toward Warwick: "Manner and Guiding," pp. 231, 233.
9. Warwick and Louis linked: Chastellain, V, p. 466; Basin, II, p. 274; *Chants historiques et populaires*, ed. by Le Roux de Lincy, Paris, 1857, pp. 159–64.
10. Chastellain, V, pp. 466–67; Commynes, I, p. 198.
11. *Cal. Mil. Papers*, I, pp. 117–18.
12. *Lettres de Louis XI*, IV, pp. 130–31.
13. "Manner and Guiding," pp. 234–36; Ellis, Series 2, I, p. 135.
14. Warkworth, notes, pp. 60–62.
15. *Coventry Leet Book*, II, p. 358.
16. Warkworth, p. 10.
17. Happenings in London: see *Great Chron.*, pp. 211–12 and notes, p. 431; Fabyan, pp. 658–59; Warkworth, p. 11.

VI THE LANCASTRIAN (1470–1471)

1. THE GRAND ALLIANCE

1. See, for example, Warkworth, p. 12.
2. *Cal. Mil. Papers*, I, p. 137; Chastellain, V, p. 494.
3. Warwick's appointments and King Henry's accessibility: in addition to *Cal. Pat. Rolls*, 1467–77; *Cal. Close Rolls*, 1468–76; and *Foedera*, XI, see Scofield, I, pp. 543–45 and notes to those pages.
4. Composition of Henry's council: I infer that Russell and Sharp were members of the council since they were among those appointed to negotiate with the French ambassadors (*Foedera*, XI, pp. 681–90). There is no indication of any prominent lord (save Clarence) being a member of the council except for Henry Bourchier, Earl of Essex (see note 8 below). It seems probable that Warwick would feel compelled to appoint a council amenable to his will.
5. Ellis, Series 2, I, p. 139.
6. Jasper Tudor at Westminster: Vergil, pp. 134–35; Warrants for Issues, 49 Henry VI, November 3 and 9, and Fine Roll 49 Henry VI, m. 7, November 14 (Scofield, I, p. 544, n. 2).
7. See a letter (in which the time element is somewhat confused) written by a merchant of Cologne, Gerhard von Wesel, *Hanserecesse*, 1431–76, II, vi, ed. by G. von der Ropp, Leipzig, 1890, pp. 415–16. See also Scofield, I, p. 545 and n. 5. Hatclyf resumed his diplomatic work for Edward as soon as Edward reclaimed his throne: see, for example, *Foedera*, XI, pp. 716–19.
8. I infer Essex's membership in the council from the fact that he was appointed one of the commissioners to treat with the French ambassadors (*Foedera*, XI, pp. 681–90).
9. Harleian MS. 543, f. 172.
10. Ellis, Series 2, I, p. 140; Scofield, I, p. 546 and n. 2.
11. See particularly *The Great Chron.*, p. 213; also R. J. Mitchell, *John Tiptoft*, London, 1938, and Scofield, I, p. 547.

12. (1) *Rot. Parl.*, V, pp. 462–63; (2) Warkworth, p. 12.
13. See Power and Postan. It seems likely that Warwick collected customs under the parliamentary grant made to Henry VI in 1453 rather than under the grant made to Edward IV in 1465 (see *Rot. Parl.*, V). For the first years of his reign, Edward had claimed the grant of 1453 as his warrant for collecting customs (Scofield, I, p. 365).
14. *London Journal*, 7, ff. 225, 230b–231; Warrants for Issues, 49 Henry VI, December 18 (Scofield, I, p. 542, n. 2).
15. See George Ashby's Poems, ed. by Mary Bateson, Early English Text Society (Extra Series, LXXVI), London, 1899. That the lines refer to Warwick is my own conjecture.
16. Attitude and actions of Charles of Burgundy: Commynes-Lenglet, II, p. 196, and IV, pp. 416–18; Commynes-Dupont, III, pp. 271–72; Dom U. Plancher, *Histoire générale et particulière de Bourgogne*, Dijon, 1739–81, IV, p. cclxxxix; Commynes, I, pp. 206–11.
17. *Great Chron.*, p. 211, which indicates that the Earl went on to Calais, but, under the circumstances, this seems unlikely.
18. Warwick's envoy to Duke Charles: Warrants for Issues, 49 Henry VI, November 12 (Scofield, I, p. 553, n. 1).
19. Waurin, III, p. 43.
20. V, pp. 487–91 (and Louis' spreading the news).
21. *Cal. Mil. Papers*, I, p. 144.
22. *Cal. Mil. Papers*, I, p. 144.
23. The French embassy and its instructions: *Foedera*, XI, p. 667; Waurin, III, pp. 196–204.
24. See De Maulde, "Un Essai d'Exposition Internationale en 1470," *Académie des Inscriptions et Belles-Lettres: Comptes Rendus . . . 1889* (4th Series, XVII), Paris, 1890, pp. 183–89; also De Maulde, "Marchandises Convoyées en Angleterre," *Bibliothèque de l'Ecole des Chartes*, LVII (1896), Paris.
25. English trade under Warwick's regime: see Power and Postan for tables showing the frightening slump in England's foreign commerce.
26. The assembly of burgesses at St. Paul's: Fabyan (p. 660) says that the meeting of Parliament, begun at Westminster, was "prorogued to Paul's" and continued till Christmas. A letter written by the French ambassadors on February 6 (see note 29 below) shows clearly that Parliament was called back into session in late January or very early February and that the burgesses were meeting in special session. I conjecture from Fabyan's statement that it was this special session which met at St. Paul's (that is, within the limits of the city of London, where—Warwick perhaps sensed—they would feel more comfortable than at Westminster).
27. In addition to *Cal. Pat. Rolls*, 1467–77, pp. 228, 232, 237, see Writs of Privy Seal, file 780, nos. 11058, 11092 (Scofield, I, p. 545, n. 1).
28. Communications of the French ambassadors: Bibl. Nat., Legrand Collections, MS. français 6978, f. 47; see Calmette and Périnelle, p. 129, and Scofield, I, p. 560.
29. The French ambassadors' letter of February 6 and Warwick's postscript: Calmette and Périnelle, P.J. no. 42, pp. 323–25.

30. The confirmation by Parliament is necessarily conjectural but seems safe to assume. The treaty signed: *Foedera*, XI, pp. 681–90.
31. *Cal. Mil. Papers*, I, pp. 149–50.
32. For Langstrother, see *Foedera*, XI, p. 693, and Warrants for Issues, 49 Henry VI, February 16 (Scofield, I, p. 564, n. 1); the orders to Wenlock I assume from the fact that he joined Queen Margaret's party and accompanied her to England (see *Historie of the Arrivall*, p. 23, p. 25—fully identified in notes to Chap. 2, Barnet).
33. The 17,000 crowns: De Maulde (see note 24 above).
Changing rate of exchange: Waurin, III, p. 211 (The Duchess of Burgundy's letter, discussed in notes to Chap. 2, Barnet).
Warwick's use of Commissions of Array: *Coventry Leet Book*, II, p. 362.
34. V, pp. 489–90.
35. See *A Relation of the Island of England*, ed. by C. A. Sneyd, Camden Society, 1870.
36. *Cal. Mil. Papers*, I, p. 76 (Camuglio to the Duke of Milan, April 18, 1461). For an example of Exeter's savage recklessness, see text, pp. 55–56.
37. Exeter begging and Duke Charles' strategy: Commynes, I, pp. 191–92, 211–12.
38. Montagu's conflict of loyalties: shown by his subsequent conduct: see text, pp. 353, 363–367.
39. The warning which reached Margaret of Anjou: Calmette and Périnelle, P.J. no. 41, pp. 321–23. I conjecture Langstrother's and Wenlock's urging her to sail from Warwick's message, conveyed by the French ambassadors (see text, p. 343, 344).

Margaret's decision to cross in ships bringing home the ambassadors: Calmette and Périnelle, P.J. no. 43, pp. 325–26; see also *Cal. Mil. Papers*, I, pp. 149–51.
40. Calmette and Périnelle, p. 133, n. 5.
41. *Cal. Mil. Papers*, I, pp. 149–50.
42. Warwick's arrests: see Gerhard von Wesel's letter (identified in note 7 above).
43. *Cal. Mil. Papers*, I, p. 150, and De Maulde (see note 24 above).
44. See Gerhard von Wesel's letter (note 7 above).

2. BARNET

The fabric of this chapter is derived mainly from the *Historie of the Arrivall of Edward IV in England* (ed. by John Bruce, Camden Society, 1838), a detailed narrative, written by a follower of King Edward who was an eyewitness of events and designed to set forth the official Yorkist view of Edward's return. A copy of this account was apparently sent to Charles of Burgundy; Waurin follows it and a French abridgement survives, printed in Commynes-Dupont, III, pp. 282–83 and translated in *Archaeologia*, XXI, p. 15. French sources and other English sources also supply important pieces of information, particularly Warkworth, *The Great Chron.*, documents in the Historical Manuscripts Commission reports, the *Paston Letters*, and Commynes, I.

1. Mil. amb.: *Cal. Mil. Papers*, I, pp. 150–51.
   Louis' wine: Calmette and Périnelle, p. 133.
2. HMC, *Rutland*, I, pp. 2–5.
3. HMC, *ibid*.
4. Gerhard von Wesel's letter (note 7 above).
5. For Lancastrian attempts to hold London and Edward's activities in the city, April 11–13, see particularly Gerhard von Wesel's letter; a letter written by Margaret, Duchess of Burgundy (identified in note 9, below); *Great Chron.*; Commynes, I; Le Roux de Lincy; and *Political Poems and Songs*, ed. by T. Wright, Rolls Series, London, 1861, II.
6. George Neville's pardon is dated April 10, the day before the King entered the city. See *Foedera*, XI, p. 709, and Warkworth, notes, pp. 63–64.
7. Warwick's state of mind and his letter to Louis: Basin, II, p. 274—"De quibus prioribus treugis cum praedictus Comes de Warvich certior factus foret, qui decimo post eas firmatas die adhuc in humanis agebat, tantum doluisse fertur, tantum moestitiae luctusque duxisse, ut paene in desperationem ceciderit. Quod per suas litteras satis indicasse ferebatur, quas ad eumdem Ludovicum de ea re scripsit, in quibus ei proditionis, perfidae, atque perjurii crimina exprobrabat. Sed cum talium, ut diximus, artifex expertissimus fuisset, satis dignum suis meritis fuerat, ut etiam in retia consimilis aucupis traderetur."
8. The *Croyland Chron.* says that the Lancastrians hoped to take Edward by surprise while he was celebrating Easter in the city (p. 464).
9. The Battle of Barnet: I have reconstructed the battle from my own study of the ground, pursued in the light of three accounts—presumably based on the reports of eyewitnesses—which were composed very shortly after the conflict: the *Historie of the Arrivall;* a letter which Edward's sister Margaret, Duchess of Burgundy, wrote to her mother-in-law from information given her by an Englishman who left London at noon on the day after the battle (Waurin, III, pp. 210–15); and the report sent home by the Cologner, Gerhard von Wesel. For a discussion of these sources and of my conclusions drawn from them, see Kendall, *Richard the Third*, pp. 527–28.

   That Warwick fought on foot at the bidding of his brother, the Marquess Montagu, is disclosed by Commynes, I, p. 214.
10. Leroux de Lincy, pp. 159–73; the English translation is mine.
11. *Cal. Mil. Papers*, I, p. 159 (July 6).

EPILOGUE

1. Charles of Burgundy's ambitions were inflamed by constant reading in the lives of the great warriors of ancient times. After his defeat at Grandson, his jester—surely a relative of Lear's!—mordantly commented on his master's obsession in the cry, "My Lord, we are well Hannibaled this time!"

Index

**PHOENIX
PRESS**

GENERAL EDITORS:
SIMON SCHAMA AND ANTONIA FRASER

*Phoenix Press publishes and re-publishes hundreds of the very best new
and out of print books about the past. For a free colour catalogue listing
more than 500 titles please*

telephone: +44 (0) 1903 828 503
fax: +44 (0) 1903 828 802
e-mail: mailorder@lbsltd.co.uk
or visit our website at www.phoenixpress.co.uk

The following books might be of interest to you:

The Wars of the Roses

JOHN GILLINGHAM

A dazzling account of peace and conflict in 15th century England
which emphasises the military over the political history of the Wars
of the Roses.

Paperback
UK: £12.99   288pp + 16pp b/w   1 84212 274 6
USA: $19.95
CAN: $29.95

Prince of Princes
The Life of Potemkin
SIMON SEBAG MONTEFIORE

'A headlong gallop of a read' said Antony Beevor about this massive
new biography of Catherine the Great's lover and co-ruler;
conqueror of the Ukraine and Crimea. Exhaustively researched
and beautifully written. 'Magnificent' *Independent*, 'Superb', *Daily
Telegraph*, 'Splendidly written' *Sunday Telegraph*, 'This well
researched and highly ambitious biography has succeeded
triumphantly in re-creating the life of an extraordinary man'

Antony Beevor, *Sunday Times*. Shortlisted for the Duff Cooper
Memorial Prize and the Samuel Johnson Prize.

Paperback
UK: £9.99   656pp + 24pp col. b/w   1 84212 438 2

Dr Johnson's London
LIZA PICARD

The first paperback edition of this celebrated account of London
from 1740–1770. With erudition and wit, Liza Picard extracts
nuggets from all sorts of contemporary records to expose the substance of everyday life in the biggest city in Europe – houses and
coffee-houses, climbing boys and gardens, medicine, toothpaste
and gin, sex, food, manners, etiquette, crime and punishment; the
practical realities of everyday life in the mid 18th century.

Paperback
UK: £9.99   384pp + 32pp col. b/w   1 84212 437 4

Empire
The British Imperial Experience From 1765 to the Present
DENIS JUDD

'Wonderfully ambitious . . . a pungent and attractive survey of the
British Empire from 1765 to the present.' *London Review of Books*,
'An indispensable one-volume source.' John Keegan

Paperback
UK: £14.99   544pp + 24pp b/w + Maps   1 84212 498 6
USA: $21.95
CAN: $31.95

The Rise of the Greeks
MICHAEL GRANT

The irrepressible Michael Grant takes the reader on an intriguing
detective trail to understand the world of the early Greeks. With
fluency and scholarship he shows how the extraordinary epoch
between 1000 and 495BC was one of the most creative in history.

Paperback
UK: £12.99   416pp + 16pp b/w + Maps   1 84212 265 7
USA: $19.95
CAN: $29.95

Paperback
UK: £14.99   684pp + Maps   1 84212 477 3
USA: $21.95
CAN: $31.95

Londinium
JOHN MORRIS

The authoritative account of earliest London from pre-Roman Britain to the Age of Arthur, examining subjects as diverse as food, religion, politics and sport.

Paperback
UK: £14.99   400pp + 8pp b/w   0 75380 660 6

The Birth of the Modern
World Society 1815–1830
PAUL JOHNSON

An examination of how the matrix of the modern world was formed. 'A work of this kind stands or falls . . . on the richness of its material, the scope of its coverage, the intelligence of its arguments, and on all these counts this book not merely stands, but towers above any other history of the period.' *Sunday Telegraph*

Paperback
UK: £11.99   1120pp   1 85799 366 7

Collision of Empires
Britain in Three World Wars 1793–1945
A. D. HARVEY

'Delightfully opinionated, well-documented insights into the three wars which constituted the rise, stagger and fall of the British Empire.' Andrew Roberts, *The Times*

Paperback
UK: £14.99   800pp   1 85799 125 7

History of the Dutch-Speaking Peoples 1555–1648
PIETER GEYL

An unforgettable portrait of Dutch life during the sixteenth and seventeenth centuries, this new paperback edition combines the two volumes *The Revolt of the Netherlands 1555–1609* and *The*

The Classical Greeks
MICHAEL GRANT

The Golden Age of ancient Greek city-state civilization lasted from 480 to 336BC, the period between the first wars against Persia and Carthage and the accession of Alexander the Great. Never has there been such a multiplication of talents and genius within so limited a period and Michael Grant captures this astonishing civilization at the height of its powers.

Paperback
UK: £12.99 352pp + 16pp b/w 1 84212 447 1
USA: $19.95
CAN: $29.95

The Fall of the Roman Empire
MICHAEL GRANT

The fall of the western Roman empire was one of the most significant transformations throughout the whole of human history. Michael Grant explores the past with clarity and depth.

Paperback
UK: £12.99 256pp 1 85799 975 4

The Muslim Discovery of Europe
BERNARD LEWIS

A lively exploration of the sources and nature of Muslim knowledge of the West. 'No one writes about Muslim history with greater authority, or intelligence, or literary charm than Professor Bernard Lewis.' Hugh Trevor-Roper, *Sunday Times*

Paperback
UK: £14.99 352pp + 28pp b/w 1 84212 195 2

The Age of Arthur
JOHN MORRIS

A history of the British Isles from 350 to 650, 'the starting point of future British history'. 'From the resources of a mind vastly learned in the documents of the Arthurian age, John Morris has created more than the most devoted of Arthurian enthusiasts could have hoped for . . . Winston Churchill would have loved this book.' *TLS* years of academic and intellectual invention. 'He combines lively opinion and a distinguished historian's erudition, with a first-class journalist's clarity and eye for the revealing anecdote . . . Irresistible.' *USA Today*

Paperback
UK: £16.99   832pp   1 84212 229 0

The Seekers
The Story of Man's Continuing Quest to Understand his World
DANIEL J. BOORSTIN

The final volume in the trilogy looks at the great men in history who sought meaning and purpose in our existence from Moses, Plato and Socrates through to Marx, Toynbee, Carlyle and Einstein. 'This completion of the trilogy on humanity's quest for understanding confirms Boorstin's rank as one of the giants of 20th century American scholarship.' George F. Will

Paperback
UK: £12.99   320pp   1 84212 228 2

Barbarossa
The Russian–German Conflict 1941–1945
ALAN CLARK

The classic account of the war on the Eastern Front, written by the eminent military historian, diarist and politician Alan Clark.

Paperback
UK: £14.99   544pp + 16pp b/w   1 84212 434 X

Second World War
MARTIN GILBERT

A new edition of the first total, global history of the Second World War, by the foremost historian of the twentieth century. 'Gilbert's epic is a remarkable achievement.' *Daily Express*

Paperback
UK: £18.99   864pp + 130 b/w photos + 102 maps   1 84212 262 8

Netherlands in the Seventeenth Century 1609–1648 of Pieter Geyl's magnificent History.

Paperback
UK: £16.99   640pp + Maps   1 84212 225 8
USA: $24.95
CAN: $36.95

The European Powers 1900–1945
MARTIN GILBERT

Martin Gilbert analyses the dramatic changes that altered the face of Europe from the strong and prosperous European Empires of 1900 to a new order reeling from the effect of two wasteful wars with influence transferred to the United States and the Soviet Union.

Paperback
UK: £12.99   316pp + 16pp b/w + Maps   1 84212 216 9
USA: $19.95
CAN: $29.95

The Discoverers
A History of Man's Search to Know the World and Himself
DANIEL J. BOORSTIN

This Pulitzer Prize-winning saga of human discovery, the first in the trilogy, is the story of countless Columbuses. 'A new and fascinating approach to history . . . rich in unknowns and surprises' Barbara Tuchman. 'A ravishing book . . . [with] a verve, an audacity and a grasp of every sort of knowledge that is outrageous and wonderful . . . I can't think of any other living writer who could have attempted, let alone accomplished it.' Alistair Cooke, 'An adventure story . . . great fun to read.' *New York Times*

Paperback
UK: £16.99   768pp   1 84212 227 4

The Creators
A History of Heroes of the Imagination
DANIEL J. BOORSTIN

A panoramic yet minutely detailed history of the arts from Homer and Giotto to Picasso and Virginia Woolf encompassing 3,000

The Klemperer Diaries, Volumes I & II

1933–1945

VICTOR KLEMPERER

A single paperback edition of the two volumes *I Shall Bear Witness* and *To the Bitter End* of Victor Klemperer's diaries of his experiences as a Jew in Nazi Germany. 'Klemperer's diary deserves to rank alongside that of Anne Frank', *Sunday Times*, 'Few English readers will fail to be moved as I was – ultimately to the point of tears.' Niall Ferguson, *Sunday Telegraph*

UK: £16.99   1070pp   1 84212 022 0

Eleanor of Aquitaine

MARION MEADE

A compassionate and comprehensive account of the life of Eleanor of Aquitaine, a woman of enormous intelligence and titanic energy. The wife of King Louis VII of France and then of King Henry II of England and mother to Richard Coeur de Lion and King John, she became the key political figure of the 12th century. A stunning biography of one of the most exciting and powerful personalities of all time.

Paperback
UK: £14.99   416pp + 12pp b/w   1 84212 490 0